Adult Mortality in Latin America

The International Union for the Scientific Study of Population Problems was set up in 1928, with Dr Raymond Pearl as President. At that time the Union's main purpose was to promote international scientific co-operation to study the various aspects of population problems, through national committees and through its members themselves. In 1947 the International Union for the Scientific Study of Population (IUSSP) was reconstituted into its present form.

It expanded its activities to:

- stimulate research on population
- develop interest in demographic matters among governments, national and international organizations, scientific bodies, and the general public
- foster relations between people involved in population studies
- disseminate scientific knowledge on population

The principal ways through which the IUSSP currently achieves its aims are:

- organization of worldwide or regional conferences
- operations of Scientific Committees under the auspices of the Council
- organization of training courses
- publication of conference proceedings and committee reports.

Demography can be defined by its field of study and its analytical methods. Accordingly, it can be regarded as the scientific study of human populations primarily with respect to their size, their structure, and their development. For reasons which are related to the history of the discipline, the demographic method is essentially inductive: progress in knowledge results from the improvement of observation, the sophistication of measurement methods, and the search for regularities and stable factors leading to the formulation of explanatory models. In conclusion, the three objectives of demographic analysis are to describe, measure, and analyse.

International Studies in Demography is the outcome of an agreement concluded by the IUSSP and the Oxford University Press. The joint series is expected to reflect the broad range of the Union's activities and, in the first instance, will be based on the seminars organized by the Union. The Editorial Board of the series is comprised of:

John Cleland, UK   Henri Leridon, France

John Hobcraft, UK   Richard Smith, UK

Georges Tapinos, France

Adult Mortality in Latin America

Edited by
IAN M. TIMÆUS
JUAN CHACKIEL
LADO RUZICKA

CLARENDON PRESS · OXFORD
1996

Oxford University Press, Walton Street, Oxford OX2 6DP

Oxford New York
Athens Auckland Bangkok Bombay
Calcutta Cape Town Dar es Salaam Delhi
Florence Hong Kong Istanbul Karachi
Kuala Lumpur Madras Madrid Melbourne
Mexico City Nairobi Paris Singapore
Taipei Tokyo Toronto
and associated companies in
Berlin Ibadan

Oxford is a trade mark of Oxford University Press

Published in the United States
by Oxford University Press Inc., New York

British Library Cataloguing in Publication Data
Data available

Library of Congress Cataloging-in-Publication Data
Data available

ISBN 0–19–828994–4

1 3 5 7 9 10 8 6 4 2

Typeset by Best-set Typesetter Ltd., Hong Kong
Printed in Great Britain
on acid-free paper by
Bookcraft, (Bath) Ltd., Midsomer Norton, Bath

Contents

Contributors

CECILIA ALBALA	Universidad de Chile, Santiago, Chile
ELÍAS ANZOLA-PÉREZ	Pan American Health Organization, Washington, DC, USA
LUCILLE C. ATKIN	The Ford Foundation, Mexico City, Mexico
SHRIKANT I. BANGDIWALA	University of North Carolina, Chapel Hill, NC, USA
JOSÉ LUIS BOBADILLA	The World Bank, Washington, DC, USA
CYNTHIA BOSCHI-PINTO	Fundaçao Oswaldo Cruz, Rio de Janeiro, Brazil
A. DAVID BRANDLING-BENNETT	Pan American Health Organization, Washington, DC, USA
EUCLIDES A. CASTILHO	Fundaçao Oswaldo Cruz, Rio de Janeiro, Brazil
JUAN CHACKIEL	Centro Latinoamericano de Demografia, Santiago, Chile
DIRK JASPERS FAIJER	Centro Latinoamericano de Demografia, Santiago, Chile
TOMAS FREJKA	United Nations Economic Commission for Europe, Geneva, Switzerland
JULIO FRENK	Instituto Nacional de Salud Pública, Cuernavaca, Mexico
WENDY GRAHAM	London School of Hygiene and Tropical Medicine, London, England
GLORIA ICAZA	Universidad de Chile, Santiago, Chile
MARLO LIBEL	Pan American Health Organization, Washington, DC, USA
ALAN LOPEZ	World Health Organization, Geneva, Switzerland
RAFAEL LOZANO	Instituto Nacional de Salud Pública, Cuernavaca, Mexico
ELIDA MARCONI	Ministerio de Salud y Acción Social, Buenos Aires, Argentina

AMÉRICO MIGLIÓNICO	Pan American Health Organization, Washington, DC, USA
CHRISTOPHER MURRAY	Harvard University, Cambridge, Mass., USA
HERNÁN ORELLANA	Centro Latinoamericano de Demografia, Santiago, Chile
RENATE PLAUT	Pan American Health Organization, Washington, DC, USA
DANUTA RAJS	Instituto Médico Legal, Santiago, Chile
MANUEL RINCÓN	Centro Latinoamericano de Demografia, San José, Costa Rica
LUIS ROSERO-BIXBY	Princeton University, Princeton, USA
MAGDA RUIZ	Instituto Nacional de Salud, Bogotá, Colombia
LADO RUZICKA	Retired
DIANA OYA SAWYER	Universidade Federal de Minas Gerais, Belo Horizonte, Brazil
SUSANA SCHKOLNIK	Centro Latinoamericano de Demografia, Santiago, Chile
HARMEN SIMONS	Universidad Autónoma de Honduras, Tegucigalpa, Honduras
CÉLIA L. SZWARCWALD	Fundaçao Oswaldo Cruz, Rio de Janeiro, Brazil
ERICA TAUCHER	Universidad de Chile, Santiago, Chile
IAN M. TIMÆUS	London School of Hygiene and Tropical Medicine, London, England
JACQUES VALLIN	Institut National D'Etudes Démographiques, Paris, France
LAURA WONG	Universidade Federal de Minas Gerais, Belo Horizonte, Brazil

Part I

Background

1   Introduction

IAN M. TIMÆUS
London School of Hygiene and Tropical Medicine, London, England

ALAN LOPEZ
World Health Organization, Geneva, Switzerland

Towards the end of the 1970s, the International Union for the Scientific Study of Population (IUSSP) decided to establish a series of Scientific Committees devoted to the study of mortality. This decision was motivated to some extent by concern in international demographic and public health circles about the stagnation of the pace of mortality decline in several countries at different stages of mortality transition. Three Committees were set up in turn to further the scientific study of mortality within the IUSSP, the first on Biology and the Length of Life chaired by John Pollard, the second on Biological and Social Determinants of Mortality chaired by Lado Ruzicka, and the third, which completed its mandate in 1989, on Comparative Mortality Changes chaired by Stan D'Souza.

Despite the economic recession that hit much of the developing world during the 1980s, child mortality continued to decline in most countries (Hill and Pebley, 1989; Cleland *et al.*, 1992). With primary health care strategies now well established in most of the developing world, the likelihood of survival to adult ages has been increasing. Concomitant with this trend, there has been an increase in interest in the health and mortality of adult populations. This has been manifested in several ways, including the establishment of programmes to meet the health and social services needs of ageing populations better and the conduct of major international studies of the health of adults, such as that completed recently by the World Bank (Feachem *et al.*, 1992).

Recognizing this trend, at its General Conference in New Delhi in 1989 the IUSSP created a Scientific Committee on Adult Mortality, chaired by Alan Lopez of the World Health Organization. The programme of work defined by the committee represents a significant departure from that of previous mortality committees in that the interdisciplinary nature of mortality analyses was emphasized and, in particular, the inter-relationship between demography and epidemiology. Both sciences have as a foundation the description, quantification and explanation of mortality trends, patterns and differentials. All too often, perhaps reflecting the general lack of public health experience among demographers, demographic enquiry has been limited to description and quantification, leaving explanation to other sciences. In this respect, the interaction of demographers and epidemiologists can only be mutually beneficial and promote, for demographers at least, a much greater understanding of the underlying causes of mortality change.

The fostering of interdisciplinary linkages and exchanges in the study of mortality was a principal objective of the first Scientific Seminar of the Adult Mortality Committee, held in Santiago, Chile from 7–11 October 1991. This is reflected in both the title of the Seminar (Causes and *Prevention* of Adult Mortality in Developing Countries) and the composition of its participants: of the seventy participants, more than one third were epidemiologists or other public health specialists. Altogether, a total of twenty-seven papers were presented at the Seminar, covering a variety of topics of relevance to adult health and survival in Latin America, Asia, and Africa. The desire of the IUSSP Adult Mortality Committee to promote this interdisciplinary exchange is also reflected in the cosponsors for the Seminar, namely the Latin American Demographic Centre (CELADE) and the Pan American Health Organization (PAHO). These two organizations respectively represent the principal centres of demographic and public health expertise in the Latin American Region and the success of the Seminar owes much to their collaboration and support. More information on the Seminar and papers presented at it can be found in the report on the Seminar prepared for the IUSSP (Gribble, 1991).

The present book is based on the papers and discussion from the Seminar. The contents, however, differ in important respects from the papers presented in Santiago. To begin with, although the study of adult mortality has become increasingly important in Latin America due to the widespread success in the conquest of childhood diseases, it is equally important in other developing countries (for example, in East Asia). To investigate adequately, in an interdisciplinary fashion, adult mortality trends throughout the developing world would have required a greatly expanded Seminar and is clearly outside the scope of a single book. The Committee, therefore, decided to focus the present volume on Latin America, thereby complementing previous publications of the IUSSP Mortality Committee that have focused more on Africa or Asia (for example, Vallin *et al.*, 1990; Van de Walle *et al.*, 1992). On this basis, several papers presented at the Seminar have been omitted since their focus was on other parts of the developing world. In other cases, it was necessary to select from among two or more papers on closely related topics to avoid duplication. Furthermore, to preserve a degree of balance among the major diseases considered in the volume, two additional chapters were commissioned for the book dealing primarily with the emergence of non-communicable diseases. In addition, the papers that have been retained from the Seminar differ significantly from those presented originally, reflecting the cumulative comments of discussants, participants at the Seminar, reviewers, and the editors of the book.

1. Organization of the Contents

The structure of this book reflects the major issues of concern for an inter-disciplinary analysis of adult mortality in a group of developing countries at different stages of mortality transition. The first section of the book provides an overview of demographic trends and differentials in the Latin American region from a public health perspective, that sets the stage for the subsequent detailed analyses. The second section of the book is concerned with data collection and methods. Two of the chapters in this section examine the utility of vital registration as an information support for the design, implementation, and evaluation of disease and injury prevention programmes. For populations in which vital statistics data are deficient, on the other hand, chapters in this section discuss alternative approaches to the measurement of adult mortality based on indirect methods for the analysis of survey data.

The third section of the book comprises studies of mortality transition and the accompanying epidemiologic transition. It is in the examination of mortality change that demography (mortality studies) and epidemiology (population epidemiology) share common objectives and methods. Beyond this point on the spectrum of public health enquiry, analyses must become disease or condition specific if they are to meet the needs of intervention programmes. This need thus defines the content of the fourth major section of the book, which is concerned with disease-specific and injury-specific analyses. The chapters in this section cover a range of public health issues of importance for adult health and mortality in Latin America, including major infectious diseases, non-communicable diseases, the reproductive health of women, and external causes of death.

2. Background

In Chapter 2, Chackiel and Plaut provide an overview of the demographic trends in Latin America that represent the context for research into adult health and assess the scale of excess mortality by age compared with low mortality populations. Their analysis emphasizes the diversity of the situations of Latin American populations, both at the national level and within countries. The region as a whole is characterized by declining fertility and child mortality, slowing population growth, and the gradual ageing of populations. On the other hand, the least developed Latin American countries and the poor of nearly every country still experience high fertility and child mortality. Thus the region faces the challenge of dealing with the causes and consequences of ill health in a growing adult population while still struggling to control the infectious diseases of childhood. Chapter 2 also emphasizes that the rapid development of a high degree of urbanization distinguishes Latin America from much of the rest of the developing world. While urbanization has probably accelerated the speed of the transition in fertility and mortality in the region, it has also contributed to the emergence of new challenges to public health.

3. Data Collection and Methods

In Chapter 3, Jaspers and Orellana assess the value of vital statistics data for cause-specific studies of adult mortality. Both the completeness of death registration and the reporting of causes of death remain deficient in most Latin American countries. Nevertheless, because coverage of adult deaths is higher than of child deaths, studies of cause-specific mortality in adulthood are worth attempting in nearly half the countries in the region. While only Venezuela has managed to improve the coverage of death registration significantly since the 1960s, certification of deaths by doctors is rising and the proportion of deaths from ill-defined causes declining. Unfortunately, in many countries, variation between administrative areas in the quality of these data represents a major obstacle to comparative study at the sub-national level. In the following chapter, Marconi emphasizes that the poor quality of vital statistics data and their limited use in the formulation of health policy represent two halves of a self-perpetuating cycle. She describes a research project investigating maternal mortality in Argentina that integrated the objectives of evaluating the quality of cause of death certification, generating improved data and applying the findings of the research to the improvement of service provision. Valuable information was generated for health planning that, in turn, can be used to justify efforts to improve the vital statistics system.

In countries where vital statistics are lacking or deficient, adult mortality data collected in surveys can be a valuable addition to those from routine sources. In Chapter 5, Timæus presents new survey-based methods for measuring adult mortality that use a question about orphanhood before and after first marriage. Estimates are presented for four of the countries that asked the relevant questions in their Phase I Demographic and Health Survey. The method seems to have worked well and provides both a more recent estimate of adult mortality than other indirect techniques and a historical series of estimates that extends back more than thirty years. The main substantive conclusion of the chapter is that adult mortality may have been more severe in the 1950s than was concluded by earlier studies but has fallen more rapidly since. If this is true, some official life tables and projections in use at present may be based on overly pessimistic forecasts of adult mortality. Simon and his collaborators discuss applications of the sisterhood method in Latin America. This is a technique that uses survey data to estimate maternal mortality. The authors conclude that it has provided robust estimates of the lifetime risk of dying from maternal causes. The sisterhood method is strategically important because misclassification biases often lead to gross underestimates of maternal mortality from the vital statistics system. In a Chilean application, the sisterhood method yielded a maternal mortality ratio over five times that indicated by registration data.

4. The Transition in Adult Mortality

In Chapter 7, Frenk, Bobadilla and Lozano provide an overview for Latin America of the epidemiologic transition, or process of change occurring in health conditions. Demographic ageing, partial success in the control of communicable disease, and the growth of risk factors for chronic disease are combining to produce increasingly complex health profiles and patterns of causes of death in which non-communicable diseases and injuries figure prominently. While certain trends are common to the region as a whole, Frenk and his colleagues, like other contributors to this volume, emphasize the diversity of the region and heterogeneous experience of different social groups. The epidemiologic transition in the poorer countries is not just occurring later than elsewhere but is following a different route. Vallin's research places these changes in a global context and considers possible future developments. Those developing countries that have achieved high life expectancies are characterized by relatively high infant mortality and low adult mortality compared with the developed world (Figure 8.1 and Table 8.2). In the future, as the scope for further reductions in early-age mortality is exhausted, further gains in life expectancy will depend increasingly on the trend in adult mortality. This has been declining steadily in some countries, such as Chile and Uruguay, but stagnating in others, including Mexico and Venezuela. All the major groups of causes of death except infectious and respiratory disease appear to contribute to these divergent trends. Even in those developing countries in which adult mortality is still falling, however, the gains may be fragile: for example, Vallin suggests, the 1980s saw a cessation or reversal of the decline in Costa Rica.

In Chapter 9, Rosero considers Costa Rica's epidemiologic transition in much more detail. The country experienced a spectacular decline in adult mortality between 1920 and 1990. Some adverse trends arose temporarily in the 1960s but, using somewhat different measures from Vallin, Rosero concludes that, although the pace of mortality decline did slow sharply for young adults in Costa Rica in the 1980s, it accelerated for those aged 50–79 years. The decline in adult mortality was largely accounted for initially by reductions in communicable disease mortality and more recently by declining mortality from injuries and cardiovascular disease. While women have benefited most, it is men who have lower mortality than in many developed countries. Cardiovascular disease mortality and lung cancer mortality are particularly low. However, mortality from other diseases, including stomach cancer, stroke, diabetes, traffic accidents, and cervical cancer, is relatively high, which suggests that there is scope for further reductions in adult mortality. It is noteworthy that both trends and geographical differentials in adult mortality differ from those in child mortality. Moreover, with a few exceptions, it is difficult to relate adult mortality to indicators of socioeconomic development or the timing of health interventions.

5. Causes of Adult Death: Issues for Prevention

In the first of the chapters on communicable diseases, Murray discusses the epidemiology and demographic impact of tuberculosis. This disease is concentrated in adults and has played a major role in the overall decline in mortality, yet it remains the most important infectious cause of death in the world other than acute diarrhoea and lower respiratory tract infections (World Bank, 1993). A clear understanding of the natural history of tuberculosis, particularly the lengthy delay that usually occurs between primary infection and the development of clinical disease, is essential to correct interpretation of trends in its impact. Despite the existence of cost-effective interventions based on chemotherapy that can interrupt transmission of the disease, tuberculosis is declining more slowly in the developing world today than in Europe before the introduction of chemotherapy. Moreover, as infection with HIV spreads, tuberculosis infection is likely to increase.

In Chapter 11, Sawyer examines malaria in the Amazon Region of Brazil. The incidence of malaria in this region is almost the highest in the Americas and the region accounted for over half the notified cases of malaria reported to PAHO in 1990. While Murray emphasizes the importance of knowledge of the biology of tuberculosis for interpretation of demographic data on its impact, Sawyer argues that the rapid growth in malaria cases in Brazil over the last thirty years can only be understood in terms of the nature of the drive made to develop the Amazon region and the forces that push settlers to migrate into the region. Moreover, the detailed age and sex profile of mortality from the disease in different States reflects varying patterns of economic activity. While mortality from malaria remains fairly low, due to an active control programme and low levels of resistance to the available drugs, it is tending to increase. Moreover, the burden of ill-health and health sector costs imposed by the disease are substantial. The problem could become much more severe if integrated measures to tackle the disease are not mounted, including encouraging the consolidation of human settlement in areas that are already occupied.

Chapters 12 and 13 consider two further infectious diseases that, like tuberculosis and malaria, are emerging or re-emerging as major public health problems as the end of the century approaches. The first is AIDS. Chapter 12 focuses on Brazil, which had reported the third highest number of AIDS cases in the world by 1990. At that time, the majority of patients were homosexual or bisexual men but heterosexual transmission and transmission through intravenous drug use are increasing. The authors estimate that somewhere between 50,000 and 300,000 individuals were seropositive in Brazil in 1990. The impact of the epidemic on overall mortality is already evident. Death rates for young men rose in Rio de Janeiro and São Paulo in the late 1980s and, among men aged 25–44 years in São Paulo, AIDS is estimated by the authors to cause the loss of more years of life than accidents or cancer and about half the loss resulting from intentional injuries. The following chapter describes the cholera epidemic in the Americas in 1991. The epidemic began in Peru in January and spread inexorably to fourteen countries by the end of the year. Over 80 per cent of 390,000 cases reported and 2900 of the 4000 deaths were in Peru: this represents one of the largest cholera epidemics ever reported. The low case-fatality rates reflect an excellent response by the region's health services but the epidemic resulted in hundreds of millions of dollars of health care expenditure and massive indirect costs. Cholera is an archetypical disease of poverty and its resurgence in Latin America reflects the economic crisis of the previous decade and the deterioration of public services. Major efforts and expenditure will be required to control the disease's spread and limit its effects during the 1990s.

In Chapter 14, Taucher and her coauthors examine trends and differentials in chronic disease mortality in Chile during the 1970s and 1980s. The decline in adult mortality over the period is accounted for largely by cardiovascular disease and stomach cancer, with a smaller contribution from cirrhosis of the liver. Mortality from cancers of the gall-bladder and breast cancer rose. Substantial differentials in non-communicable disease mortality exist between regions, urban and rural areas, and social groups. Some of these are associated with environmental factors, in particular the air and water pollution associated with copper refineries, while others are consistent with what is known about the influence of lifestyle factors from research in the developed world. Certain differentials and trends are more puzzling: for example, lung cancer mortality has risen and cardiovascular mortality fallen simultaneously. It is hypothesized this may be explained by the heterogeneity of Chilean society; the decline in cardiovascular mortality could be accounted for by conditions such as rheumatic heart disease, that are associated with poverty, while the rise in lung cancer mortality is probably linked to increases in smoking among the more affluent.

Chapters 15 and 16 focus on maternal mortality. Rajs compares the number of maternal deaths in different countries with those that would be expected, based on the death rates prevailing in that country with a similar level of fertility that has the lowest maternal mortality. Even after introducing this partial control for both the proportion of births that are high risk and socio-economic development into the analysis, she documents massive differentials across the Americas. The structure of causes of maternal death is dominated by direct obstetric causes everywhere but varies markedly within this category between countries. Thus, while inadequate maternal health care and unsafe

and illegal abortions are problems across the region, efforts to reduce maternal mortality should be based on different strategies and activities in each
country. In the following chapter, Frejka and Atkin consider the contribution
of induced abortions to maternal mortality in more detail. Their figures
suggest that one induced abortion may be performed in Latin America for
every two or three live births. While official statistics indicate that around 17
per cent of maternal deaths are abortion related, the actual proportion is
probably double this. Somewhere between 83 and 250 deaths occur per
100,000 abortions. Almost all these deaths could be avoided. Furthermore,
health complications resulting from induced abortions may well account for
the majority of morbidity related to pregnancy and childbirth. Even without
liberalization of abortion legislation, much could be done to improve the
quality of services and referral systems.

The last two chapters of the book focus on the external causes of death.
Deaths from injuries, in particular violent deaths among young men, are a
major public health problem in Latin America. Anzola-Pérez and Bangdiwala
present an overview of trends across the region. Mortality from external
causes is of the same order of magnitude as that from other major cause-of-
death groupings such as cardiovascular disease or cancer. Levels and trends in
mortality from the various external causes, particularly violence, differ greatly
between countries. In general, however, increasing mortality from traffic accidents and violence is offsetting declining mortality from other external causes.
Thus, as all-cause mortality declines, mortality from accidents and violence is
becoming relatively more important. They have a disproportionate impact on
young adults, the poor, and men. The final chapter comprises a detailed
discussion of mortality from accidents and violence in one of the countries
where they are most significant, Colombia. According to Ruiz and Rincón,
armed political conflict, and the growth in criminal activity that has occurred
in this context, have led to a massive growth in deaths from violence: the
homicide death rate (including, in the authors' definition, deaths resulting
from the intervention of agencies of the state) tripled for men during the 1970s
and 1980s. Mortality from accidents has also risen. These trends are of considerable demographic significance. They have reduced the increase in male
life expectancy by about one quarter over the last twenty-three years and
produced an unusually large differential between the life expectancy of men
and women.

6. Concluding Comments

As this overview of the contents of the book has shown, several themes
unite the discussion in the different chapters. The findings support the most
important conclusions of the World Bank's comparative study of adult health
in the developing world (Feachem *et al.*, 1992). In particular, even at low levels

of life expectancy, non-communicable disease mortality is higher than communicable disease mortality among adults. Moreover, declines in non-communicable diseases make a substantial contribution to the transition in adult mortality, although the specific causes and mechanisms involved are still poorly understood. Nevertheless, the communicable diseases decline more rapidly, leading to an increase in the relative importance of mortality from non-communicable disease and injuries. Having made these general points, we would emphasize the growing complexity and diversity of health conditions in Latin America. To a considerable extent, this can be related to environmental differences, to variation between countries in their level and pattern of development, and to social inequalities within countries. Some diseases of adulthood are common problems across the region and certain interventions are likely to be cost-effective priorities everywhere. Nevertheless, it would be wrong to assume that the public health problems indicated by such broad categories as maternal mortality, cancer, or injuries are the same in every Latin American country. Thus, the scope for global-priority setting, as exemplified by the package of interventions that has been promoted to improve child survival, is clearly diminishing.

A second theme is that, as for children, the communicable diseases remain major adult health problems in Latin America. Mortality from these diseases has declined greatly, accounting for much of the overall decline in mortality, but is still higher than in the developed world. Moreover, the burden of ill-health and costs to the health sector imposed by communicable diseases remain heavy. Several infectious diseases seem likely to become more prevalent during the coming decade. AIDS is of special concern but tuberculosis, cholera, and malaria remain major problems, despite probably having had more public health effort directed at them over the past 150 years than any other disease except smallpox. Public health strategies to control these diseases will need to become more focused, with more equitable delivery of health services, if further progress is to be achieved.

Third, while it is beyond doubt that the overall decline in adult mortality can be linked to socio-economic development and the expansion of the health sector, little is known about the exact risk factors and interventions involved. Therefore, some actions that could promote further improvements in adult health may not have been identified yet. The case studies of Costa Rica and Chile both emphasize this point. Many of the trends and differentials that they document may be explicable in terms of risk factors identified by epidemiological research in the developed world but few hard data exist that could establish this. For example, a decrease in cardiovascular mortality accounts for a substantial part of the recent decline in adult mortality in both countries. It is unclear, however, whether this is linked to the changes in risk factors and clinical care that have been important in developed countries (which are themselves incompletely understood) or whether the clinical spectrum of disease classified under this heading is different in Latin

America and has responded to other, less clearly defined facets of socio-economic development.

Fourth, while it is clear that the general trend in Latin America is toward lower overall mortality from the non-communicable diseases and most forms of injury, evidence exists for some countries of adverse trends in specific causes of death. These encompass diverse conditions, including cancers of the lung, gall-bladder and breast, diabetes, traffic accidents, and violence. While urbanization and the adoption of less healthy lifestyles underlie the rise of these causes of death, such developments should not be regarded as an inevitable consequence of socio-economic development. Far from being 'diseases of affluence', many of these conditions disproportionately affect the poor within any country. Effective interventions are available that address many such health problems, although they often lie outside the field of responsibility of ministries of health (World Bank, 1993). Unfortunately, the prevention of non-communicable diseases and injuries is still a neglected priority in many Latin American countries. Urgent action is needed to control rising cigarette consumption, for example, to prevent an epidemic of lung cancer on the scale of that experienced by the more developed regions of the world.

A final theme relates to the state of the vital statistics system and other data sources that can be used to document health conditions in Latin America. The existence of this book is testimony to the fact that, after careful evaluation and adjustment, data do exist that can support research to inform policy on adult health. Even the statistics reported here, however, tend to be heavily qualified and to extend this kind of study to all the countries of the region and all diseases of public health significance is impossible at present. While general efforts to improve health information systems would be welcome, much also could be done with limited additional resources to reorient existing activities to improve the pertinence, quality, timeliness, and dissemination of the statistics that they are producing.

To conclude this introduction, we would like to thank all the participants at the Seminar in Santiago for their critical comments and suggestions. These have helped considerably to focus the chapters that follow and thereby to increase their relevance to public health issues. If this book can help to inform debate, improve data collection, and promote further research relevant to more effective public health action, then it will have served its purpose. We also thank the Minister of Health of Chile for his interest in the Seminar and his remarks at the closing session. The Seminar was made possible through the generous financial support of several institutions, including PAHO, CELADE, the Population Council and UNFPA, all of whose assistance is acknowledged gratefully here. A particular expression of gratitude is extended to CELADE for hosting the Seminar and especially to Juan Chackiel, Chief, Demography Area, who organized the Seminar and contributed so much to its success. Lastly, the editors thank Kate Cox and Evelyn Dodd, who undertook much of the work involved in preparing the manuscript for submission to the publisher.

References

Cleland, J., G. Bicego, and G. Fegan (1992), 'Socioeconomic inequalities in childhood mortality: the 1970s to the 1980s', *Health Transition Review*, 2: 1–18.

Feachem, R. G. A., T. Kjellstrom, C. J. L. Murray, M. Over, and M. A. Phillips (eds.) (1992), *The Health of Adults in the Developing World*, Oxford University Press, New York.

Gribble, J. N. (1991), 'Seminar on causes and prevention of adult mortality in the developing countries, Santiago, Chile, 7–11 October 1991', *IUSSP Newsletter*, 43: 18–37.

Hill K., and A. R. Pebley (1989), 'Child mortality in the developing world', *Population and Development Review*, 15: 657–87.

Vallin, J., S. D'Souza, and A. Palloni (eds.) (1990), *Measurement and Analysis of Mortality: New Approaches*, Clarendon Press, Oxford.

Van de Walle, E., G. Pison, and M. Sala-Diakanda (eds.) (1992), *Mortality and Society in Sub-Saharan Africa*, Clarendon Press, Oxford.

World Bank (1993), *World Development Report 1993: Investing in Health*, Oxford University Press, New York.

2 Demographic Trends with Emphasis on Mortality

JUAN CHACKIEL
Centro Latinoamericano de Demografía, Santiago, Chile

RENATE PLAUT
Pan American Health Organization, Washington, DC, USA

1. Introduction

The purpose of this chapter is to outline the demographic context in which adult mortality is developing in Latin America. The objective is to understand better the factors that influence health and disease and the implementation of preventive policies. In Section 2, general demographic trends and the most important changes that have occurred in the last few decades are described, emphasizing the diverse situations in the countries of the region. This leads to a typology that groups countries according to the stage that their demographic transition has reached.

As the overall focus of this book is on the adult population, an analysis of the current age distribution of the population in Latin America and future prospects is carried out in Section 3. Section 4 is dedicated to analysing the strong tendency towards urbanization that has occurred in the region, which is related to the demographic transition. Urbanization is one of the most important factors in understanding the changes in fertility and mortality. As well as heterogeneous demographic behaviour between countries, there also exist strong contrasts within them. Social inequalities are expressed in demographic trends that differ between population sectors, as discussed in Section 5. These differences are illustrated through variables that are more thoroughly documented than adult mortality: fertility and infant mortality.

From Section 6 on, mortality trends are analysed more deeply. The overall behaviour of this variable, measured through life expectancy at birth, as well as through sex, age and cause of death structures, indicates the pattern of change and emerging situation. Section 7 deals with excess mortality at different levels of life expectancy at birth in the countries of the region, according to a model composed of the lowest observed mortality rates. Finally, some comments are presented, motivated by the challenges arising from the situation described.

2. Demographic Situation and Trends

2.1. General Situation

On 11 July 1987, our planet reached a total population of 5 billion persons and, since then, 480 million more have been added. Latin America, with 447 million in 1992, accounts for less than 10 per cent of the world total. This situation will not change substantially before the end of the century, when the region's population will be around 510 million, growing at a rate slightly higher than the world average. Six Latin American countries account for nearly 80 per cent of its total population, that is 351 million persons. These are: Brazil with slightly more than 153 million; Mexico with 88 million; Argentina and Colombia with more than 33 million each; Peru with 22 million, and Venezuela with 20 million. The other fourteen countries account for the remaining 95 million (Table 2.1).

Latin America is presently undergoing a demographic transition process in which mortality has fallen markedly and fertility is now following the same trend. Thus, the region's average annual growth rate reached its highest level

Table 2.1. Total population by country, 1980–2000 (in thousands)

	1980	1985	1990	1995	2000
Latin America	349,198	389,520	430,182	471,025	51,093
Argentina	28,237	30,331	32,322	34,264	36,238
Bolivia	5,581	6,342	7,171	8,074	9,038
Brazil	121,286	135,564	149,042	161,382	172,777
Colombia	26,525	29,481	32,300	35,101	37,822
Costa Rica	2,284	2,642	3,034	3,424	3,798
Cuba	9,679	10,078	10,608	11,091	1,504
Chile	11,145	12,122	13,173	14,237	15,272
Ecuador	8,123	9,309	10,547	11,822	13,090
El Salvador	4,525	739	5,172	5,768	6,425
Guatemala	6,917	7,963	9,197	10,621	12,222
Haiti	5,353	5,865	6,486	7,180	7,959
Honduras	3,662	4,383	5,138	5,968	6,846
Mexico	67,046	75,594	84,486	93,670	10,255
Nicaragua	2,802	3,229	3,676	4,443	5,169
Panama	1,956	2,180	2,418	2,659	2,893
Paraguay	3,147	3,693	4,277	4,893	5,538
Peru	17,295	19,417	21,550	23,854	26,276
Dominican Republic	5,697	6,416	7,170	7,915	8,621
Uruguay	2,914	3,008	3,094	3,186	3,274
Venezuela	15,024	17,164	19,321	21,483	23,622

Source: CELADE, current estimates and population projections.

at the beginning of the 1960s (2.9 per cent), to drop to 2.1 per cent in the 1980s. It is estimated that the growth rate for the current decade will be 1.7 per cent annually, which means that 80 million persons will be added by the year 2000. The fact that the region will continue to grow relatively rapidly is due to the inertia produced by the large number of women in their fertile years. This results from past high fertility and leads to large numbers of births despite the decreasing number of births per woman.

Demographic developments from the 1950s to the 1970s were accompanied by sustained economic growth in the majority of the countries, as is evident from the increase in per capita Gross National Product (GNP), from US$ 950 in 1950 to US$ 2070 in 1980. This created expectations about improvements in living conditions across all sectors of society. It is in this context, along with other factors of varying importance including family planning programmes, that the decrease of the average number of births per woman has begun to take place.

The economic crisis that affected the region during the 1980s produced a sustained fall in per capita GNP between 1980 and 1989. This situation, which is obviously not uniformly serious across countries, generated a deterioration in the living conditions of the population and increased levels of poverty and indigence (ECLAC, 1990). We emphasize that, at the moment when the crisis was at its height, most of the countries were already undergoing a demographic transition which apparently did not suffer any changes. Thus the important decrease in mortality and subsequent fall in fertility have occurred to some extent independently of socio-economic conditions. For instance, the decrease in mortality between the 1930s and 1970s has been linked to advances in the medical field (discovery of pesticides, antibiotics and vaccines), sanitation, the emergence of public health systems (for example 'Caja del Seguro Social' in Costa Rica and 'Servicio Nacional de Salud' in Chile), and programmes directed at specific groups and problems, such as maternal and child health.

Another of the traits that characterizes the Latin American population is its relatively high level of urbanization, a fact that has made it stand out from other less developed regions for a long time. In 1950, 60 per cent of Latin Americans inhabited areas that were considered to be rural, but currently only 30 per cent do so. It is forecast that, by the end of the century, three-quarters of the population will live in urban areas. This process is considered to be one of the factors that facilitated the demographic transition. It allowed relatively rapid propagation of the education system, new cultural patterns, and modern technology, resulting in relatively fast decreases in mortality and fertility.

The other factor in population change is international migration, which has become important in the last few years in the many countries that have social and political conflicts. This factor, however, will not be considered in this chapter because it has a minor impact upon population growth and structure and because of the high level of uncertainty about future trends.

2.2. Country Typology According to Demographic Transition

There exists a diversity of demographic behaviour among the countries of the region. This is also evident within countries between geographic areas and social sectors. For instance, at the national level differences exist of more than four children per woman in the total fertility rate and more than fifteen years in the life expectancy at birth. These facts suggest the need to group countries to make the analysis of demographic tendencies easier. In order to construct a typology of countries, we refer to the concept of 'demographic transition'. This refers to the process observed in different societies which consists of evolution from high levels of fertility and mortality to a situation of low levels in these variables.

Therefore, Latin American countries can, with a few exceptions, be grouped in an empirical way in the following manner:

Group I.   *Incipient Transition* Countries with high fertility and high mortality (annual average growth rate of 2.5 per cent): Bolivia and Haiti.

The total fertility rate in this group of countries is over 4.5 children per woman, with a tendency toward a slight decrease during the period (Table 2.2). High fertility is linked to socio-economic and cultural factors that are expressed in the scant use of contraceptives by couples, ignorance and lack of access to modern procedures. For example, the Bolivian Demographic and Health Survey of 1989 shows that 68 per cent of women in their fertile years knew of some modern method of contraception, but only 12 per cent used one and only 30 per cent used any method at all, either modern or natural (Demographic and Health Surveys, 1991).

Mortality, measured by life expectancy at birth, is approximately 54 years, which indicates that, in spite of important improvements (from 39 years in the early 1950s), the situation is far behind what has been achieved in developed countries and many developing countries. This level of life expectancy at birth is around 20 years less than in the more favoured countries of Latin America, which implies a lag of between 30 and 40 years if average yearly gains for this indicator are considered (Table 2.3).

Group II.   *Moderate Transition* Countries with high fertility and moderate mortality (annual average growth rate of 3 per cent): El Salvador, Guatemala, Honduras, Nicaragua, Paraguay.

As in the previous group, overall fertility is high, with over 4.5 children per woman in most countries (Table 2.2). Demographic and Health Surveys reveal limited use of modern contraceptive methods, although in some countries use is higher than in the countries of Group I. In El Salvador (1985), 45 per cent of women in their fertile years were using modern contraceptives; in Guatemala (1987) 19 per cent were using them; and in Paraguay (1990) 24 per cent.

Rising life expectancy at birth, with higher values than those observed in

Table 2.2. Total fertility rates for countries grouped according to stage of demographic transition, 1950–2000

Countries	1950–55	1960–65	1970–75	1980–85	1985–90	1995–2000
Latin America	5.9	6.0	5.0	3.9	3.4	2.8
Group I						
Bolivia	6.8	6.6	6.5	5.5	5.0	4.1
Haiti	6.3	6.3	5.8	5.2	5.0	4.6
Group II						
El Salvador	6.5	6.9	6.1	5.0	4.5	3.6
Guatemala	7.1	6.9	6.5	6.1	5.8	4.9
Honduras	7.1	7.4	7.4	6.2	5.6	4.3
Nicaragua	7.4	7.4	6.8	6.0	5.6	4.5
Paraguay	6.8	6.8	5.7	4.8	4.6	4.1
Group III						
Brazil	6.2	6.2	4.7	3.8	3.2	2.4
Colombia	6.8	6.8	4.7	3.5	2.9	2.5
Costa Rica	6.7	7.0	4.3	3.5	3.4	3.0
Ecuador	6.9	6.9	6.1	4.7	4.1	3.2
Mexico	6.8	6.8	6.4	4.3	3.6	2.8
Panama	5.7	5.9	4.9	3.5	3.1	2.7
Peru	6.9	6.9	6.0	4.7	4.0	3.2
Dominican Republic	7.4	7.3	5.6	4.2	3.8	3.0
Venezuela	6.5	6.5	5.0	3.9	3.5	2.9
Group IV						
Argentina	3.2	3.1	3.2	3.2	3.0	2.7
Cuba	4.1	4.7	3.6	1.9	1.8	2.0
Chile	5.1	5.3	3.6	2.8	2.7	2.6
Uruguay	2.7	2.9	3.0	2.6	2.4	2.3

Source: CELADE, current estimates and population projections.

Group I, is typical of this stage of transition, although levels are still characteristic of less developed countries. In the 1985–90 period, this indicator was estimated to average 63 years, that is nearly 10 years more than in Group I, but 9 years less than in the most advanced group (Table 2.3).

Group III.   *Transition in Progress* Countries with moderate fertility and low or moderate mortality (annual average growth rate of 2.2 per cent): Brazil, Colombia, Costa Rica, Ecuador, Mexico, Panama, Peru, Dominican Republic, Venezuela.

This group accounts for the majority of the Latin American population. It comprises half of the countries of the region, including those with the largest populations. This means that there is diverse behaviour within the group, which can be seen, for example, in the fact that the average annual rate of growth varies from 2 per cent to 2.6 per cent.

The most notable feature of these countries is the pronounced decrease in fertility over the last 25 years. Total fertility fell from 6.5 children per woman to 3.5 in that period, that is an average decrease of 46 per cent. In some cases, such as Costa Rica, Colombia, and Dominican Republic, the decrease was around 50 per cent (Table 2.2). In the countries with the greatest change in birth rates, knowledge of modern contraceptive methods among women in their fertile years is nearly 100 per cent. Except in Peru and Ecuador, which still have total fertility rates of over four children per woman, the use of

Table 2.3. Life expectancy at birth for countries grouped according to stage of demographic transition, 1950–2000

Countries	1950–55	1960–65	1970–75	1980–85	1985–90	1995–2000
Latin America	51.8	57.2	61.3	65.2	66.7	69.3
Group I						
Bolivia	40.4	43.5	46.7	56.2	58.8	63.4
Haiti	37.6	43.6	48.5	52.7	54.7	58.4
Group II						
El Salvador	45.3	52.3	58.9	57.2	62.4	68.3
Guatemala	42.1	47.0	54.0	59.0	62.0	67.2
Honduras	42.3	47.9	54.0	61.9	64.0	67.5
Nicaragua	42.3	48.6	55.2	59.3	62.4	68.4
Paraguay	62.6	64.4	65.6	66.4	66.9	67.7
Group III						
Brazil	51.0	55.9	59.8	63.4	64.9	67.5
Colombia	50.6	57.9	61.6	67.2	68.2	70.2
Costa Rica	57.3	63.0	68.1	73.8	75.3	76.8
Ecuador	48.4	54.7	58.9	64.3	65.4	67.7
Mexico	50.8	58.6	62.9	67.1	68.8	71.5
Panama	55.3	62.0	66.3	71.0	72.1	73.3
Peru	43.9	49.1	55.5	58.6	61.4	67.0
Dominican Republic	46.0	53.6	59.9	64.1	65.9	69.0
Venezuela	55.2	61.0	66.2	69.1	69.7	71.0
Group IV						
Argentina	62.7	65.5	67.3	69.7	70.6	72.0
Cuba	59.5	65.4	71.0	74.2	75.2	76.1
Chile	53.8	58.1	63.6	71.0	71.5	72.5
Uruguay	66.3	68.4	68.8	70.9	72.0	72.8

Source: CELADE, current estimates and population projections.

modern contraceptives is over 45 per cent (Demographic and Health Surveys, 1991).

This group of countries, which is representative of Latin America, shows an increase of 14 years in life expectancy in the last 25 years to an average life-span of 67 years. In terms of this indicator, there is great diversity between countries, with some belonging more properly to the previous group. The most advanced countries are Costa Rica and Panama. According to their life expectancy, they are similar to the countries that have advanced most in the process of demographic transition (Table 2.3). Some countries of this group will reach a life expectancy at birth of 70 years by the end of the century, a lifespan that has been set as the goal of the World Health Organization in its action plan *Health for All in the Year 2000* (PAHO/WHO, 1980).

Group IV.   *Advanced Transition* Countries with low fertility and moderate and low mortality (annual average growth rate of one per cent): Argentina, Chile, Cuba, and Uruguay.

Of the countries with the most advanced transitions, Cuba and Chile must be distinguished from Argentina and Uruguay. While these latter two countries have had low birth rates and moderate death rates for a long time, in Cuba and particularly in Chile, the greatest progress was made only recently. Thus, not only is Cuba the country with the highest life expectancy at birth in Latin America (Table 2.3), but its population is concentrated in the ages with low death rates. On the other hand, Argentina and Uruguay have higher death rates, partially due to the fact that they have age structures produced by historically low fertility.

The current total fertility rate in Cuba of 1.8 children puts that country in the position of being unable to replace its population in the long term, which could lead to negative natural growth rates. This has not occurred, to date, due to the inertia of its age structure.

It is important to note that the life expectancy at birth of around 75 years, achieved by some countries of the region, is similar in level to developed countries. It is notable that this has occurred in some countries in the absence of economic and social development that benefits all population groups.

3. The Age Distribution of the Population

Population by age group is perhaps the most important demographic variable for policy design and the elaboration of plans and programmes for meeting the social needs of the population, including health care. The most useful age groups to consider depend on the purpose of the analysis and the actions to be taken. The term functional age group is used to refer to groups such as those less than 6 years old, representing the pre-school ages; those aged 6–24 years, representing the school ages (and, within this group, it is possible to create classifications according to schooling cycles); those aged 15–64 years, the potentially active age group; those aged 15–49 years, for the group of fertile women; and those aged 60 or 65 years and over, representing the elderly population. The chapter on mortality in the book *Health Conditions in the Americas* (PAHO, 1990), uses the groups 0–4 years, 5–14, 15–39, 40–64, and 65 years and over, but also presents a detailed analysis of those aged less than 1 year and other groups of special interest. Several definitions of adulthood exist but, for the purpose of this chapter, adults are defined as being 15–64 years old.

It is very important to take both the absolute and relative growth of the total population into account. In order to address unmet and new social demands, it is necessary to understand how a given population is distributed and how it is growing in terms of the different age groups. As might be expected, the general tendency is toward an ever more elderly age structure, with the percentage of children aged less than 15 years decreasing and the percentage of the population aged 65 years and older increasing.

The process of ageing in the countries of the region bears a direct relationship to the stage of their demographic transition. More precisely, the age structure of a country's population also locates that country within the process of demographic change. Thus, in the first stage of transition, which corresponds to a situation of high birth and death rates, the population has a high percentage of children and young people and a very low number of persons in the third age. In Group I, the percentage of those less than 15 years is around 42 per cent, while those aged 65 and older account for 4 per cent. In this case, the adult population represents around 55 per cent of the total (Table 2.4).

In the following stage of transition (Group II), in which mortality decreases while fertility drops very little, the population becomes younger, with a greater percentage of children. This occurs because the greatest decrease in the mortality occurs among very young children, producing the same effect as an increase in fertility. This brings as a consequence a drop in the percentage of the population in the third age (to 3 per cent) and in adulthood (to 52 per cent) (Table 2.4).

The countries in Group III, which are defined as having a transition in progress, already have a lower percentage of their population aged under 15 years (36 per cent in 1990). This proportion is still high as a result of high fertility in the past, which has produced a large number of women in the fertile ages. The decrease in the proportion of children is linked to an increase in the proportion in the central age span to 60 per cent, while the proportion aged 64 years is 4 per cent.

In the countries in the most advanced phase of the transition, the percentage of old people is already twice that of the countries in the early stages. Countries in this group have, in general, less than 30 per cent of their population under the age of 15 and almost 10 per cent of the population in the third age;

Table 2.4   Population aged 15–64 years: size (in thousands), percentage of total population and growth rate (per cent), for countries grouped according to stage of demographic transition. 1960, 1990 and 2000[a]

Countries	1960			1990			2000		
	Population	%	r	Population	%	r	Population	%	r
Latin America	112,676	53.86	2.57	255,843	59.47	2.34	321,223	62.87	1.96
Group I									
Bolivia	1,850	53.95	2.25	3,942	54.96	2.88	5,217	57.72	2.62
Haiti	2,112	55.53	1.34	3,612	55.69	2.10	4,480	56.29	2.32
Group II									
El Salvador	1,335	51.95	2.59	2,724	52.66	3.12	3,644	56.71	2.52
Guatemala	2,034	51.32	2.65	4,726	51.39	3.19	6,519	53.34	3.25
Honduras	1,017	52.55	2.92	2,679	52.15	3.49	3,792	55.39	3.27
Nicaragua	740	49.25	2.84	1,805	49.11	4.48	2,747	53.15	3.63
Paraguay	870	49.04	2.46	2,397	56.05	2.93	3,221	58.16	2.83
Group III									
Brazil	38,842	53.51	2.81	90,392	60.65	2.25	112,782	65.28	1.78
Colombia	8,032	50.39	2.82	19,541	60.50	2.35	24,540	64.88	1.82
Costa Rica	611	49.40	3.49	1,799	59.29	2.77	2,347	61.80	2.39
Ecuador	2,259	51.19	2.93	6,001	56.89	2.98	7,986	61.01	2.45
Mexico	18,377	50.31	3.01	49,227	58.27	2.63	63,247	61.67	2.19
Panama	580	52.50	2.72	1,457	60.26	2.39	1,826	63.11	1.98
Peru	5,288	53.25	2.54	12,621	58.57	2.65	16,247	61.83	2.19
Dominican Republic	1,626	50.31	2.94	4,212	58.74	2.37	5,332	61.85	2.15
Venezuela	3,860	51.45	3.38	11,417	59.09	2.80	14,914	63.13	2.17
Group IV									
Argentina	13,180	63.68	1.52	19,070	60.97	1.53	22,809	62.94	1.26
Cuba	4,239	60.69	1.45	7,299	68.80	0.60	7,737	67.26	0.64
Chile	4,253	55.86	2.05	8,347	63.36	1.49	9,756	63.88	1.62
Uruguay	1,624	64.00	1.05	1,938	62.62	0.81	2,078	63.47	0.70

[a] Growth rates corresponds to the quinquennium initiated in mentioned year.

Source: CELADE, current estimates and population projections.

therefore, about 62 per cent of their population is between 15 and 64 years of age (Table 2.4).

The age structure of population has evolved slowly. During the 1950s, 41 per cent of the region's population were children (first phase of transition). During the 1960s, there was an increase in the proportion of children due to the decrease in child mortality. At present, the population under 15 years of age represents 36 per cent of the total and the region has a high percentage of young adults (third phase of transition). Even if the fertility rate continues to decline rapidly in the future, because of the slowness of the ageing process by the year 2010 Latin America will still have a little less than 30 per cent of children and the countries of Groups I and II will have more than 35 per cent.

The effects of demographic changes are more remarkable if we consider absolute or relative growth in the different age spans. In countries that are in the incipient and moderate phase of transition, the annual growth rate is high and similar in all age groups, while in absolute terms children exceed by up to ten times the population of the third age. In countries that have advanced further in the transition, the growth rate of the population over 64 is four times that of the under 15 age group (2 per cent and 0.5 per cent respectively), which, in absolute values, means a 30 per cent greater increase in people of the third age over children. As the adult population maintains a high growth rate and comprises a wider age span (15 to 64 years), it is increasing by a larger number of people (Table 2.4).

In terms of the social demands that will need to be faced in the next decade, 80 per cent of the total population that Latin America will gain in the decade of the 1990s will be in the central age span, representing 65 million people (Table 2.4). Those aged less than 15 will absorb 10 per cent of the growth (8 million) and the elderly population will contribute a similar figure. In this sense, the most outstanding feature of the region at present is the coexistence of demands from different age groups. Although the effects of the high fertility level of the past are still being felt, we can already perceive the signs of ageing. Furthermore, it is important to anticipate the changes that will occur in the longer term in order not to suffer the negative experiences of the countries that have advanced in transition, but have not been able to cope with increasing demands in terms of social security and health care for the adult and elderly population.

One interesting development is the association that exists between the age structure of the population and the corresponding mortality level and epidemiologic profile. In Sections 5 and 6, the association between the relative age distribution of the population and deaths is analysed, as well as the cause of death structure. The ageing of the population is just one of the factors that plays a role in the increase in the relative importance of chronic diseases.

4. Urbanization

The process of demographic transition in Latin America has taken place in parallel with a marked process of urbanization. In a very few years, the region has changed from being predominantly rural to having its population concentrated in urban areas. In 1950, 60 per cent of the population lived in rural areas. Today, only 30 per cent remain there. Moreover, it is estimated that by the end of the century three-quarters of the population will live in what are considered to be urban areas. In absolute terms, this means that in the last forty years the urban population has multiplied five times, while the rural population has not quite tripled. This rapid urban increase is a product of both natural population growth, which was particularly high in the 1950s and 1960s due to sharp decreases in death rates, migration to the cities and the re-classification of additional localities as urban.

Intense urbanization makes the Latin American transition different from that of the rest of the developing world. Those Asian countries undergoing rapid transitions with pronounced decreases in fertility have not experienced such intense urbanization. This is important as it could indicate that the transition process in Latin America is closely linked to migration to the cities, where new cultural patterns are adopted and resources are more readily available, while, in rural areas, conditions conducive to high fertility and mortality often persist.

Even though urbanization is characteristic of the whole region, great diversity exists between individual countries. In 1950, only four countries were predominantly urban (Argentina, Chile, Uruguay, and Venezuela). By 1990, approximately half the countries had 70 per cent of their populations in urban areas. Only five countries still have more than half their population in rural areas: Haiti, Guatemala, El Salvador, Honduras, and Paraguay. Bolivia, Costa Rica, Panama, and Ecuador have roughly half their population in each type of area. Brazil, Colombia, and Mexico, with around 70 per cent of their population now urban, set the pace for Latin America. As mentioned above, there is an association between urbanization and the process of demographic transition. Thus, while Group I has less than 40 per cent of its population in urban areas, Group IV has double that value.

In general, the rate of urban population growth has slowed. This reflects both decreases in birth rates and changes in the direction of internal migration. In many countries, rural–urban migration is probably giving way to other types of movement, both inter-urban and rural–rural. Nevertheless, urban growth rates continue to be very high, compared with rural rates. On average, the latter are seven times lower than urban rates and they have been negative for a long time in many countries. In the next decade, 77 million people will be added to Latin America's urban areas and only 3 million to its rural areas.

Perhaps because of the size of the population that is affected, environmental problems in urban areas, especially those in big cities, appear to be alarming. The concentration of the population in big cities has constituted one of the most visible associations between demographic dynamics and their conse-quences on the environment. The cities of Mexico, São Paulo and Santiago are examples of urban agglomerations that face serious problems of air pollution, as well as other threats to health such as water pollution, accidents, and violence.

5. Differentials in Demographic Behaviour

Thus far, we have analysed the demographic situation of the countries of the region at the national level. However, as in other fields, these data hide tremendous diversity. Within countries, population segments at every stage of demographic transition coexist; that is sub-populations with very high fertility and mortality coexist with others which have completed the transition process. We illustrate these differences in terms of fertility and infant mortality:

(a) *Fertility* By way of example, Figure 2.1 presents fertility data for countries in different stages of transition and classifies the population in terms of the level of education attained by the head of household. Fertility by place of residence and by occupation of head of household behave in a similar

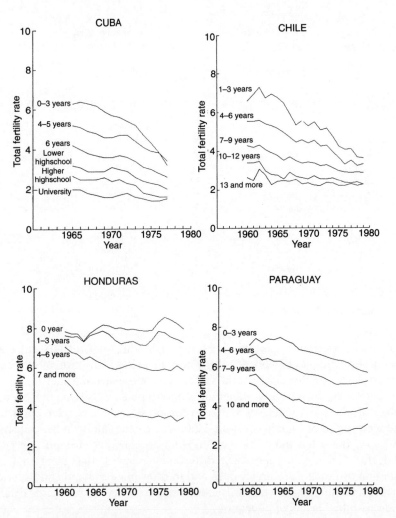

Fig. 2.1.   Total fertility rate by mother's education, 1960–80, selected countries
Source: CELADE, IFHIPAL Project.

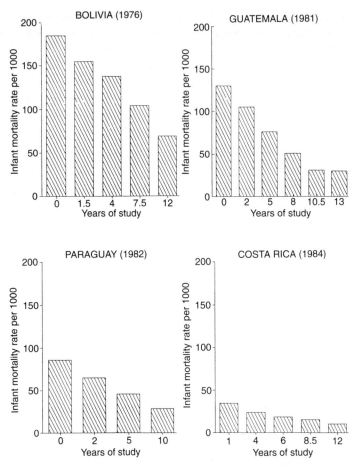

Fig. 2.2. Infant mortality rate by mother's education, selected countries
Source: CELADE, IMIAL Project.

fashion (Chackiel and Schkolnik, 1990). In general, total fertility rates are higher in rural areas and in households whose head has a low level of schooling and who works in the agricultural sector. The most striking fact is that, in those countries in the early stages of demographic transition, the average number of children of the most deprived social sectors is over eight and has tended to rise or remain constant. Countries further along in the transition process, on the other hand, have a tendency to converge around fairly low total fertility rates, although some differential persists. It is clear that any population or health care policy designed to offer maternal and child services or to affect fertility must necessarily extend those services to rural areas and to women with low levels of education.

(b) *Infant mortality* Differences in infant mortality within national populations are rooted in the sharp contrasts in living conditions that prevail. Health care services should be concerned to identify high risk groups in order to give them priority attention. By way of illustration, Figure 2.2 presents estimates of infant mortality in countries at different stages of transition, classified by educational level of the mother. The children at greatest risk are found in rural areas and have illiterate mothers. In certain cases, the children of these mothers have four times the risk of dying of children of university-educated mothers. Other variables also reveal sharp contrasts, for example ethnic origin—the children of indigenous peoples face high death rates.

In spite of the urbanization process and due, in part, to higher rural fertility in countries belonging to Groups I and II, half or more births occur among the rural population. These births are exposed to greater risk of death and generate approximately two-thirds of the national totals of infant deaths. Moreover, in countries with high death rates, the majority of infant deaths occur among the children of illiterate mothers (between 60 and 80 per cent), because of their disadvantaged living conditions and higher fertility. The fact that, among the poorest, more children are born and die creates a dramatic situation in terms of the demand for maternal and child health care. To this must be added the chain of social problems linked to the high frequency of adolescent pregnancies. These often lead to abortions, with consequent threats to the mothers' health, and unwanted births. Even though reliable figures are not available, mortality caused by pregnancies and births is many times higher in Latin America than in developed countries. The majority of these deaths could be prevented.

6. Changes in the Level and Structure of Mortality

As seen in Section 2, the countries of Latin America have experienced a substantial reduction in the level of general mortality over the past 35 years, as indicated by the increase in life expectancy at birth from 51.8 years in 1950–5 to 66.6 years in 1985–90 (Table 2.3). This gain of almost 15 years—a little over 2 years per quinquennium—has reduced the gap in life expectancy between Latin America and the English-speaking countries of North America from 17.3 to 9.5 years. Within Latin America, however, there still exists a difference of 22 years in life expectancy at birth between the highest and lowest mortality countries (Table 2.3).

In 1985–90 mortality in Latin America was lower than in all other developing regions of the world, with the exception of Eastern Asia. Nevertheless, life expectancy remains at the level that the United States of America achieved 40 years ago. In addition, the magnitude of Latin America's gain in the last 35 years is comparable with that which the United States attained starting from the same mortality level over an equal number of years, from 1910–15 to 1945–50. In the United States, however, this advance was made before many of the life-prolonging technologies available today had been developed and in spite of the fact that the United States participated in two world wars during the period (PAHO, 1990).

While in Canada and the United States the gain in life expectancy per quinquennium was greater in the period 1970–5 to 1985–90 than during the 20 preceding years, the same was true for only 4 out of the 20 countries of Latin America (Bolivia, Honduras, Chile, and Uruguay). If major efforts are not implemented to accelerate the current pace of mortality reduction, Latin America will not have reached the life expectancy that the United States has at present, even 35 years from now (PAHO, 1990).

The increase in life expectancy at birth has resulted from decreases in mortality at all ages, but the largest—and historically earliest—gains stemmed from the reduction in mortality among children under 5 years of age and, especially, in infant mortality. The differentially greater decrease of the risk of dying at an early age is reflected in the fact that the mortality structure has aged faster than the population structure. This can be seen in Table 2.5, which provides demographic indicators for Guatemala, Mexico, Argentina, Chile, Cuba, and Costa Rica, ordered according to their life expectancy at birth in 1985–90.

With increasing life expectancy and population ageing, the burden of mortality shifts progressively from the younger to older age groups. Thus, in Guatemala, with a life expectancy at birth of 62 years, 45 per cent of the population is under 15 years old, and over one half of all deaths occur in this age group. Where life expectancy has surpassed 75 years, as in Cuba, the proportion of children under 15 years of age in the population has decreased to 23 per cent, but deaths in this group have declined much further, and account for only 5 per cent of all deaths. (In Canada, 21 per cent of the population and 2 per cent of deaths are under 15 years of age.) At the other extreme of age, the oldest population groups account for an increasing proportion of deaths as overall mortality declines. Where life expectancy is low, 3 per cent of the population and 19 per cent of the deceased are 65 years of age or older, but, where life expectancy at birth is 75 years, this group is about 9 per cent of the population and contributes almost two-thirds of all deaths. Thus, although driven primarily by fertility, the population's age structure also reacts to age-specific and, as will be seen, cause-specific changes in mortality, albeit after a longer time-lag (PAHO, 1990; United Nations, 1991).

The relationship between changes in the level and structure of mortality can be illustrated by the model shown in Table 2.6. The model is based on the mortality history of Costa Rica and Cuba, and represents adequately mortality experience in the countries of Latin America. It can be seen that the largest reduction in both absolute and relative terms has been achieved by the youngest age group. As life expectancy at birth increases from 50 to 75 years, the risk of dying among children under 5 years of age has decreased by 37 deaths per 1000 from 40.8 to 3.9, a reduction of 90 per cent. For the next two age groups

Table 2.5.   Demographic indicators for selected countries of Latin America

Indicator	Country[a]					
	Guatemala	Mexico	Argentina	Chile	Cuba	Costa Rica
Total fertility rate						
1985–1990	5.8	3.6	3.0	2.7	1.8	3.4
1950–1955	7.1	6.8	3.2	5.1	4.1	6.7
Life expectancy at birth						
1985–1990	62.0	68.8	70.6	71.5	75.2	75.3
1950–1955	42.1	50.8	62.7	53.8	59.5	57.3
Annual growth rate (%)						
1985–1990	2.9	2.2	1.3	1.7	1.0	2.8
1950–1955	2.9	2.8	2.0	2.2	1.8	3.5
Percent urban population						
1990	38.1	72.7	85.9	84.6	74.8	46.7
Population age structure						
(1990)	100.0	100.0	100.0	100.0	100.0	100.0
0–14	45.4	38.0	29.9	30.6	22.7	36.5
15–44	41.3	47.4	42.8	48.6	51.4	47.6
45–64	10.1	10.9	18.2	14.8	17.4	11.7
65 and over	3.2	3.7	9.1	6.0	8.5	4.2
Mortality age structure						
(year)	(1984)	(1986)	(1987)	(1987)	(1988)	(1988)
0–14	54.5	23.3	9.1	9.8	5.1	15.0
15–44	14.9	18.5	8.1	11.7	11.8	13.2
45–64	12.0	19.2	22.8	21.3	19.3	17.9
65 and over	18.7	39.1	60.1	57.2	63.8	53.9

[a] These countries were selected because they illustrate different mortality patterns, different stages in the process of demographic transition and have data of acceptable reliability (each country reports over 5000 deaths per year, and under-registration is estimated to be less than 20%).

Source: CELADE, current estimates and population projections; PAHO, Technical Information System.

mortality is lower and the absolute gains have been lower too—2.5 deaths per 1000 children aged 5–14 years, and 4.4 deaths per 1000 adults aged 15–39 years. Nevertheless, these declines represent improvements of 89 per cent and 80 per cent, respectively. For the older adults (40–64 years) mortality rates are higher but progress has been relatively slow, with a 64 per cent reduction. After childhood the risk of dying increases steadily with age and thus is higher for those aged 65 years or more than for adults under 65 years of age, although important gains are to be expected here as well (PAHO, 1990).

To assess progress made, current age-specific mortality rates—consisting of the average of the rates reported for the three most recent years—were compared with the rates recorded for 1965 (Figure 2.3). To emphasize the challenge for the future, these figures also show as a reference a set of more favourable rates, consisting of the lowest age-specific mortality rates recorded for each sex since 1978 in those countries of the Americas reporting at least 5000 deaths per year and with under-registration of deaths estimated to be less than 10 per cent. The reference rates are provided in Appendix Table 2.A1 (Uemura, 1989).

It can be seen that the pathways leading to longer life expectancy have differed between the countries shown. In Cuba, most advances for both sexes had already been achieved by 1965. In the other five countries, gains have occurred since 1965 for all age groups, with the exception of 25–34-year-old men in Guatemala. In general, these gains have been more pronounced for women than for men, especially in Chile and Costa Rica. Current rates in Costa Rica are close to the lowest rates recorded in the Americas for adult men and women, while Guatemala faces the most striking gap between its current mortality and these reference rates.

Changes in the level and structure of mortality by sex and age are closely related to changes in mortality from specific causes. When life expectancy at birth was below 50 years, over two-thirds of all deaths were due to communicable diseases (infectious and parasitic diseases, meningitis, acute respiratory infections, pneumonia, and influenza), and over 60 per cent of deaths from these diseases occurred before age 15. Communicable diseases represented the number one health priority, as they still do in many developing countries. Over time, the improvement in general living conditions and specific biomedical advances contributed to a dramatic reduction of mortality from these diseases, particularly in the age group of the population most vulnerable to them, namely children under 5 years of age. In countries where life expectancy at birth approaches 75 years, over two-thirds of all deaths are caused by non-communicable diseases and external causes.

Table 2.6. Mortality rates by age, according to life expectancy at birth, Cuba–Costa Rica model

Life expectancy at birth	Mortality rates by age (per 1000)				
	0–4	5–14	15–39	40–64	65+
50	40.8	2.8	5.5	16.9	91.0
55	33.5	2.2	4.3	14.2	84.0
60	26.2	1.6	3.2	11.5	77.1
65	18.5	1.0	2.2	9.2	72.1
70	10.6	0.6	1.6	7.6	66.3
75	3.9	0.3	1.1	6.1	59.7

Source: CELADE in PAHO (1990).

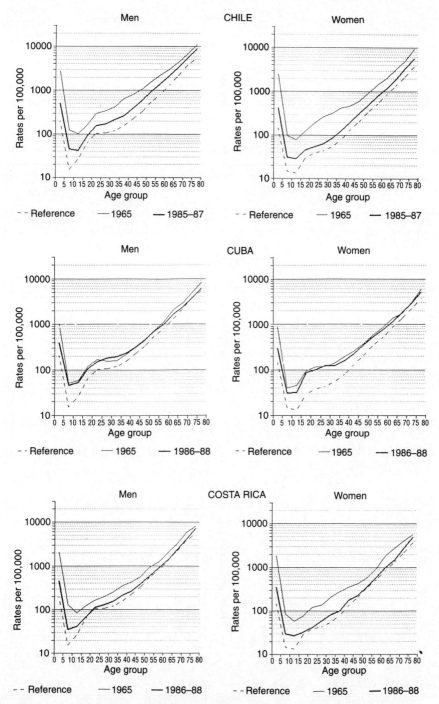

Fig. 2.3. Age-specific mortality rates, 1960s and 1980s, selected countries
Source: PAHO Technical Information System.

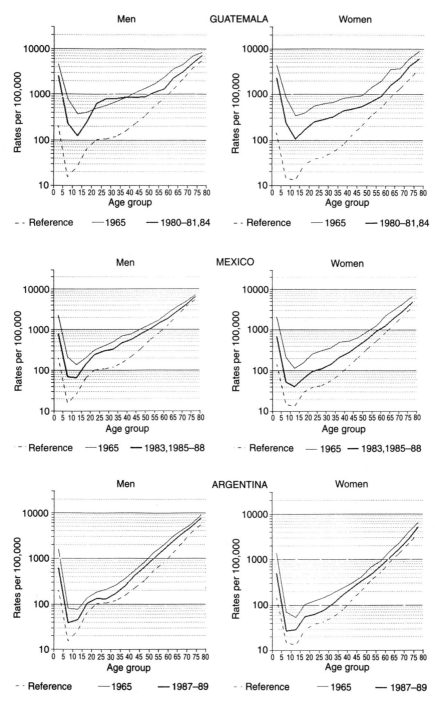

Within the communicable diseases category, the most important causes of death are intestinal infections (diarrhoea), followed by acute respiratory diseases and diseases preventable by immunization. As a single cause grouping, diarrhoeal disease mortality has decreased more rapidly than mortality from all other causes combined. This decline has contributed more than decreases in all other cause groups to the reduction in mortality of children under 5 years of age and in mortality at all ages, and thus to the increase of life expectancy at birth. Nevertheless, diarrhoea persists as a problem of disease and death for large population segments, reflecting poor nutrition and sanitation (PAHO, 1991*b*). The recent outbreaks of cholera further attest to this situation (PAHO, 1991*c*).

Today, the persistence of high mortality from the communicable diseases as a group, and from diarrhoeal disease in particular, has become synonymous with underdevelopment and poverty. In Canada, the country with the highest life expectancy in the Americas, communicable diseases are now responsible for around 4 per cent of deaths at all ages, and 2 per cent or less of deaths in adults (15–44 and 45–64 years). In many countries of Latin America, however, these advances are far from being attained. In Guatemala, almost one half of all deaths are still due to communicable diseases and most of those occur before age 5. This situation probably exists in several other countries of the region, where life expectancy at birth continues to be low and precarious living conditions still prevail for the vast majority of the population. The impact of AIDS, an emerging problem among young adults, is not yet reflected in the data shown.

The structure of mortality by broad groups of causes (as defined by the Pan American Health Organization for international comparisons) is shown in Table 2.7 for deaths at all ages, and for adults aged 15–44 and 45–64 years. The definitions of the groups and the ICD codes are provided in Appendix Table 2.A2. Consistent with the age structure of the population, the relative importance of tumours, diseases of the circulatory system, and injury and poisoning is increasing. Together, these causes account for over two-thirds of all deaths in countries where life expectancy at birth has reached or surpassed 75 years.

Most deaths from non-communicable disease occur in the population aged 65 years and over, but their frequently lengthy and sometimes incapacitating course starts at much earlier ages. Although the importance of non-communicable disease mortality relative to total deaths has increased, rates for most such causes have tended to decline, at least up to age 44. The risk of dying from cardiovascular disease appears to be beginning to decrease in several countries, but not before reaching epidemic proportions in the 45–64 year age group, especially among men. On the other hand, mortality rates for the cancers as a group are increasing, especially in those 45 years of age and older. Of special concern are cancer of the reproductive organs in women and cancer of the lung in men, which is also beginning to increase in women.

Table 2.7. Mortality structure by broad groups of causes, selected countries of Latin America around 1987

Cause groups[a]	Country					
	Guatemala 1984	Mexico 1986	Argentina 1987	Chile 1987	Cuba 1988	Costa Rica 1988
All ages						
Total	100.0	100.0	100.0	100.0	100.0	100.0
1. Communicable diseases	44.7	17.8	6.4	12.2	6.6	6.9
2. Neoplasms	4.2	9.7	18.5	20.8	19.6	21.9
3. Diseases of circulatory system	7.5	19.1	46.0	29.9	43.7	29.6
4. Conditions originating in perinatal period	16.3	5.0	3.8	2.7	1.4	5.2
5. External causes	6.8	16.3	6.9	13.0	12.2	11.4
6. All other diseases	20.6	32.0	18.5	21.4	16.6	25.0
Age 15–44 years						
Total	100.0	100.0	100.0	100.0	100.0	100.0
1. Communicable diseases	33.1	8.9	6.7	7.4	2.9	3.7
2. Neoplasms	5.3	7.2	16.5	15.8	13.1	20.0
3. Diseases of circulatory system	6.9	8.2	23.9	8.6	14.1	12.2
5. External causes	29.1	50.2	33.7	50.6	52.7	43.0
6. All other diseases	25.7	25.5	19.2	17.6	17.2	21.0
Age 45–64 years						
Total	100.0	100.0	100.0	100.0	100.0	100.0
1. Communicable diseases	33.2	8.7	4.8	7.6	3.4	3.4
2. Neoplasms	11.5	16.3	27.8	31.1	28.0	32.7
3. Diseases of circulatory system	15.1	19.9	41.9	25.0	40.7	27.4
5. External causes	8.9	14.3	7.1	12.2	10.9	11.2
6. All other diseases	31.2	40.8	18.4	24.1	17.0	25.3

[a] Percentages based on total deaths from defined causes only. Definitions of cause groups and ICD codes are provided in Appendix Table 2.A2.

Source: PAHO (1991a).

Deaths from accidents and violence are increasing in prominence among young adults, especially men. Over one half of deaths from external causes occur among those aged 15–44 years and their relative importance is growing among persons under 15 years of age.

The broad grouping of causes of death chosen is intended to facilitate a general overview of the changing epidemiologic profile in these countries, so far as this is possible using mortality data alone. By its nature, it does not do justice to diseases which by themselves carry limited relative weight in the mortality structure. Many of these are thrown together in the last group, 'all other diseases', which includes diabetes mellitus, chronic bronchitis and other chronic pulmonary disease, chronic liver disease and cirrhosis, diseases of the urinary system and other diseases that increase in importance as the population ages. Also included in this last group is maternal mortality which, although decreasing, is vastly under-reported and continues to be exceedingly high in most of Latin America. Maternal mortality has been almost completely eliminated in the developed world. Its persistence at high levels in Latin America reflects poor coverage and deficient quality of care for pregnant women.

7. Excess Mortality

According to current population and mortality projections, it is estimated that 34 million deaths will occur in Latin America during the last decade of the twentieth century. One way of assessing excess mortality has been illustrated already by comparing current sex and age-specific mortality rates with the lowest rates observed in countries of the same hemisphere (Figure 2.3). Over one half of the deaths are in excess of those that would occur if the reference rates had prevailed in every country. But rates tell only part of the story, as even moderate excess rates may be responsible for heavy burdens of excess mortality when they affect a large proportion of the population. This will be illustrated by standardized mortality ratios (SMRs), defined as the number of deaths observed in a given population, relative to the number of deaths expected under specified assumptions—in this case represented by the lowest observed age-sex-specific rates—in a population with the same age-structure. Computation of the SMRs was restricted to the population under 80 years of age, because death is more difficult to postpone after this age and the data become increasingly less reliable (Plaut and Roberts, 1989).

As shown in Table 2.8, the overall SMR for Guatemala is 446 per cent, meaning that according to currently prevailing mortality rates, 446 deaths occur in the population of Guatemala for every 100 deaths that would occur if the reference rates applied to that population. The situation is even worse for children under 15 years of age and is worse for girls than for boys. More than twelve boys and almost sixteen girls die according to current rates, instead of

Table 2.8. Standardized mortality ratios (%) by sex and broad age group, selected countries of Latin America, 1990[a]

Country	Age in years				
	Under 80	Under 15	15–44	45–64	65–79
Both sexes					
Guatemala	445.7	1362.1	559.2	193.7	149.9
Mexico	200.0	414.8	257.2	174.0	125.8
Argentina	157.8	305.1	165.9	165.1	138.1
Chile	164.2	261.9	161.3	159.1	151.6
Cuba	135.1	205.4	178.6	135.2	119.1
Costa Rica	130.1	229.4	123.8	110.3	119.2
Men					
Guatemala	415.1	1217.4	564.8	191.2	133.4
Mexico	199.5	389.0	263.5	177.8	118.1
Argentina	166.2	293.5	154.9	186.0	144.2
Chile	168.9	250.0	165.4	170.6	153.8
Cuba	124.3	202.0	154.7	128.1	108.0
Costa Rica	126.8	222.5	121.0	108.6	115.8
Women					
Guatemala	494.8	1572.1	547.1	197.6	175.0
Mexico	200.8	452.5	243.8	168.5	135.5
Argentina	146.6	321.8	189.2	135.2	130.9
Chile	157.9	279.2	152.6	143.4	149.2
Cuba	152.3	210.4	229.4	146.1	136.0
Costa Rica	135.3	239.3	129.9	112.9	123.8

[a] All deaths estimated for 1990 population using average rates from three most recent years available for currents deaths (numerator), and reference rates for expected deaths (denominator).

Source: PAHO, Technical Information System.

the single child of each gender that would die if the reference rates had prevailed. Although lower than in Guatemala, the SMRs in all other countries of the region are higher for this age group than for any other. The SMRs are also very high for young adults, especially in Guatemala. In that country, Mexico and Chile they are higher for men than for women, reflecting the impact of accidents and violence, especially in urban settings. After age 45, most of the SMRs are lower for both sexes and the differences between countries become less pronounced.

The examination of specific causes responsible for excess adult mortality and the approaches required for their prevention is beyond the scope of this chapter, as is assessment of the number of deaths that could be prevented if existing effective technology were to be made available to all those who need

it (Taucher, 1978). However, the approach used here allows excess mortality to be identified and studied in considerable detail.

8. Comments

The summary findings presented attempt to provide an impression of the diversity of countries in Latin America in terms of some of their demographic characteristics. Differentials inside the countries are even more pronounced. With few exceptions, distribution of income and access to social resources are still highly inequitable and large segments of the population live in extremely depressed conditions. If this situation is to be alleviated, provisions must be made now to meet the needs of a population that will become larger, older, and more concentrated in urban areas. Demographic trends must be watched closely and planning must start promptly if sufficient employment opportunities, as well as adequate housing, education, social security, and health services are to be available for all population groups.

The persistence of precarious living conditions is reflected in health problems such as diarrhoea and other diseases of poverty which continue to prevail in most countries of Latin America but have been conquered in developed societies. On the other hand, in all countries there are signs that the burden of mortality from causes associated with adulthood is increasing as a result of the growth in the proportion of adults in an ageing population structure. Such causes of death should not be considered 'diseases of development': the risk of dying from non-communicable disease and, even more so, the risk of accidental or violent death are considerably higher among the poor than among those who are socially better off.

Changes in the level and structure of mortality by age and sex are closely related to changes in the cause-specific probabilities of being exposed to and suffering disease or injury and ultimately dying from them. A high level of mortality reflects the impact of negative forces acting on population groups rendered vulnerable by their biological characteristics or an adverse physical and social environment. A better understanding of excess mortality in terms of who dies prematurely, where, when, and from what causes, should facilitate the development of targeted interventions that will yield longer and healthier lives.

It is a basic tenet of epidemiology that neither exposure to health insults nor vulnerability to them are randomly distributed throughout the population but, rather, that certain population groups are at higher risk than others because of their general or specific circumstances. It is one of the challenges of epidemiology to identify the circumstances and factors that influence health and disease and the population groups most exposed to them, in order to understand better the mechanisms involved. Epidemiology needs to participate more in devising, implementing, and advocating strategies that may enhance the population's resistance to disease and promote health in general, as well as in designing interventions either to counteract specific factors that contribute to disease (and injury) or, at least, to reduce disease severity and case-fatality. Undoubtedly, effective health promotion and disease prevention should make the greatest possible contributions to enhancement of the quality of life and avoidance of suffering from unnecessary illness. Nevertheless, since disease and injury will never be eliminated entirely, it is a further challenge to public health to ensure the availability of adequate health care to those who need it. Untimely death is but the ultimate expression of failure at any or all of these possible points of intervention.

Policy-makers and administrators responsible for the health of the public in the countries of the region will face the double challenge of dealing with the causes and consequences of an increasing, and increasingly costly, burden of ill health in a growing adult population, while still having to struggle with those problems of childhood which, in the light of current knowledge and available technology, should have been resolved long ago.

Appendix 2.1

Table 2.A1. Reference rates for estimating avoidable mortality[a]

Age in years	Men			Women		
	Country	Year	Rate[b]	Country	Year	Rate[c]
Under 5	Canada	1988	200.2	Canada	1985	144.4
5–9	Puerto Rico	1986	15.4	Puerto Rico	1989	14.7
10–14	Canada	1989	26.4	Puerto Rico	1987	13.2
15–19	Costa Rica	1986	64.1	Costa Rica	1987	28.8
20–24	Costa Rica	1986	103.3	Costa Rica	1985	38.4
25–29	Uruguay	1985	107.3	Canada	1987	43.0
30–34	Costa Rica	1983	119.3	Canada	1987	55.1
35–39	Canada	1985	155.5	Canada	1987	78.8
40–44	Canada	1989	222.0	Canada	1988	130.9
45–49	Costa Rica	1983	328.9	Costa Rica	1986	207.7
50–54	Costa Rica	1983	542.1	Canada	1989	342.3
55–59	Costa Rica	1988	807.7	Costa Rica	1988	522.7
60–64	Costa Rica	1987	1,327.1	Canada	1989	869.6
65–69	Cuba	1978	2,177.9	Canada	1989	1354.8
70–74	Cuba	1983	3,763.5	Canada	1989	2206.6
75–79	Puerto Rico	1979	5,479.3	Canada	1989	3678.1
80+	Cuba	1983	12,174.0	Canada	1989	9713.3

[a] Lowest values for sex- and age-specific mortality rates, reported since 1978 in countries of the Americas with at least 5000 deaths reported per year, and under-registration estimated to be less than 10%.
[b] Age-specific rates per 100,000 men.
[c] Age-specific rates per 100,000 women.
Source: PAHO Technical Information System.

Table 2.A2. Definition of groups of causes of death according to the International Classification of Diseases

1. Communicable diseases	All categories in Chapter I, i.e. all infectious and parasitic (diseases 001–139), and, in addition, meningitis (320–322), acute respiratory infections (460–466), and pneumonia and influenza (480–487).
2. Neoplasms:	All categories in Chapter II, i.e. all malignant as well as benign neoplasms, carcinoma in situ, neoplasms of

Table 2.A2. *Continued*

---

	uncertain behaviour and those of unspecified nature, that is (140–239).
3. Diseases of the circulatory system:	All categories in Chapter VII, i.e. acute rheumatic fever, chronic rheumatic heart disease, hypertensive disease, ischemic heart disease, diseases of pulmonary circulation and other forms of heart disease, cerebrovascular disease, diseases of arteries, arterioles and capillaries, of veins and lymphatics, and other diseases of the circulatory system (390–459).
4. Certain conditions originating in the perinatal period:	All categories in Chapter XV, i.e. maternal conditions and obstetric complications affecting the fetus or newborn, slow fetal growth, fetal malnutrition and immaturity, birth trauma, hypoxia, asphyxia, other respiratory conditions of fetus and newborn, infections specific to the perinatal period, and other and ill-defined conditions originating in the perinatal period (760–779).
5. External causes of injury and poisoning:	All categories in Chapter XVII, code E, i.e. all accidents, suicide, homicide, legal intervention, injury undetermined whether accidentally or purposely inflicted, and injury resulting from operations of war (E800–E999).
6. 'All other diseases':	All other defined causes not included in groups 1 through 4 (remainder of 001–779).

Note: Proportional mortality by cause is based on total deaths from defined causes; that is, the denominator excludes deaths coded as due to Symptoms, signs and ill-defined conditions (ICD-9: 780–799).

Source: PAHO (1990).

References

Chackiel, J., and S. Schkolnik (1990), 'América Latina: Transición de la fecundidad en el período 1950–1990', Seminar on Fertility Transition in Latin America, CELADE/IUSSP/CENEP, Buenos Aires, Argentina.

Demographic and Health Surveys (1991), *Newsletter*, 4(1): 12, IRD/Macro International, Columbia, Md.

Economic Commission for Latin America and the Caribbean (ECLAC) (1990), *Magnitud de la pobreza en América Latina en los años ochenta*, Santiago, Chile.

Pan American Health Organization (PAHO) (1990), *Health Conditions in the Americas, 1990 Edition*, Vol. I, Scientific Publication No. 524, Washington, DC.

——(1991*a*), *Health Statistics from the Americas, 1991 Edition, Mortality Since 1960*, Sci. Publ. No. 537, Washington, DC.

——(1991*b*), 'Mortality due to infectious intestinal diseases in Latin America and the Caribbean, 1965–1990', *Epidemiological Bulletin*, 12(3): 1–6, Washington, DC.

——(1991c), 'Cholera situation in the Americas. An update', *Epidemiological Bulletin*, 12(4): 11–13.

——and World Health Organization (WHO) (1980), *Health for All by the Year 2000. Strategies*, Official Paper No. 173, PAHO, Washington, DC.

Plaut, R., and E. Roberts (1989), 'Preventable mortality: Indicator or target? Applications in Developing Countries', *World Health Statistics Quarterly*, 42(1): 4–15.

Taucher, E. (1978), *Chile: Mortalidad desde 1955 a 1975. Tendencias y causas*, Series A, No. 162, CELADE, Santiago, Chile.

Uemura, K. (1989), 'Excess mortality ratio with reference to the lowest age-sex-specific death rates among countries', *World Health Statistics Quarterly*, 42(1): 26–41.

United Nations (1991), *World Population Prospects 1990*, Department of International Economic and Social Affairs, New York.

Part II

Data Collection and Methods

3 Evaluation of Vital Statistics for the Study of Causes of Death

DIRK JASPERS FAIJER and HERNÁN ORELLANA
Centro Latinoamericano de Demografía, Santiago, Chile

1. Introduction

Various studies have examined the quality of vital statistics data on deaths and their causes in Latin America (see, for example, Chackiel, 1987). The most recent work of this kind is the Pan American Health Organization (PAHO) publication on health conditions in the Americas (PAHO, 1990). Although these studies are very useful for the analysis of overall mortality, they are of limited use for the study of adult mortality. This chapter takes a deeper look at the problems presented by the data on adult mortality (defining the adult population as those aged 15 years or more) and causes of death among adults in Latin America. First, vital statistics coverage by age and sex is reviewed for those Latin American countries for which the necessary information is available. Then, the problem of ill-defined causes of death is addressed and an estimate of total unavailable information on causes of death, compared with total estimated deaths, is presented.

This analysis is based on the information in the PAHO databases corresponding to the 9th Revision of the International Statistical Classification of Diseases, Injuries, and Causes of Death (ICD), which covers the years 1979–88 (WHO/PAHO, 1978), together with data available in national and international annual statistical reports. This makes it possible to include sixteen or seventeen of the twenty countries, which compose the Latin American region, in the analysis. In order to facilitate work with the PAHO database, a new database was created within the REDATAM (Retrieval of data for small areas by microcomputer) system, which is a package developed by the UN Latin American Demographic Centre for processing census information (CELADE, 1990). To establish the quality of the available information on causes of death, data on medical certification of deaths are analysed briefly. Problems that arise in studies at sub-national levels are also mentioned. Finally, other issues which must be faced in the analysis of mortality by causes of death are reviewed; for example, incompatibilities between different revisions of the ICD, the treatment of ill-defined causes of death and the availability and management of data.

2. Coverage of Death Registration Systems

When beginning any study of mortality based on the information contained in vital statistics, the first question to be answered is what percentage of deaths are registered? In seeking to answer this question for the twenty countries of the region, the preliminary problem must be faced of the availability of data, which varies greatly from country to country. Only a few countries make their statistical information readily available. Others do not possess the data and/or do not make them available. Moreover, the data may be dispersed among the publications of various institutions (both national and international) and the statistics in different publications may not agree. Given this situation, the decision was made to work with the PAHO database for 1979–88, which is not only relatively complete but available on tape. It is important to note that this database contains no information on three countries (Bolivia, Haiti, and Nicaragua) and that, for other countries, the number of years on which information is available varies. The only country for which there is information for every year of the 9th Revision of the ICD (1979–88) is Cuba. The other two countries for which the information is fairly complete are Costa Rica (1980–8), and Panama (1979–87).

An estimate of total registered deaths was made for each country for the 1980–5 period (from mid-1980 to mid-1985), assuming that the years for which data were available in the database are representative of the whole period. For example, total registered deaths in Guatemala during this period were estimated on the basis of 1980, 1981, and 1984. Registered deaths for other periods were estimated from other sources, both national and international. These estimates are compared with the number of deaths expected by age for each period analysed, corresponding to the deaths implicit in the current population projections for each country. Obviously these estimates might differ from the deaths that actually occurred, particularly in those countries where mortality estimates for the period 1980–5 are forecasts or where population estimates are not very reliable. It is not believed that this affects the major conclusions of this chapter.

The coverage of the vital statistics system with respect to the registration of deaths is very uneven in Latin America. Some countries record nearly all deaths and publish the data. In others, either the number of registered deaths is not even known or only 50 per cent of deaths are recorded. In order to summarize the situation in Latin America, the following classification system was adopted, based on the available information and the criteria used in other studies. Coverage of registered deaths is rated as follows (see Table 3.1):

- 'good' when coverage is greater than 90 per cent;
- 'satisfactory' when it is between 80 and 89 per cent;

Table 3.1. Classification of Latin American countries by coverage of mortality statistics

Classification	Coverage									
	Total				Broad age groups 1980–5					
	1960–65	1975–80	1980–85[a]	1987[b]	0–14			15 and over		
					T	M	F	T	M	F
Good	3	7	5	3	3	3	2	8	10	7
Satisfactory	5	3	4	2	2	3	3	4	1	4
Unsatisfactory	4	2	3	2	5	4	5	2	4	3
Deficient	7	8	5	—	7	7	7	3	2	3
No information	1	—	3	13	3	3	3	3	3	3

[a] According to the PAHO database.
[b] Only seven countries provide information for this year in the PAHO database.

- 'fair' when it is between 70 and 79 per cent;
- 'deficient' when it is lower than 70 per cent, or
- 'no information'.

In the 1980–5 period, less than half of Latin American countries had statistics which can be considered to be good or satisfactory (with less than 20 per cent under-registration). Eight countries still have omission rates higher than 30 per cent. Furthermore, no country managed to improve coverage greatly between 1960 and 1985 (see Table 3.2) except Venezuela, which lowered the omission rate from 25 per cent to less than 10 per cent by 1980 (although it should be noted that the omission rate rose again to 13 per cent in the following five-year period). Cuba would seem to be a similar case but the high level of under-registration in the 1960–5 period must be seen as an exception in the light of that country's excellent statistical tradition, as this period covers the years following the revolution of 1959 (Chackiel, 1987). In Colombia, although the omission rate appears to have dropped from 27 to 15 per cent between 1975 and 1985, sources other than the PAHO database, which contains data on Colombia for only 1981, 1984, and 1985, produce an estimated omission rate of 24 per cent, indicating little change.

As might be expected, there is a clear relationship between the level of under-registration and life expectancy at birth, because both reflect a country's socio-economic situation. This can be seen in Figure 3.1, in which the under-registration rates for all Latin American countries are arranged with respect to their life expectancy at birth (from the highest to the lowest value). There are

Table 3.2. Under-registration of deaths, ill-defined causes and total with no information, 1969–88

	Under-registration					Ill-defined causes				Total without information		
	1960–5[a]	1975–80[b]	1980–5[b]	1980–5[d]	1987[d]	1965[a]	1978[a]	1980–5[d]	1987–8	1960–5	1978	1980–5
Argentina	5.8	2.1	5.2	4.1	—	12.4	4.3	3.2	—	17.5	6.3	7.2
Bolivia	64.1	62.7	64.7	—	—	23.2	—	—	—	72.4	—	—
Brazil	34.4	19.6	23.5	29.0	—	39.7	—	21.4	—	60.4	—	44.2
Colombia[c]	10.1	26.5	24.1	14.9	1.1	13.5	8.6	6.5	2.3	22.2	32.8	20.4
Costa Rica[c]	11.7	13.7	7.5	7.5	-0.6	9.2	8.0	5.7	0.2	19.8	20.6	12.8
Cuba	26.4	4.3	6.3	6.4	10.6	1.6	0.0	0.3	8.1	27.6	4.3	6.7
Chile[c]	3.7	6.3	1.4	1.5	—	7.7	10.8	8.7	—	11.1	16.4	10.1
Dominican Republic[c]	54.6	44.8	41.3	41.4	—	32.1	31.9	17.5	—	69.2	62.4	51.7
Ecuador	12.8	18.9	22.5	22.4	28.1	21.7	16.5	15.7	15.0	31.7	32.3	34.6
El Salvador[c]	28.3	31.4	33.6	34.0	—	34.4	28.5	21.5	.	53.0	51.0	48.2
Guatemala	12.7	4.9	6.8	10.7	—	16.0	18.2	12.4	—	26.7	22.2	21.8
Haiti	—	79.5	—	—	—	—	—	—	—	—	—	—
Honduras	49.8	51.0	40.4	48.5	—	41.0	34.0	36.2	—	70.4	67.7	67.1
Mexico	11.3	9.3	12.2	12.5	—	18.6	8.9	5.4	5.2	27.8	17.4	17.2
Nicaragua	56.4	39.0	—	—	—	19.9	27.0	—	—	65.1	55.5	—
Panama	25.2	25.2	25.7	25.7	21.1	18.6	10.8	9.6	8.2	39.1	33.3	32.8
Paraguay	58.5	31.1	47.6	43.2	—	25.8	19.4	21.6	—	69.2	44.5	55.5
Peru	42.6	35.7	—	52.5	—	13.7	8.4	7.7	—	50.5	41.1	56.2
Uruguay	6.0	2.9	1.2	3.5	0.4	6.7	6.9	7.9	6.2	12.3	9.6	11.1
Venezuela	24.8	9.4	13.3	12.7	17.0	25.0	14.2	12.2	13.2	43.6	22.3	23.4

Sources:
[a] Chackiel, 1987 (except countries marked[c]).
[b] From the national Vital Statistics Reports or the United Nations *Demographic Yearbook*, various volumes.
[c] From reports on each country's projections.
[d] Information from the PAHO's database (9th Revision).

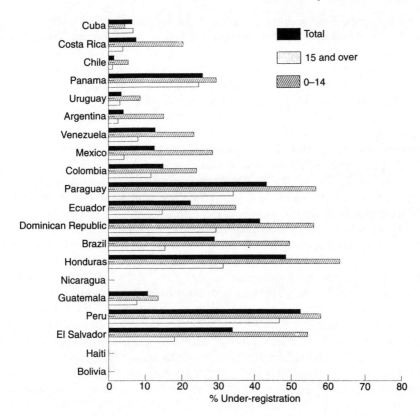

Fig. 3.1. Under-registration of child and adult deaths, 1980–5

two exceptional countries. On the one hand, Guatemala has relatively complete vital statistics, despite its moderately high mortality level. This fact has been noted in a number of studies (Chackiel, 1987) and is explained by the long tradition of vital registration in that country, which is rooted in the country's role as Captaincy General in the era of Spanish colonization. However, recent estimates suggest a deterioration in death registration coverage. In Panama, the opposite situation prevails. The country has one of the lowest mortality levels in the region, but the level of under-registration is high. This is even more noteworthy in the light of the fact that Panama has a good reputation in statistical matters in terms of both the regularity of population and housing censuses and the efficiency with which it makes detailed vital statistics available.

The under-registration of adult deaths (of persons aged 15 years or more) is much lower than that of child deaths in all countries except Cuba (see Figure 3.1). This implies that there are a relatively large number of countries in which vital statistics are sufficiently complete to make the study of adult mortality possible: twelve countries have an omission rate for adult deaths lower than 20 per cent. Equally, it is clear that opportunities for mortality studies in the under-15 age group are much more limited. Only three countries have an omission rate of less than 10 per cent for deaths in childhood.

While substantial and systematic differences in the overall level of omissions by sex are not characteristic of Latin America, there is some tendency to register adult male deaths more fully than deaths of women. In Brazil, which is the extreme case, only 6 per cent of male deaths go unrecorded but the omission rate rises to 26 per cent for women (see Table 3.3). The estimated omission rate for broad age groups behaves similarly to the sex ratios by age usually observed in censuses. There are two low points: the first among young adults (between 15 and 35 years old) and the second in the open-ended age group. Omissions are most common in the age groups 0–14 years and also among those aged approximately 50 to 70 years. This trend is clearer among men than women. In particular, the earlier low point in omission rates among women is not found in all countries, implying that there tends to be a marked difference by sex in the omission of deaths among young adults.

The similarity between the age pattern of under-registration of deaths and that of enumerated sex ratios is probably not coincidental. On the one hand, the errors which affect censuses may also operate in death registration systems while, on the other, errors in a census may affect estimates of both mortality and the corrected population by sex and age. Moreover, it is striking that in some countries there appears to be over-registration of deaths in certain age groups, which does not seem likely. One explanation for apparent over-registration in the young adult male age group (for example, in Guatemala, Venezuela, and Uruguay) may be a deficit in the expected number of deaths arising from under-estimation of the young male population (which would indicate a greater rate of omission in censuses than that implied in population estimates and projections) and/or over-estimation of the death rates for those age groups. On the other hand, the apparent over-registration of deaths at age 75 years and above in some countries can be explained partially by the widespread tendency to exaggerate the ages of older persons when they die, as this tends to exceed age exaggeration in population censuses. This phenomenon will cause a deficit of registered deaths in immediately younger age groups, for example ages 60 to 74, which could explain the second apparent peak in the level of omissions. In this case, however, the apparent over-registration could also be explained by under-estimation of the death rate among those aged 75 years and above and/or by under-estimation of the population in these age groups. Although the possibility that death rates among the very old in Latin America are under-estimated has been noted frequently, a focused study in one Latin American country verified the relatively low death rate for that group (García, 1990).

The discussion so far presents an overview for Latin America. The trends

Table 3.3. Under-registration, ill-defined causes and total with no information, by sex and broad age groups, 1980–5

| | % under-registration | | | | | | % ill-defined | | | | | | % no information | | | | | |
| | 0–14 | | | 15 and over | | | 0–14 | | | 15 and over | | | 0–14 | | | 15 and over | | |
	M	W	T	M	W	T	M	F	T	M	F	T	M	F	T	M	F	T
Argentina	14.4	16.3	15.0	2.4	3.5	2.6	6.5	6.6	6.5	2.7	2.5	2.6	20.0	21.8	20.5	5.0	5.9	5.1
Bolivia	—	—	—	—	—	—	—	—	—	—	—	—	—	—	—	—	—	—
Brazil	52.8	44.7	49.5	5.9	26.1	15.4	24.6	26.0	25.2	19.7	21.1	20.3	64.4	59.1	62.2	24.4	41.7	32.6
Colombia	25.7	21.6	24.0	8.7	15.0	11.5	5.6	6.1	5.8	5.8	7.9	6.7	29.9	26.4	28.4	14.0	21.7	17.4
Costa Rica	19.7	21.1	20.3	2.7	5.3	3.9	4.9	4.7	4.8	5.5	6.5	5.9	23.6	24.8	24.1	8.1	11.5	9.6
Cuba	4.5	4.2	4.4	7.1	6.2	6.7	0.5	0.5	0.5	0.3	0.3	0.3	5.0	4.7	4.9	7.4	6.5	7.0
Chile	5.7	5.1	5.4	-0.5	3.0	1.1	7.9	8.0	7.9	8.0	9.9	8.8	13.1	12.7	12.9	7.5	12.6	9.8
Domin. Rep.	55.9	56.2	56.0	29.4	29.4	29.4	11.5	11.8	11.7	21.8	26.3	23.8	61.0	61.4	61.1	44.8	48.0	46.2
Ecuador	37.2	31.8	34.8	11.5	18.2	14.6	11.4	12.6	12.0	16.2	21.3	18.5	44.4	40.4	42.6	25.8	35.6	30.4
El Salvador	54.9	53.8	54.4	21.1	11.8	18.0	11.6	12.9	12.2	19.3	36.2	25.3	60.1	59.8	60.0	36.3	43.7	38.7
Guatemala	13.7	13.2	13.5	0.4	17.2	7.7	11.2	11.4	11.3	11.3	16.9	13.5	23.4	23.1	23.3	11.7	31.2	20.2
Haiti	—	—	—	—	—	—	—	—	—	—	—	—	—	—	—	—	—	—
Honduras	63.5	62.7	63.1	28.4	35.0	31.4	32.7	33.1	32.9	34.7	44.3	38.9	75.4	75.0	75.2	53.2	63.8	58.1
Mexico	28.7	28.0	28.4	3.6	4.9	4.2	5.0	5.5	5.2	4.8	6.4	5.5	32.3	32.0	32.1	8.2	11.0	9.5
Nicaragua	—	—	—	—	—	—	—	—	—	—	—	—	—	—	—	—	—	—
Panama	29.6	29.2	29.4	22.5	27.3	24.6	11.3	11.6	11.5	8.4	9.5	8.9	37.6	37.4	37.5	29.0	34.2	31.3
Paraguay	57.1	56.0	56.6	36.9	30.9	34.1	20.3	20.7	20.5	19.9	23.9	21.9	65.8	65.1	65.5	49.5	47.4	48.5
Peru	58.7	57.3	58.0	48.3	45.1	46.8	5.7	5.7	5.7	7.2	8.9	8.1	61.1	59.7	60.4	52.0	50.0	51.1
Uruguay	7.0	10.7	8.6	1.0	5.5	3.1	8.9	9.5	9.1	7.7	6.1	7.0	15.3	19.2	16.9	8.6	11.3	9.9
Venezuela	24.8	21.2	23.3	8.4	7.5	8.0	11.9	12.9	12.3	11.1	13.4	12.1	33.7	31.4	32.7	18.6	19.9	19.1

Source: Calculations on the basis of the data available in the PAHO database (9th Revision).

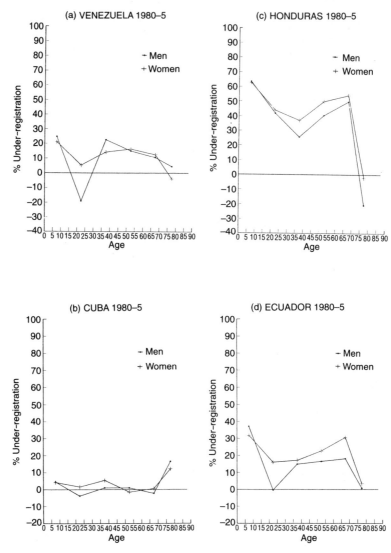

Fig. 3.2.   Under-registration of deaths by age and sex, selected countries, 1980–5

mentioned are clearer in countries with satisfactory or fair rates of omission (see, for example, Venezuela and Ecuador in Figure 3.2) than countries with better ratings. The latter countries, that is those with registration systems considered to be of good quality, are characterized by omission rates that are less differentiated by age. In particular, under-registration in the open-ended age group does not differ much from that estimated for other older age groups.

What is more, in some of these countries, for example Cuba (see Figure 3.2), more deaths are omitted in the open-ended age group of 75 years and above.

In countries with higher mortality and greater under-registration, the low rate of omission in the open-ended age group is particularly striking. In several countries there is even over-registration for that group, as noted earlier, for example, Honduras in Figure 3.2. A focused study to test the possible explanations mentioned could clarify the situation. It is notable that those countries whose mortality has been estimated on the basis of vital statistics, that is those with low mortality plus Guatemala, do not show this striking drop in under-registration for the open-ended age group.

3. Ill-Defined Causes of Death

To study mortality, it is not enough to know the age and sex of the deceased. For in-depth analysis, it is also necessary to investigate causes of death. The same factors that explain why not all deaths are recorded also explain, at least partially, why causes of death are not defined precisely. The situation is worse in those instances where the deceased did not receive medical attention prior to death. Consequently, the degree to which causes of death are well defined is also an indirect and approximate measure of the availability and use of public health services.

As with under-registration, the degree to which the causes of registered deaths are known varies from country to country. There is less variation than in the case of registration coverage, perhaps because the majority of those whose deaths are recorded belong to the more favoured socio-economic strata and receive medical attention prior to death. At any rate, there is a relationship between the degree of under-registration and the proportion of causes of death that are ill-defined, as shown in Figure 3.3. Two countries present somewhat anomalous situations. One is Peru and the other Honduras. Both have omission rates around 45 per cent, but Honduras also has a very high percentage of ill-defined causes (around 37 per cent), while in Peru the cause of death is known for more than 90 per cent of registered deaths. The latter situation usually occurs only in countries with omission rates of less than 20 per cent. The exceptional pattern in Peru is explained by the socio-economic characteristics of the deceased: the deaths in question occur mainly in urban areas.

Although the overall situation with respect to the degree of under-registration has not changed very much since 1960, somewhat greater optimism is possible in the case of ill-defined causes of death. Between 1960 and 1985, significant reductions in the percentage of ill-defined causes recorded were observed in the great majority of countries (see Table 3.2). While cover-

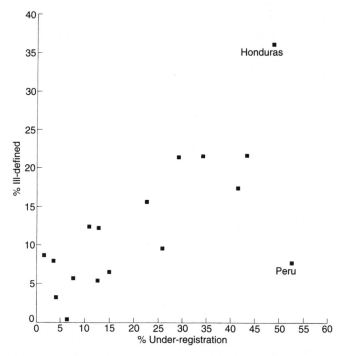

Fig. 3.3. Relationship between death under-registration and reporting of ill-defined causes of death, 1980–5

age of adult deaths is considerably better than of deaths in the 0–14 age group, in the case of ill-defined causes of death no general pattern emerges (see Table 3.3). Differences between age groups in the percentage of deaths from ill-defined causes are generally small, but tend to increase slightly with age to peak in the open-ended group of 80 years and above. Causes of death among men are recorded better than those among women in fourteen out of seventeen countries, the exceptions being Cuba, Argentina, and Uruguay. This difference between the sexes increases in adulthood (see Figure 3.4). The greatest differences between the sexes occurs usually in the fertile ages, while differences are minimal in the older age groups. Figure 3.5 clearly shows the behaviour of ill-defined causes of death by sex and age in two of the fourteen countries in which this striking fact was observed. Part of this difference might be explained by the relatively greater importance of accidents among male deaths. However, bearing in mind the greater under-registration of women's deaths at these ages in several countries, a link between this phenomenon and maternal mortality, which is known to be under-registered, might also explain this difference between the sexes. A more detailed analysis of this matter is needed.

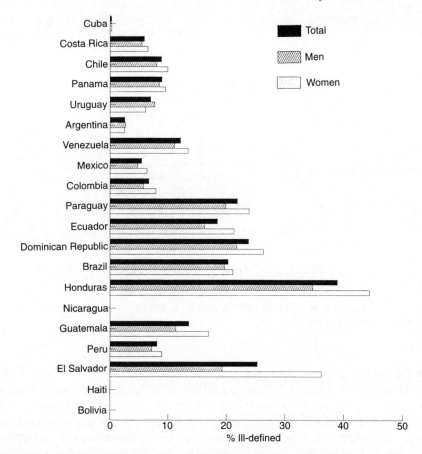

Fig. 3.4. Proportion of reported adult deaths with ill-defined causes, by sex, 1980–5

4. Totals with 'No Information' with Respect to Causes of Death

On the basis of the findings of the first two sections of this chapter, which deal with under-registration and ill-defined causes, the overall percentage of deaths whose cause is unknown was calculated, creating a percentage termed the total with 'no information' (the results of this exercise are found in Tables 3.2 and 3.3).

Given that improvements in the registration of causes of death have been observed in the majority of countries, the scope for studying mortality by cause of death has improved slightly in the region, especially between 1960 and 1980. Thus, while in the 1960–5 period, only four countries presented statistics which allowed for analysis of mortality by cause of death with a reasonable degree of

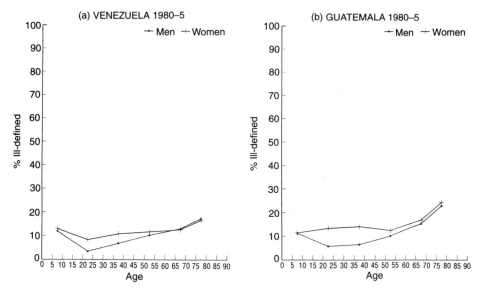

Fig. 3.5. Proportion of reported deaths with ill-defined causes, by age and sex, selected countries, 1980–5

reliability, this number rose to five in the 1975–80 period and to six in the following five-year period (Figure 3.6). Reflecting the relatively high rates of coverage for adult deaths, if knowledge of the cause of death for 80 per cent of all deaths is considered the minimum acceptable, studies of adult mortality by cause of death could be carried out in the following seven countries: Argentina, Costa Rica, Cuba, Chile, Mexico, Uruguay, and Venezuela. Colombia and Guatemala could be added to this list for studies of adult male mortality (see Table 3.3 and Figure 3.7). In contrast, only one country has data on cause of death for more than 90 per cent of deaths among those less than 15 years of age.

5. Medical Certification

The percentage of total deaths for which no information about cause of death is available and, especially, the percentage of ill-defined causes should be interpreted as preliminary indicators of the quality of the data. In order to obtain a more direct indicator of this, it is also useful to examine the proportion of deaths certified by a physician, because it can be presumed that the disease that caused the death is diagnosed better in such cases, although not always correctly (see, for example, Puffer and Griffith, 1968).

Table 3.4 presents percentages of deaths with medical certification for

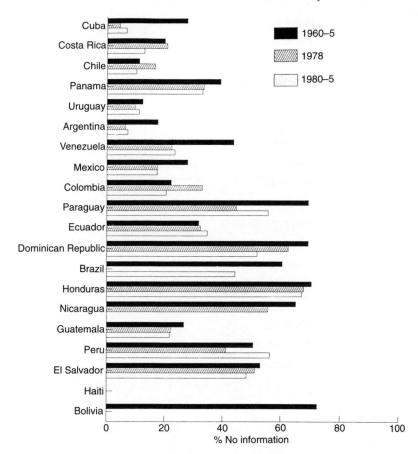

Fig. 3.6.   Proportion of all deaths for which a cause is not reported, selected periods

selected years. As can be seen, this information is very scarce for many countries of the region. Great heterogeneity among countries is observed, with values ranging from 38 to 100 per cent in recent years. Once again, countries with lower mortality levels and lower under-registration have better data. As with ill-defined causes of death, the information has tended to improve over time. There is a relationship between the percentage of deaths with no medical certification and the percentage of ill-defined causes, although not perhaps such a clear one as might have been expected (Figure 3.8). The major exceptions are Guatemala and Peru, which also have unexpected levels of coverage, and Costa Rica.

As has been noted in other studies (Chackiel, 1987), the low percentage of deaths that are medically certified in Costa Rica, according to the statistics

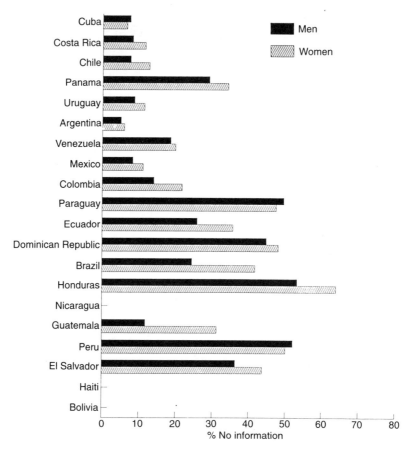

Fig. 3.7.   Proportion of all adult deaths for which a cause is not reported, by sex, 1980–5

available in international annual reports, is striking. Thanks to access to a database in the REDATAM system which contains the original records of deaths registered in the years 1985 and 1988, it is possible to ascertain that the published figures do not refer to total medical certification but to those cases in which there was 'medical care' (that is, the percentage of deaths in which the illness that eventually ended in death was treated medically). In order to obtain an internationally comparable percentage of deaths with medical certification, the category 'no medical care but with medical certification' must be added, which raises the percentage by 20 per cent. For example, in 1985, the actual percentage of deaths registered with certification is about 94 per cent, not the 75 per cent that appears in the annual reports (the percentages for 1988 are 96 and 76 per cent, respectively). The real percentage of deaths

Table 3.4. Percentage of reported deaths with medical certification for selected countries, 1960–85[a]

Country	Year					
	1960	1970	1975	1980	1985	Last available
Argentina	—	—	—	98.9	—	99.3 (82)
Colombia	47.5	65.7	72.1	80.9	83.6	88.6 (88)
Costa Rica	48.5	56.7	61.0	62.2	74.7[b]	76.0 (88)[b]
Cuba	—	—	—	100.0	—	100.0 (83)
Chile	72.1	72.6	83.4	89.6	91.0	93.6 (88)
Dominican Republic	48.6	48.6	36.8	—	—	38.9 (76)
Ecuador	34.1	43.6	49.6	64.5	76.4	77.1 (87)
El Salvador	—	35.7	37.1	51.3	46.5	46.5 (84)
Guatemala	—	21.8	—	37.9	—	37.9 (80)
Mexico	—	75.8	78.5	87.0	—	87.9 (81)
Panama	46.9	—	69.3	77.5	81.1	83.3 (88)
Paraguay	—	—	36.2	—	—	36.2 (74)
Peru	44.2	—	—	—	—	66.6 (78)
Uruguay	—	99.7	—	—	—	99.8 (78)
Venezuela	—	79.4	—	—	—	83.1 (77)

[a] The percentages for each country correspond to available information. In some cases, the year to which the table refers, or approximately that year, is used directly. In others, an average of the two or three years around the year presented are used.
[b] These percentages correspond to 'with medical care'; the percentages 'with medical certification' should be 94.0 and 96.5, respective (see text).

with medical certification is therefore much closer to what one would expect for Costa Rica in light of the development of that country's health services. Moreover, it is interesting to note that an autopsy was performed in the case of 71 per cent of deaths without medical care but accompanied by medical certification.

Given the focus of this book on adult mortality, it was decided to examine the percentage of registered deaths with medical certification among those over 15 years of age. The only data available pertain to Colombia, Costa Rica (thanks to the database), Chile (Castillo and Mardones, 1986a and 1986b) and Panama. In the countries with higher mortality and/or omission rates, Colombia and Panama, the proportion of adult deaths that are certified by a physician is relatively high, reaching levels over 80 per cent in both cases, while in the 0–14 age group this proportion is less than 75 per cent. In Chile and Costa Rica, such clear differences are not observed, although the same tendency is present. Finally, as noted for ill-defined causes, the percentage of deaths without medical certification is higher for the open-ended age group in all the four countries studied.

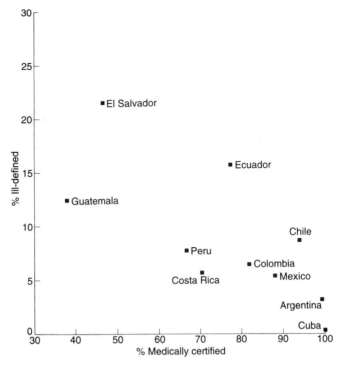

Fig. 3.8. Relationship between the proportion of deaths with ill-defined causes and the proportion medically certified, 1980–5

Given the lack of data with respect to medical certification in many countries, it is interesting to analyse the relationship between the percentage of deaths with ill-defined causes and the percentage of those without medical certification in order to assess the capacity of the percentage of ill-defined causes to serve as a general indicator of the quality of the data. Such analysis, by age group, confirms that the lower the percentage of ill-defined causes, the higher the percentage with medical certification (see Figure 3.9(*a*) and (*b*)). For the purpose of learning more about the quality of the data, it would be helpful if countries published data with respect to medical care and autopsies by age and sex and, in so far as possible, by cause (for example, at least with respect to ill-defined causes). According to the information used for this study, the only country that has published this kind of data in fairly complete form until now is Panama.

The analysis presented so far is based on an indirect evaluation of the coverage of death registration and some general indicators for data quality. Much more information could have been presented if direct evaluation of the coverage and content of the data on registered deaths had been carried out

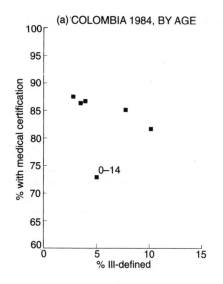

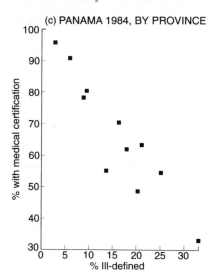

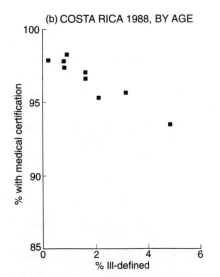

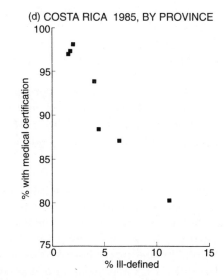

Fig. 3.9.   Relationship between the proportion of deaths with ill-defined causes and the proportion medically certified by age or province, selected countries in the 1980s

recently, such as the studies undertaken in the 1960s and early 1970s by Puffer and others (Puffer and Griffith, 1968; Puffer and Serrano, 1973). One of the conclusions, at that time, was that only 67 per cent of the causes of selected urban adult deaths were classified correctly.

6. Analysis of Mortality at Sub-National Levels

Given the significance of analyses of mortality in different geographical sub-divisions of a country for the purpose of health programme evaluation and design, it is important to note that differences in death registration within countries can be very significant, both in terms of coverage and in relation to the percentage of ill-defined causes.

Differences within a country can produce a situation in which it is impractical to carry out analysis at the national level, because the data are very unreliable at that level, but possible to study certain geographical units. This is the case in Brazil, for example, which lacks a significant amount of information at the national level, especially for the female population, although statistics for some states, for example São Paulo, are fairly complete. On the other hand, some countries have relatively acceptable statistics at the national level despite very considerable regional differences. This is the case in Argentina, for example, where some isolated provinces have omission rates in excess of 30 per cent (Somoza and Muller, 1988). Moreover, there is reason to doubt the quality of the information about the habitual residence of the deceased, given that, as in the case of birth records, it seems that many informants declare the habitual residence to have been the place of death (for example, the location of the hospital where the deceased received his last medical attention).

Regional differences in the percentage of ill-defined causes of death and the percentage of deaths recorded with medical certification also exist. Thus, in Chile in 1983, for example, the percentage of ill-defined causes of death varied from 1 to 32 per cent between the nineteen regional Health Services and the percentage without medical certification from 2 to 35 per cent (Castillo and Mardones, 1986a, 1986b). This obviously renders inter-regional analysis difficult. A similar situation can be observed in Panama. In 1984, 98 per cent of recorded deaths were medically certified in urban areas but only 60 per cent in rural areas. In Colombia in 1984, the proportion of deaths with certification in the various administrative regions varied from 34 to 100 per cent (see Figure 3.9). Even in a country like Costa Rica, which has very good health indicators, significant differences exist. In 1985, the percentage of deaths from ill-defined causes varied between 2 and 11 per cent in the seven provinces and the percentage with no medical certification between 2 and 20 per cent.

7. Other Problems Arising in the Use of Vital Statistics to Study Mortality by Cause

In the study of mortality by cause of death, the researcher faces a number of practical and methodological problems. Some of these, such as the difficulty of obtaining data, the coverage of death registration systems and the quality of the information measured in terms of the percentage of ill-defined causes and the existence of medical certification, are dealt with in earlier sections. Differences in the coverage and quality of the data at the sub-national level have also been discussed. In this section, other relevant topics are raised.

The first problem is how to deal with the basic information. Difficulties arise from the format in which data is available, that is whether it is in printed tables or on tape (data are available on microcomputer diskettes for only a few countries). Machine-readable data are ideal but, at the present time, few researchers have access to such data or to computers with tape drives. However, working with printed data imposes numerous limitations, beginning with the limited level of detail in the available tables (see Table 3.5 for a summary of the kind of information available in printed form for the countries studied). If the data are presented in summary form, for example for principal causes of death, they are easier to process but the detail of the analysis is limited. On the other hand, while more detailed information such as causes disaggregated to four digits offers additional possibilities for analysis, the difficulties involved in processing so much data means that very few researchers can take advantage of them. These problems may explain, at least partially, why so few studies of causes of death have been carried out in the Latin American region: to date, most studies have been carried out as postgraduate theses and a small number as part of the routine work of public agencies.

If studies cover different revisions of the ICD, the researcher faces another tedious task: that of making the different revisions of the ICD, each of which covers a period of approximately ten years, compatible. To perform this task rigorously, it is necessary to know causes of death to the third digit ('category' or 'heading') and fourth digit ('sub-category' or 'sub-heading') for both revisions. Comparison of two revisions can produce the following situations (Vallin, 1988; Orellana and Villalón, 1990):

- One category in a given revision may have exactly the same content in the subsequent revision;
- One category may be broken down into different categories;
- Various categories may become one category;
- One category may be fragmented into several segments (composed of sub-categories), each one of which is distributed among diverse categories which, moreover, receive portions from other categories.

Even if all the necessary information is available, analysis is difficult because rules of correspondence between the various revisions for categories and sub-categories have not been established. This makes the task of establishing compatibility especially difficult when dealing with the fourth situation just mentioned. Once category and sub-category compatibility has been established, it is necessary to analyse the trend of those categories which exhibit irregularities from one revision to another. Thus, the results of the process of

Table 3.5. Published information on causes of death, according to ICD revision and detail of these data, by country

Country	7th Revision		8th Revision		9th Revision	
	List	Detail	List	Detail	List	Detail
Argentina	B	Age	Large groups	Total	56 groups	Age
Bolivia	A	Age	—		—	
Brazil	B	Total	Detail 3 digits	Age	Detail 3 digits	Age
Colombia	A	Age	A	Age	56 groups	Age
Cuba	A and B	Age	A	Age	Selected causes	Age
Costa Rica	10 main causes	Total	10 main causes	Age	Main causes	Large groups
Chile	A	Age	A	Age	Detail 3 digits	Age
Dominican Republic	B	Age	B	Age	—	
El Salvador	Detail 3 digits	Age	Detail 3 digits	Age	56 groups	Age
Ecuador	A	Age	A	Age	Detail 3 digits	Age
Haiti	10 large groups	Age	—		Detail	Age
Honduras	Detail 3 digits	Total	A	Age	56 groups	Different
Mexico	Special groupings	Total	Special groupings	Total	12 groups	Total
Nicaragua	B	Age	—		—	
Panama	B	Age	A	Age	56 groups	Age
Peru	A	Age	—		—	
Venezuela	Detail 4 digits	Age	Detail 4 digits	Age	Detail 4 digits	Age

Note: For each country, data for at least one year in each revision are available.
(—) No information is available for any year covered by the revision.

establishing compatibility are different from country to country. (The studies by Vallin (1988) and Orellana and Villalón (1990) discuss in detail the possibilities and limitations of the process of establishing compatibility.) The actual situation becomes even more intractable as very few countries possess the detailed information necessary. Moreover, the way that the information is presented also changes in many countries when a new revision is produced. In Argentina, for example, while causes of death were presented in broad groups in the 8th Revision, the basic tabulation list of fifty-six causes was used for the 9th Revision. Obviously, lack of detail and changes in format make the task of establishing compatibility even more difficult (although much depends on the objectives of a particular study). In order to avoid the problems involved in establishing compatibility, especially the tedious work involved, a number of studies of causes of death have examined the relatively short period of time covered by a single revision.

Finally, when a new revision is adopted there may be an increase in ill-defined causes for a few years, because the codification of causes also changes. It is worth noting, however, that analysis of the percentages of ill-defined causes by calendar year in Latin American countries fails to reveal this phenomenon in the majority of countries. The explanation must be that other factors, such as medical treatment, are decisive in determining the volume of ill-defined causes and much more important than the introduction of new rules of codification. The exceptions are Cuba, Costa Rica, and Chile. In these countries a slight increase in ill-defined causes occurs for the years 1979, 1980, and 1981, compared with 1978 and with later years.

When the analyst is faced with ill-defined causes, the question immediately arises of what to do with them. This question is particularly important in the analysis of mortality trends over periods in which the weight of ill-defined causes is very variable and in comparison of geographic areas showing significant differences in this respect. In studies of trends, ill-defined causes have often been treated as another group of causes. This has meant that change in mortality over time is attributed, in part, to a decrease in the 'cause' known as 'ill-defined causes'. For example, in Guatemala, between the periods 1969–70 and 1978–9, more than 10 per cent of the 5.6 year increase in life expectancy at birth (0.6 per year) is 'explained' by the decrease in the incidence of ill-defined causes (Díaz, 1987). This problem is usually less serious in countries with good statistics because this percentage does not change much over time. Nevertheless, it can pose difficulties for studies carried out at sub-national levels. As noted above, even in countries whose statistics are considered to be good, such as Costa Rica and Chile, there are significant differences at the level of internal geographical regions.

As Chackiel (1987) pointed out, it would be worthwhile evaluating the proposed procedures for redistributing ill-defined causes along the lines suggested by Lederman (1955) and the adaptations proposed by Vallin (1988). Moreover, it would be worthwhile studying this problem in each country with sufficiently reliable statistics on causes of death and making the results available to potential users and researchers. A similar suggestion could be made with respect to the process of establishing compatibility among different revisions of the ICD. In this way, research on causes of death could be increased significantly, because many potential researchers are currently reluctant to investigate the subject because of the practical problems involved.

Providing the potential researcher with registration statistics in a form which would permit rapid and easy processing would also augment the number of relevant studies. For example, the research presented here was made much easier by the use of a database of all the information on causes of death available for Latin America for the 1980s. The information in the PAHO database was transferred from tape to diskette for microcomputer processing by the REDATAM system, which made it possible to cross-tabulate the necessary variables. However, since the PAHO database contains aggregated data, its usefulness is restricted by the limited number of variables included (country, year, sex, age, cause, and number of persons deceased according to those variables). For all of these reasons it is to be recommended that databases be created for each country, using the original information (that is each entry should correspond to one person who has died) in a format which would allow for work with a system such as REDATAM. A database for Costa Rica with these characteristics was used in the research presented here and made it possible to recover information for the years 1985 and 1988.

In view of the fact that the new REDATAM-PLUS system has just become available, even more ambitious databases can be imagined. These would be created by adding to the information on deaths, data such as birth records, data on the population by sex and age, and health service statistics, which would help explain mortality processes. Making all these possible tools available to users would increase knowledge about (adult) mortality, which could lead to improved health conditions for everyone.

8. Conclusions

Even though, in general terms, registration of deaths in Latin America displays important deficiencies, it is nevertheless possible to carry out research on mortality and causes of death among adults in many countries. This is because information on causes of death is more widely available for adults than for those under 15 years of age. It is worth emphasizing that the data for adults are of higher quality for the male population. The difference between the sexes with respect to ill-defined causes is concentrated in the young adult age group (or fertile ages) in nearly all countries, which suggests that it may be related to the under-estimation of maternal mortality. With respect to under-registration by age, relatively serious problems appear in young adult age groups (mainly among men) and in the age group 75 years and above. These problems differ in intensity from country to country, according to the level of mortality and the quality of the statistics.

The percentage of causes of death verified by medical certification is another indicator of data quality. Important differences between countries are observed, together with a clear association between this variable and the percentage of deaths from ill-defined causes. Both indicators improved to some degree between 1960 and 1985. The selected indicators reveal important differences not only between countries but also within countries. Such significant discrepancies exist that the scope for studies by geographic region is limited, even though such studies are highly important for the elaboration of effective public health programmes.

Finally, there are other problems of a practical nature that obstruct the study of causes of death, such as the effort involved in establishing compatibilities between two or more revisions of the ICD, dealing with ill-defined causes and obtaining and processing the data. Apart from improving the coverage and quality of vital statistics, an attempt should be made to solve practical problems with respect to data processing by making registration statistics available on diskette with a computer package, such as REDATAM-PLUS, thereby providing rapid and easy access to the information.

References

Castillo, B., and G. Mardones (1986*a*), 'Defunciones por causas mal definidas en los servicios de salud en Chile', *Revista Médica de Chile*, 114(4): Sociedad Médica de Chile, Santiago, Chile.

——(1986*b*) 'Certificación médica de las defunciones en los servicios de salud de Chile', *Revista Médica de Chile*, 114(7): Sociedad Médica de Chile, Santiago, Chile.

Centro Latinamericano de Demografía (CELADE) (1990), *REDATAM Informa*, 1(2): (LC/DEM/G.99), Santiago, Chile.

Chackiel, J. (1987), 'La investigación sobre causas de muerte en la América Latina', *Notas de Población*, 44: (LC/DEM/G.61), CELADE, Santiago, Chile.

Díaz, E. (1987), *Causas de muerte en Guatemala, 1960–1979*, (LC/DEM/CR/G.17), CELADE, San José, Costa Rica.

García, V. (1990), *Mortalidad y características socio-económicas de la tercera edad*, CELADE, Universidad de Costa Rica, Dirección General de Estadística y Censos, San José, Costa Rica.

Lederman, S. (1955), 'La répartition des déces de causes indeterminées', *Revue de l'Institut International de Statistique*, 23(1/3).

Orellana, H., and G. Villalón (1990), *Compatibilización de las revisiones séptima, octava y novena de la Clasificación Internacional de Enfermedades: aplicación a Chile, 1960–1985*, Instituto Nacional de Estadísticas, Santiago, Chile.

Pan American Health Organization (PAHO) (1990), *Health Conditions in the Americas*, 2 vols., Scientific Publication No. 524, Washington, DC.

Puffer, R., and G. W. Griffith (1968), *Patterns of Urban Mortality*, Sci. Publ. No. 151, PAHO/WHO, Washington, DC.

——and C. Serrano (1973), *Patterns of Mortality in Childhood*, Sci. Publ. No. 262, PAHO/WHO, Washington, DC.

Somoza, J., and M. Muller (1988), 'Tablas de mortalidad 1980–1981: total y jurisdicciones', *Estudios INDEC*, 10: Instituto Nacional de Estadística y Censos, Buenos Aires, Argentina.

Vallin, J. (1988), *Seminario sobre causas de muerte: aplicación al caso de Francia*, (LC/DEM/G.55), CELADE/INED, Santiago, Chile.

World Health Organization (WHO) and Pan American Health Organization (PAHO) (1978), *International Statistical Classification of Diseases, Injuries and Causes of Death*, i, Sci. Publ. No. 353, Washington, DC.

4 Use of Vital Statistics on Maternal Deaths in Argentina

ELIDA MARCONI

Ministerio de Salud y Acción Social, Buenos Aires, Argentina

1. Introduction

Mortality statistics are part of a vital statistics system that provides data that are seldom used in the countries of Latin America. While most such data are incomplete, of poor quality, outdated, and dispersed among various institutions that are often not part of the health sector, they are potentially useful for those researchers who are aware of their existence and can use them within their limitations.

The institutions that produce them generally use such data for descriptive purposes. The analytic content of such studies has been of limited value to potential users. A self-perpetuating situation exists in which the fragmentary nature of the data serves as an excuse for their under-utilization. This contributes to perpetuation of the poor quality of the data, owing to the scant attention paid to their compilation, processing and analysis.

Nevertheless, many research projects on mortality have now been or are being undertaken in the region in general, and in the Argentine Republic in particular, using data from registration statistics. The results of these research efforts are very useful for orienting activities related to the organization of health services, the prevention and mitigation of damage to health, and the evaluation of the quality of the vital statistics system and its contribution to making data more complete, reliable, and timely.

This chapter presents both a description of the quality of mortality data in the Argentine System of Vital Statistics and research on maternal

Principal researcher: Dr Jorge C. Vinacur. Researchers: Dr María Rosa Allub de Cortigiani, Dr Omar Althabe, Dr Fernando Althabe, Dr Federico Carlos Collia, Dr Graciela Cuman, Dr Jorge Josipovic, Elida Marconi, María de las Mercedes Méndez Alonso, Inés Moreno, Dr Pedro Sarrasqueta, María Cristina Uthurralt. Methodology consultant: Luis R. Acosta. Mention must be made of the valuable cooperation provided to the research team by Catalina N. Fratalochi and Susana H. Masseroni (both from the Institute of Sociology of the National University of Buenos Aires) and the architect Wilma G. Zipper (of the Department of Health Statistics, Health Secretariat, Ministry of Health and Social Welfare).

mortality undertaken within the area of the Federal Capital, based on direct measurement using data from death statistics reports cross-checked with corresponding medical histories (corroboration). After an evaluation of the initial results and an adjustment of the methodology, the research has been extended to three other provinces in the country: Tucumán, Córdoba, and Corrientes.

2. The Vital Statistics System as a Source of Data

The System of Vital Statistics (SVS) in Argentina operates nationwide. Until 1968 it was the direct responsibility of the Statistics and Census Office (currently the National Institute of Statistics and Censuses—INDEC). After 1968 this responsibility was transferred to the health sector. Although a number of provinces had already adopted international recommendations for medical certification of the cause of death, it was in 1968 that this model was introduced throughout the national territory. The International Statistical Classification of Diseases, Injuries and Causes of Death (ICD) is now used for the codification of cause of death.

The Department of Health Statistics within the Ministry of Health and Social Welfare is the agency that centralizes, consolidates and disseminates data submitted by the provinces. It also has responsibility for supervising and helping to improve the system. Responsibility for SVS lies with the health sector in eighteen provinces and under the jurisdiction of the provincial departments of statistics and censuses in the remaining six. The vital information covered by SVS—births, deaths, foetal deaths and marriages—is registered for administrative, legal and statistical purposes by the administrative units known as the 'Register of Vital Statistics and Status of Persons' of each province. At the national level there is no organization that sets standards and regulates the functioning of these units. However, to improve the quality of data on mortality and morbidity, a National Commission on Health Statistics has been set up, together with a committee of professionals and technicians with wide experience in the use of the ICD.

3. Quality of Data

3.1. Completeness of Death Registers

Jorge Somoza (undated), in a technical report on the construction of life tables, presents some estimates of omissions from the registers. According to his report, the registers are complete in only five provinces (Federal Capital, Buenos Aires, Córdoba, Mendoza, and Santa Fe). In the remaining provinces, the degree of under-registration varies, with omissions being more marked for children under 5 years of age (3 per cent nationally) than in the age group 5 to 79 years (2.1 per cent nationally). The highest levels of under-registration for children under 5 occurred in Santiago del Estero and Santa Cruz-Tierra del Fuego. Table 4.1 shows the relationship between the number of deaths registered and projected by province, from which the corresponding percentages of omissions for age groups 0–4 years and 5–79 years were deduced.

3.2. Quality of Medical Certification

Certification of the cause of death is a very important item on the death certificate and one of the most complex. Various factors influence the validity

Table 4.1. Relationship between recorded and projected deaths for age groups 0–4 and 5–79 by province, Argentine Republic, 1980–1

Province	Age group	
	0–4	5–79
Federal Capital	1.09	1.00
Buenos Aires	1.03	1.00
Catamarca	0.93	0.81
Córdoba	1.03	1.00
Corrientes	0.96	0.93
Chaco	0.93	0.97
Chubut	0.91	0.98
Entre Ríos	0.94	0.91
Formosa	0.88	0.95
Jujuy	0.84	0.97
La Pampa	0.84	0.89
La Rioja	0.94	0.79
Mendoza	1.00	1.00
Misiones	1.00	1.00
Neuquén	0.92	0.88
Río Negro	0.92	0.91
Salta	0.94	0.91
San Juan	0.90	0.90
San Luis	0.85	0.85
S. Cruz/T. Fuego	0.57	0.96
Santa Fe	0.98	1.00
Stgo. del Estero	0.67	0.61
Tucumán	0.99	0.96
Argentine Republic	0.97	0.98

Source: Somoza (undated).

of this information, such as whether the deceased received medical attention, whether the death took place in an institution, and whether a doctor certified the cause of death or an autopsy was performed. The certification of the cause of death is a datum validated by the existence of a clear diagnosis, the performance of an autopsy, a correct summary of the pathologies and death process, and a clear written account of all this in a statistical report.

Table 4.2 shows that 98.6 per cent of the 249,882 deaths registered in the Argentine Republic in 1987 were certified by a doctor. This indicator is at

Table 4.2. Medically certified deaths and deaths due to ill-defined causes by province of occurrence, Argentine Republic, 1987

Province	Total	With medical certification	Ill-defined	% with medical certification	% ill-defined
Argentine Republic	249,882	246,294	5,141	98.6	2.1
Federal Capital	42,687	42,687	70	100.0	0.2
Buenos Aires	92,095	92,095	443	100.0	0.5
Catamarca	1,132	1,037	83	91.6	7.3
Córdoba	21,883	21,201	226	96.9	1.0
Corrientes	5,121	3,856	272	75.3	5.3
Chaco	5,243	5,229	280	99.7	5.3
Chubut	1,819	1,817	62	99.9	3.4
Entre Ríos	7,969	7,968	247	100.0	3.1
Formosa	1,906	1,864	96	97.8	5.0
Jujuy	3,049	2,889	388	94.8	2.7
La Pampa	1,698	1,698	10	100.0	0.6
La Rioja	1,222	1,180	46	96.6	3.8
Mendoza	9,101	9,098	97	100.0	1.1
Misiones	4,160	4,160	191	100.0	4.6
Neuquén	1,637	1,621	49	99.0	3.0
Río Negro	2,577	2,574	86	100.0	3.3
Salta	4,773	4,700	316	98.5	6.6
San Juan	3,526	3,521	31	99.9	0.9
San Luis	1,711	1,703	26	99.5	1.5
Santa Cruz	739	739	18	99.1	2.4
Santa Fe	24,026	23,761	967	98.9	4.0
Stgo. del Estero	3,951	3,258	727	82.5	8.4
Tucumán	7,690	7,633	407	99.3	5.3
Tierra del Fuego	167	5	3	3.1	1.8

Source: Ministry of Health and Social Welfare, Health Secretariat, Department of Health Statistics.

least 99 per cent in fourteen provinces. Of the total number of deaths, 2.1 per cent were attributed to 'ill-defined signs, symptoms and morbid states', although there are notable differences among provinces. While in the Federal Capital, Buenos Aires, La Pampa, and San Juan the number of such deaths was under 1 per cent, in Jujuy and Santiago del Estero the figure was over 10 per cent. If cases with inconsistencies between cause of death and age and sex of the deceased and codes not included in the classification of diseases are added to the of deaths in the ill-defined group, the percentage rises to 2.3 per cent.

Another problem with the cause of death certification is the weight of certain categories that, although not classified by the ICD as deaths due to ill-defined causes, are nevertheless terminal states which could be the consequence of diverse pathologies. One of them is often registered on the death certificate as the only cause of death: cardiorespiratory failure. This corresponds to the category 427 of the 9th Revision of the ICD which covers cardiac dysrythmia. In 1980, the percentage of total deaths listed under this code varied, depending on the province, between 2.7 per cent and 13.4 per cent. In addition, category 428 (heart failure) has a significant weight (between 5 per cent and 11.7 per cent, depending on the province).

Table 4.3 shows the number of deaths of women aged 15 to 49 registered in the Argentine Republic in 1987, and the number and percentage of deaths due to ill-defined causes for this age group. Out of a total of 9953 deaths of this group, 2.4 per cent were attributed to 'ill-defined signs, symptoms and morbid states', a percentage somewhat higher than that recorded for all deaths. Significant differences exist between provinces. In four of them no deaths in the category 'ill-defined causes' were registered. In addition, the total number of such deaths was under 1 per cent in the Federal Capital, Buenos Aires, Córdoba, Mendoza and San Juan. However, in Chaco the percentage was 6.0 per cent, in Jujuy 8.2 per cent, in Salta 7.9 per cent and in Santiago del Estero 19.0 per cent. As with total deaths, when inconsistencies between cause of death, age and sex of the deceased, and codes not included in the ICD are included, the percentage of deaths in the ill-defined group rises to 2.8 per cent. Maternal deaths constitute perhaps one of the most under-registered categories of causes of death for women aged 15 to 49. In addition to those placed in the ill-defined group, even in countries with good mortality records many maternal deaths are attributed to other causes.

This discussion suggests that time and resources should be devoted to an analysis of the components of ill-defined causes, for example, through comparison of the death certificate with other sources of data. In this way information would be obtained on the composition of this category without excluding it. The research on maternal mortality, using the direct method discussed in Section 4 of this chapter, has helped to clear up doubts about the quality of the medical certification in Argentina.

Table 4.3. Deaths of women aged 15–49 years due to ill-defined causes by province of occurrence, Argentine Republic, 1987

Province	Total	Ill-defined	% ill-defined
Argentine Republic	9953	236	2.4
Federal Capital	1386	4	0.3
Buenos Aires	3278	4	0.1
Catamarca	56	—	—
Córdoba	849	4	0.5
Corrientes	289	5	5.2
Chaco	317	19	6.0
Chubut	121	3	2.5
Entre Ríos	302	10	3.3
Formosa	140	6	4.3
Jujuy	220	18	8.2
La Pampa	65	—	—
La Rioja	58	1	1.7
Mendoza	412	2	0.5
Misiones	259	10	3.9
Neuquén	92	1	1.1
Río Negro	122	6	4.9
Salta	343	27	7.9
San Juan	175	1	0.6
San Luis	70	1	1.4
Santa Cruz	42	—	—
Santa Fe	776	43	5.5
Santiago del Estero	210	40	19.0
Tucumán	362	21	5.8
Tierra del Fuego	9	—	—

Source: Ministry of Health and Social Welfare, Health Secretariat, Department of Health Statistics.

4. Investigating Maternal Mortality using the Vital Statistics System

Despite the problems with the SVS data, various studies have been and are being undertaken in the Argentine Republic using this data source. Such research has had two objectives: first, to support decision-making in the health sector (specifically in programmes for health damage prevention), second, to provide guidelines for improving the Vital Statistics System. Better utilization of data thus contributes to a gradual improvement of the system. To illustrate this, a research project on maternal mortality has been selected that fully met this double objective and demonstrated the usefulness of vital statistics data, particularly mortality statistics. It is based on the direct measurement of maternal mortality, comparing and matching data from different data sources (statistical reports of deaths and medical histories).

4.1. General Considerations

During the period 1987–9, a research project on maternal mortality was conducted in the Federal Capital within the institutional framework of the National Health Secretariat/National Department of Maternal and Child Welfare, with the support of the Department of Health Statistics and sponsorship by the Pan American Health Organization (PAHO). This experience was later extended to other provinces, namely, Tucumán, Córdoba and Corrientes. The research team consisted of professionals from the two departments mentioned and advisors from the same departments.

Several factors determined the selection of the general line of work initiated by the National Department of Maternal and Child Welfare in 1985, which led finally to the implementation of the research project. On the one hand, despite its decline during the last two decades, the maternal mortality rate in Argentina had not fallen to the desired level. This is an indicator of the severe harm suffered by women of childbearing age. Deaths due to complications during pregnancy, delivery and the post-partum period are among the leading five causes of total deaths of women aged 15 to 40 in both the country as a whole and in most provinces.

In 1985 the maternal mortality rate was approximately 60 per 100,000 live births. Its distribution among the different regions of the country shows differentials that reflect inequalities in access to and the quality of available health services. Tables 4.4 and 4.5 document the characteristics of this problem, comparing the trienniums 1968–70 and 1978–80. It is striking that a problem of this magnitude exists in a country that achieved low levels of birth and fertility a long time ago (the crude birth rate has been below 30 per 1000 since 1930). It is also of significance that, in addition to social, economic, and cultural factors, the availability and quality of services are important determinants of maternal mortality, particularly in a country where more than 90 per cent of deliveries occur in health institutions. Various studies have shown that most deaths due to pregnancy, delivery, and post-partum complications could be prevented.

It has always been suspected that maternal mortality rates calculated from SVS statistics underestimate the problem because of under-registration of this cause of death. In other words, deaths due to maternal causes are registered as other causes. Indirect estimates, based on secondary information, justify a strong presumption of under-registration of maternal causes. The belief that the real maternal mortality rate is greater than the one registered was thus a significant motive for the research. The issue was to determine the magnitude of the under-registration and its distribution by cause. The final report on the

Table 4.4. Age-specific maternal mortality rates, Argentine Republic, 1968–70 and 1978–80 (per 100,000 live births)

Age group	1968–70	1978–80
15–19	135.3	66.1
20–24	80.5	44.8
25–29	99.9	55.7
30–34	167.3	89.2
35–39	271.2	170.2
40–44	356.9	200.6
45–49	235.8	170.8
Total	140.3	75.0

Source: Ministry of Health and Social Welfare, Health Secretariat, National Department of Maternal and Child Welfare, Department of Health Statistics.

Table 4.5. Maternal mortality rates by cause (per 100,000 live births)

Cause of death	1968–70	1978–80	% variation
Pregnancy ended in abortion	38.0	24.0	−37
Haemorrhage	26.3	11.8	−55
Hypertension	20.4	13.4	−34
Sepsis	11.9	7.6	−36
Other causes	43.7	18.2	−64
Total	140.3	75.0	−47

Source: Ministry of Health and Social Welfare, Health Secretariat, National Department of Maternal and Child Welfare, Department of Health Statistics.

study was drawn upon in the preparation of this chapter (Ministry of Health and Social Welfare, 1989).

4.2. Hypothesis and Objectives

Starting from the main hypothesis that there is under-registration of maternal causes due to the certification methods used and the interpretation of the certificates, the principal objectives of the research are as follows: to ascertain the degree of under-registration of maternal causes and discover the real structure of maternal mortality in the Federal Capital; to identify factors associated with such mortality in order to determine which of them could be controlled through health services; and to design a method to be applied in studies of other provinces. These objectives were formulated with the intention that the results of the research should lead to improvements in the organization of health services, thus helping to reduce the present level of maternal mortality.

4.3. Materials and Methods

This retrospective study of maternal mortality used as its main data source the death certificates (statistical reports of deaths) of women aged 14 to 49, who died in 1985 in the Federal Capital. These certificates are part of SVS. The Capital was selected as a pilot area for the testing and adjustment of a method to be extended to other provinces.

The Federal Capital has a fairly complete mortality register in terms of the recording of deaths and is one of the five provinces in the country with a complete register (as indicated in Section 3.1 of this chapter). It also has 100 per cent coverage by medical certification and few deaths in the category 'ill-defined signs, symptoms and morbid states' (0.2 per cent).

The year 1985 is the period of reference, since information for that year was the most up-to-date available when the research began and had been coded and entered into a computer data base. Thus the research required no alteration in the routines of the corresponding SVS statistical unit. The selection of ages 14 to 49 years as the reproductive age range took into account methodological recommendations on maternal mortality indicators and the distribution of births by age of the mother. The other data source used was the medical histories registers of the health establishments (public, private, and belonging to the social security system) in which the deaths in question occurred.

The method involved identifying and evaluating under-registration by comparing the cause recorded on the death certificate with the background information and other data recorded in the medical history file of the deceased woman. Thus, the study involves the direct measurement of maternal mortality and the cross-checking of the death certificate against the corresponding medical history.

The data registered and selected from the medical history were transcribed on a specially designed form. These forms included information on the personal identity of the deceased (from the death certificate), data from the medical history and the autopsy report, and the cause of death identified using the medical history (including a confidential report from the researcher describing aspects of the medical attention received which could have had a significant bearing on the outcome). Researchers who specialize in obstetrics reviewed the medical histories.

The entire medical team evaluated and revised the information case by case.

Social scientists working in the Department of Health Statistics, who formed part of the research team, ensured that the protocols were filled out completely and consistently and retrieved the information (death certificates and protocols with data from the medical histories) for making social profiles of the deceased women.

Death certificates of women aged 14 to 49 who died in the Federal Capital in 1985 were selected, eliminating those with errors in the reporting of age. This produced a final total of 1590 certificates for consideration from the 1608 selected originally. The medical researchers revised the death certificates and reclassified the reported causes of death based on the application of appropriate medical criteria. In this way the total number of death certificates was divided into two subgroups: the first comprising certificates with 'clearly defined' clinical causes and the second certificates with 'ill-defined' clinical causes. Clinically 'well defined' causes of death include those cases in which, irrespective of the final cause of death, an illness (for example, sepsis, diabetes, myocardium infarct, neoplasia) or specific syndrome (for example, chronic renal insufficiency, cerebrovascular accident) was registered that could have caused death. Clinically 'ill-defined' causes of death include those cases in which only a final non-specific cause of death is given (for example, non-injury-related cardiorespiratory failure) or an unspecific syndrome of numerous diseases that may cause death (for example, acute pulmonary oedema, shock, respiratory failure). For the group of clinically 'clearly defined' causes of death the following categories were established: tumours; cardiovascular pulmonary failure; infections; maternity-related; violence (accidents, homicides and suicides); and other causes. Each of these categories was then coded according to the 9th Revision of the ICD. The deaths were classified according to place of habitual residence, age group and place of occurrence.

Tables 4.6, 4.7 and 4.8 show the distribution of registered deaths of women aged 14 to 49 classified according to cause and age group, place of death (whether at home or in an institution) and residence of the deceased. Within the category of clinically 'clearly defined' deaths, the most frequent causes, in decreasing order of occurrence, are tumours, cardiovascular pulmonary diseases, violence, and infections (Table 4.6). The number of deaths increases with age for all causes except those that are maternity-related. The proportion of clinically 'ill-defined' deaths also increases with age, which might indicate a need to determine whether there is a relationship between the age of the deceased and the nature of the certification (Table 4.6). Seventy-eight per cent of deaths within the age group considered occurred in health institutions (Table 4.7). The distribution of deaths differs according to place of death: deaths due to tumours usually occur in institutions, while deaths due to violence figure prominently among non-institutional deaths. Deaths registered as maternity-related all took place in institutions. They totalled 41 cases, whose place of occurrence was almost equally divided between public and private institutions (20 and 21 respectively). Deaths classified as clinically 'ill-defined'

Table 4.6. Registered deaths of women aged 14 to 49, classified according to age group and cause, Federal Capital, 1985

Cause of death	Age group				
	14–19	20–29	30–39	40–49	Total
Clinically clearly defined					
Tumours	14	39	131	312	496
Cardiovascular-pulmonary	4	28	56	117	205
Accidents, homicides and suicides	31	41	62	50	184
Infections	11	31	39	59	140
Maternity-related	2	17	19	3	41
Other	15	43	49	77	184
Subtotal	77	199	356	618	1250
Clinically ill-defined	13	47	85	195	340
Total	90	246	441	813	1590

Source: Ministry of Health and Social Welfare (1989).

Table 4.7. Registered deaths of women aged 14 to 49 years, classified according to cause and place of occurrence, Federal Capital, 1985

Cause of death	Institutional		Non-institutional		Total	
	Number	%	Number	%	Number	%
Clinically clearly defined						
Tumours	426	34.3	70	20.3	496	31.2
Cardiovascular-pulmonary	191	15.4	14	4.0	205	12.9
Accidents, homicides and suicides	81	6.5	103	29.7	184	11.5
Infections	136	10.9	4	1.2	140	8.8
Maternity-related	41	3.3	—	—	41	2.6
Other	154	12.4	30	8.5	184	11.6
Subtotal	1029	82.8	221	63.7	1250	78.6
Clinically ill-defined	214	17.2	126	36.3	340	21.4
Total	1243	100.0	347	100.0	1590	100.0

Source: Ministry of Health and Social Welfare (1989).

constitute a significant proportion of the total (21.4 per cent). Such deaths represent a substantial proportion of those occurring outside institutions (36.3 per cent). The low proportion of such deaths within institutions (17.2 per cent), however, should be noted (Table 4.7).

Regarding the residence of deceased women, 50 to 70 per cent of deaths were of residents of the Federal Capital, with the exception being deaths due to infections and maternity-related causes. Thus residents of the Federal Capital accounted for only 25 per cent of deaths certified as maternal deaths (Table 4.8). This reflects the fact that maternal death is more likely in complicated obstetric situations or cases where there is a shortage of hospital beds.

4.4. Comparison of Death Certificates and Medical Histories

Only deaths occurring in institutions were considered for comparative purposes. The large number of deaths occurring in institutions in the Federal Capital, the dispersion of deaths among different medical establishments, and the resources available for the research made it impossible to compare all the institutional death certificates with the corresponding medical histories. The cases to be compared were therefore selected based on the experience of the medical team, as to which causes were likely to conceal maternal deaths. Thus, the objective universe of the study is defined as 326 cases comprising:

- All certificates of infectious causes recorded as sepsis (51 certificates).
- All certificates of cardiovascular pulmonary causes recorded as

Table 4.8.   Registered deaths of women aged 14 to 49, classified according to residence of the deceased, Federal Capital, 1985

Cause of death	Residents of the Federal Capital	Residents of the province of Buenos Aires	Residents of other provinces	Residents of other countries	Unknown	Total
Clinically clearly defined						
Tumours	284	180	30	2	—	496
Cardiovascular-pulmonary	100	85	20	—	—	205
Accidents, homicides and suicides	121	54	7	1	1	184
Infections	54	70	16	—	—	140
Maternity-related	10	30	1	—	—	41
Other	93	78	13	—	—	184
Subtotal	662	497	87	3	1	1250
Clinically ill-defined	235	90	14	—	1	340
Total	897	587	101	3	2	1590

Source: Ministry of Health and Social Welfare (1989).

cerebrovascular accidents, hypertension, haemorrhage, or hypovolemic shock (92 certificates).

- All certificates reporting a maternal death, in order to obtain a more precise description of the structure of causes (40 certificates following the exclusion of one case upon verification that the certification did not correspond to the circumstances of this framework).
- Certificates reporting clinically ill-defined causes were sampled (simple random sampling): one certificate stating an ill-defined cause for each certificate reporting a clearly defined non-maternal cause (143 certificates).

In 29 per cent of the cases comprising the objective universe no comparison was possible due to the loss of the medical histories for one reason or another. Therefore a method was designed for processing the universe of certificates and medical histories as if it were a simple random sample, thus making it possible to estimate the total number of·maternal deaths for the Federal Capital in 1985.

Table 4.9 shows that of the medical histories sought, only 71 per cent were located. This proportion differed according to the administrative category of the establishment (81 per cent in the public sector and 63 per cent in the private sector). This difference is even greater for deaths certified as maternity-related (95 per cent and 53 per cent respectively). This highlights the need to establish an order of priority within medical registers, particularly in the private sector.

Table 4.9. Medical histories reported according to cause and subsector of occurrence, Federal Capital, 1985

Cause of death	Subsector of occurrence					
	Public		Private		Total	
	S^a	F^b	S^a	F^b	S^a	F^b
Clinically clearly defined	89	74 (83)	94	57 (61)	183	131 (72)
Maternity-related	21	20 (95)	19	10 (53)	40	30 (75)
Infections	29	24 (83)	22	13 (59)	51	37 (73)
Cardiopulmonary	39	30 (77)	53	34 (64)	92	64 (70)
Clinically ill-defined	59	46 (78)	84	56 (67)	143	102 (72)
Total	148	120 (81)	178	113 (63)	326	233 (71)

[a] Medical histories sought.
[b] Medical histories found (percentage).

Source: Ministry of Health and Social Welfare (1989).

5. Results

5.1. Magnitude of Under-Registration

Table 4.10 shows the proportion of misclassified maternal deaths by recorded cause of death in the cases for which medical histories were found. The magnitude of misclassification varies according to the recorded cause. After cross-checking with medical histories, 25 additional deaths were added to the 40 maternal deaths registered on death certificates, making a total of 65 cases. Thus, of the total of 65 maternal deaths identified through cross-checking, 38.5 per cent were not registered as such on the death certificate. If the same distribution of causes characterized the medical histories that were not located (93) as those that were, the total number of maternal deaths would increase to 75. On this assumption, under-registration of maternal deaths rises to 53.3 per cent (since 35 maternal deaths would not be recorded as such on the death certificate).

In 1985 in the Federal Capital, according to data from death certificates, one maternal death occurred for every 2000 births, that is to say, a rate of maternal mortality of 50 per 100,000 live births. However, taking the results of the cross-check against the located medical histories into account, the ratio should be one maternal death for every 1250 births, or a rate of 79.2 per 100,000 live births. Moreover, extrapolating the results of the cross-checking process to the medical histories that were not found, the ratio should be one maternal death for every 1100 births, increasing the rate to 91.4 per 100,000 live births.

Table 4.11 shows the distribution of maternal deaths by clinical cause, permitting the analysis of the difference, in absolute values and in percentages, between deaths registered on death certificates and those deaths not registered. Irrespective of which service attends abortion complications, this cause of death tends to be under-registered as the Argentine Penal Code considers deliberate abortion, with very few exceptions, a punishable act. In the other categories of causes, the extent of under-registration varies, depending on the

Table 4.10 Misclassification of maternal deaths in the located medical histories by recorded cause of death

Cause of death	Medical histories found	Maternity-related deaths	Percentage of maternal deaths
Cardiopulmonary	64	5	7.81
Infections	37	8	21.62
Ill-defined	102	12	11.76
Total	203	25	12.32

Source: Ministry of Health and Social Welfare (1989).

Table 4.11. Maternal deaths according to clinical cause, by whether registered

Cause of death	Registered		Unregistered		Total	
	N	%	N	%	N	%
Abortion	23	92	2	8	25	100
Sepsis	5	36	9	64	14	100
Haemorrhage	4	57	3	43	7	100
Hypertension	2	50	2	50	4	100
Cardiovascular	3	37	5	63	8	100
Systemic	0	—	4	100	4	100
Anaesthesia-related accidents	3	100	0	—	3	100
Total	40	62	25	38	65	100

Source: Ministry of Health and Social Welfare (1989).

time that elapsed between delivery and death. As this period increases, mothers tend to be treated by services other than obstetric care ones. In such circumstances the significance of post-partum complications tends to be relegated to a secondary position.

It should be emphasized that these results arise from a special analysis of deaths occurring in institutions. If adequate information was available about the total number of deaths of women at childbearing age, for whatever reason, occurring within or outside an institution, it may be assumed that the level of under-registration of maternal deaths detected would be higher.

5.2. Structure of Maternal Mortality

Table 4.12 compares the distribution of maternal mortality according to clinical cause and as registered on the death certificate and determined after cross-checking against the medical history. These figures reveal the importance of abortion and sepsis not related to abortion. Eighty-six per cent of deaths are related to the post-partum stage and 14 per cent to pre-existing morbidity. Comparing the two distributions by cause (registered cause compared with the results of cross-checking), it is clear that abortion is the leading cause in both groups of maternal deaths and that the others are ordered in a similar manner. Moreover, the significance of causes related to the attention received during pregnancy and at delivery (excluding abortion) is clear.

5.3. Social Profile of the Deceased Women

To elucidate health/disease processes and identify social differences in the group of corroborated maternal deaths, which would be useful in pursuing

Table 4.12. Distribution of maternal mortality by medical cause, based on data from the medical history and the death certificate

Cause of death	Medical history		Death certificate (%)
	Number	(%)	
Abortion	25	38.5	57.5
Sepsis	14	21.5	12.5
Cardiovascular	8	12.3	7.5
Haemorrhage	7	10.8	10.0
Hypertension	4	6.2	5.0
Systemic	4	6.2	0.0
Anaesthesia-related accidents	3	4.6	7.5
Total	65	100.0	100.0

Source: Ministry of Health and Social Welfare (1989).

both intra- and extra-sectoral lines of research, it was decided to elaborate a social profile of the universe of deceased women. For this profile only secondary and fragmentary information was available. A detailed analysis was conducted of information on social variables on the death certificate and in the medical history form after completing the cross-checking or corroboration exercise (occupation, education, description of housing, and usual residence of the deceased woman).

The limitations of these data were overcome by complementing them with indirect survey methods. For cases where there was no social information in either source or where such information was incomplete or contradictory, an inspection was carried out of the facilities in the area of residence of the deceased women and of external aspects of their housing. This method has been tested in other social research and permits the recovery of relevant data for social profiling, while respecting the ethical principle on which the research team based its work: to refrain from collecting information at the household level to complement routine data merely to improve the description of the phenomenon. All the women dying of maternal causes were characterized socially in this way (for more information see Ministry of Health and Social Welfare, 1989).

Table 4.13 summarizes the information on maternal deaths according to where the deaths occurred and the social status of the deceased. The women were divided into those from the lower and those from the middle class or social sector. The lower sector is divided further into two strata: those living in a relatively poor situation (RPS) and those living in a relatively good situation (RGS). In general, the findings confirm what had been anticipated: most of

Table 4.13. Maternal deaths in public and private establishments according to
social status

Subsector	Low class		Middle class	Data unavailable[b]	Total
	RPS[a]	RGS[a]			
Public	15	13	3	5	36
Private	7	12	6	4	29
Total	22	25	9	9	65

[a] RPS: relatively poor situation. RGS: relatively good situation.
[b] Cases in which visual inspection was impractical (because of unlocated addresses or residences in
  the interior of the country) and no other data appeared on the death certificate or in the medical
  history form that would permit classification.
Source: Ministry of Health and Social Welfare (1989).

these women are from the lower class. Of 65 maternal deaths certified as such
during the cross-checking or comparison exercise, 72 per cent of the deceased
belonged to the lower class or social group and 14 per cent to the middle class
or social group (in 14 per cent of the cases no data could be found to determine
this). Of the 47 deaths classified as from the lower class or social group, 60
per cent occurred in public establishments. On the other hand, 66 per cent
of deaths within the middle class or social group took place in private
establishments.

One significant fact should be noted and considered in any programme for
the reduction of maternal mortality. Half the deaths occurring in the lower
class or social group were of women covered by social security. This supports
the idea that, under current conditions, legal coverage by the social security
system does not eliminate the risk inherent in social status. In addition, the
physical location of the residence of the deceased and the services by which
they were first treated further strengthen the belief that the populations most
at risk have services with less capacity, in both qualitative and quantitative
terms, to solve health problems.

6. Final Considerations

The information resulting from the application of this method was specially
processed by a medical team that analysed both the characteristics of mortality
and the problems observed in the health services (in terms of organization of
resources, service criteria and attitude of the population to using the services),
with a view to promoting actions within health service establishments that help
to prevent or mitigate harm to women. The findings derived from the social
profiles of deceased women, in terms of the relationship between the risks

faced by a given population group, the geographical location of that group and of the health services available to them, together with the characteristics of such services and the role played by legal coverage by social security, should not be ignored when approaching the problem of programming health actions that respond to the differing risks inherent in these conditions. Finally, the objective of describing the research presented here has been to point out the value of mortality statistics, in particular, and of vital statistics, in general, in research aimed at the prevention and reduction of damage to health, in this case represented by maternal mortality.

References

Ministry of Health and Social Welfare (1989), *Study of Maternal Mortality: Analysis of the Underregister of Maternal Deaths in the Federal Capital (1985)*, Health Secretariat, National Department of Maternal and Child Welfare, Department of Health Statistics, WHO/PAHO, Buenos Aires, Argentina.

Somoza, J. (undated), *Technical Report on the Construction of Life Tables by Province, 1980–1981*, Centre for Population Studies, Buenos Aires, Argentina.

5 New Estimates of the Decline in Adult Mortality since 1950

IAN M. TIMÆUS

London School of Hygiene and Tropical Medicine, London, England

1. Introduction

Only in a handful of Latin American countries is the registration of deaths effectively complete (Chackiel, 1990). In the rest of the region, it is necessary to apply indirect techniques of analysis to estimate adult mortality. A wide range of methods exist for measuring adult mortality in countries with limited and defective data. Those based on intercensal survival are perhaps the oldest of all indirect techniques. Moreover, during the last twenty years, two further approaches to the measurement of adult mortality in the absence of reliable registration statistics have been explored. The first set of techniques is based on questions about the survival of specific relatives that can be asked in single-round surveys and censuses. The second comprises a range of methods that can be used to evaluate and adjust data on recent deaths obtained from deficient vital registration systems or household surveys.

Straightforward procedures for calculating indices of adult mortality from the survival of parents (Brass and Hill, 1973), first spouses (Hill, 1977) and siblings (Hill and Trussell, 1977) were developed during the 1970s. At about the same time, Brass (1975) proposed using the growth balance equation to adjust data on recent deaths. Further important methodological advances occurred around 1980. Brass and Bamgboye (1981) derived a way of estimating the time reference of estimates of mortality obtained from orphanhood and widowhood data, while Zlotnik and Hill (1981) proposed calculating synthetic cohort estimates of orphanhood from data collected on two separate occasions. These developments facilitated interpretation of data on the survival of relatives in countries where the level of adult mortality was changing. In addition, a range of new methods that can be used to evaluate data on recent deaths was devised (Brass, 1979; Courbage and Fargues, 1979; Preston and Hill, 1980; Preston *et al.*, 1980; Bennett and Horiuchi, 1981). The United

I am grateful to Juan Chackiel for providing both a copy of CELADE's (1989) life tables and an explanation of how those for the countries considered here were constructed.

Nations' (1983) manual on indirect estimation incorporated much of this work and marked the coming of age of the field: during the 1980s attention has focused on the refinement and assessment of existing methods of estimation (Blacker, 1984; Blacker and Mukiza-Gapere, 1988; Hill, 1984; Palloni and Heligman, 1986; Palloni *et al.*, 1984; Timæus, 1986, 1987, 1991*a*).

Techniques based on the survival of relatives can measure only the broad trend in adult mortality and provide no information about the age pattern of mortality within adulthood. Estimates of adult mortality obtained from orphanhood data about children are sometimes biased downward by under-reporting of parental deaths (the 'adoption effect'). The widowhood method, in turn, has yielded mixed results and often overestimates recent mortality. For analysis of data on recent deaths to be feasible, on the other hand, information must be collected from a large sample and the majority of events must be reported (Preston, 1984). The first criterion rules out asking about recent deaths in surveys such as those conducted by the Demographic and Health Surveys (DHS) programme. The second vitiates many data collection efforts that supposedly cover entire populations but fail to achieve reporting that is 50 per cent complete.

Thus, there is no fully satisfactory way of measuring adult mortality in the absence of accurate registration statistics. Asking questions about the survival of relatives on household survey questionnaires has its limitations but provides estimates at minimal cost. Depending on the context, the results may be the only source of data on adult mortality or a useful external check on the validity of estimates obtained from other data collection systems. New methods for analysing orphanhood data have been proposed recently that circumvent some of the limitations of the approach.

Chackiel and Orellana (1985) suggest supplementing the question about the survival of mothers with one about the date of orphanhood. With this item of information it is possible to calculate the time location of the mortality estimates directly, without resorting to Brass and Bamgboye's (1981) proce-dure, and also to construct synthetic cohorts from data collected in a single survey. This question has yielded promising results in some Latin American applications (Chackiel and Orellana, 1985) but has performed poorly in sub-Saharan Africa, where respondents appear unable to supply accurately the dates when their parents died (Timæus, 1991*b*).

This chapter focuses on a second technique for obtaining more up-to-date mortality estimates than those yielded by the basic orphanhood method. The approach also avoids some of the biases that can affect the basic method. It is based on a supplementary question about whether orphanhood occurred before or after marriage. This provides some indication of the timing of parental deaths but makes fewer demands on respondents than the question proposed by Chackiel and Orellana (1985). Rather than having to recall the date when their parent died, respondents have only to indicate the relative timing of two major events in their lives. After a brief explanation of the techniques proposed for the analysis of such data, the chapter uses them to investigate the decline in adult mortality since 1950 in four Latin American countries.

2. Sources of Data

Adult mortality can be estimated from both orphanhood before marriage and orphanhood since marriage. Data on fathers provide estimates of male mortality and data on mothers estimates of female mortality. Only data on respondents aged 25 years or more can be analysed. At younger ages, the relationship between parental survival and life table survivorship is sensitive to the exact shape of the first marriage distribution. For age groups in which most women have married, in contrast, the estimates depend on the average timing of first marriages but not on their distribution around the mean.

The information on orphanhood before marriage used to estimate life table survivorship is the proportion of ever-married respondents in each five-year age group who had living mothers or fathers when they first married ($_5S_x^m$). For orphanhood since marriage, information on two adjoining age groups is used. It comprises the proportion of those respondents who had a living mother or father at first marriage whose mothers or fathers still remain alive ($_5S_x/_5S_x^m$). With complete reporting, multiplication of the proportion of respondents with a living mother or father at marriage by the proportion whose parent has survived since marriage should yield the proportion who still have living parents ($_5S_x$).

Questions about whether ever-married women lost their parents before or after their first marriage were asked in about half the surveys conducted during Phase I of the DHS programme. They included several enquiries in Latin American countries. This chapter focuses on the application of the new methods to data from Colombia, Ecuador, the Dominican Republic, and Peru. The basic data used in the analysis are presented in Table 5.A1.

In all four countries, the results obtained using the new methods are compared with estimates of survivorship extracted from life tables constructed by CELADE (1989). This comparison is of particular interest for Colombia and Ecuador because the life table estimates of adult mortality are based on vital statistics data generated by systems that register the majority of adult deaths. Thus, once the registration statistics have been adjusted by means of the growth balance equation, they represent an independent source of information on adult mortality. In the Dominican Republic, several sources of data on adult mortality were used to construct CELADE's (1989) life tables, including maternal orphanhood estimates for the 1970s, while in Peru the estimates of adult mortality are based solely on orphanhood data. Nevertheless, the comparison between the new estimates and those incorporated in the life tables is of interest even in Peru because the lengthy series of estimates yielded by the new techniques suggests a different interpretation of the earlier data from that adopted by CELADE.

3. Methods of Analysis

In an extension of methods proposed for analysing data on lifetime orphanhood (Hill and Trussell, 1977; United Nations, 1983; Palloni and Heligman, 1986; Timæus, 1992), regression models have been estimated for the calculation of conditional survivorship in adulthood from proportions of female respondents with parents surviving to the respondents' first marriage and since their marriage. The models are presented in Table 5.A2. An exposition of the theoretical basis of these methods, the derivation of the estimation procedures and the calculation of the time location of the estimates has been published elsewhere (Timæus, 1991*c*). This material is not reiterated here, though the following paragraphs outline the main features of the approach. Estimates from data on lifetime orphanhood and orphanhood in synthetic cohorts based at age 20 are also calculated using new sets of coefficients (Timæus, 1991*b*, 1992). These are based on the same assumptions as the coefficients in Table 5.A2.

To use the equations, estimates are required of both the cohort mean age at marriage of the female respondents ($\bar{m}$) and the period mean age at childbearing of their mothers or fathers ($\bar{M}$). The first item of information can be calculated directly from the retrospective reports of age at first marriage obtained by the DHS surveys. As such reports are prone to recall errors, other evidence was examined as well, but it was eventually decided to estimate $\bar{m}$ from these data. Because the secular trend to later marriage and truncation of the experience of younger cohorts tend to offset each other, a single estimate of $\bar{m}$ is used for respondents of all ages.

Estimates of mean ages at childbearing should refer to the experience of the parents and thus to fertility patterns in the middle decades of this century. The estimates used for women are based on a range of evidence, with most emphasis being given to the fertility patterns reported retrospectively in the World Fertility Survey (WFS) birth histories. Information on the relative ages of women of childbearing age and their husbands is required to estimate the timing of male fertility. Because husbands' ages were not collected in the DHS surveys, estimates are again based on WFS data. The approach adopted was to calculate the differences between both the singulate mean ages at marriage of men and women and the median ages of currently married men and currently married women. An estimate of the mean age of men at the birth of their children was then obtained by adding the average of these two differences to the value of $\bar{M}$ calculated for the mothers.

Data on orphanhood before marriage yield estimates of $l(45)/l(25)$ for women and $l(55)/l(35)$ for men, representing the parents' survivorship from about their mean age at childbearing to about their average age when their daughters marry. Data on orphanhood since marriage yield estimates of $l(25 + n)/l(45)$ for women and $l(35 + n)/l(55)$ for men, where n is the age dividing the two age groups of respondents considered and the measures represent survivorship from about the parents' average age when the respondents married to their average age when the data were collected. As an illustration, applications of the procedures to Colombian data on maternal orphanhood before marriage and paternal orphanhood since marriage are shown in Tables 5.1 and 5.2.

Approximate estimates of the time location (T) of the survivorship ratios can be obtained using the procedures developed by Brass and Bamgboye (1981) and by Brass (1985). The latter approach is used here. For orphanhood before marriage, the index of the age at which exposure starts (M) is either the mothers' mean age at childbearing ($\overline{M}$) or the fathers' mean age at the concep-

Table 5.1. Estimation of adult female mortality from orphanhood before marriage, Colombia

Age n	Proportion not orphaned before marriage $_5S^m_n$	Survivorship from age 25 to 45 $_{20}P_{45}$	Mortality level α	Survivorship from age 15 to 60 $_{45}P_{15}$	Date
25	0.9115	0.9214	−0.633	0.770	1970.7
30	0.9082	0.9213	−0.631	0.770	1965.7
35	0.8949	0.9098	−0.547	0.742	1960.7
40	0.8684	0.8854	−0.389	0.685	1955.6
45	0.8320	0.8514	−0.201	0.614	1950.4

Table 5.2. Estimation of adult male mortality from orphanhood since marriage, Colombia

Age n	Proportion not orphaned since marriage $_5S_{n-5}/_5S^m_{n-5}$	Survivorship from age 55 to 35 + n $_{35+n}P_{55}$	Mortality level α	Survivorship from age 15 to 60 $_{45}P_{15}$	Date
30	0.8855	0.7954	−0.442	0.705	1982.3
35	0.7734	0.6603	−0.507	0.728	1980.5
40	0.6406	0.5010	−0.587	0.755	1979.3
45	0.5097				
Averages			−0.512	0.729	1980.7

tion of their live-born children ($\bar{M} - 0.75$). The index of the duration of exposure (N) is the respondents' mean age at marriage ($\bar{m}$) for maternal orphanhood and $\bar{m} + 0.75$ for paternal orphanhood. On average the parents' exposure ceased $N - \bar{m}$ years ago, where N is the mid-point of the age group of respondents considered. Using Brass's (1985) notation, one obtains for maternal orphanhood estimates:

$$T = (N - \bar{m}) + {}_{\bar{m}}g_{\bar{M}}. \tag{1}$$

where ${}_{\bar{m}}g_{\bar{M}}$ is the time reference relative to $\bar{m}$ of mortality estimates based on deaths before $\bar{m}$, calculated using the formula proposed by Brass (1985). As Table 5.1 illustrates, the time references of the different mortality estimates span a twenty-year period, commencing some thirty-seven years before the data were collected.

For orphanhood since marriage, the index of the age at which exposure starts is $\bar{M} + \bar{m}$ and the index of the duration of exposure is $n - \bar{m}$, where *n* is the age dividing the two age groups of respondents considered. Therefore:

$$T = {}_{n-\bar{m}}g_{\bar{M}+\bar{m}}. \tag{2}$$

As the fathers' exposure to the risk of death begins well after the birth of their daughters, Equation (2) applies to estimates of both men's and women's mortality. The estimates obtained from orphanhood since marriage in different age groups all refer to the period four to eight years before the data were collected (see Table 5.2). Rather than trying to measure trends over this period, it is probably more realistic to average the results to obtain a single estimate of mortality for about six years ago.

The indices obtained from data on lifetime orphanhood, orphanhood before marriage and orphanhood since marriage measure survivorship over varying age ranges in early adulthood and middle age. To compare the measures and examine mortality trends, they must be translated into a common index of mortality. Different analysts have used various indices for this purpose. In this chapter, results are presented in terms of the life table probability of surviving from age 15 to 60 (${}_{45}p_{15}$). This is a straightforward measure of the overall level of adult mortality that does not incorporate any assumptions about the severity of old age mortality. To calculate ${}_{45}p_{15}$ from the survivorship ratios yielded by the regression models, it is necessary to fit one-parameter model life tables to them. In this chapter relational-logit model life tables are used based on the General Standard (Brass, 1971). Other systems of models would yield similar results for the range of ages with which we are concerned (15 to 75 years). Moreover, the life tables published by CELADE (1989) suggest that, in the four countries considered, the General Standard is probably a reasonable representation of the pattern of mortality at these ages for the period 1950 to 1985.

4. Results

4.1. Colombia

Estimates of the mortality of adult men and women in Colombia, presented in terms of the probability of surviving from age 15 to age 60, are shown in Figure 5.1. The estimates based on maternal orphanhood before marriage and paternal orphanhood since marriage are taken from Tables 5.1 and 5.2. The direct estimates, based on civil registration statistics adjusted for under-reporting, have been taken from the quinquennial life tables published by CELADE (1989).

Two features of the orphanhood results deserve emphasis. Firstly, a very high estimate of women's mortality was obtained from data on the lifetime orphanhood of respondents aged 15–19 years. Only a minority of this age group are married and the estimate presumably reflects the selection of orphaned girls for early marriage. Therefore this estimate was discarded. Secondly, the results obtained from data on lifetime orphanhood reflect mortality over a limited period of time, centred on a date about twelve years prior to their collection. In contrast, analysis of information on the timing of orphanhood relative to marriage, yields estimates that span the entire period between 1950 and 1980.

The estimates for the 1970s, based on lifetime orphanhood, and those for 1980, based on orphanhood since marriage, agree fairly well with the vital statistics data as to the overall level of mortality. However, the orphanhood estimates indicate slightly higher mortality for men and a wider gender differential in adult mortality. According to the registration data, only modest

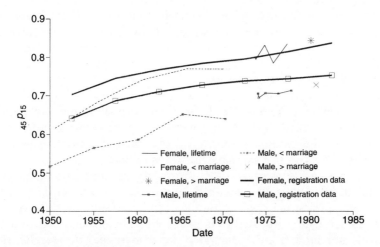

Fig. 5.1.   Trends in adult mortality in Colombia

improvements in adult survivorship occurred between 1950 and 1985, the decline slowed after 1960 and men benefited less than women. In contrast, the orphanhood estimates indicate that survivorship has risen rapidly and continuously from a much lower level and that men and women have benefited more or less equally. The estimates from orphanhood before marriage, in particular, suggest that male mortality in the 1950s and 1960s was much heavier than it appears according to the adjusted registration data on which CELADE based its life tables.

To determine definitively whether the orphanhood or registration-based estimates of adult male mortality in Colombia are to be preferred would require a detailed re-assessment of the registration statistics, the adjustment procedures applied to them and other sources of demographic data on Colombia. While this investigation is not attempted here, the following paragraphs outline why the paternal orphanhood method is unlikely to have overestimated mortality substantially.

One possibility that can be discounted is that the discrepancies between the two sources arise from the imprecision of the procedures used to estimate survivorship from orphanhood. Because the incidence of orphanhood before marriage reflects survivorship over a limited range of ages, this technique is one of the more robust variants of the orphanhood method. Even if the age pattern of mortality within adulthood in Colombia prior to 1970 was very unusual, this would affect the estimates of $_{20}p_{35}$ and their conversion into $_{45}p_{15}$ by only a few per cent. Moreover, though the regression model can underestimate $_{20}p_{35}$ if fathers' ages at childbearing are much more dispersed than is assumed, only an unusually wide distribution, of the type found in highly polygynous societies, could account for an important part of the discrepancy between the orphanhood and registration statistics.

One factor that can lead to the overestimation of mortality from data on orphanhood before marriage is the use of too low a value for the mean age of men at the birth of their children. In Colombia, one would have to raise the estimate of $\overline{M}$ for men by 1.5 years merely to reduce the gender differential in adult mortality to the size indicated by the vital statistics data. Only an implausibly high estimate of $\overline{M}$ would raise survivorship to the level indicated by the registration data. As this would also have a broadly comparable effect on the estimates obtained from lifetime orphanhood and orphanhood since marriage, revising the results in this way would merely shift the discrepancy between the two series of estimates forwards in time.

Similar considerations suggest that the discrepancy between the two sets of estimates of male mortality cannot be explained by errors in the estimation of the timing of first marriage. Although raising the value of $\overline{m}$ increases the level of survivorship estimated from orphanhood before marriage and lowers the level estimated from orphanhood since marriage, the results are not particularly sensitive to this measure. Such an adjustment might further improve the consistency between the orphanhood and registration estimates of female mortality but cannot explain the inconsistencies in the estimates for men.

The other possible source of error in the orphanhood-based estimates of men's mortality is over-reporting of orphanhood in childhood. Reconciliation of the two sources would require that about a quarter of women who stated that their father died before they married had living fathers. It is difficult to see why inaccurate reporting should occur on this scale. The daughters of some divorced and widowed women might believe mistakenly that their father died when they were children, but not nearly 5 per cent of the entire population.

Thus, to summarize this discussion, there are a number of factors that might lead to the overestimation of men's mortality from orphanhood data. Even if several such factors were acting in combination, it seems unlikely that estimates of survivorship as low as those obtained for Colombia in the 1950s and 1960s would result if the actual level of survivorship was that suggested by the registration statistics. Moreover, unless the only error is over-reporting of orphanhood before marriage, such an account implies that reasonable agreement between more recent estimates and the registration data occurs only because they are affected by a further set of offsetting errors. It seems more likely that the registration of adult male deaths in the 1950s and 1960s was less complete than has been realized until now.

4.2. Ecuador

Orphanhood and registration-based estimates of adult mortality in Ecuador are shown in Figure 5.2. As in Colombia, a high proportion of married teenage girls have lost their mother. In Ecuador, this group of women also suffers from

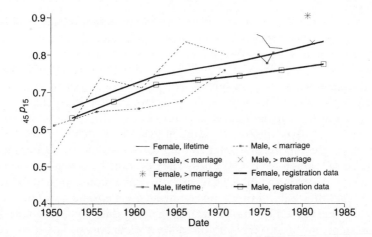

Fig. 5.2.   Trends in adult mortality in Ecuador

a high level of paternal orphanhood. Thus, both mortality estimates based on orphanhood in this age group have been discarded. Furthermore, the estimates of female survivorship obtained from data on the lifetime orphanhood of respondents in their twenties also indicate appreciably higher mortality than those obtained from older respondents. They may also be biased downwards by an association between orphanhood and ages at marriage and should perhaps be discounted. If this is done, the orphanhood estimates tell a fairly consistent story. Although more erratic than those for Colombia, they suggest that survivorship of both men and women in Ecuador rose steadily between 1950 and 1980.

Comparison of the orphanhood estimates with those derived from the registration statistics, reveals that the two sources yield broadly comparable results for the 1950s and 1960s. They agree less well for the following decade. While the registration data suggest that recent improvements in adult survivorship have been modest, the data on lifetime orphanhood and orphanhood since marriage suggest that survivorship has continued to rise rapidly and that mortality in now substantially lower for both men and women than is indicated by CELADE's (1989) life tables.

Once again, it seems unlikely that the discrepancy between the two series stems from the imprecision of the estimation procedure or the use of an inappropriate value of $\bar{M}$ or $\bar{m}$ to calculate the orphanhood estimates. The translation of the recent estimates into $_{45}p_{15}$ is more sensitive to the age pattern of mortality than it is for data on orphanhood before marriage. However, the registration-based survivorship ratios for age ranges that correspond exactly to those obtained from the regression models suggest that this potential problem does not distort the results shown in Figure 5.2. Secondly, even if the mean age at childbearing has been overestimated by two years for each sex, the orphanhood data still imply higher survivorship than the registration data.

It is possible that the estimates from lifetime orphanhood and orphanhood since marriage are in error because some women claim that parents who died recently are still alive. It seems unlikely, however, that respondents would do this on a large scale but report accurately about parents who died before they married. Secondly, while substantial exaggeration of ages would affect the results in the same way, for women this problem is not as characteristic of data on Latin America populations as it is of data on Africa and Southern Asia. Moreover, if the orphanhood data were affected by either of these errors one would expect the reports of women in their forties to indicate lighter mortality than those of women in their thirties. They do not. Thus, while it is possible that a series of errors and biases have led the orphanhood method to underestimate recent mortality, serious consideration must also be given to the possibility that the life tables based on registration data underestimate recent improvements in the survivorship of adults in Ecuador.

4.3. Dominican Republic

Estimates of adult mortality in the Dominican Republic are shown in Figure 5.3. Lifetime data on maternal orphanhood were collected in the 1975 WFS survey and lifetime data on both maternal and paternal orphanhood in the 1980 National Fertility Survey (NFS) and 1986 DHS study. The DHS enquiry also collected information on the timing of orphanhood relative to marriage. Using the WFS and NFS data, one can calculate synthetic indices of maternal orphanhood for the period 1975–80 (Timæus, 1991*b*). As the DHS data refer only to ever-married women, this has not been attempted for the period 1980–6.

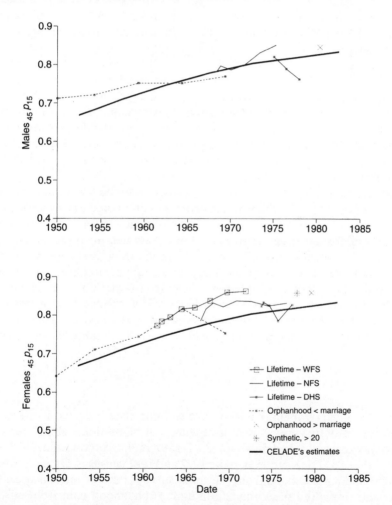

Fig. 5.3.   Trends in adult mortality in the Dominican Republic

There are a number of minor problems with the DHS data. Information on women aged 15–19 in the DHS survey again indicates very high mortality and has been discarded. Secondly, women aged 25–9 reported fewer living mothers in the DHS survey than one would expect on the basis of the other information available. The impact of this on both the most recent estimate obtained from orphanhood before marriage and the estimates from lifetime orphanhood is clear. It is also notable that older women in the DHS reported that rather high proportions of their fathers survived to their marriage. Women aged 45–9 years actually reported that, when they first married, fewer of their mothers than fathers were alive. As well as affecting the results from orphanhood before marriage, this feature of the data underlies the surprising trend in the estimates of men's mortality calculated from the data on lifetime orphanhood collected by the DHS. It does not affect the estimate based on orphanhood since marriage.

If one ignores the estimates of men's mortality based on orphanhood before marriage, the orphanhood data collected in the DHS agree quite well with those collected in earlier enquiries and indicate a plausible gender differential in adult mortality. The close agreement between the estimate of women's mortality obtained from orphanhood since marriage and the synthetic cohort estimate is particularly impressive given that they are derived from data collected by means of different questions, posed in different surveys and analysed in different ways.

The estimates for both men and women also tie up quite well with CELADE's (1989) life tables, which are based on intercensal survival for the period up to 1970 and a combination of vital statistics data and data on lifetime orphanhood for the more recent past. Having said this, the orphanhood-based estimates consistently suggest that female survivorship is slightly higher than in the life tables adopted by CELADE. This could be accounted for in many ways and only an in-depth study of all the data now available could determine which estimates are to be preferred. Finally, it is notable that in this application, unlike those for Colombia and Ecuador, the new estimates provide support for the idea that the pace of decline in adult mortality has slowed since 1970.

4.4. Peru

Estimates of survivorship based on orphanhood data collected in a series of enquiries in Peru are shown in Figure 5.4. Questions about maternal orphanhood were asked in the 1976 Demographic Survey, the 1977 WFS survey, the 1986 DHS survey and the 1972 and 1981 censuses. Data on paternal orphanhood are available from the three surveys but not the censuses. Estimates are presented based on the lifetime orphanhood data from all these sources, the data on orphanhood before and since marriage provided by the DHS survey and synthetic indices of maternal orphanhood during the period

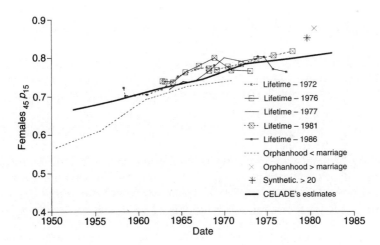

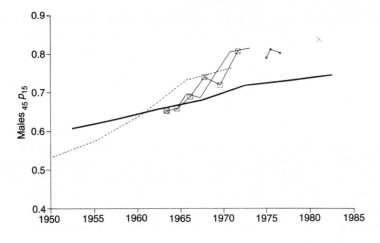

Fig. 5.4. Trends in adult mortality in Peru

1977–81. Once again, the DHS data on married teenage girls indicate very high mortality and have been discarded. As in Ecuador, lifetime data on the maternal orphanhood of respondents in their twenties also indicate rather high mortality.

If the data supplied by younger respondents in the DHS are ignored, all the estimates of women's mortality based on lifetime data agree closely. They also tie up well with the estimates based on orphanhood before and since marriage. By using a slightly higher value of $\overline{m}$ to calculate the new estimates, one could produce an even more consistent series. As in the Dominican Republic, DHS data on orphanhood since marriage yield a level of survivorship very similar to that in the synthetic cohort constructed from data collected in earlier enquiries. The estimates for males are broadly consistent with those for females and indicate slightly higher mortality. There is some indication that too few deaths of fathers were reported for children in both the 1976 and 1977 surveys. Depending on why this occurred, the DHS data on orphanhood before marriage might also underestimate mortality. Those on orphanhood since marriage should not be affected.

The life tables constructed by CELADE (1989) for Peru are based on estimates for the 1960s and early 1970s. The new estimates from orphanhood before and after marriage provide measures of adult mortality in the 1950s and late 1970s that were lacking before. These lengthy series of results make it much easier to assess the long-term trend in mortality. They suggest that it has undergone a rapid decline. It seems likely that levels of survivorship in adulthood were lower in the 1950s than CELADE assumed, but that survivorship is now higher than they predicted. There is no evidence that the rate of increase in adult survivorship has slowed over time.

5. Discussion

One aim of the collection of orphanhood data in the DHS surveys was the estimation of adult mortality (Institute for Resource Development, 1987). In practice, the basic information on lifetime orphanhood is of limited value for this purpose. This is because the data are available only for ever-married women. In Latin America, as elsewhere (Timæus, 1991c), women who have lost a parent tend to marry young. This is presumably, at least in part, because both early orphanhood and early marriage are concentrated among socio-economically disadvantaged groups. As a result, the information on lifetime orphanhood collected by the DHS programme yields little more than a single estimate of the level of adult mortality, based on the responses of age groups that have largely completed first marriage and referring to about a dozen years before the data were collected.

In the large subset of those countries asking about orphanhood, that asked about its timing relative to marriage, one can achieve much more. Information supplied by older women about orphanhood since marriage can be used to estimate the level of male and female adult mortality some six years earlier. These data are unlikely to be distorted by the 'adoption effect' and, as most women marry before age 25, the estimates are robust to selection biases stemming from any association between orphanhood and age at marriage (Timæus, 1991c). While the issue has yet to be studied in Latin America, in sub-Saharan Africa a question about the timing of orphanhood relative to marriage has proved a more robust way of producing an up-to-date estimate than asking about the dates when parents died (Timæus, 1991c).

Information on orphanhood before marriage produces estimates of mortality that reach back more than thirty-five years into the past. The more recent results are a valuable check upon those obtained from lifetime orphanhood for about fifteen years before the data were collected and the lengthy series of estimates yielded by the method provides an improved basis for assessing mortality trends and predicting the future.

The four applications of the new orphanhood methods presented here emphasize that, as with all techniques for estimating adult mortality in the absence of adequate vital registration statistics, critical assessment of the results is important. In three of the applications, estimates based on maternal and paternal orphanhood since marriage agree well with one another and with all the other evidence as to the level and trend in adult mortality. In Ecuador, the orphanhood data are internally consistent but disagree with those based on registration statistics. As one might expect, estimates obtained from orphanhood before marriage seem less precise. In Ecuador they are somewhat erratic, in the Dominican Republic they suggest that female mortality was higher than male mortality in the 1950s, while in Colombia they suggest much higher male mortality than estimates derived from civil registration statistics. In Colombia, at least, the information on orphanhood before marriage may be correct. Taken together, however, the applications suggest that orphanhood before marriage provides only a broad indication of more distant trends in adult mortality.

The new estimates of adult mortality presented for four Latin American countries present a picture of the history of decline in adult mortality in these populations that differs from that accepted up till now. They suggest that the decline in adult mortality has been both rapid and substantial. Only in the Dominican Republic is there evidence that the pace of decline has slowed since the 1950s or early 1960s. During the 1950s, male mortality in Colombia and the mortality of both sexes in Peru was probably higher than suggested by earlier studies. By 1980, adult mortality in Ecuador and Peru may have fallen to a lower level than anticipated.

6. Conclusions

Although more detailed and accurate demographic data are available for Latin America than for most other parts of the less developed world, in some countries orphanhood data still represent the most reliable information available on adult mortality. In other countries, they are a valuable adjunct to data obtained from vital registration. Further investigations may or may not support the suggestion that the decline in adult mortality since 1950 in many Latin American countries has been more substantial than believed previously. Either way, it is clear that by collecting data on orphanhood one gains a valuable external source of information that can contribute to the assessment of routinely collected data.

The scepticism that developed about the orphanhood method in the early

1980s (e.g. Hill, 1984), still informs the thinking of many experts (e.g. Sullivan, 1990). Results presented here and elsewhere (Timæus, 1991c) suggest that by asking an additional question about whether parents died before or after respondents married one can overcome many of the limitations of the method. Surveys conducted in the first phase of the DHS programme generated a wealth of data on adult mortality in this way at minimal cost. The opportunity to collect more such data in most Phase II DHS surveys has already been missed. It should not be neglected in future.

Appendix 5.1

Table 5.A1. Proportions of parents alive
Colombia

Age	Survival of mothers			Survival of fathers		
	At survey	At marriage	Since marriage	At survey	At marriage	Since marriage
15–19	0.9070			0.8547		
20–24	0.9213			0.8183		
25–29	0.8520	0.9115	0.9347	0.7141	0.8065	0.8855
30–34	0.8306	0.9082	0.9145	0.6264	0.8100	0.7734
35–39	0.7148	0.8949	0.7987	0.4925	0.7688	0.6406
40–44	0.6066	0.8684	0.6986	0.3852	0.7557	0.5097
45–49	0.4337	0.8320	0.5213		0.7245	

Note: $\overline{M}_f$ = 27.2 years, $\overline{M}_m$ = 32.1 years, $\overline{m}$ = 20.1 years. Date of survey: 1986.88.

Ecuador

Age	Survival of mothers			Survival of fathers		
	At survey	At marriage	Since marriage	At survey	At marriage	Since marriage
15–19	0.8945			0.8744		
20–24	0.9122			0.8150		
25–29	0.8754	0.9249	0.9464	0.8329	0.8853	0.9408
30–34	0.8475	0.9361	0.9054	0.7000	0.8344	0.8389
35–39	0.7818	0.8824	0.8860	0.6357	0.8216	0.7736
40–44	0.6897	0.8939	0.7715	0.5199	0.8170	0.6364
45–49	0.5355	0.7908	0.6771		0.7951	

Note: $\overline{M}_f$ = 27.1 years, $\overline{M}_m$ = 31.2 years, $\overline{m}$ = 20.0 years. Date of survey: 1987.13.

Table 5.A1. *Continued*

Dominican Republic

Age	Survival of mothers			Survival of fathers		
	At survey	At marriage	Since marriage	At survey	At marriage	Since marriage
15–19	0.9276			0.8832		
20–24	0.9227			0.8359		
25–29	0.8592	0.9182	0.9358	0.7878	0.8934	0.8818
30–34	0.8359	0.9406	0.8886	0.7225	0.8823	0.8188
35–39	0.7724	0.9118	0.8470	0.6237	0.8816	0.7075
40–44	0.6577	0.8978	0.7325	0.4964	0.8656	0.5735
45–49	0.5628	0.8619	0.6529		0.8598	

Note: $\overline{M}_f$ = 26.3 years, $\overline{M}_m$ = 32.4 years, $\overline{m}$ = 18.3 years. Date of survey: 1986.83.

Peru

Age	Survival of mothers			Survival of fathers		
	At survey	At marriage	Since marriage	At survey	At marriage	Since marriage
15–19	0.9071			0.8429		
20–24	0.8804			0.8562		
25–29	0.8347	0.8930	0.9347	0.8023	0.8752	0.9167
30–34	0.7945	0.8825	0.9002	0.7276	0.8532	0.8528
35–39	0.7107	0.8644	0.8222	0.5851	0.7989	0.7324
40–44	0.6115	0.8217	0.7442	0.4268	0.7580	0.5630
45–49	0.4828	0.7968	0.6060		0.7289	

Note: $\overline{M}_f$ = 28.0 years, $\overline{M}_m$ = 32.0 years, $\overline{m}$ = 20.5 years. Date of survey: 1986.83.

Table 5.A2. Coefficients for orphanhood estimation

1. Coefficients for maternal orphanhood after marriage

Estimation of $l(25 + n)/l(45)$ from proportions of mothers alive among women with living mothers when they married

$$l(25 + n)/l(45) = \beta_0(n) + \beta_1(n)\overline{M} + \beta_2(n)\overline{m} + \beta_3(n)_5S_{n-5}/_5S_{n-5}^m + \beta_4(n)_5S_n/_5S_n^m$$

n	$\beta_0(n)$	$\beta_1(n)$	$\beta_2(n)$	$\beta_3(n)$	$\beta_4(n)$	R^2
30	0.5617	0.00836	−0.00261	−1.1231	1.4199	0.964
35	0.0476	0.01396	−0.00536	−0.3916	1.1354	0.966
40	−0.3715	0.01966	−0.00744	0.5394	0.5286	0.976
45	−0.6562	0.02587	−0.00716	1.0208	0.1789	0.987
50	−0.8341	0.03045	−0.00561	1.1898	0.0541	0.990

Table 5.A2. *Continued*

2. Coefficients for paternal orphanhood after marriage

Estimation of $l(35 + n)/l(55)$ from proportions of fathers alive among women with living fathers when they married

$$l(35 + n)/l(55) = \beta_0(n) + \beta_1(n)\overline{M} + \beta_2(n)\overline{m} + \beta_3(n)_5S_{n-5}/_5S_{n-5}^m + \beta_4(n)_5S_n/_5S_n^m$$

n	$\beta_0(n)$	$\beta_1(n)$	$\beta_2(n)$	$\beta_3(n)$	$\beta_4(n)$	R^2
30	0.0676	0.01588	−0.00633	−1.2070	1.8284	0.979
35	−0.5459	0.02273	−0.01083	−0.2509	1.3867	0.980
40	−0.8674	0.02622	−0.01135	0.6057	0.7198	0.974

3. Cofficients for maternal orphanhood before marriage

Estimation of $l(45)/l(25)$ from proportions of women with living mothers when they married

$$l(45)/l(25) = \beta_0(n) + \beta_1(n)\overline{M} + \beta_2(n)\overline{m} + \beta_3(n)_5S_n^m + \beta_4(n)\overline{m}_5S_n^m$$

n	$\beta_0(n)$	$\beta_1(n)$	$\beta_2(n)$	$\beta_3(n)$	$\beta_4(n)$	R^2
25	−0.9607	0.00418	0.04466	1.8178	−0.04291	0.988
30	−0.9921	0.00429	0.04700	1.8428	−0.04501	0.988
35	−1.0129	0.00433	0.04822	1.8607	−0.04611	0.988
40+	−1.0206	0.00434	0.04861	1.8680	−0.04648	0.988

4. Coefficients for paternal orphanhood before marriage

Estimation of $l(55)/l(35)$ from proportions of women with living fathers when they married

$$l(55)/l(35) = \beta_0(n) + \beta_1(n)\overline{M} + \beta_2(n)\overline{m} + \beta_3(n)_5S_n^m + \beta_4(n)\overline{m}_5S_n^m$$

n	$\beta_0(n)$	$\beta_1(n)$	$\beta_2(n)$	$\beta_3(n)$	$\beta_4(n)$	R^2
25	−1.2719	0.01060	0.04480	1.8383	−0.04007	0.969
30	−1.2977	0.01068	0.04652	1.8530	−0.04124	0.969
35	−1.3203	0.01070	0.04769	1.8726	−0.04225	0.970
40+	−1.3232	0.01070	0.04783	1.8753	−0.04238	0.970

References

Bennett, N. G., and S. Horiuchi (1981), 'Estimating the completeness of death registration in a closed population', *Population Index*, 47: 207–21.

Blacker, J. G. C. (1984), 'Experience in the use of special mortality questions in multipurpose surveys: the single-round approach', in: *Data Bases for Mortality Measurement*, United Nations, New York.

Blacker, J. G. C., and J. Mukiza-Gapere (1988), 'The indirect measurement of adult mortality in Africa', in: *African Population Conference, Dakar, 1988*, International Union for the Scientific Study of Population, Liège, Belgium.

Brass, W. (1971), 'On the scale of mortality', in: W. Brass (ed.) *Biological Aspects of Demography*, Taylor & Francis, London.

——(1975), *Methods for Estimating Fertility and Mortality from Limited and Defective Data*, Occasional Publication, International Program of Laboratories for Population Statistics, Chapel Hill, NC.

——(1979), 'A procedure for comparing mortality measures calculated from intercensal survival with the corresponding estimates from registered deaths', *Asian and Pacific Census Forum*, 6(2): 5–7.

——(1985), 'Further simplification of time location estimates for survivorship of adult relatives reported in a survey', in: *Advances in Methods for Estimating Fertility and Mortality from Limited and Defective Data*, Centre for Population Studies Occasional Paper, London School of Hygiene and Tropical Medicine, London.

——and E. Bamgboye (1981), *The Time Location of Reports of Survivorship: Estimates for Maternal and Paternal Widowhood and the Ever-Widowed*, Centre for Population Studies Research Paper No. 81–1, London School of Hygiene and Tropical Medicine, London.

——and K. Hill (1973), 'Estimating adult mortality from orphanhood', in: *International Population Conference, Liège, 1973*, International Union for the Scientific Study of Population, Liège, Belgium.

Centro Latinamericano de Demografía (CELADE) (1989), *Latin American Life Tables*, Demographic Bulletin, 44, Santiago, Chile.

Chackiel, J. (1990), 'Studies of cause of death in Latin America: the current situation and future perspectives', in: J. Vallin, S. D'Souza, and A. Palloni (eds.) *Measurement and Analysis of Mortality: New Approaches*, Clarendon Press, Oxford.

——and H. Orellana (1985), 'Adult female mortality trends from retrospective questions about maternal orphanhood included in censuses and surveys', in: *International Population Conference, Florence, 1985*, International Union for the Scientific Study of Population, Liège, Belgium.

Courbage, Y., and P. Fargues (1979), 'A method for deriving mortality estimates from incomplete vital statistics', *Population Studies*, 33: 165–80.

Hill, K. (1977), 'Estimating adult mortality levels from data on widowhood', *Population Studies*, 31: 75–84.

——(1984), 'An evaluation of indirect methods for estimating mortality', in: J. Vallin, J. H. Pollard, and L. Heligman (eds.) *Methodologies for the Collection and Analysis of Mortality Data*, Ordina, Liège, Belgium.

——and T. J. Trussell (1977), 'Further developments in indirect mortality estimation', *Population Studies*, 31: 313–33.

Institute for Resource Development (1987), *Model "A" Questionnaire*, Basic Documentation, 1, Columbia, Md.

Palloni A., and L. Heligman (1986), 'Re-estimation of the structural parameters to obtain estimates of mortality in developing countries', *Population Bulletin of the United Nations*, 18: 10–33.

—— M. Massagli, and J. Marcotte (1984), 'Estimating adult mortality with maternal orphanhood data: analysis of sensitivity of the techniques', *Population Studies*, 38: 255–79.

Preston, S. H. (1984), 'Use of direct and indirect techniques for estimating the completeness of death registration systems', in: *Data Bases for Mortality Measurement*, United Nations, New York.

—— A. J. Coale, J. Trussell, and M. Weinstein (1980), 'Estimating the completeness of reporting of adult deaths in populations that are approximately stable', *Population Index*, 46: 179–202.

——and K. Hill (1980), 'Estimating the completeness of death registration', *Population Studies*, 34: 349–66.

Sullivan, J. M. (1990), 'The collection of mortality data in WFS and DHS surveys', in: J. Vallin, S. D'Souza, and A. Palloni (eds.) *Measurement and Analysis of Mortality: New Approaches*, Clarendon Press, Oxford.

Timæus, I. M. (1986), 'An assessment of methods for estimating adult mortality from two sets of data on maternal orphanhood', *Demography*, 23: 435–50.

——(1987), 'Estimation of fertility and mortality from WFS household surveys', in: J. Cleland and C. Scott (eds.) *The World Fertility Survey: An Assessment*, Clarendon Press, Oxford.

——(1991a), 'Measurement of adult mortality in less developed countries: a comparative review', *Population Index*, 57: 552–68.

——(1991b), 'Estimation of mortality from orphanhood in adulthood', *Demography*, 27: 213–27.

——(1991c), 'Estimation of adult mortality from orphanhood before and since marriage', *Population Studies*, 45: 455–72.

——(1992), 'Estimation of adult mortality from paternal orphanhood: a reassessment and a new approach', *Population Bulletin of the United Nations*, 33: 47–63.

United Nations (1983), *Indirect Techniques for Demographic Estimation*, Manual X, Department of International Economics and Social Affairs, New York.

Zlotnik, H., and K. Hill (1981), 'The use of hypothetical cohorts in estimating demographic parameters under conditions of changing fertility and mortality', *Demography*, 18: 103–22.

6 Experience with the Sisterhood Method for Estimating Maternal Mortality

HARMEN SIMONS
Universidad Autónoma de Honduras, Tegucigalpa, Honduras

LAURA WONG
Universidade Federal de Minas Gerais, Belo Horizonte, Brazil

WENDY GRAHAM
London School of Hygiene and Tropical Medicine, London, England

SUSANA SCHKOLNIK
Centro Latinoamericano de Demografía, Santiago, Chile

1. Introduction

It has recently been estimated that, worldwide, about 500,000 women die each year of causes related to pregnancy and childbirth (Royston and Lopez, 1987). Of these maternal deaths almost 99 per cent take place in

The authors would like to acknowledge the collaborating organizations and individuals and the funding agencies involved in the three applications of the sisterhood method reported in this chapter. The participating institutions in the Temuco survey, Chile, were La Universidad de la Frontera de Temuco (UFRO); La Pontificia Universidad Católica (PUC), sede Temuco; La Fundación Instituto Indígena (FII); El Instituto Nacional de Estadística (INE); Programa de Extensión y Apoyo en Salud Materno Infantil (PEASMI); and El Centro Latinoamericano de Demografía (CELADE). The survey in Lima, Peru was funded by the Diarrhoeal Diseases Control Programme of the World Health Organization, Geneva. The principal investigators were Dr Alex Aguirre and Dr Allan G. Hill. We gratefully acknowledge their kind permission to present the data on maternal mortality and for their assistance in the analysis and interpretation. Thanks are also due to the collaborators in this study from the Ministry of Health in Lima and to the fieldworkers. The participating institutions in the study in Avaroa, Bolivia, were El Consejo Nacional de Población (CONAPO), Bolivia; El Servicio de Información y Acción en Población (SIAP); UNICEF; and CELADE.

The collaborative work on the sisterhood method between CELADE and the London School of Hygiene and Tropical Medicine which resulted in this chapter was funded by the Pan American Health Organization, CIDA (Canada), and the British Overseas Development Administration. Finally, the authors would like to thank Dr Samuel Preston, Director of the Population Studies Center, University of Pennsylvania, for his comments on the method used to calculate the number of sisters ever-exposed to the risk of dying from maternal causes used in the Temuco and Avaroa studies; Dr Juan Chackiel, Head of the Demographic Section, CELADE; and Professor William Brass, Emeritus Professor of Medical Demography, London School of Hygiene and Tropical Medicine, for supporting and encouraging our interest in maternal mortality.

developing countries. The share of Latin America in these tragic figures is estimated to be 34,000 or almost 7 per cent of the estimated total (Starrs, 1987). The majority of these deaths could be prevented with appropriate health care. Maternal mortality figures among the four or five most important causes of death for women in the childbearing ages and specific studies have revealed alarmingly high maternal mortality rates in several developing countries. For all these reasons, the reduction of maternal mortality has now become a high priority in strategies for *Health for All by the Year 2000*, both for the World Health Organization (WHO), on a worldwide scale, and for the Pan American Health Organization (PAHO) in the Latin American context.

While it is now widely acknowledged that there exist great differences in levels of maternal mortality, both within and between developing and developed countries, accurate information concerning this phenomenon is grossly deficient. This lack of information tends to be most serious in those areas in which maternal mortality is likely to be highest.

2. Measuring Maternal Mortality

Maternal mortality usually refers to deaths which occur among women during pregnancy or within forty-two days of its termination, without regard to the duration or localization of the pregnancy, from any cause related to or aggravated by the pregnancy itself or attendant on it, but not from accidental or incidental causes (WHO, 1977). This operational definition of maternal mortality permits its measurement from conventional sources of (cause-specific) mortality data such as vital registration and health-services statistics. In most developing countries these data sources are neither complete nor reliable. The lack of reliable information constitutes a major obstacle for health planners in the development of adequate strategies aimed at reducing this problem.

Over the last twenty years, a number of indirect methods have been developed for application in areas with poor statistical infrastructure. The rationale underlying all these methods is identical. Straightforward questions on the survival of close relatives are asked in a census or sample survey and simple statistics (i.e. proportions of surviving relatives classified by standard age groups of respondents) are calculated, which, by reference to demographic models, can be transformed into conventional life table measures of mortality.

Recently, demographers have turned their efforts towards the measurement of maternal mortality as an essential prerequisite to the planning, management and evaluation of intervention programmes and the judicious allocation of scarce resources. In response to growing interest and concern about maternal mortality, W. Brass and W. Graham, from the London School of Hygiene and

Tropical Medicine, developed in late 1987 a new and relatively simple procedure for providing a community-based estimate of the level of maternal mortality in societies with limited alternative sources. The main objective of this chapter is to describe and discuss the results of three applications of the method in Latin America. Although detailed accounts of the sisterhood method are available elsewhere (Graham and Brass, 1988; Graham, Brass and Snow, 1989), a short description of it is given in the next section along with the definitions used in the remainder of this chapter.

3. The Sisterhood Method

Maternal mortality is often expressed as a *ratio*, that is the number of maternal deaths per 100,000 live births. Another indicator is the maternal mortality *rate*, which relates maternal deaths to women in their reproductive period, usually expressed per 10,000. The appropriateness and source of the denominators used in these measures of the level of maternal mortality have been discussed in detail elsewhere (Graham and Airey, 1987). The origin of the numerator is generally regarded as the more serious problem. In several developing countries identification of maternal deaths in the community solely through the vital registration system has been found to lead to serious underestimation (Walker *et al.*, 1986; Grubb *et al.*, 1988). Similarly, deaths located solely through the health services are subject to serious selection biases with consequent effects on the derived estimates. Hence, the need for alternative and complementary methods.

Graham and Brass (1988) have proposed one such alternative method. Using model fertility and mortality distributions, a simple procedure was devised for converting the proportions of sisters dying of pregnancy-related causes reported by adults during a population-based census or survey into conventional measures of maternal mortality. This procedure has been named the 'Sisterhood Method'. The method is based on a series of questions in a single-round census or survey aimed at obtaining the following information:

- number of sisters (born to the same mother) who have ever been exposed to the risk of pregnancy and, hence, to the risk of dying of maternal causes;
- the number of sisters ever exposed to this risk who are dead; and,
- of those dead, the number who died while they were pregnant, during childbirth or in the puerperium.

The declared proportions of sisters dying from maternal causes among all sisters who survived to childbearing age are adjusted to provide a retrospective estimate of maternal mortality. The key simplifications of the relationship between sibling survival and age of respondent which provide a starting point for developing the sisterhood method are:

- first, the expected birth order position of any individual is central and thus, on average, they have equal numbers of younger and older siblings;
- second, the age difference between siblings and any index man or woman can be accurately modelled by a symmetrical distribution about a mean of zero.

It can be shown that the proportion of sisters dying of maternal causes, $\pi(i)$, reported by adults of age i in a single-round census or sample survey, can be related to the probability of dying of maternal causes between the age of first exposure to the risk of pregnancy and i, $q(i)$. The sisterhood method transforms the empirically observed $\pi(i)$, for every five-year age group of respondents, into estimates of the probability of dying by the end of the reproductive period, $q(w)$, using the adjustment factors, termed $A(i)$ in this chapter developed by Graham and Brass (1988).

A set of values for the $A(i)$ (see Table 6.1) was derived by combining a model of maternal mortality by age of woman with a fixed (symmetric) distribution of the differences between the ages of sisters and respondents. A major simplification arose from discovering that age patterns of maternal mortality can be fitted remarkably well by a relational Gompertz model with the Booth (1984) fertility standard and the parameters $\alpha = -0.5$ and $\beta = 0.8$. On the assumption that the same parameters of location and shape are satisfactory for all populations, acceptable adjustment factors for estimating $q(w)$ from observed $\pi(i)$ can be calculated from this model of $q(i)$ in combination with a fixed distribution for the difference between the ages of sisters and respondents, $\Theta(z)$. Thus:

Table 6.1. Adjustment factors A(i) for estimating q(w) from π(i)

Age of respondent (i)	A(i)	Age of respondent (i)	A(i)
12.5	0.048	42.5	0.802
15.0	0.073	45.0	0.856
17.5	0.107	47.5	0.900
20.0	0.151	50.0	0.934
22.5	0.206	52.5	0.958
25.0	0.270	55.0	0.975
27.5	0.343	57.5	0.986
30.0	0.421	60.0	0.992
32.5	0.503	62.5	0.996
35.0	0.585	65.0	0.998
37.5	0.664	67.5	0.999
40.0	0.737	70.0	1.000

Source: Graham and Brass (1988).

$$\pi(i) = \int \Theta(z) \cdot q(i + z)dz \qquad (1)$$

can be tabulated as a proportion of q(w), for an appropriate series of *i* values.

The resulting estimates of q(w), the lifetime risk, may be translated into a more conventional measure, the Maternal Mortality Ratio (maternal deaths to 100,000 live births), by the following approximation:

$$MMR = 1 - (1 - q(w))^{(1/TFR)} \qquad (2)$$

where MMR is the maternal mortality ratio and TFR is the total fertility rate.

As the information gathered concerns events which occurred at various points in the past, a relevant consideration is the time-period to which each estimate of q(w) refers. An equation was derived (Graham and Brass, 1988) from the general formula of Brass and Bamgboye (1981) which can be used to estimate the time location of each q(w) separately or, alternatively, when owing to small sample sizes only a single, global estimate of Q(w) is possible, the point in time to which this aggregate measure refers. The formula proposed for the time location, T(i) for a respondent aged *i* is:

$$T(i) = \frac{\int \Theta(z) \cdot \int^{i+z} q(x)dx\,dz}{\int \Theta(z) \cdot q(i + z)dz} \qquad (3)$$

Values of T(i) for relevant ages of respondents, *i*, are presented in Table 6.2.

4. Selected Applications of the Sisterhood Method

The first application of the sisterhood method was carried out in The Gambia. The basic information was obtained from a field study carried out in Septem-

Table 6.2.   Estimates of time-location for the sisterhood method

Age of respondents (i)	T (years)	Age of respondents (i)	T (years)
17.5	5.7	47.5	17.5
22.5	6.8	52.5	21.2
27.5	8.1	57.5	25.6
32.5	9.7	62.5	30.3
37.5	11.7	67.5	35.2
42.5	14.3	72.5	40.2

Source: Graham and Brass (1988).

ber 1987 in six rural villages in the Farafenni area. The British Medical Research Council has maintained a rural population surveillance system for several years in this area which provided an opportunity to check the results from the sisterhood method against data recorded by this independent system. The sample included slightly over 2000 persons, 15 years and over, belonging to different ethnic groups (Graham, Brass and Snow, 1989).

To illustrate the relative ease with which this method can be applied, a case from Latin America is discussed in detail in the next section. Reference is then made to other field experiences in Latin America.

4.1. Temuco, Province of Cautín, Chile

Information for this study was obtained through the Experimental Census of Indigenous Communities, 'Censo experimental de reducciones indígenas', which was carried out between October and December 1988 in the districts of Labranza, Molco, Maquehue and Metrenco located in the province of Cautín, Chile. In the four selected districts, located near the city of Temuco, capital of Cautín, 13,560 persons were interviewed, grouped in 2850 households.

The population studied, all of Mapuche origin, is characterized by a young age structure and low educational level. It is mainly involved in agricultural activities. Over the past fifteen years this population has had intermediate levels of mortality and fertility, with an infant mortality rate of about 70 per 1000, a female life expectancy at birth of 58 years and a total fertility rate of nearly 4.5 children. More recently, the infant mortality rate was reported to have declined to 45 per 1000 live births and the total fertility rate to 3.9 children (Oyarce *et al.*, 1989).

The following three questions were asked of the entire population of 12 years and over, in order to obtain the necessary data:

- How many sisters do you have, born to the same mother, who are currently alive?
- How many sisters, born to the same mother, are now dead?
- How many sisters died during:
  - pregnancy
  - childbirth
  - the puerperium?

The main difference compared with the original method is that the total number of sisters ever born was obtained, irrespective of whether those who died reached the childbearing ages—defined as 15 years and over in this case. The main reasons for this change were, firstly, that the simplification of the questions may, in some cases, ease the fieldwork and, secondly, that it is possible to apply other indirect techniques to these data in order to estimate female adolescent and adult mortality (Hill and Trussell, 1977).

The information obtained from the first two questions cannot be related directly to the data from the third one. To proceed, it is necessary to determine the proportion of sisters who were ever exposed to the risk of becoming pregnant and hence to the risk of dying of maternal causes. To arrive at this number an estimate of $l(15)$, the life table probability of surviving till age 15, is needed, which is then used to determine the proportion of sisters who were ever at risk classified by age group of respondents, termed N(i) in this chapter. In the original specification of the sisterhood method, this step is not necessary since the number of sisters reaching age 15 is ascertained directly from the respondents.

Applying the sibling survival method of Hill and Trussell (1977), the maternal orphanhood method and the child survival method, a best estimate of 0.86 for $l(15)$ was obtained which corresponds to West Level 16 in the Coale and Demeny (1983) model life tables. This level is more or less consistent with that estimated for the Mapuche population from data provided by the 1982 national census (Oyarce *et al.*, 1989).

The basic data and calculations are shown in Table 6.3, with the two key items being:

- all sisters who ever reach the age of 15 classified by five-year age group, *i*, of the respondents, N(i), and
- number of maternal deaths, also by five-year age group, *i*, of the respondents, r(i).

With this information, an observed $\pi(i)$ is calculated as r(i)/N(i) or, in other words, the proportion of sisters dead from maternal causes by age group of the respondents. In order to estimate q(w) from $\pi(i)$ the adjustment factors A(i) are used, as shown in column 6 of Table 6.3, which represent the values for the mid-point of each five-year age group.

When the number of sisters at risk of maternal death in each age group of respondents is large enough, each q(w) can be considered as a separate estimate of maternal mortality for a different point in time. Differences in q(w) by age of the respondents can then be interpreted in terms of response errors, limitations of the assumptions or time trends. However, when sampling errors are an important consideration, data should be aggregated to obtain a single, overall best estimate, Q(w). Two alternative procedures may be considered for aggregating the data:

(a) the expected maternal deaths by the end of the reproductive period can be calculated by *dividing* the number of maternal deaths r(i) by the adjustment factor A(i). By summing these expected maternal deaths and dividing them by the total number of sisters at risk, $\Sigma N(i)$, a single, global estimate, Q(w), is obtained. Proceeding in this manner, however, a relatively high weight is attached to the information derived from younger respondents where the number of maternal deaths is small and 1/A(i) is large. In these circumstances,

Table 6.3. Estimation of maternal mortality using the sisterhood method, Temuco, 1988

Age groups i	Number of respondents	Total number of sisters NT(i)	Total sisters exposed to risk of maternal death[a] N(i)	Maternal deaths r(I)	Adjustment factors A(I)	Sister-units of risk exposure B(i) = N(i)*P(i)	Life time risk of maternal death q(w) = r(i)/B(i)
15–19	1468	3,869	3,327	20	0.107	356	0.0562
20–24	1173	3,576	3,075	23	0.206	633	0.0363
25–29	924	2,874	2,472	15	0.343	848	0.0177
30–34	794	2,563	2,204	23	0.503	1,109	0.0207
35–39	479	2,374	2,042	24	0.664	1,356	0.0177
40–44	604	1,762	1,515	20	0.802	1,215	0.0165
45–49	590	1,739	1,496	21	0.900	1,346	0.0156
50–54	539	1,563	1,344	26	0.958	1,288	0.0202
55–59	483	1,338	1,151	13	0.986	1,135	0.0115
60+	1390	3,510	3,019	68	1.000	3,019	0.0225
Total	8714	25,168	21,645	253		12,305	0.0206[b]

[a] Calculated as N(i) = NT(i)*(15), with l(15) = 0.86.
[b] Calculated as the sum of r(i) divided by the sum of B(i).

systematic and sampling errors cannot be ignored. For this reason the following procedure is generally preferable.

(b) Instead of dividing r(i) by A(i), the number of sisters potentially at risk of dying of maternal causes, N(i), is *multiplied* by the adjustment factors, that is N(i)*A(i), to arrive at 'sister units of risk exposure' of maternal death, B(i). An estimate of Q(w) is then obtained by summing the r(i) across all age groups and dividing this by the sum of the B(i):

$$Q(w) = \Sigma r(i)/\Sigma B(i) \qquad (4)$$

It is worth mentioning that both procedures yield the same results as far as the individual q(w)s are concerned. However, when cumulation is used to obtain a single value, Q(w), the results are different. The procedure is illustrated in Table 6.3.

As can be observed from the last column of the table, which presents the separate estimates of q(w), the values are relatively stable, albeit slowly declining, across age groups from 25–9 to 45–9. In the youngest age groups, q(w) is much higher. This phenomenon has been observed in all the applications of the method so far. It is likely that it can be attributed to the considerable adjustments which need to be made to the data from the first two age groups of respondents in order to extrapolate the observed mortality from maternal causes among sisters to that expected by the end of the childbearing period. Equally, after the age of 50, the values of q(w) are more erratic, probably reflecting memory recall errors.

Since a more reliable estimate of the lifetime risk of maternal mortality can be derived by aggregating the data, it was decided to calculate Q(w) from those q(w)'s with more or less consistent values. Using respondents aged from 25 to 49 years, an estimate of 0.0176 was obtained. This means that, for every fifty-seven women entering the reproductive period, one will die of maternal causes before reaching the end of the childbearing period. Translating this probability into the more conventional maternal mortality ratio, a value of 403 per 100,000 live births is obtained using a total fertility rate of 4.4 corresponding to the same time as the estimate of Q(w), that is 12.7 years prior to data collection. If, as in this case, the data are aggregated in order to arrive at a single estimate of the lifetime risk, the corresponding time-location can be obtained by using the following formula:

$$\Sigma\{T(i)*B(i)\}/\Sigma B(i) \qquad (5)$$

where the T(i) are the time-location values for the individual age groups used in the calculation of Q(w) (Table 6.2). It is interesting to note that small variations in the value of $l(15)$ hardly affect the final estimates of Q(w) or, alternatively, the maternal mortality ratio. Thus, if a $l(15)$ of 0.814, corresponding to West Level 14 in the model life tables of Coale and Demeny (1983) had been used, the MMR would be only slightly higher: 424 maternal deaths per 100,000 live births instead of 403. Likewise, a $l(15)$ of 0.901 (West

Level 18) would have resulted in a MMR of approximately 383, that is, a difference of less than 5 per cent from the figure derived from using a $l(15)$ of 0.860.

These findings can be compared with data provided by vital registration, which is generally reliable in Chile for all-cause mortality. In the province of Cautín (the smallest administrative division available), data for the years 1982–4 yield an estimate of 74 maternal deaths per 100,000 live births. This contrasts sharply with the 403 per 100,000 obtained from the sisterhood method. One possible explanation for the discrepancy may relate to misclassification biases in the cause-specific vital registration data. Maternal mortality is well known to be subject to under-registration and misreporting in official statistics for several reasons, of which illegal abortion is one of the most important (Royston and Armstrong, 1989). A study carried out in several Latin American cities over twenty years ago revealed that maternal deaths were often reported as being due to other causes, in particular disguising the number of deaths due to abortions (Puffer and Griffith, 1967). In Santiago, for example, the study found the proportion of maternal deaths related to abortion to be an alarming 53 per cent.

4.2. *Other Applications of the Sisterhood Method in Latin America*

The sisterhood method has been applied in two other studies in Latin America with which the authors have had some involvement. One was in the peripheral districts of Lima, Peru and the other in the province of Avaroa, Oruro, Bolivia. In the first study the data were collected in conjunction with a study conducted in thirty recently-settled areas on the periphery of Lima in October 1987 that was primarily concerned with child mortality. Fieldwork for the second study was carried out in September 1988.

The results of the Lima experiment are described in detail elsewhere, together with the problems encountered (Graham and Brass, 1988). Only the final estimates of maternal mortality are mentioned here. Estimates for the MMR vary from 253 to 286 maternal deaths per 100,000 live births, according to the denominator used. This range reflects uncertainty over the population at risk in this study deriving from the sequence of questions asked. These concerned sisters reaching the age of 15 years and, of these, sisters ever-married or cohabiting. Thus births outside marriage or union may not have been included in the study. The result is an estimate whose validity is restricted to the ever-married or cohabiting population. There may also have been misinterpretation on the part of the respondents as to which of their sisters the question on maternal deaths referred. The total fertility rate used to translate the Q(w) into an MMR is also questionable: it seems to be rather low for this population.

The procedure used in the case of Bolivia was very similar to that applied in the case of the Mapuche population in Cautín. The correction procedure described earlier in the chapter was used to arrive at the number of sisters ever exposed to the risk of pregnancy-related death. In this case a $l(15)$ of 0.68 was used, which corresponds to South Level 10 in the Coale and Demeny (1983) model life tables. Based on the results from age groups in which the separate $q(w)$ estimates are reasonably consistent, namely 25 years and over, a $Q(w)$ was found of 0.0811, a 1 in 12 risk of dying of maternal causes during the childbearing ages. This corresponds to an MMR of 1121 deaths per 100,000 live births. A total fertility rate of 7.5 was used which is consistent with the estimated level of fertility about 15 years prior to data collection. This extremely high level of maternal mortality is in line with the high level of overall and infant mortality observed in this part of Bolivia. The region is one of the poorest parts of the country, with limited health services and extremely high fertility (Wong *et al.*, 1990). National statistics for Bolivia, based on vital registration, suggest a maternal mortality ratio for the period 1973–7 of only 480 per 100,000 live births; this is the second highest ratio for tropical South America (WHO, 1986).

5. Conclusions and Recommendations

It is widely known that in most of the developing world cause-specific mortality statistics are either non-existent or of poor quality. This holds in particular for maternal deaths, which are often seriously under-reported or misclassified. Recently an indirect estimation procedure has been developed (Graham and Brass, 1988) which can be used to provide data that complement those from routine sources. The results of the applications of the method described in this chapter highlight the possible extent of under-registration and/or misclassification of cause of death in official statistics in the case of maternal mortality. The results from the three countries vary substantially from an MMR of 253 per 100,000 live births in Lima, Peru to an MMR of 1121 in Avaroa, Bolivia, but the sisterhood method consistently produces higher figures than other data sources. In the case of Cautín, Chile, for example, the MMR obtained from the sisterhood method was over five times higher than the MMR calculated from more recent vital registration data. Studies in other regions of the world where estimates from community-based surveys have been compared with those from vital registration have found similar discrepancies. For example, in Jamaica a population survey produced an estimate of maternal mortality which was over double the official figure (Walker *et al.*, 1986).

This chapter has stressed the importance of wording questions about sisters carefully in order to arrive at a denominator which adequately reflects women at risk. Clearly, the questions should be adapted to suit local conditions. For example, in societies with high levels of pre-marital fertility it may be necessary to ask about all sisters old enough to bear children, which essentially means including all sisters who have reached the age of 15 (taken to be the average age at menarche). In other situations it may be imprudent to ask about maternal deaths among unmarried sisters. For the studies in Temuco and Oruro the questions referred to all sisters, irrespective of their age at the time of the data collection. These questions were used to ease comprehension on the part of the respondent and to allow the application of other indirect techniques for mortality estimation. It is shown in this chapter that this variant, apart from being very easy to apply, yields plausible and robust results. Although additional information about general mortality is needed, this does not present a difficulty since the majority of demographic surveys collect such data. In addition, it is demonstrated here that the data from the sisterhood method are robust to the selection of the value of $l(15)$ used in the adjustment.

As regards the estimation of Q(w), the aggregate figure for the probability of dying of maternal causes by the end of the reproductive period, careful consideration should be given to the selection of the range of age groups of respondents over which data are included. This chapter shows that the results from the two youngest respondent age groups produce estimates of q(w) which differ considerably from those for older groups, especially respondents aged 25 to 49 years. Any decision to exclude the data from respondents aged less than 25 years in the calculation of Q(w) must also take into account the size of the sample and thus the sampling errors of estimates based on a subset of the data. A similar argument may be put forward in the case of the exclusion or inclusion of the data from the older age groups, where problems of memory recall may produce distortions in the results and where the backwards shift in the time-location of the Q(w) estimate that results from their inclusion may be regarded as a disadvantage. The sisterhood method seems, in short, to produce robust estimates of the life-time risk of dying of maternal causes, Q(w) and the q(w)'s for five-year age groups of respondents. Estimates of the MMR, a less refined measure, but a popular indicator of the obstetric risk of death, can be derived from the results of the sisterhood method. It must be noted, however, that this derivation is sensitive to the value of the total fertility rate used: small deviations in the total fertility rate can cause considerable variations in the estimate(s) of the MMR. Moreover, in situations where there has been a recent drop in fertility, the total fertility rate should refer to the same period as the estimate(s) of Q(w) or q(w). Of course, these problems are not peculiar to the sisterhood method but general difficulties with obtaining estimates of the MMR from figures on lifetime risk.

As a recent addition to the array of indirect techniques for mortality estimation, the sisterhood method is still at a comparatively early stage in its evolution. Further refinements and adaptations to the basic method will continue to be made as experience with its application accumulates. Developments can be expected with regard to analytical procedures, including refinement of the adjustment factors; field techniques for data collection; inclusion of additional questions, such as place of death; and methods for evaluating the derived estimates of maternal mortality.

References

Booth, H. (1984), 'Transforming Gompertz's functions for fertility analysis: the development of a standard for the Relational Gompertz function', *Population Studies*, 38(3): 495–506.

Brass, W., and E. A. Bamgboye (1981), *The Time Location of Reports of Survivorship: Estimates for Maternal and Paternal Orphanhood and the Ever-widowed*, CPS Research Paper No. 81–1, London School of Hygiene and Tropical Medicine, London.

Coale, A. J., and P. Demeny (1983), *Regional Model Life Tables and Stable Populations*, 2nd edn, Academic Press, New York.

Graham, W., and P. Airey (1987), 'Measuring maternal mortality: sense and sensitivity', *Health Policy and Planning*, 2(4): 323–33.

—— and W. Brass (1988), 'Field performance of the sisterhood method for measuring maternal mortality', Paper presented in the Seminar 'Recolección y procesamiento de datos demográficos en América Latina', IUSSP, May 1988, Santiago, Chile.

—— —— and R. W. Snow (1989), 'Estimating maternal mortality: the sisterhood method', *Studies in Family Planning*, 20(3): 125–35.

Grubb, G. S., J. A. Fortney, S. Saleh, S. Gadalla, A. El-Baz, P. Feldblum, and S. M. Rogers (1988), 'A comparison of two cause-of-death classification systems for deaths among women of reproductive age in Menoufia, Egypt', *International Journal of Epidemiology*, 17(2): 201–7.

Hill, K., and J. Trussell (1977), 'Further developments in indirect mortality estimation', *Population Studies*, 31(2): 313–34.

Oyarce, A. M., M. I. Romaggi, and A. Vidal (1989), *Cómo viven los Mapuches: Análisis del Censo de 1982*, PAESMI-CELADE, Santiago, Chile.

Puffer, R. R., and W. G. Griffith (1967), *Patterns of Urban Mortality*, Scientific Publication No. 151, Pan American Health Organization, Washington, DC.

Royston, E., and S. Armstrong (1989), *Preventing Maternal Deaths*, World Health Organization, Geneva, Switzerland.

—— and A. Lopez (1987), 'On the assessment of maternal mortality', *World Health Statistics Quarterly*, 40: 214–24.

Starrs, A. (1987) 'La prevención de la tragedia de las muertes maternas', paper presented at the International Conference on Safe Motherhood, WHO/World Bank/UNFPA, Nairobi, Kenya.

Walker, J. A., D. E. C. Ashley, A. M. McCaw, and G. W. Bernard (1986), 'Maternal Mortality in Jamaica', *The Lancet*, i: 456–8.

World Health Organization (WHO) (1977), *International Classification of Diseases. Manual of International Statistical Classification of Diseases, Injuries and Causes of Death*, Geneva, Switzerland.

——(1986), *Maternal Mortality Rates: A Tabulation of Available Information*, 2nd edn., Geneva, Switzerland.

Wong, L. R., H. Simons, W. Graham, and S. Schkolnik (1990), 'Estimaciónes de mortalidad materna a partir del método de Sobrevivencia de Hermanas: experiencias en América Latina', *Notas de Población*, año XVIII, 50, CELADE, Santiago, Chile.

Part III

The Transition in Adult Mortality

7 The Epidemiological Transition in Latin America

JULIO FRENK
Instituto Nacional de Salud Pública, Cuernavaca, Mexico

JOSÉ LUIS BOBADILLA
The World Bank, Washington, DC, USA

RAFAEL LOZANO
Instituto Nacional de Salud Pública, Cuernavaca, Mexico

1. Introduction

At least for the past half century, most Latin American countries have been experiencing a complex transformation of their health conditions. The changes have had profound implications for the organization of health and other social services. In these countries, the transformation is expressed by an epidemiological pattern where the sharp decline in the level of mortality has been accompanied by a differentiation of its causes. Mortality levels are lower but the composition by causes of death is much more complex. Thus, communicable diseases, malnutrition, and reproductive health problems have lost their previous predominance, but still maintain a major position in the epidemiological profile. At the same time, the absolute and relative importance of non-communicable diseases and injury have increased.

The growing complexity of the health profiles of these nations can also be seen in the organization and functioning of their health systems. Generally speaking, these systems have not solved old problems, like insufficient population coverage, urban concentration of resources, technological lag, and low productivity. At the same time, they face new challenges posed by the building and expansion of institutions, greater diversity of human resources, increasing costs, and inadequate quality of care.

This chapter analyses the health situation in some selected Latin American countries. Using information on mortality by cause of death, it is shown that epidemiological profiles vary significantly over time and among countries.

2. Conceptual Framework

One of the earliest works that specifically tried to analyse the health implications of demographic and economic transitions was published by

Frederiksen (1969) more than two decades ago. Nevertheless, it was Omran who, in 1971, coined the term 'epidemiologic transition' and thus made way for a major breakthrough in our understanding of the dynamics of causes of death (Omran, 1971). Almost simultaneously, and apparently in an independent way, Lerner (1973) presented a paper postulating a 'health transition', a broader concept than the one used by Omran, since it included elements of the social conceptions and behaviours regarding health determinants.

Few conceptualization and research activities were carried out during the decade that followed those pioneering works, though some of their particular aspects, such as the analysis of cause of death, produced multiple empirical results. In contrast, recent years have witnessed a rediscovery of the epidemiologic transition, with many groups of researchers, national institutions, and international agencies becoming interested in this concept as a useful explanation of the major changes that have occurred in the health of populations.

Since the work of the original authors, the concepts introduced by them have often been used in a rather loose manner. The main confusion arises from exchanging the terms 'epidemiologic transition' and 'health transition'. In a previous paper (Frenk *et al.*, 1989*b*), it was proposed that the latter should be considered a broader concept, of which the former is a component. In an abstract sense, the study of health in populations comprises two major objects: on the one hand, the health conditions of the population; on the other hand, the response to those conditions. According to this simplifying dichotomy, the health transition may be divided into two main components. The first one is the epidemiologic transition strictly speaking, which is defined as the long-term process of change in the health conditions of a population, including changes in the patterns of disease, disability, and death. The second component, which may be called the health care transition, refers to the change in the patterns of the organized social response to health conditions.

Another cause of confusion often comes from including, in the definition of epidemiologic transition, processes that really constitute mechanisms through which such transition occurs. This confusion may be observed particularly in connection with fertility change. Since the original work by Omran (1971), there has been a tendency to include fertility decline as a defining element of the different epidemiologic transition models. This tendency is even more explicit in a revision of his ideas by Omran himself (1983). As we try to demonstrate later, fertility decline is one of the main mechanisms through which prevailing morbidity and mortality patterns change, but is not itself part of the definition of the epidemiologic transition.

3. Sources of Information and Methods of Analysis

The population data used in this paper are taken from estimates produced by CELADE (1987) jointly with governmental institutions of Latin America. Up to 1980, information is derived from population censuses; from then on, the population data are projections. Such population projections are derived from a single set of assumptions about the evolution of mortality and international migration, and from the 'middle or recommended' assumptions concerning fertility.

The fertility data used in this work are derived from analyses by CELADE (1987), Miro (1984), and Chackiel and Schkolnik (1990). Information from these sources is already processed, so its quality is taken for granted. Information on deaths used in the analysis of the epidemiologic transition in selected Latin American countries is derived from two sources. In the case of Uruguay, Cuba, Costa Rica, Chile, Guatemala, and Mexico, information comes from vital statistics. Mortality data for the rest of the countries studied are taken from the series entitled *Health Conditions in the Americas* published by PAHO (PAHO, 1956, 1962, 1970, 1974, 1978, 1986, 1990). These data are part of PAHO's Technical Information System and are supplied each year by member governments.

Eight countries are available for analysis that satisfy a rigorous check of the quality of mortality information, using standard markers to assess this (Chackiel, 1987). The countries are Argentina, Uruguay, Chile, Venezuela, Guatemala, Mexico, Costa Rica, and Cuba. Nevertheless, the improvement in the quality of death certification and the slow decrease of under-registration led us to consider including seven more countries, which allows us to study about 90 per cent of all deaths in Latin America. This group includes Brazil, Colombia, Panama, Ecuador, Peru, the Dominican Republic, and El Salvador. The last three have the poorest quality data.

The methods employed in this analysis of the epidemiologic transition are the following:

(a) In order to document change in the cause of death structure over the period of study, we examine the proportional change of six different causes: tuberculosis, diarrhoea, pneumonia, cancer, cardiac disease, other chronic diseases, and injuries (intentional and non-intentional).

(b) To illustrate the duration and timing of mortality changes, the Mortality Profile Ratio is proposed (MPR). This index is the ratio of the mortality rate due to communicable diseases (ICD 9th Revision first group and pneumonia) to the mortality rate due to the major non-communicable diseases (neoplasms and cardiac disease). The index uses age-adjusted rates. If the MPR is greater than one, it represents a mortality profile with a dominance of communicable diseases; if it is smaller than one, it represents a profile with a dominance of non-communicable diseases.

(c) The countries studied are classified according to three different criteria: modernization level, fertility decline, and mortality profile.

We next explain the first two criteria. Mortality profiles are analysed in detail later in the chapter.

Classification by level of modernization. The heterogeneity of Latin American countries makes it difficult to generalize about the transformations accomplished and complicates the task of comparing social realities. Nevertheless, the selected countries can be grouped into categories according to the achieved extent of economic and social modernization. In this respect, CEPAL (1989) proposes a three-group classification of countries based on urbanization, education, and changes in the occupational structure:

(a) Those characterised by incipient modernization, having just emerged from their agricultural stage. These countries display remarkable changes in their occupational structure and population distribution.

(b) Those undergoing partial but rapid modernization. These countries experienced swifter changes than expected: 'instead of slowly developing technology and organizational structures . . . they were able to adopt, being "newcomers", models already developed by industrialized countries . . .' (CEPAL, 1989).

(c) Those characterised by advanced social and economic modernization that have experienced changes dating back to the first half of this century.

Classification by level of fertility decline. Based on demographic changes, the countries under study can be classified into four main groups (Chackiel and Schkolnik, 1990):

(a) Those experiencing a very advanced fertility transition (TFR < 3.0): Argentina, Uruguay, Cuba and Chile.

(b) Those presenting an advanced transition (3.0 < TFR < 4.5): Brazil, Colombia, Costa Rica, Ecuador, Mexico, Panama, Peru, Dominican Republic, and Venezuela.

(c) Those presenting an intermediate fertility transition (4.5 < TFR < 5.5): El Salvador.

(d) Those presenting an incipient transition (TFR > 5.5): Guatemala, where fertility began to drop after the rest of the countries.

For this paper we consider El Salvador and Guatemala together and define them as countries characterized by an early transition.

In countries at an advanced stage of modernization, fertility rates have been decreasing since the 1950s. In contrast, in countries experiencing late modernization, such rates started declining in the 1970s, after remaining almost static at high levels for years. Countries undergoing incipient modernization still have high fertility rates. For example, Guatemala and El Salvador exhibit only a quantitative increase of the population with little alteration of the population structure. In contrast, the group with advanced demographic transition shows an important qualitative as well as quantitative modification. The proportion of people under 15 years is slowly decreasing, resulting in the well-known phenomenon of population ageing.

According to Chackiel and Schkolnik (1990) the fertility transition is not homogeneous within the countries; it is much more advanced in urban areas, above all in the big cities and particularly among the upper and middle sectors.

As in the case of mortality, we have to speak of transitions in the plural (Murray and Chen, 1991), due to the heterogeneity of the demographic and health process in Latin America as a whole and within each country.

4. Some Attributes of the Epidemiologic Transition in Latin America

There are five main attributes of the epidemiologic transition that need to be analysed in order to describe differences among countries. These are: changes in the age structure of mortality; changes in the predominant causes of death; duration and timing of these changes; social distribution of health profiles; and sequence of epidemiological eras. They are briefly described for a selected group of Latin American countries in the following paragraphs.

Change of the age structure of mortality. At the onset of the epidemiologic transition, most deaths occur among children under 15 years old. During the transition the burden of death shifts into older age groups. This process is due to the fact that communicable diseases and malnutrition problems mainly affect children. With the control of infectious diseases, the survival of children increases more rapidly than that of adults and the elderly.

The age structure of mortality has changed in all Latin American countries over the past twenty years. Except for Guatemala, Peru, Bolivia, and Haiti, all countries have reduced the age-specific mortality rates of children under 15 years old. By 1979, some countries reported 30 to 50 per cent of deaths among children under 15; by 1986, in all countries these deaths represented less than 20 per cent of the total. Correspondingly, the percentage of deaths among the elderly (60 years and over) increases.

Changes in the predominant causes of death. The mortality decline that accompanies the start of the transition is concentrated on communicable diseases, which tend to be displaced by non-communicable diseases, injuries, and mental illnesses. Figure 7.1 shows data on the proportion of deaths from selected causes in six countries. The proportion of all deaths due to communicable diseases was about 10 per cent in Argentina around 1960. Thirty years later the contribution of these causes of death accounted for less than 5 per cent of deaths. In Cuba, Costa Rica, and Chile around 1960, 15 to 30 per cent of deaths were due to communicable diseases, which is compatible with poor living conditions. By the mid 1980s, the contribution of infectious diseases was around 5 per cent of all deaths. In contrast, Guatemala and Mexico still had a comparatively high proportion of deaths from infectious disease in 1985. Mexico shows a decline from about 30 per cent in 1960 to 13 per cent in 1985, whereas Guatemala maintains 30 per cent of deaths attributable to infectious diseases over that period.

The increase of non-communicable diseases can be observed in Figure 7.1 in all six countries. Not surprisingly, the rise of non-communicable diseases and injuries mirrors the decline of communicable diseases as causes of death.

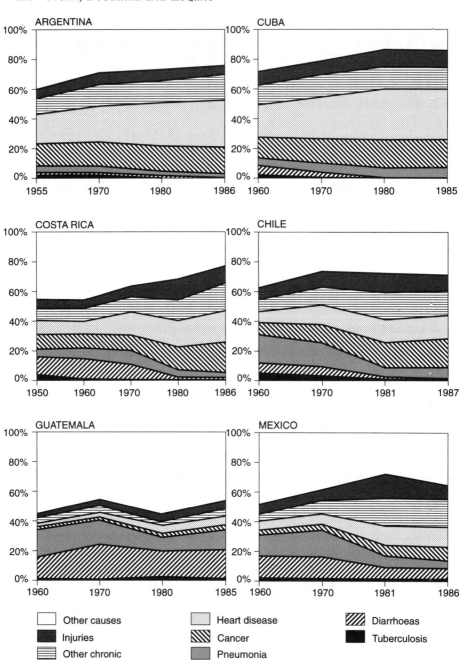

Fig. 7.1. Relative distribution of deaths, by cause, in selected Latin American countries, *c.* 1955–86
Source: PAHO, *Health Conditions in the Americas*, various dates.

Three slightly different groups of countries can be distinguished. Argentina and Cuba represent the first group. At the beginning of the period, less than 50 per cent of deaths in these countries were due to non-communicable diseases. By the year 1985 this proportion was around 70 per cent. The second group comprises Costa Rica and Chile, with an increase in the respective percentage from 30 to 60 per cent in the same period. In the third group, Mexico started with 20 per cent in 1960 and reached 50 per cent in 1985 while, in Guatemala, the increase during this period was from 10 to 19 per cent.

Duration and timing of changes. In his seminal article, Omran (1971) recognizes that there may be different transition models. He specifically describes three: the 'classical or Western model', characteristic of Europe and North America; the 'accelerated model', illustrated by Japan, and the 'contemporary or delayed model', typical of some developing societies such as Sri Lanka and Chile. The criteria used in this classification are the historical time at which the transition starts and the pace at which each country goes through the stages. Omran selected the starting point and the velocity of the epidemiologic transition in Western Europe as the standard for comparison. The experiences of other countries are then labelled according to the way they differ from the European standard.

It is worth noting that Omran (1971) and other authors (Frenk *et al.*, 1989*a*; Jamison and Mosley, 1991) have concentrated their description of the epidemiologic transition on the characteristic shift in predominance from communicable to non-communicable diseases. The complete description of this shift is difficult for most Latin American countries, since long-term time series of mortality rates by causes of death are not available. For this reason the duration and timing of the shift is inferred from the available information, which covers the period from 1959 to 1985. In order to describe those two attributes we have estimated the mortality profile ratio (MPR), as described before. Figure 7.2 shows the mortality profiles for fifteen countries, divided into four groups.

Panel (a) shows three countries that in 1959 had values under one and reached values close to 0.2 by the year 1986. This pattern of change—starting from the control of infectious diseases some time in this century and advancing clearly through the epidemiologic transition in less than 100 years—is similar to the accelerated model, according to the original description by Omran (1971). Panel (b) shows six countries that by 1959 had values between 1.2 and 2.5. In all of them the ratio declined to values around 0.5 by 1986. In other words, in these countries, for each death due to communicable diseases there are about two deaths due to non-communicable diseases. This pattern is different from the one above because the starting point can be traced to an earlier period in the former group of countries. They probably started the effective control of communicable diseases in the past century or in the first decade of the present.

Panels (c) and (d) show countries that started their transition late, probably

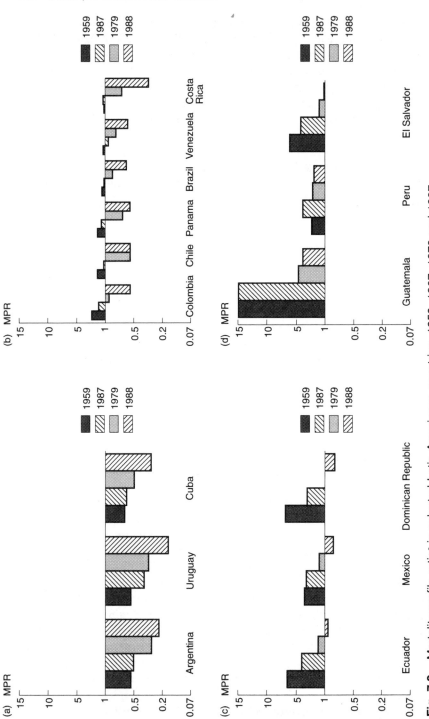

Fig. 7.2.   Mortality profile ratio[a] in selected Latin Americana countries. 1959, 1967, 1979 and 1987
[a] The mortality profile ratio (MPR) was constructed by dividing the mortality rate due to infections and parasitic diseases (including ICD 9th group and pneumonia) by the mortality rate due to cardiovascular diseases and neoplasms.

in the second quarter of this century. In Panel (c) these countries have barely managed to cross the value of one, while countries in Panel (d) still had values above one in 1986. Guatemala once again shows extreme values; it started in 1959 with a ratio around 17, the highest of all countries shown in Figure 7.2, and by the year 1986 had a ratio close to five, which is still the highest. The model of the epidemiologic transition shown by countries in Panels (c) and (d) does not fit any of the models presented by Omran (1971). The 'transitional' model later introduced by Omran (1983) is probably typical of African countries that started the decline of mortality rates after 1950. All of the countries in Panels (c) and (d) have shown important reductions of their mortality rates since the beginning of the century. Their pattern fits well the 'protracted polarized' model suggested recently for Mexico and outlined in the next paragraph (Frenk *et al.*, 1989*b*).

Social distribution of health profiles. The duration and timing of the epidemiologic transition for a given country reflects an average of diverse transitions occurring among different social groups within the country. Changes are likely to be slower among those living in rural areas than among urban inhabitants. As countries move along the path of transition, health inequalities, particularly those reflected in child mortality and communicable diseases, become more acute, producing what we have labelled as the 'epidemiologic polarization'. Important as it may be, this process is not described further in this paper due to the scarcity of available information. Empirical evidence of health inequalities has been provided for Costa Rica (Rosero, 1985; Behm and Robles, 1990), Honduras (Guzmán, 1990), and Mexico (Bobadilla *et al.*, 1990*a*, 1990*b*, 1993) in recent publications but only in relation to child mortality. Even though polarization may be present in all countries that undergo the epidemiologic transition, for Latin America it is likely to be of paramount importance owing to the region's history of inequalities in the distribution of wealth.

Sequence of epidemiological eras. During the past century all the industrialized countries have completed the shift from an epidemiological era characterized by the preponderance of communicable diseases to one characterized by non-communicable diseases. Nevertheless, age-specific mortality rates for many non-communicable diseases still vary considerably among these countries. Furthermore, the emergence of AIDS and the re-emergence of other sexually-transmitted diseases suggest that communicable diseases will play an important role in the foreseeable future.

In many Latin American countries some communicable diseases, like malaria and dengue fever, were thought to be under control. Unfortunately, the incidence rate for both diseases has increased considerably in the past ten years. In the case of malaria, for example, the number of reported cases by the late 1980s was nine times higher than the number reported in the period 1955–60. In addition, there is evidence that the decline in the infant mortality rate in many countries has slowed and, in northern Brazil, an increase in the infant mortality rate has been reported. It has been suggested (Frenk *et al.*, 1989*b*) that the re-emergence of some communicable diseases represents an actual regression, suggesting the possibility of a 'countertransition'. In addition, the 'protracted-polarized' model is characterized by a substantial degree of overlap between epidemiological eras, as is shown in Figure 7.2.

5. Mechanisms of the Epidemiologic Transition

Three major mechanisms are involved in the epidemiologic transition (Mosley *et al.*, 1990). They are changes in risk factors, which affect the incidence of disease; fertility decline, which alters age structure; and improvements in health care technology and organization, which modify case-fatality rates.

Changes in risk factors. This mechanism acts mainly on the chance of acquiring a disease, that is, on the incidence rates of illness. Many of these changes are related to the model of development exhibited by the countries of the region, including the change from societies where agricultural production prevails into societies where services and industrial production are predominant; the change in population distribution, from rural areas to urban areas, with the consequent concentration of economic activities; and increasing pauperization of vast sectors of the population (Miro, 1984).

Jamison and Mosley (1991) consider the urbanization process a basic determinant of the change in the health picture. On the one hand, they associate it with the reduction in the risk of acquiring infectious diseases, owing to improvement of sanitary conditions; on the other hand, they link it to the upsurge of new health problems due to changing life conditions and styles (Susser, 1981). Other important socio-economic changes include educational expansion; increasing involvement of women in the work force, leading to marked modifications of family and community dynamics; and improvements in average nutrition, housing conditions, and sanitary services, which produce decreasing health risks (McKeown, 1976; Evans *et al.*, 1981).

As mentioned earlier, most economic, social, and cultural changes usually identified with 'modernization' play a dual role: they promote a reduction in the incidence of infectious diseases and problems derived from reproduction but may increase the importance of certain non-communicable diseases and non-intentional injuries. For instance, the introduction of basic urban infrastructure and the adoption of hygienic measures produce an important decrease in the exposure to enteropathogenic micro-organisms and, therefore, in the incidence of gastrointestinal infections. Also, adoption of effective contraceptive methods reduces fertility and alters reproductive patterns by diminishing pregnancy rates in women more than 35 years old and lengthening the time span between births. There is evidence that such changes influence maternal and neonatal survival, reducing exposure to high-risk pregnancy (Fortney, 1987; Bobadilla *et al.*, 1990*b*).

Regarding the negative effects, the working and living conditions of many urban residents give rise to a higher incidence of occupational, traffic, and home injuries. Similarly, the adoption of unhealthy consumption and behaviour patterns may increase the risk of sickness and death from certain diseases. The practical relevance of these findings is that less-developed countries should not view the increase of degenerative diseases as evidence of 'progress', but as a stimulus to develop preventive strategies immediately to obviate going through the same negative experiences as industrialized nations (Soberón *et al.*, 1986).

Fertility decline. This process, which is part of the demographic transition, implies a shift from a situation in which fertility is dominated by natural and biological factors to another, in which fertility is controlled to a large extent by the will of couples. In Latin America, this mechanism is essential to understanding the epidemiologic transition. The analysis of the evolution of fertility in the twentieth century shows a late decrease in most of the countries, that has reached a rate of decline never seen before in Latin America (Miro, 1982). The incipient shift noticed in the 1950s gained powerful momentum in the 1970s. Only four countries out of the many that had high total fertility rates (higher than 5.5 children per woman) in 1950 maintain this level (Bolivia, Guatemala, Nicaragua, and Honduras). The remaining countries exhibit middle-range total fertility rates; most of them have an average of less than 4.5 children per woman. Those countries that in 1950 had middle-range fertility now have low fertility, as is the case of Chile, Argentina, Cuba, and Uruguay (PAHO, 1990).

From the point of view of the epidemiologic transition, the major effect of fertility decline is the resulting change in age structure. The growing proportion of adults and elderly raises the relative importance of non-communicable diseases and injuries. Table 7.1 shows age structure changes for Latin America as a whole.

Improvement in case-fatality rates. Several changes in the size, distribution, organization, and technological content of the health services have contributed to the epidemiologic transition. During the last century, medical research and technological development have resulted in major advances in the effective treatment of many diseases, both infectious and non-communicable. An important part of improved survival is due to the decrease of case-fatality rates achieved by the application of effective diagnostic and therapeutic technologies.

Some interventions, such as chemotherapy for pulmonary tuberculosis, antibiotic therapy for acute respiratory diseases or oral rehydration salts for acute diarrhoeal diseases, do not affect the risk of acquiring disease but only the chance of dying for those already sick. In fact, in the case of chronic diseases, the introduction of this kind of intervention in populations elicits the paradoxical effect of increasing total morbidity by prolonging the average duration of disease (Donabedian, 1973). Conversely, interventions such as

Table 7.1. Changes in age structure in Latin America

Age group	Population[a]					
	1950		1980		2010	
	No.	%	No.	%	No.	%
Young people (0–4 years)	65	48.7	138	39.3	183	29.6
Adults (15–59 years)	86	54.1	191	54.3	379	61.4
Elderly (60 + years)	8	5.2	23	6.4	55	9.8
Total	159	100.0	352	100.0	617	100.0

[a] in millions.
Source: CELADE (1987).

immunization influence the chance of acquiring disease. The main effect of both types of interventions in underdeveloped countries has been to reduce the proportion of deaths caused by infectious and parasitic diseases, thus contributing to the initial stages of the epidemiologic transition. In further stages of the transition, technological innovations may elicit a reduction in case-fatality rates or even (though this is more difficult) lower the incidence of some non-communicable diseases. This, along with some other factors, produces an epidemiologic pattern which Olshansky and Ault (1986) describe as the delay of deaths caused by degenerative diseases.

The three mechanisms are not uniform across all nations or regions. Indeed, each of the mechanisms analysed, as well as their interrelations, establish important differences in the epidemiologic dynamics of a country. This emphasizes the need for thorough study of the specific qualities of such dynamics.

6. Discussion and Conclusions

There is a growing recognition of the diversity of countries in the developing world. It is clear from the discussion in this chapter that it is impossible to generalize about levels and trends of health indicators in Latin America. We have shown that the epidemiologic transition is occurring in all the countries studied, but at different paces and with different characteristics.

It is a challenge to explain why countries vary so greatly in their transitional experiences (Frederiksen, 1969). According to the mechanisms proposed previously, changes in fertility rates and in living conditions should account for most of the variation. Indeed, if countries are classified independently according to modernization level, fertility decline, and mortality profile, the resulting groups are remarkably similar. Table 7.2 shows the countries studied classified according to the three different dimensions. The first group, with advanced economic modernization, includes seven countries. Four of them are classified as 'very advanced' in terms of their fertility transition. Another four are advanced in their mortality profile, meaning that by 1986 they had a MPR < 0.5 (Figure 7.2). Costa Rica, Panama, and Venezuela are advanced in terms of modernization, but not in the fertility transition. Although Chile is advanced in terms of modernization and fertility decline, it does not quite meet the criterion for an advanced mortality profile. The second group, with six countries, is characterized by partial but rapid modernization. This is matched by these countries' advanced fertility transition and, except for Peru, mixed mortality profile. Two countries, El Salvador and Guatemala, are classified as being in an incipient process of modernization. Their fertility and mortality declines are in the incipient stages too.

Table 7.2. Economic modernization, fertility transition and the mortality profile in selected Latin American countries

Economic modernization[a]	Fertility transition[b]	Mortality profile
I. Advanced	I. Very advanced	I. Advanced
Argentina	Argentina	Argentina
Uruguay	Uruguay	Uruguay
Cuba	Cuba	Cuba
Chile	Chile	Costa Rica
Costa Rica		
Panama		
Venezuela		
II. Partial & rapid	II. Advanced	II. Mixed
Panama	Costa Rica	Venezuela
Brazil	Venezuela	Brazil
Colombia	Brazil	Colombia
Mexico	Colombia	Mexico
Dominican Republic	Mexico	Dominican Republic
Ecuador	Dominican Republic	Ecuador
Peru	Ecuador	
	Peru	
III. Incipient	III. Early	III. Incipient
El Salvador	El Salvador	Peru
Guatemala	Guatemala	El Salvador
		Guatemala

[a] *Source*: CEPAL (1988).
[b] *Source*: Chackiel and Schkolnik (1990).

The quality and completeness of data on causes of death also differ among the countries studied here. Two errors are more likely to occur among the less developed countries. The first is incomplete counting of deaths, which is usually concentrated in children under 1 year of age. This probably means that infectious diseases are underestimated for El Salvador, Guatemala, and Peru. The second error refers to the percentage of ill-defined conditions, which tends to be higher when the quality of death certification is low. Other countries with suboptimal vital statistics are Brazil, Panama, Venezuela, Ecuador, and Mexico. Despite the possible errors in the data, it is unlikely that better statistics would change the main conclusions of this paper, namely, that the epidemiologic transition in Latin America varies among countries, and that the variations permit classification of the countries into distinct models as a heuristic device in the initial search for explanation of the epidemiologic transition.

Health planning in the period 1950–79 relied, in most Latin American countries, on estimates of health needs derived from population size. Since economic growth was, for the most part, greater than population growth, the plan was often to do more of the same. The economic crisis of the 1980s, the rapid changes in the age structure of the population, the rise in the prevalence of risk factors for communicable diseases, and the escalation of health care costs are demanding a comprehensive review of priorities and criteria used to allocate resources in the health sector (Jamison and Mosley, 1991).

The attention given to infant health and infectious diseases in most Latin American countries has to continue, but, at the same time, more attention should be directed to the health needs of older children, adults and the elderly. It is of paramount importance to identify the most important health needs of each group and the extent to which the available interventions are effective. In particular, questions should be asked with regard to the model of organized social response to adult morbidity, which by and large has been dominated by hospital treatment of cases.

Prevention of chronic diseases and injuries is neglected in the health plans of most developing countries, partly because there is widespread scepticism regarding the efficacy of educational campaigns and partly because many of the interventions are outside the sphere of action of the ministries of health, as is the case of taxing tobacco or regulating the use of seat belts. In addition, the effects of these preventive measures probably only become apparent many years after they have been implemented, making them politically less attractive than other measures whose results can be demonstrated in the short term.

It has become clear in the past decades that the definition of development should include universality of benefits and progress. Latin American countries hold the dubious privilege of being the champions of inequality. Health inequalities are not unique to this region. What is outstanding is the magnitude of the inequalities and the widening differences between extreme social groups. Health policies directed towards reducing inequalities are essential for

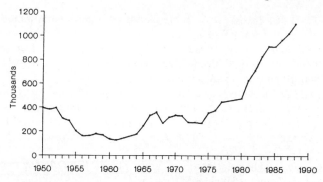

Fig. 7.3. Cases of malaria in Latin America, 1950–88
Source: PAHO *Health Conditions in the Americas*, various dates.

any plan aimed at contributing to development. Since governments are seldom willing to reduce the benefits of the well-off (at least explicitly), policies should call for positive discrimination in health programmes, so that disadvantaged groups receive more and first. Again, the criteria used to define priority social groups need to be country-specific.

More research is required to describe the epidemiologic transition at the local level in different countries. More detailed analyses of the quality of information are also warranted. Finally, more detailed analysis is required to convert the concept of the epidemiologic transition into an organizing tool for planning and budgeting health programmes.

References

Behm, H., and A. Robles (1990), 'Costa Rica: el descenso reciente de la mortalidad en la infancia por grupos socioeconomicos', in: *Factores sociales de riesgo de muerte en la infancia*, CELADE, Santiago, Chile.

Bobadilla, J. L., L. Schlaepfer, and J. Alagón (1990a), *Family Formation Patterns and Child Mortality in Mexico*, The Population Council and Institute for Resource Development/Macro Systems, New York.

——and A. Langer (1990b), 'La mortalidad infantil en México: un fenómeno en transición', *Revista Mexicana de Sociología*, 52(1): 111–32.

——J. Frenk, T. Frejka, R. Lozano, and C. Stern (1993), 'The epidemiological transition and health priorities', in: D. T. Jamison, W. H. Mosley, A. R. Measham, and J. L. Bobadilla (eds.) *Disease Control Priorities in Developing Countries*, Oxford Medical Publications, New York.

Centro Latinamerico de Demografía (CELADE) (1987), 'América Latina: proyecciones de población, 1950–2025', *Boletín Demográfico*, 40.

CEPAL (1989), 'Transformación ocupacional y crisis social en América Latina', United Nations, Santiago, Chile.

Chackiel, J (1987), 'La investigación sobre causas de muerte en la América Latina', *Notas de Población*, 15(44): 9–30.

——and S. Schkolnik (1990), 'América Latina: transición de la fecundidad en el período 1950–1990', IUSSP Conference on the Transition of Fertility in Latin America 1990, Buenos Aires, Argentina.

Donabedian, A. (1973), *Aspects of Medical Care Administration: Specifying Requirements for Health Care*, Harvard University Press, Cambridge, Mass.

Evans, J. R., K. L. Hall, and J. Warford (1981), 'Shattuck Lecture—health care in the developing world: problems of scarcity and choice', *New England Journal of Medicine*, 305: 1117–27.

Fortney, J. A. (1987), 'The importance of family planning in reducing maternal mortality', *Studies in Family Planning*, 5: 109–15.

Frederiksen, H. (1969), 'Feedbacks in economic and demographic transition', *Science*, 166: 837–47.

Frenk, J., J. L. Bobadilla, J. Sepúlveda, and M. Lopez-Cervantes (1989*a*), 'Health transition in middle-income countries: new challenges for the organization of services', *Health Policy and Planning*, 4: 29–39.

——T. Frejka, J. L. Bobadilla, C. Stern, J. Sepúlveda, and M. V. José (1989*b*), 'The epidemiological transition in Latin America', *International Population Conference, New Delhi*, Vol. 1, International Union for the Scientific Study of Population, Liège, Belgium.

Guzmán, I. M. (1990), 'Honduras: diferencias socioeconomicas en las tendencias de la mortalidad en la niñez, 1974–1983', *Factores sociales de riesgo de muerte en la infancia*, CELADE, Santiago, Chile.

Jamison, D., and H. Mosley (1991), 'Diseases control priorities in developing countries: health policy responses to epidemiological change', *American Journal of Public Health*, 81(1): 15–22.

Lerner, M. (1973), 'Modernization and health: A model of the health transition', paper presented at the annual meeting of the American Public Health Association, San Francisco, Calif.

McKeown, T. (1976), *The Modern Rise of Population*, Edward Arnold, London.

Miro, C. (1982), *Las tendencias recientes de la fecundidad en America Latina y sus implicaciones*, Comision de Población y Desarrollo, CLACSO, Cuernavaca, Mexico.

——(1984), 'America Latina: Transición demográfica y crisis económica, social y política', in: *Memorias del congreso latinoamericano de población y desarrollo*, Vol. 1, UNAM-El Colegio de Mexico-PISPAL, Ciudad de México, Mexico.

Mosley, W. H., D. T. Jamison, and D. A. Henderson (1990), 'The health sector in developing countries: prospects for the 1990s and beyond', *Annual Review of Public Health*, 11: 335–58.

Murray, C. J. L., and L. C. Chen (1991), 'The health transitions: dynamics and patterns of mortality change', in: L. C. Chen, A. Kleinman, J. Potter, and J. Caldwell (eds.) *Health and Social Transitions. An International Perspective*, forthcoming.

Olshansky, S. J., and B. A. Ault (1986), 'The fourth stage of the epidemiologic transition: the age of delayed degenerative diseases', *Milbank Memorial Fund Quarterly*, 64(3): 355–91.

Omran, A. R. (1971), 'The epidemiologic transition: a theory of the epidemiology of population change', *Milbank Memorial Fund Quarterly*, 49: 509–38.

——(1983), 'The epidemiologic transition theory. A preliminary update', *Journal of Tropical Pediatrics*, 29: 305–16.

Pan American Health Organization (PAHO) (1956), *Health Conditions in the Americas*, Scientific Publication No. 24, Washington, DC.

——(1962), *Health Conditions in the Americas*, Sci. Publ. No. 64, Washington, DC.

——(1970), *Health Conditions in the Americas*, Sci. Publ. No. 207, Washington, DC.

——(1974), *Health Conditions in the Americas*, Sci. Publ. No. 287, Washington, DC.

——(1978), *Health Conditions in the Americas*, Sci. Publ. No. 364, Washington, DC.

——(1986), *Health Conditions in the Americas*, Sci. Publ. No. 500, Washington, DC.

——(1990), *Health Conditions in the Americas*, Sci. Publ. No. 524, Washington, DC.

Rosero, L. (1985), 'Determinantes del descenso de la mortalidad infantil en Costa Rica', in: *Demografía y epidemiología en Costa Rica*, Asociación Demográfica Costarricense, San José, Costa Rica.

Soberón, G., J. Frenk, and J. Sepúlveda (1986), 'The health care reform in Mexico: before and after the 1985 earthquakes', *American Journal of Public Health*, 76: 673–80.

Susser, M. (1981), *Industrialization, Urbanization and Health. An Epidemiological View. Selected Papers*, Oxford University Press, New York.

8 Causes of Adult Death in Low-Mortality Developing and Developed Countries

JACQUES VALLIN

Institut National D'Etudes Démographiques, Paris, France

Health status has long been considered a key indicator of level of development. However, many of the countries classified as 'developing' by the different international organizations now have life expectancies similar to those termed 'developed' (Vallin, 1985). Table 8.1 shows all the countries with more than 300,000 inhabitants in which men's mean length of life in 1985 was higher than in the former USSR, the country that trails at the bottom of the developed group.

The 'developing' countries are indicated in bold type. They account for thirty-one of the sixty-seven countries in the list. It is true that, as regards health, the former USSR and Eastern Europe have been at a disadvantage for the past two or three decades, compared with the rest of the developed world. Thus to include them is perhaps to set the life expectancy that constitutes the limit of 'low mortality' too low. In 1985, male life expectancy at birth was only 64.2 years in the USSR, 65.3 in Hungary, and 66.5 in Poland, whereas in all other developed countries, with the exception of Portugal, it exceeded 70 years. In most of the thirty-one developing countries in Table 8.1, life expectancy was below 70 years. However, nine of them were among the thirty-five countries which had exceeded this limit. Unsurprisingly, the lowest mortality developing countries are Cyprus, which is more European than Middle-Eastern, and Hong Kong, one of the four 'dragons' of Far East capitalism. But it is noteworthy that these two countries join Japan, Iceland, and Sweden in the life expectancy vanguard. More surprising still is the case of Cuba, where male life expectancy equals that of the Netherlands and Norway, and is far ahead of the 'big four' countries of Western Europe (i.e. the former Federal Republic of Germany, England and Wales, France, and Italy). In addition, Costa Rica is ahead of France, while Jamaica, Puerto Rico and Kuwait are all in front of Belgium. Among the developing countries which have not yet achieved such life expectancies, but are well above that of the USSR, we find China, Mexico, Chile, Argentina, and Venezuela.

When we consider women's life expectancy at birth, the comparison is somewhat less favourable to the developing world. There are only fourteen developing countries among the forty-nine countries with a mean length of

Table 8.1. Life expectancy at birth in countries where it was higher than in the ex-USSR (males) or in Hungary (females), 1985, countries with over 300,000 inhabitants

Males		Females		Males		Females	
Japan	74.8	Japan	80.5	**Singapore**	70.0	Germany (DR)	75.5
Iceland	74.0	Iceland	80.2	**Panama**	69.7	**Guadeloupe**	75.3
Cyprus	73.9	Switzerland	80.0	Portugal	69.6	**Singapore**	75.0
Sweden	73.8	Canada	79.8	Germany (DR)	69.1	**Uruguay**	74.9
Hong Kong	73.8	Sweden	79.7	**Venezuela**	68.7	Czechoslovakia	74.8
Switzerland	73.5	Norway	79.6	Albania	68.5	Poland	74.8
Israel	73.5	France	79.4	**Uruguay**	68.4	**Reunion**	74.8
Spain	73.1	Spain	79.4	**United Arab Emirates**	68.4	Bulgaria	74.4
Canada	73.0	Netherlands	79.2	ex-Yugoslavia	68.3	**Chile**	73.9
Norway	72.8	**Hong Kong**	79.2	Bulgaria	68.2	Albania	73.8
Netherlands	72.7	Luxembourg	78.9	**Guadeloupe**	68.0	**Argentina**	73.6
Cuba	72.7	Australia	78.8	**Sri Lanka**	68.0	ex-Yugoslavia	73.6
Italy	72.4	Italy	78.8	Czechoslovakia	67.4	**Panama**	73.5
Australia	72.3	Finland	78.5	**Malaysia (peninsular)**	67.4	Romania	73.3
Greece	72.2	United States	78.2	**China**	67.3	ex-USSR	73.3
England & Wales	72.2	Germany (FR)	78.0	**Trinidad & Tobago**	66.9	Hungary	73.2
Martinique	71.9	**Cyprus**	77.8	Romania	66.9	**Kuwait**	73.0
Denmark	72.6	Denmark	77.5	**Argentina**	66.9	**Venezuela**	72.8
Germany (FR)	71.5	England and Wales	77.5	**Guyana**	66.6	**Malaysia (peninsular)**	72.7
Costa Rica	71.5	Austria	77.5	Poland	66.5	**Korea (Rep. of)**	72.0
France	71.3	**Puerto Rico**	77.3	**Chile**	66.5	**Sri Lanka**	72.0
United States	71.2	Scotland	77.0	**Surinam**	66.4	**Mauritius**	71.9
Luxembourg	71.0	Israel	77.0	**Reunion**	66.2	**Korea (DPR of)**	71.8
New Zealand	71.0	**Costa Rica**	76.9	**Paraguay**	65.7	**United Arab Emirates**	71.7
Malta	70.8	New Zealand	76.8	**Korea (DPR of)**	65.4	**Trinidad & Tobago**	71.6
Jamaica	70.8	Belgium	76.8	Hungary	65.3	**Guyana**	71.6
Austria	70.8	Northern Ireland	76.5	**Qatar**	65.2	**Surinam**	71.4
Puerto Rico	70.3	Greece	76.4	**Korea (Rep. of)**	65.0	**Mexico**	71.4
Kuwait	70.3	**Jamaica**	76.2	**Bahrain**	65.0	**Paraguay**	70.3
Northern Ireland	70.1	**Cuba**	76.1	**Mexico**	64.9	**China**	69.9
Ireland	70.1	**Martinique**	76.1	Lebanon	64.7	Lebanon	68.8
Finland	70.1	Malta	76.0	**Mauritius**	64.5	**Bahrain**	68.4
Belgium	70.0	Portugal	75.8	ex-USSR	64.2	**Qatar**	67.6
Scotland	70.0	Ireland	75.6				

life exceeding that of Hungary, the worst developed country as regards women's mortality. Hong Kong drops back to tenth position and Cyprus to seventeenth.

Thus, although many developing countries have now achieved the life expectancy levels of the developed world, the sex profiles of mortality are very different and women's advantage over men is much more pronounced in the latter group. Women's relatively fragile position in developing countries is perhaps a lingering mark of 'underdevelopment'. Another characteristic which can be interpreted in the same way is infant mortality, which remains high compared with the mean length of life.

In Figure 8.1, the infant mortality rate is plotted against life expectancy at birth for the sexes combined for each of the countries in Table 8.1. Western industrialized countries contrast with developing countries and Eastern Europe. What is most striking about this figure is not the existence of a relationship between the two indicators, but the fact that this relationship is very elastic. With very few exceptions, developing countries systematically have much higher infant mortality for a given level of life expectancy, than developed ones. At life expectancies of 74 to 75 years, infant mortality rates range from 6.4 to 11.2 per 1000 in Austria, Finland, Denmark, England and Wales, the United States, and the Federal Republic of Germany, but from 15.3 to 18.9 per 1000 in Costa Rica, Cuba and Martinique.

This difference can be brought into sharper focus by examining the product of life expectancy at birth and infant mortality, which is equivalent to the ratio of the infant mortality rate (m_0) to the life table death rate (m_i):

$$r = m_0 e_0 = \frac{m_0}{m_i}$$

and illustrates the relative risk of dying in infancy. Table 8.2 provides this ratio for the countries in Table 8.1, grouped into developing countries, developed countries other than Eastern Europe, and Eastern European countries including the former USSR.

For all industrialized countries in the West, apart from Greece and Portugal

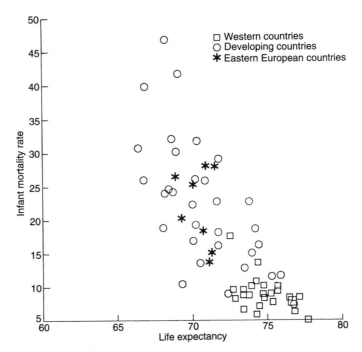

Fig. 8.1. Relationship between the infant mortality rate and life expectancy at birth in low-mortality countries, 1985, both sexes

Table 8.2.   Ratio of the infant mortality rate to the life table death rate

Industrialized countries		Developing countries		Eastern Europe and ex-USSR	
Japan	0.427	Hong Kong	0.574	Czechoslovakia	0.995
Finland	0.468	Singapore	0.674	Bulgaria	1.098
Malta	0.521	Trinidad and Tobago	0.734	Poland	1.307
Sweden	0.522	Cyprus	0.910	Hungary	1.413
Switzerland	0.530	Jamaica	0.970	ex-USSR	1.788
Denmark	0.589	Reunion	0.973	Romania	1.795
Canada	0.604	Martinique	1.132	ex-Yugoslavia	2.001
Netherlands	0.608	Guadeloupe	1.175	Albania	2.006
France	0.625	Malaysia	1.191		
Finland	0.641	Cuba	1.228		
Norway	0.645	Paraguay	1.285		
Spain	0.648	Kuwait	1.318		
Germany (FR)	0.665	Chile	1.369		
Iceland	0.678	Costa Rica	1.402		
Belgium	0.690	Sri Lanka	1.575		
Scotland	0.691	Panama	1.647		
Germany (DR)	0.696	Mauritius	1.650		
England and Wales	0.702	Korea (DPR of)	1.681		
Northern Ireland	0.704	Puerto Rico	1.697		
Luxembourg	0.705	Korea (Rep. of)	1.699		
Australia	0.748	Bahrain	1.748		
United States	0.777	United Arab Emirates	1.835		
Italy	0.779	Venezuela	1.847		
New Zealand	0.798	Qatar	2.058		
Austria	0.830	Surinam	2.101		
Israel	0.895	Uruguay	2.107		
Greece	1.048	China	2.223		
Portugal	1.290	Argentina	2.248		
		Lebanon	2.677		
		Guyana	2.902		
		Mexico	3.203		

where economic development has lagged behind, the ratio is less than 1. It is generally between 0.5 and 0.8 but falls to around 0.4 in Japan. On the other hand, in most low-mortality developing countries, the ratio exceeds 1, often by a wide margin. In more than half these countries it exceeds 1.5 and, in Mexico, 3. Once more, the exceptions test the rule: on the one hand, they comprise countries which are not really 'underdeveloped' (e.g. Hong Kong, Singapore) and, on the other, those where infant mortality is perhaps underestimated (e.g. Trinidad and Tobago, Jamaica). Eastern Europe is similar to the developing countries, with ratios ranging from 1 to 2.

If, for a given level of life expectancy, infant mortality is higher in the developing countries, this means that their adult mortality is lower. Whereas trends in infant mortality largely determine life expectancy up to a level of 65 or 70 years, beyond this point adult mortality plays the major role (see, for example, the case of France in Table 8.3). The fact that developing countries have relatively low adult mortality, compared with their infant mortality, is an advantage when this 65 to 70 year limit is crossed: the reduced weight of infant mortality, even if not as striking as in the developed world, then allows the relatively low adult mortality to have a major impact. Countries in this situation rapidly achieve the highest levels of life expectancy. This is what happened in Italy. The North, which is more developed economically than the South, had higher levels of life expectancy until infant mortality became less important and the Southern regions raced ahead because of their lower adult mortality (Caselli and Egidi, 1979, 1980*a*; Vallin, 1981). It has also occurred in certain Mediterranean countries, in particular Greece, which have gained headway over north-western Europe (Caselli *et al.*, 1992; Caselli and Egidi, 1980*b*; Nizard and Vallin, 1970; Vallin and Chesnais, 1974).

The future is more difficult to predict, since spectacular increases in life expectancy can no longer be achieved by reducing infant mortality further. In developing and developed countries alike, future progress will depend on adult mortality, particularly in the older age groups. This has diminished rapidly over the past few decades in most industrialized countries and there

Table 8.3. Contributions of early mortality (0–29 years) and adult mortality (30 years+) to the increase in life expectancy, in France[a]

Period	Total increase	Increase due to mortality at ages		% due to adult mortality
		0–29	30+	
Males				
1819–69	3.45	3.50	−0.05	0.0
1869–1909	8.17	8.20	−0.03	0.0
1909–39	8.42	6.84	1.58	18.8
1939–69	10.96	6.54	4.42	40.3
1969–89	5.01	1.31	3.69	73.8
Females				
1819–69	4.20	3.58	0.63	15.0
1869–1909	10.09	8.72	1.37	13.6
1909–39	10.53	7.26	3.27	31.1
1939–69	10.51	6.48	6.03	48.2
1969–89	5.53	1.18	4.36	78.8

[a] Using Pollard's (1982) method to estimate each contribution.

Table 8.4. Selection of the developing countries in Table 8.1 for analysis of recent cause-specific adult mortality trends

Country	'Complete' registration	Over 400 deaths at ages 60–4	Cause-of-death data for the 1980s
Cyprus	yes		
Hong Kong	yes	yes	yes
Cuba	yes	yes	yes
Martinique	yes		
Trinidad and Tobago	yes	yes	yes
Costa Rica	yes	yes	yes
Jamaica	yes	yes	
Puerto Rico	yes	yes	yes
Kuwait	yes		
Singapore	yes	yes	yes
Panama			
Venezuela	yes	yes	yes
Uruguay	yes	yes	yes
United Arab Emirates			
Guadeloupe	yes		
Sri Lanka	yes		
Malaysia (peninsular)	yes		
China			
Argentina	yes	yes	yes
Guyana	yes		
Chile	yes	yes	yes
Surinam	yes		
Reunion	yes		
Paraguay			
Korea (DPR of)			
Qatar			
Korea (Rep. of)			
Bahrain			
Mexico	yes	yes	yes
Lebanon			
Mauritius	yes	yes	yes

are no signs of this trend slowing down. Will the low-mortality developing countries be able to hold on to their advantage in this field, so that, like Japan, they will soon be up with the leaders? Or will they again be overtaken on the path to this new stage in the health transition? The study of recent mortality trends and cause of death patterns at adult ages may perhaps give us an inkling of what the future holds.

Complete and reliable mortality data are not available for all the countries in Table 8.1. For many developing countries, the data used earlier are estimates and there is no statistical basis for a more detailed breakdown. Although it is not always a sufficient guarantee, according to the United Nations' *Demographic Yearbook*, twenty-two of these thirty-one developing countries had death registration coverage of 90 per cent or more. The low numbers of adult deaths in small populations with a very narrow-summited population pyramid also has to be considered. Those with fewer than 400 deaths at ages 60–4 have been eliminated, which leaves fifteen countries. The basic requirement for further analysis is the availability of cause-of-death statistics. The World Health Organization (WHO) data file covers all fifteen countries, but two of them, Malaysia and Sri Lanka, have to be discarded because information for the 1970s and 1980s is very incomplete. The different stages of this selection process are shown in Table 8.4. Twelve countries were finally retained: one in Africa (Mauritius), nine in Latin America (Argentina, Chile, Costa Rica, Cuba, Mexico, Puerto Rico, Trinidad and Tobago, Uruguay, Venezuela) and two in Asia (Hong Kong and Singapore). Of course, even for these selected countries, cause of death data are not necessarily completely reliable.

To compare these developing countries with the industrialized ones, the easiest solution is to take some typical examples of the developed world, while bearing in mind what we know of its diversity (Caselli *et al.*, 1992; Caselli and Egidi, 1980*b*; Brouard and Lopez, 1985). With Japan, the United States, West Germany, England and Wales, France, Italy, Sweden and Hungary (representing Eastern Europe) the field seems well covered.

1. The Standardized Mortality Rate at Ages 30–85

In the following analysis, the standardized mortality rate at ages 30–85 is used as an indicator of adult mortality. It is calculated from the mortality rates by five-year age group and WHO's European model age structure, which seems suitable in this low-mortality context.

During the last twenty years, adult mortality has fallen by 20 to 25 per cent for men and 25 to 35 per cent for women in the industrialized countries. The exceptions are Hungary, where there has been a 4 per cent rise for men and a 16 per cent fall for women, and Japan, where there has been a decrease of 37 and 44 per cent for men and women respectively (Table 8.5).

Progress has been less obvious and less homogeneous in the developing countries. It is true that there has been a spectacular drop in the mortality of men in Chile, Cuba and Hong Kong, which resemble Japan rather than the other industrialized countries, but in only three other countries (Singapore, Argentina, Uruguay) was a reduction of roughly 20 per cent observed. Elsewhere, there was either a very slight fall (Puerto Rico, Trinidad and Tobago) or a slight rise (Mauritius, Costa Rica, Mexico, Venezuela). For women, the decline was general—apart from Venezuela and Argentina, where there was

Table 8.5. Changes in the standardized mortality rate at ages 30–80 over the last two decades

Country	Males			Females		
	1968	1987	Change (%)	1968	1987	Change (%)
Developing countries						
Mauritius	247	264	7	179	160	−11
Argentina[a]	250	207	−17	136	135	−1
Chile	269	184	−32	197	124	−37
Costa Rica	185	186	1	161	126	−22
Cuba	236	156	−34	202	124	−39
Mexico[b]	184	192	4	153	141	−8
Puerto Rico[b]	203	186	−8	153	114	−25
Trinidad and Tobago[c]	291	268	−8	219	202	−8
Uruguay[b]	233	194	−17	154	124	−19
Venezuela[c]	182	185	2	139	141	1
Hong Kong	210	148	−30	111	88	−21
Singapore	274	214	−22	153	138	−10
Industrialized countries						
Germany (FR)	257	190	−26	170	111	−35
England and Wales	252	180	−29	154	114	−26
France	236	169	−28	135	88	−35
Hungary	266	278	5	197	165	−16
Italy[b]	227	180	−21	151	106	−30
Sweden	205	166	−19	149	99	−34
United States	249	180	−28	156	109	−30
Japan	219	139	−37	144	81	−44

Notes: The last year is: [a]1985; [b]1986; [c]1983, instead of 1987.

practically no change—but it reached or exceeded 20 per cent in only six countries out of twelve and was below 10 per cent in the others. Furthermore, men's and women's mortality has not always followed the same pattern. In Argentina, for instance, women's mortality has not declined, whereas men's has fallen sharply. In Puerto Rico, on the other hand, the decline has been slight for men, but considerable for women.

Further heterogeneity is introduced by relatively large annual fluctuations (Figure 8.2), in contrast to the smooth trends observed for the industrialized countries (Figure 8.3). While such fluctuations could be interpreted as a sign of the developing world's greater vulnerability to outbreaks of infectious diseases, this view can be questioned. The fluctuations may also reflect variations in the completeness of death reporting, which could be considerable in these countries. In particular, the large rise in mortality observed in Mauritius up to the beginning of the 1980s can no doubt be attributed to better death regis-

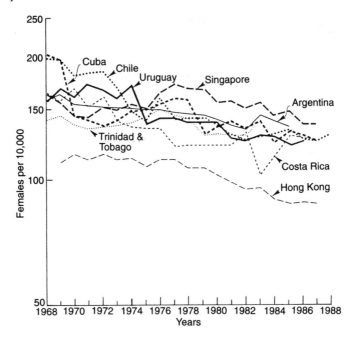

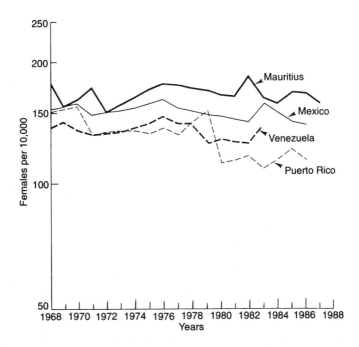

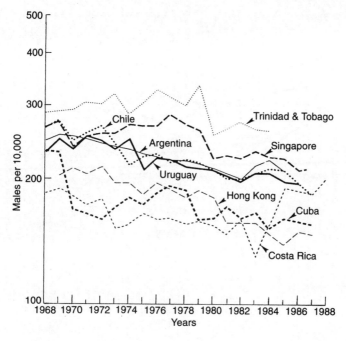

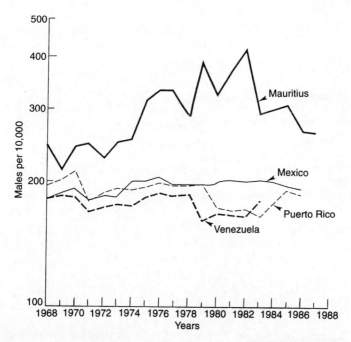

Fig. 8.2. Trends in mortality at 30–85 years in twelve low-mortality developing countries

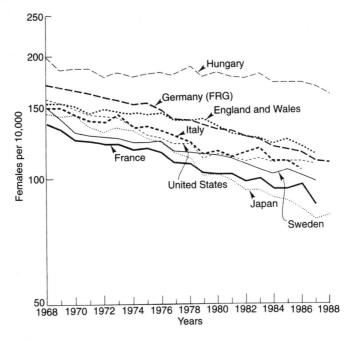

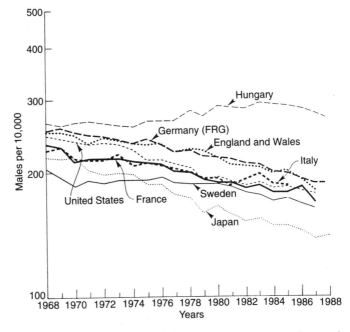

Fig. 8.3. Trends in mortality at 30–85 years in seven developed countries

tration. The same is perhaps true of Singapore and of Trinidad and Tobago, where mortality apparently does not decrease until the end of the period. The case of Costa Rica is more puzzling. Adult mortality declined steadily until 1983, then suddenly increased in 1984 and continued to rise to the end of the period, by when it had reverted to almost the level of twenty years before. All these anomalies are much more pronounced for men than for women.

Despite some uncertainty about data quality in the low-mortality developing countries, two different patterns seem to emerge: on the one hand, a clear, regular decline; on the other, quasi-stagnation. The first pattern is observed in Hong Kong, Chile and Uruguay. Argentina can no doubt also be added to the list, although data for 1970 to 1979 are lacking. Cuba and Singapore are a little more uncertain. In Cuba, adult mortality declined sharply from 1968 to 1972, but then much more moderately, while in Singapore, the drop did not start until the end of the 1970s, and is then hesitant. The second pattern, stagnation, clearly characterizes Mexico, Puerto Rico and Venezuela, but is more subdued for Puerto Rican women.

Two tendencies thus emerge among the low-mortality developing countries: in some, adult mortality is already relatively low and is declining; it can therefore take over from infant mortality and keep life expectancy at birth edging upward. These countries stand a very good chance of overtaking most of the industrialized countries in the future. In others, adult mortality is stagnating. Once the impact of rapidly declining infant mortality on life expectancy has been exhausted, they may well start to lose ground again.

Hong Kong and Chile represent examples of the first tendency (the former being much further ahead than the latter) and Mexico an example of the second. We have compared the cause of death patterns of these three countries with Japan, France and West Germany, three countries which (leaving aside Hungary) are representative of the developed world according to Figure 8.3.

It seems of interest to add Costa Rica, as an 'exception'. This country has been considered the classic example of a low-mortality developing country (Meslé, 1985) and until 1983 its adult mortality was particularly low, even beating that of Hong Kong for males (Figure 8.2). The sharp increase in 1983–4 is therefore surprising and calls for investigation.

2. Causes of Death

Nicolas Brouard has recently shown that several cause of death profiles exist in low-mortality countries (Brouard and Lopez, 1985; Brouard, 1990). In particular, Hong Kong and Singapore follow a pattern that is very different from that of the industrialized countries in general and closer to that of Japan. The aim of this study is to investigate whether recent divergent trends in adult mortality can be attributed to certain specific causes or whether they are independent of cause of death profiles.

The 8th Revision of the International Classification of Diseases (ICD) came into effect in 1968 in six of the seven countries studied here, and in 1969 in Hong Kong. The period under study is therefore covered by the last two Revisions of the ICD (8th and 9th), with the exception of 1968 in Hong Kong (7th Revision). Problems arising from statistical discontinuities between successive revisions are consequently limited. The WHO computer file provides deaths classified by the *A List* for the 7th and 8th Revisions and by the *Basic Tabulation List* for the 9th Revision. The broad groups of causes used (see Table 8.6) are those proposed by Meslé (1991) in a recent study of European mortality. The items in these groups are practically identical at the different revisions and no adjustment for discontinuity is required. These eight groups of causes are:

- infectious diseases (ICD ch. I and acute respiratory diseases);
- other diseases of the respiratory system;
- neoplasms;
- cirrhosis of the liver;
- cerebrovascular diseases;
- cardiovascular diseases;
- other diseases;
- injury and poisoning.

Table 8.6. The groups of causes: items in the A List of the 7th and 8th Revisions and the Basic Tabulation List of the 9th Revision of the ICD

Group of causes	ICD 7	ICD 8	ICD 9
Infectious diseases	001–043	001–044	010–07r
(including acute respiratory diseases)	087–092	089–092	310–312
			320–322
Other diseases of the respiratory system	093–097	093–096	313–31r
			323–32r
Neoplasms	046–060	045–061	080–17r
Cerebrovascular diseases	070	085	290–29r
Cardiovascular diseases	079–086	080–084	250–28r
		086–088	300–30r
Cirrhosis of the liver	105	102	347
Other diseases	061–069	062–079	180–24r
	071–078	097–101	330–346
	098–104	103–137	348–46r
	106–137		
Injury and poisoning	138–150	138–150	470–56r

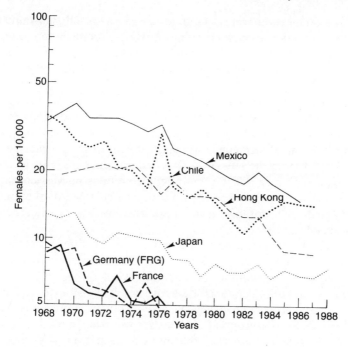

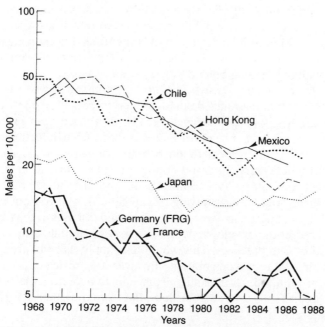

Fig. 8.4. Trends in mortality at 30–85 years from infectious and acute respiratory diseases

As with the total mortality rates, standardized cause-specific mortality rates at ages 30–85 have been calculated using WHO's European reference population. Deaths due to ill-defined conditions (ICD ch. XVI) were redistributed proportionally among the other groups before calculating the standardized rates.

For mortality from *infectious and acute respiratory diseases*, three groups of countries are observed (Figure 8.4). In Chile, Mexico and Hong Kong, the level is high and an almost synchronous decline is observed throughout the period. In France and Germany, a similar decline is observed at a lower level. The downward trend is the same in both groups of countries until around 1980, when it stops in France and Germany but continues in Mexico and Hong Kong. In Chile, the decline becomes more hesitant towards the end of the period. In Japan, the mortality level is intermediate and the decrease much less pronounced.

Thus Japan, the record holder in terms of overall life expectancy, has a higher level of adult mortality from infectious diseases than France and Germany and a less favourable recent trend. What is most pertinent to this study, however, is that infectious diseases are not responsible for the divergent trend in overall mortality between Mexico and Chile or Hong Kong. Mortality levels and trends for this group of diseases are the same in all three countries, bringing them close to Japan by the end of the period, and substantially reducing the differential with France and Germany. This is observed for both men and women. However, female mortality from infectious diseases is noticeably higher in Mexico than in Chile and Hong Kong. Excess male mortality for this group of causes is less marked than in the other two countries and Mexican women are lagging behind.

Mortality from *'other' diseases of the respiratory system*, which has fallen slightly in the industrialized countries, has increased in all three developing countries. The rise is somewhat greater in Mexico than in Chile and Hong Kong (Figure 8.5). In contrast to mortality from infectious disease, Japan's position in this respect is much better than that of Germany and France. Practitioners' reporting and coding practices may differ as regards classification of respiratory diseases into 'acute' and 'chronic'. In part this may explain the surprisingly poor showing of Japanese mortality from infectious diseases. Similarly, the rise in chronic or unspecified diseases of the respiratory system observed in the developing countries may be amplified by changes in reporting and coding practices. This would also imply that the drop in infectious disease mortality is exaggerated. However, for this category the effect would be more limited, as mortality from infectious and acute respiratory diseases is three to four times higher than that from the other diseases of the respiratory system.

Mortality from *neoplasms* varies little either from country to country or over the period (Figure 8.6). In five of the six countries it has stagnated for males and only decreased slowly for females. Mexico stands apart, with a fairly substantial rise for men and no headway at all for women. While neoplasms

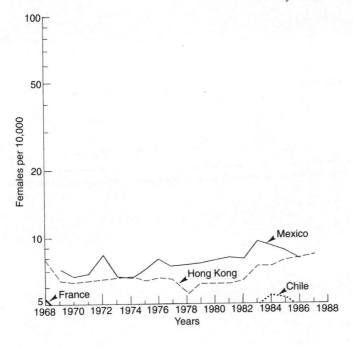

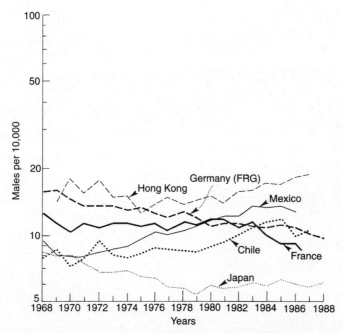

Fig. 8.5. Trends in mortality at 30–85 years from 'other' diseases of the respiratory system

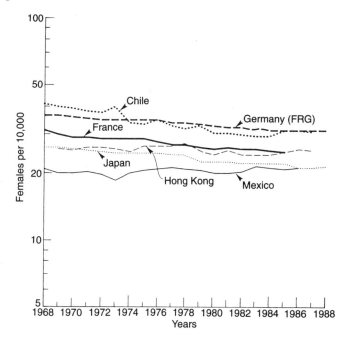

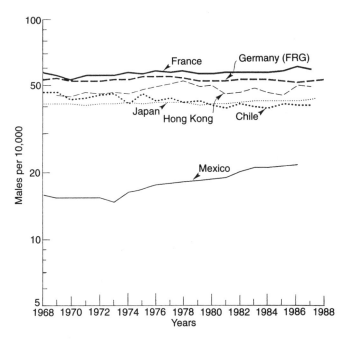

Fig. 8.6.   Trends in mortality at 30–85 years from cancer

therefore account in part for the lack of overall mortality decline in this country, their contribution is small. The level of mortality from neoplasms is lower in Mexico than in the other countries, and this difference is considerable for men. Comparison of Figures 8.4 and 8.6 shows that Mexico's disadvantageous trend as regards mortality from neoplasms cannot alone cancel out the gains made with respect to infectious diseases.

Mortality from *cirrhosis of the liver* (Figure 8.7) is only significant for males in Mexico and Chile, on the one hand, and France and Germany, on the other. The principal causes of cirrhosis of the liver are alcoholism and viral hepatitis. The latter, *ceteris paribus*, may account for the higher levels observed in the developing countries, but alcoholism is undeniably what differentiates Mexico and Chile from Hong Kong, and France and Germany from Japan. Although levels of liver cirrhosis mortality are similar in Chile and Mexico, there is a slight downward trend in the former country and a slight upward trend in the latter, which contributes to a small extent to the divergent trend in mortality between the two countries.

Mortality from *cerebrovascular diseases* (Figure 8.8) has declined sharply (even spectacularly in Japan) in the three industrialized countries. In contrast, in the four developing countries, it has stagnated or decreased only very slowly. Thus, the level in France and Germany, which in 1968 was higher than in the developing countries, is now below that of Chile and, in the case of

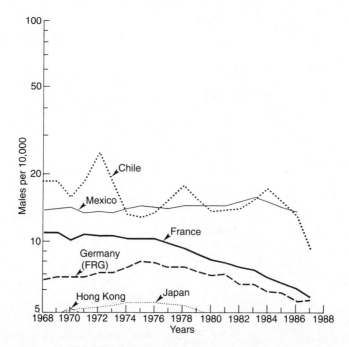

Fig. 8.7. Trends in mortality at 30–85 years from cirrhosis of the liver

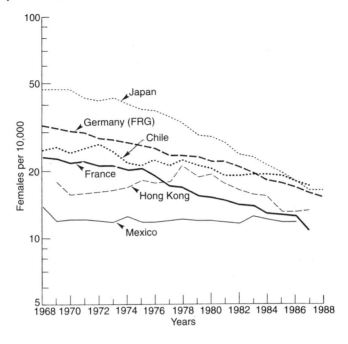

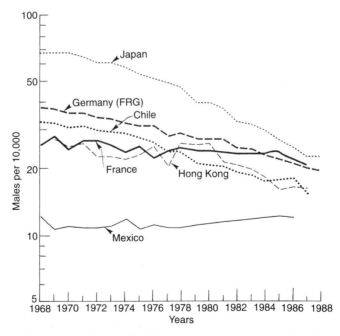

Fig. 8.8. Trends in mortality at 30–85 years from cerebrovascular disease

France, even below Hong Kong. Japan, which at the beginning of the period stood out with an exceptionally high level, is now very close to Chile. The evolution of this group of causes is now clearly unfavourable to the developing world. In addition, Mexico lags slightly behind the other developing countries, in keeping with its divergent trend in total mortality.

As regards the level of *cardiovascular mortality*, the three industrialized countries diverge. Cardiovascular mortality is almost twice as high in Germany as in Japan, with France in between, but all three countries follow the same downward trend (Figure 8.9). In the three developing countries, on the other hand, mortality levels are similar, but the trends more varied. Male cardiovascular mortality has fallen in Chile and even more sharply in Hong Kong, whereas it has risen in Mexico. For women, the decline is more general. It is recent and slight in Mexico, but started earlier and has been more substantial in Chile.

Mortality from *'other diseases'* shows a fairly distinct decline in five of the six countries (Figure 8.10). In Hong Kong, this drop is more limited for men and non-existent for women (though the level was already very low for women at the start of the period). The exception is once again Mexico, where mortality due to other causes has risen noticeably for both sexes, despite being higher initially than in the other countries. This group of causes thus plays an important part in the differential trend in mortality between Mexico and Chile.

Mortality from *injuries and poisoning* is much higher in all countries for men than for women, for whom it is relatively unimportant (Figure 8.11). The trends for both sexes are very similar. Mortality due to these causes has decreased in the three industrialized countries and in Hong Kong and Chile, but has risen in Mexico.

The case of *Costa Rica* is illustrated in Figure 8.12 for all these groups of causes. The issue is why the undeniable lead of Costa Rica, which was still clear at the beginning of the 1980s, has given way in recent years. Figure 8.12 shows that all groups of causes have contributed to this situation. For men, a perfectly synchronized rise in death rates from each cause grouping is visible in 1984. The turn-around is less sharp and more difficult to date for women. Nevertheless, for the last four years, all groups of causes show an upward trend. In contrast, all the trends were downward during the 1970s (with the exception of 'other diseases of the respiratory system', which have risen throughout the period but more rapidly since 1984). Thus, study of the different groups of causes of death throws little light on the recent deterioration of adult mortality in Costa Rica. It is a general problem, which involves infectious diseases and other causes alike, and therefore has nothing to do with the differences observed between Mexico and Hong Kong or Chile. It demonstrates the fragility of the advantage achieved by certain developing countries considered as leaders in terms of health status.

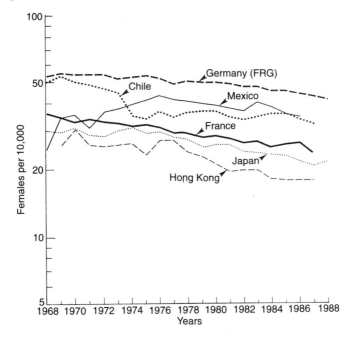

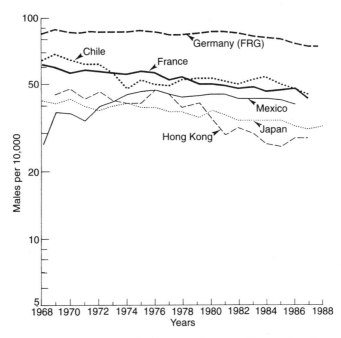

Fig. 8.9.   Trends in mortality at 30–85 years from cardiovascular disease

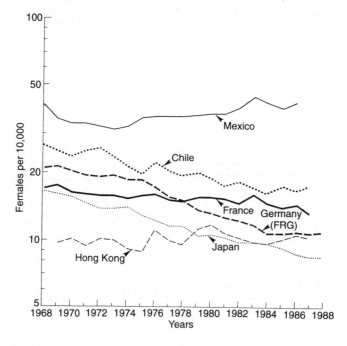

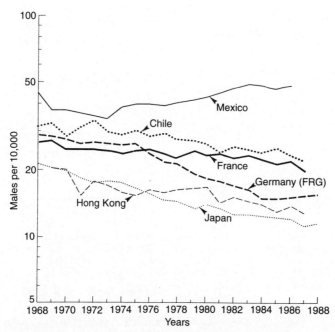

Fig. 8.10. Trends in mortality at 30–85 years from other diseases

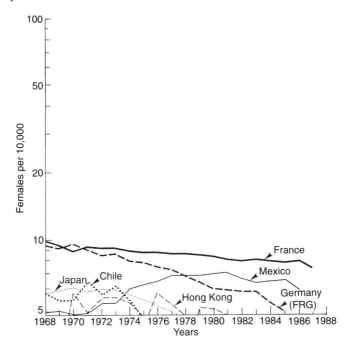

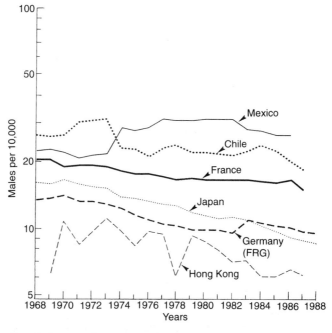

Fig. 8.11. Trends in mortality at 30–85 years from injuries and poisoning

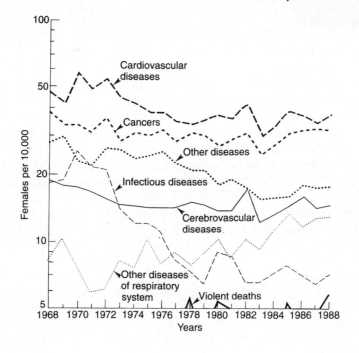

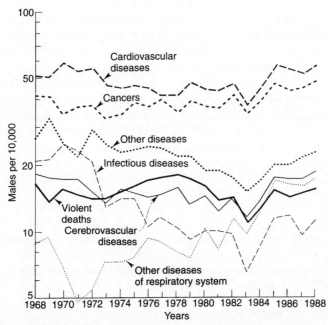

Fig. 8.12. Trends in mortality at 30–85 years for major causes of death, Costa Rica

3. Conclusions

This short analysis suggests two conclusions. Firstly, infectious diseases and diseases of the respiratory system (acute or otherwise) do not contribute to the difference observed between those developing countries where adult mortality is declining (here, Chile and Hong Kong) and those in which it is stagnant (here, Mexico). All other groups of causes have their share of responsibility. In other words, the difference is not due to those diseases whose decline marks the first stage of the epidemiological transition (infection), but to causes which underlie the headway made recently in the developed world (neoplasms, cirrhosis of liver, cerebrovascular and cardiovascular diseases, injury and poisoning). If the trends of the past few years continue, certain low-mortality developing countries—Chile and, in particular, Hong Kong—could be expected to retain their relatively high life expectancy or even to overtake most industrialized countries. Others, such as Mexico, may lag behind again once the decline in infant mortality has started to lose its impact.

Secondly, forecasting the future course of mortality among these forerunners calls for caution. We have seen that, five years ago, Costa Rica would have been placed among the top few. If the recent deterioration observed in this country is confirmed, it should be taken as a warning of the fragility of the privileged health status achieved by certain developing countries during the 1960s and 1970s.

Finally, these two conclusions are somewhat tentative. Whether we consider the recent worsening of Costa Rica's situation or the divergence between Mexico and Chile or Hong Kong, we should bear in mind that the data quality may cloud or distort the image. Although the coverage of death reporting is reputedly complete in these countries, this may not be the case. If the Mexican data, for instance, were incomplete at the end of the 1960s and coverage has improved since, this would account for at least part of the apparently unfavourable evolution of mortality. A sudden improvement in death registration in Costa Rica in 1983–4 may seem less plausible, but cannot be ruled out. In both cases, this would imply that the actual mortality levels of reputedly low-mortality developing countries have been underestimated hitherto.

References

Brouard, N. (1990), 'Classification of developed countries according to cause-of-death patterns: a test of robustness during the period 1968–74', in: J. Vallin, S. D'Souza, and A. Palloni (eds.) *Measurement and Analysis of Mortality: New Approaches*, Clarendon Press, Oxford.

——and A. Lopez (1985), 'Cause of death patterns in low mortality countries: a classification analysis', in: *International Population Conference, Florence 1985*, IUSSP, Liège, Belgium.

Caselli, G., and V. Egidi (1979), 'La géographie de la mortalité italienne: différences territoriales et milieu'. *Genus*, 35: 101–54.

—— ——(1980*a*), *Le differenze territoriali di mortalità in Italia: tavole di mortalità provinciali (1971–1972)*, Università di Roma, Rome, Italy.

—— ——(1980*b*), *Nouvelles tendances de la mortalité en Europe*, CAHED, Council of Europe, Strasbourg.

——F. Meslé, and J. Vallin (1992), 'Le triomphe de la médicine', in: J. Dupâquier and J. P. Bardet (eds.) *Histoire de la population européenne*, Arthème Fayard, Paris, France.

Meslé, F. (1985), 'Evolution des causes de décès dans quelques pays à faible mortalité', in: *International Population Conference, Florence, 1985*, IUSSP, Liège, Belgium, 407–27.

——(1991), 'La mortalité dans les pays de l'Est', *Population*, 46: 599–650.

Nizard, A., and J. Vallin (1970), 'Les plus faibles mortalités', *Population*, 25: 847–74.

Pollard, J. H. (1982), 'The expectation of life and its relationship to mortality', *Journal of the Institute of Actuaries*, 109: 225–40.

Vallin, J. (1981), 'Le développement économique est-il nuisible à la santé des hommes?' *Population*, 36: 929–33.

——(1985), 'Répartition et évolution des causes de décès dans les pays à faible mortalité', in: *International Population Conference, Florence, 1985*, IUSSP, Liège, Belgium, 379–84.

——and J.-C. Chesnais (1974), 'Evolution récente de la mortalité en Europe, dans les pays anglo-saxons et en Union soviétique', *Population*, 29: 881–98.

9 Adult Mortality Decline in Costa Rica

LUIS ROSERO-BIXBY

Princeton University, Princeton, USA

1. Introduction

Costa Rica is, along with Cuba, the country with the best health indicators in Latin America. Life expectancy at birth in Costa Rica was 77.9 years for women and 72.7 years for men in 1990, figures which are comparable with those for Western Europe and the USA. Study of the epidemiologic transition in Costa Rica has usually focused on children, reflecting the fact that the main component of mortality decline has been the prevention and control of premature deaths (Behm, 1976; Rosero-Bixby, 1986; CELADE *et al.*, 1987; Cervantes and Raabe, 1991). The greater availability of information on child health and the young age-structure of the population (in 1960, 47 per cent of the population were children under 15 years of age) have reinforced the emphasis on studying the young.

This chapter shifts the previous emphasis on childhood to focus on adult mortality. The purpose is to describe the mortality transition at adult ages, to identify its key components, and to make inferences about its likely determinants. The chapter has five sections: socio-economic and public-health background of Costa Rica; the data and methods used; decline in risks of dying in two age intervals (20–49 and 50–79 years); analysis of risks of dying by cause of death; and areal analysis of adult mortality and its correlate across 100 small geographical units.

2. Background Information on Costa Rica

2.1. Socio-Economic Background

Costa Rica is a small Central American country with a population of about 3 million. Its economy is dependent on export of tropical crops, predominantly coffee and bananas. Per capita income in 1990 was about US $1900, slightly

This paper is part of a collaborative research project into health policy of the University of Costa Rica and the Nordic School of Public Health. The project was partially supported by a grant of the Swedish Agency for Research Cooperation with Developing Countries (SAREC). Dr Leonardo Mata contributed to this paper with helpful comments.

lower than the Latin American average. Approximately one half of the population resides in rural areas and a third of the labour force is employed in agriculture. The country has had greater social than economic development: only 7 per cent of adults are illiterate, almost all children attend school, 79 per cent of the population is covered by the social security system, and 94 per cent enjoy a piped water supply (Table 9.1).

After World War II, Costa Rica enjoyed more than three decades of vigorous economic growth. The real growth in gross domestic product (GDP) was greater than 6 per cent per annum (more than 3 per cent in per capita terms) between 1950 and 1980. Moreover, welfare-oriented institutions helped to distribute the product of such progress comparatively evenly among the various social strata (González-Vega, 1985). In the early 1980s, however, international and domestic circumstances brought this continuous progress to an end. The country experienced an acute economic crisis in the 1980s, from which it has not yet recovered. Consequently, GDP and expenditure on public health per capita in 1990 were lower than in 1980. Although the main indicators of health status of the population did not deteriorate during this decade, other social indicators, such as school attendance, have decayed (Table 9.1).

2.2. The Health Sector

Significant public health programmes began in Costa Rica in the 1920s, with the creation of the Sub-Secretariat of Hygiene and Public Health in 1922; the Sub-Secretariat was promoted to ministerial level in 1929 (Meza-Lago, 1985). An ambitious social security system started in 1941 which provided, among other benefits, medical and hospital care to workers in the formal sector and, since 1955, to their families. The health sector was substantially reorganized in the early 1970s. All hospitals were transferred to the social security system, which, in turn, expanded its coverage from 39 to 70 per cent of the population over a ten-year period (Table 9.1). The Ministry of Health established a programme of primary health care to reach rural areas and urban slums (Saenz, 1985). By 1980, this programme covered 60 per cent of the Costa Rican population with services that included quarterly visits to every household by a health worker.

At present, Costa Rican medicine is highly socialized. Only 1.2 per cent of the hospital discharges come from the private sector. Coverage of public medical services is high: for example, 97 per cent of births occurred in hospitals in 1990. However, the quality of the service may be questioned. The budget outlay for health in the public sector peaked at 7.6 per cent of the GDP in 1980 and today represent 5.6 per cent of GDP (Table 9.1).

2.3. Demographic Trends

Mortality probably started to decline in Costa Rica before the end of the nineteenth century, after the cholera epidemic of 1856. In contrast, the birth

Table 9.1.   Demographic, socio-economic and health characteristics of Costa Rica, 1950–90

Indicators	1950	1960	1970	1980	1990
Demographic					
Populations (1000s)	862	1236	1731	2284	3015
Natural growth (%)	3.2	3.8	2.6	2.7	2.3
Total Fertility Rate	6.7	7.3	4.9	3.7	3.2
Under age 15 (%)	43	47	46	38	35
Socioeconomic					
Per capita GDP in 1990-US$	808	1103	1527	1999	1937
Male work force in agriculture (%)	63	59	49	35	33
Illiteracy (% in ages 15+)	21	16	13	10	7
Enrolment in primary and secondary school (% ages 5–19)	39	52	61	64	60
Health (general)					
Life expectancy at birth	55.6	62.6	65.4	72.6	75.2
Infant mortality rate (1000s)	95	80	67	21	16
Public health expenditure					
Per capita in 1990-US$	19	33	78	152	109
As % of GDP	2.2	3.0	5.1	7.6	5.6
Hospital care					
Beds per 1000 population	5.1	4.6	4.1	3.3	2.5
Discharges per 1000 population	95	101	111	117	105
Births in institutions (%)	20	49	70	91	97
Medical care					
Physicians per 10,000 people	3.1	2.8	5.6	7.8	8.9
Medically certified deaths (%)	60	65	71	84	96
Health insurance coverage (%)	8	15	39	70	79
Outpatient consultations per capita (public health services)	—	1.1	2.0	2.9	2.5
Primary health care					
Administrative coverage (%)	0	0	0	60	57
Sanitation					
Population with piped water (%)	53	65	75	83	94
Population with faeces disposal (%)	48	69	86	94	97

Source: Updated from Rosero-Bixby (1985*b*).

rate remained high until 1960 and even increased briefly in the 1950s. Consequently, population growth accelerated, reaching 3.8 per cent in 1960—one of the highest growth rates in the world. By 1960 the birth rate began to decline, which resulted in a reduced population growth (Table 9.1).

In contrast with its present very low mortality, Costa Rica's population growth (2.3 per cent) and total fertility rate (3.2 births per woman) remained moderately high in 1990. The low mortality level and a transitional age-structure with relatively large population at ages at which the risk of death is minimal, result in a crude death rate below 4 per 1000, one of the lowest in the world.

2.4. The Epidemiologic Transition

Early data suggest that at the beginning of this century mortality was lower in Costa Rica than in Latin America as a whole (Rosero-Bixby, 1985*a*). Social homogeneity inherited from colonial times, a more egalitarian distribution of land, the absence of militarism, and an emphasis on education by governments of all parties are some factors that seem to account for this initial advantage of Costa Rica (Mata and Rosero-Bixby, 1988). As in the rest of the continent, the most rapid improvement in life expectancy took place after World War II. Costa Rica's life expectancy rose sharply from 46 to 63 years between 1940 and 1960. This progress has been linked with the adoption of cost-effective tech-nologies, such as antibiotics, DDT, and vaccines, as well as to government initiatives, such as the social security system established in 1941. The standard of living in Costa Rica also increased substantially during this period (Rosero-Bixby, 1991*a*).

After modest gains in life expectancy in the 1960s, a breakthrough in the trend took place in the 1970s (Caldwell, 1986). Life expectancy rose from 65 to 73 years between 1970 and 1980, owing to a dramatic decline in the infant mortality rate from 67 to 21 per 1000. This decline has been linked mainly to the implementation of cost-effective primary health care programmes among rural populations. Conventional health interventions, favourable socio-economic circumstances, and a substantial fertility reduction have also been identified as significant factors in the improvement of child health in the 1970s (Rosero-Bixby, 1986).

In spite of the economic recession, mortality continued falling during the 1980s, but at a slower pace. Life expectancy increased from 72.6 to 75.2 years and infant mortality declined from 21 to 16 per 1000 between 1980 and 1990 (Table 9.1). This progress is intriguing since it occurred under difficult socio-economic circumstances and declining public health expenditure and services (Table 9.1).

3. Data and Methods

Most analyses in this paper are based on the risk of dying in the age groups 20 to 49 years and 50 to 79 years. These risks measure the probability of dying in those age intervals by a person that has reached the initial age of the interval.

The risks were derived from the age-specific mortality rates ($_5m_x$) and the following approximate relations (Kleinbaum *et al.*, 1982: 107):

$$Q_{(20-49)} \approx 1 - \exp\left(-5.\sum_{x=20}^{45} {}_5m_x\right)$$

$$Q_{(50-79)} = 1 - \exp\left(-5.\sum_{x=50}^{75} {}_5m_x\right)$$

The risk of dying was also computed by specific causes of death. In this case, the risk represents the probability of dying of a particular cause (or group of causes) in the corresponding age interval in the absence of other causes of death. The following relation aggregates the risks of dying by k different causes i:

$$Q = 1 - \prod_{i=1}^{k}\left(1 - Q_i\right)$$

The proportional contribution of the *i-th* cause of death to the decline in the risk of dying by all causes—the 'attributable risk decline' D_i—was estimated using the following relation:

$$D_i \approx \frac{\Delta Qi}{\Delta Q} \cdot \frac{1 - \overline{Q}}{1 - \overline{Q_i}}; \qquad \sum_i D_i = 1$$

where $\overline{Q}$ is the mean risk in the period and the operator Δ indicates the amount of change (the first difference) during the period.

The data source from which the risk of dying by all causes is drawn is a series of life tables covering the period 1920–80 (Rosero-Bixby and Caamaño, 1984). These tables include corrections for under-registration of deaths. The series was updated with life tables computed for 1985 and 1990 (not shown) employing the same procedures and adjustments as for the 1980 life table.

Seventeen groups of causes of death were defined, based on the classification into twelve groups developed by Preston *et al.* (1972). Table 9.2 presents the definitions of these groups according to the International Classification of Diseases, 5th to 9th Revisions. The age-specific death rates by cause in 1951–2 and 1961–2 come from statistical yearbooks ('Anuario Estadístico') published by the Directorate of Statistics and Censuses. For 1971–2, 1981–2 and 1989–90 the data come from computer files obtained from the Directorate of Statistics and Censuses.

The areal analysis of adult mortality is based on two cross-sections centred in 1973 and 1984 for 100 counties. Mortality rates were computed with three-year averages of deaths (i.e. 1972–4 and 1983–5) from vital statistics computer files using the census population in the age intervals 20–49 years and 50–79

Table 9.2. Definition of the groups of causes of death. International Classification of Diseases, 5th to 9th Revisions

Groups of causes of death	International Classification of Diseases Revisions				
	5th (1938)	6th (1948)	7th (1955)	8th (1965)	9th (1975)
Respiratory tuberculosis	13	1	1–8	10–12	10-12
Malaria	28	37	111–116	84	84
Diarrhoeal disease	119–120	104	571–572	8–9	8–9
Acute respiratory infections	33, 106–9	88–93	480–502	466–491	466, 480–491
Other infectious and parasitic diseases	1–12, 14–27, 30, 34–44, 177	2–36, 38–43	9–111, 117–138	0–7, 13–83, 85–136	0–7, 13–83, 85–139
Malnutrition	67–71, 73	64–65	286–293	260–9, 280–5	260–9, 280–5
Maternal	141–150	115–120	640–689	630–678	630–678
Digestive cancer	46	45–48	150–159	150–159	150–159
Respiratory cancer	47	49–50	160–163	160–163	160–163
Uterus cancer	48	52–53	171–174	180–182	179–182
Other cancer	45, 49–57, 74	44, 51, 54–60	140–9, 164–170, 175–239	140–9, 170–9, 183–239	140–9, 170–8, 183–239
Cardiovascular	58, 83, 90–103	70, 79–86	330–34, 400–68	390–458	390–459
Diabetes	61	63	260	250	250
Cirrhosis	77, 124	105	581	571	571
Automobile accidents	170	138	810–835	810–825	810–825
Other accidents and violence	163–9, 171–6, 178–195	139–150	800–9, 840–999	800–7, 830–999	800–7, 830–999
Ill-defined, senility	162, 199, 200	136–137	790–795	790–795	790–795

years as denominators. Child mortality rates were estimated from the census data on the proportions of surviving children.

The analysis considers the following explanatory variables:

(a) Socio-economic development, as estimated by an index computed from a linear combination of census data on seven indicators. These indicators with their weights indicated in parentheses are household income (1), proportion of non-agricultural activities (1), urbanization (1), women in the labour force (3), literacy (3), school attendance (2), and school attainment (2). The weights were determined with exploratory factor analysis. Detailed information from this index and the definition of the 100 counties is presented elsewhere (Rosero-Bixby, 1991*b*: ch. V).

(b) Social security, an indicator of access to medical services, is the proportion of population covered by the social security system according to the 1973 and 1984 censuses.

(c) Medically assisted deaths, a proportion computed from vital statistics.

(d) Primary health care services, as estimated by the proportion of population living in areas administratively covered by the rural and community health programs in 1984 (these programmes started in 1972).

(e) Improvement in access to secondary health care, as estimated by the proportion of population living in the catchment areas of health centres or clinics opened between 1970 and 1983.

(f) Travel time to San José in 1970 and 1984, an indicator of access to health and other services only available in the capital, estimated as the average of the times for each census tract, as assessed by supervisors of the 1984 census (unpublished information).

Multiple regression models for this areal data set are estimated with Generalized Least Squares, using as a weighting variable the square root of the population (young or older adults) in the county. This procedure purges the distortion caused by the different variance of residuals due to the different demographic size of counties (Hanushek and Jackson, 1977: 150–68). The regression models were estimated using the computer package SHAZAM.

4. Level and Trend in Adult Mortality

In 1920, a 20-year-old Costa Rican had a 40 per cent chance of dying before reaching age 50; in 1990 the risk was only 6.1 per cent for men and 3.3 per cent for women, a fall of more than 80 per cent (Table 9.3). This decline is of similar magnitude to that observed in infant mortality, which fell from 200 to 16 per 1000 during this period (Rosero-Bixby and Caamaño, 1984). Young adult mortality diminished steadily during these 70 years except in the period 1960–5, when men's mortality increased slightly. The fastest decline occurred in the 1950s when Costa Rica benefited from discoveries associated with World War II, notably antibiotics and DDT. The risk of dying for young adults diminished by about 5 per cent a year during that decade. The second fastest decline took place in the 1940s, and was probably conditioned by factors similar to those operating in the 1950s. In addition, the 1970s were highly advantageous for women, probably due to improved reproductive health conditions.

The decline in the risk of dying at older ages (50 to 79 years) was not as dramatic as that at younger ages, but was still substantial. The probability of dying in this age interval was 54 per cent among men and 40 per cent among women in 1990, about 40 per cent lower than 70 years earlier (Table 9.3). The fastest decline in mortality at older ages took place in the late 1980s, which was a period characterized by adverse socio-economic conditions and reductions in expenditure on public health. The early 1970s is another period of accelerated reduction in the mortality of this age group (Table 9.3). The temporal sequence of mortality decline among older adults is thus different from that among young adults. There is, however, some coincidence in the cohort sequence of the transition. The beneficiaries of the accelerated decline at older ages in the 1980s were the same cohorts that experienced a fast decline at young adult ages in the 1950s.

The widening of the sex differential in adult mortality, especially among

Table 9.3. Risk of dying among adults in the age groups 20–49 and 50–79 years, Costa Rica 1920–90

Year	Mortality per 1000		Sex ratio	Annual change (%)	
	Male	Female		Male	Female
Young adults (20–49 years)					
1920	402	404	0.99	−4.2	−4.2
1930	264	265	0.99	−1.0	−1.1
1940	239	238	1.00	−4.3	−4.8
1950	155	148	1.05	−4.5	−5.1
1960	99	89	1.11	0.7	−1.8
1965	102	81	1.25	−1.1	−3.9
1970	96	67	1.43	−1.8	−4.3
1975	88	54	1.62	−2.9	−4.8
1980	76	43	1.78	−3.6	−3.6
1985	64	36	1.79	−0.9	−1.4
1990	61	33	1.84		
Old adults (50–79 years)					
1920	858	853	1.01	−0.7	−0.9
1930	797	782	1.02	0.0	−0.2
1940	793	771	1.03	−0.5	−0.9
1950	751	704	1.07	−0.8	−1.6
1960	690	598	1.15	−0.2	−0.3
1965	684	588	1.16	−0.7	−1.0
1970	660	560	1.18	−1.2	−1.9
1975	621	511	1.22	−0.7	−1.4
1980	601	475	1.27	−0.7	−1.3
1985	579	446	1.30	−1.5	−2.1
1990	538	401	1.34		

Source: updated from Rosero and Caamaño (1984).

young adults, is a noteworthy feature of the mortality transition in Costa Rica and elsewhere. Until 1940 there was almost no difference in the risk of dying by sex. Since then the pace of mortality decline has been slower for men, raising their relative risk of dying in respect to women. In 1990, men had a risk of dying 84 per cent higher than women at young adult ages and 34 per cent higher at older adult ages.

How does the adult mortality transition in Costa Rica compare with other countries? The contrast with the United States suggests that the decline in Costa Rica has been extraordinary, particularly among men (Figure 9.1). In 1920, the risk of dying of young Costa Rican adults, men and women, was double that of US citizens. It was about 16 per cent higher at older adult ages. Costa Rican men closed this gap by 1960 and nowadays they have a 21 per cent

AGES 20–49

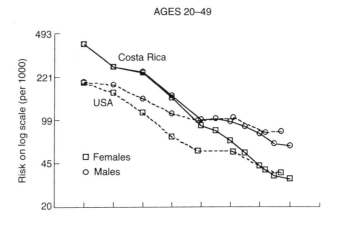

AGES 50–79

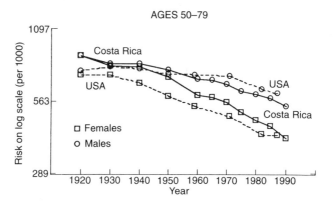

Fig. 9.1. Risk of dying in the age groups 20–49 and 50–79. Costa Rica and the USA, 1920–90
Source: Costa Rica: Table 9.2; US: National Centers for Health Statistics.

lower risk of dying than their US counterparts at young adult ages and 7 per cent lower risk at older ages (Figure 9.1). The mortality decline for Costa Rican women was relatively less steep (in spite of being faster than that of men), but it was fast enough for women to catch up with their US counterparts in the 1980s. At present, adult women in Costa Rica and the US experience approximately the same risks of dying.

A comparison with two European populations—France and the Czech Republic—suggests once again that the adult mortality decline in Costa Rica, especially among men, has been exceptional (Figure 9.2). In 1985, men's life expectancy at age 40 in Costa Rica was five years longer than in the Czech Republic and one year longer than in France, whereas that of women was two years longer than in the Czech Republic but about two years lower than in

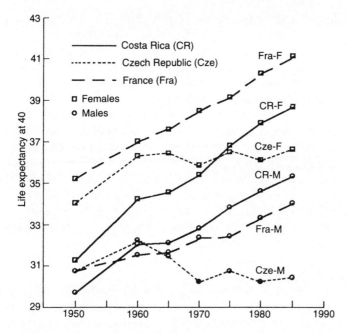

Fig. 9.2. Life expectancy at age 40 in Costa Rica, the Czech Republic and France, 1950–85
Source: Costa Rica: updated from Rosero-Bixby and Caamaño (1984); France and the Czech Republic: Rytchtaríková *et al.* (1990).

France. Figure 9.2 also illustrates that continuous progress in contemporary adult mortality is by no means the rule. In the Czech Republic, as in the rest of Eastern Europe and the former Soviet Union, adult mortality has stalled or deteriorated since the 1960s (Bourgeois-Pichat, 1985).

Another feature of adult mortality trends in Costa Rica is that the widening of the sex-gap has been less severe than in industrialized countries. Although progress in reducing adult male mortality in Costa Rica has been slower than for adult women, it was substantially faster than in industrialized countries. Conversely, although mortality decline among Costa Rican women has been substantially faster than among men, it has not been fast enough to catch up with the levels prevailing in industrialized countries.

5. Causes of Death

A salient aspect of the epidemiologic transition is the shift in cause of death patterns from infection and malnutrition to degenerative and man-made conditions as the leading causes of death (Omran, 1982). Mohs (1991) contrasts two paradigms in the explanation of this shift, the 'malnutrition paradigm' which emphasizes the improvement in living conditions, and the 'infectious diseases paradigm' which underscores the role of health interventions, especially in the lagged transitions of the less developed countries. How well does the Costa Rican cause-of-death pattern of decline in adult ages fit this picture of the epidemiologic transition?

Data available for the period since 1951 show that the cause of death profile has changed in Costa Rica in the expected direction: the importance of infections and malnutrition has declined, whereas that of degenerative and man-made conditions has increased (Figure 9.3). More specifically, the place left vacant by the decline in infectious and deficiency diseases was taken largely by accidents and violence at young adult ages (38 per cent of deaths in 1989–90) and by cardiovascular diseases at older adult ages (39 per cent of deaths in 1989–90). It is important to point out, however, that the contribution of infectious and deficiency diseases to adult mortality was somewhat limited in the past: 40 and 19 per cent of deaths in the age groups 20 to 49 years and 50 to 79 years, respectively, in 1951–2.

The proportion of ill-defined causes of death (including those classified as 'senility') gives an idea of the quality of cause of death data. This proportion was 9 and 12 per cent at young and older ages respectively in 1951–2, which is unusually low for a developing country four decades ago. Reflecting an improvement in data quality, the group of ill-defined causes declined to 2 per cent of deaths in 1989–90 in both age groups, a figure that is consistent with the fact that 96 per cent of deaths in Costa Rica were medically certified in 1990. The reduction in the proportion of ill-defined causes of death, in spite of being

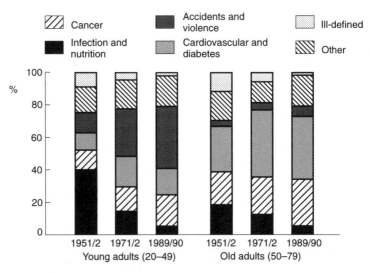

Fig. 9.3. Distribution of deaths by groups of causes: Costa Rica, adults, 1951–90

a favourable trend, is a nuisance for the study of cause-specific mortality over time. It is possible, for example, that a part of the decline in infections and malnutrition has been blurred by improved diagnosis, or that a part of the increase in the contribution of cardiovascular diseases has been an artifact of better diagnoses.

Figure 9.4 shows the evolution in the risks of dying from selected groups of causes of death, as defined in Table 9.2. The upper part of the figure presents conditions of infectious or nutritional origin. The dramatic declines in respiratory tuberculosis at young adult ages during the 1950s and in acute respiratory infections during the 1970s stand out. The virtual elimination of malaria in the 1950s was a notable achievement in both age groups. The reduction in maternal mortality in the 1960s, probably a byproduct of the fertility transition, was another noteworthy trend. The risk of dying from diarrhoeal diseases and nutritional conditions exhibits a sustained decline during the period, although it is not as fast as the aforementioned reductions. The only clear increase in mortality from diseases of infectious origin is for acute respiratory infections at older ages between 1951 and 1971. The risk of dying from these conditions rose from 33 to 60 per 1000 in these twenty years. Part of this increase could be an artifact of changes in diagnostic practices.

The lower part of Figure 9.4 shows the evolution in the risk of dying from degenerative and man-made conditions. There are several negative trends. The most serious are the increase in automobile accidents, cardiovascular diseases, and diabetes from 1951–2 to 1971–2. Mortality from automobile accidents at young adult ages underwent a seven-fold increase in this period, whereas that caused by diabetes at older adult ages underwent a three-fold increase. Mortality from respiratory cancer (chiefly lung cancer) also increases substantially, particularly for young adults in the 1960s and for older adults in the 1970s. The risk of dying from respiratory cancer in 1989–90 is three and two times greater than in 1951–2 at young and older adult ages, respectively.

The most notable trend in this group of causes of death was the sharp decline in cardiovascular mortality in the 1970s (Figure 9.4). The decline was one of 38 per cent and 25 per cent at young and older adult ages respectively during the decade. Major declines in diabetes, accidents and violence (including automobile accidents) also took place during this decade. The large reduction in mortality from cancer of the uterus (chiefly cervical neoplasms) in the 1960s has been linked to screening programmes implemented, in part, along with family planning services (Rosero-Bixby and Grimaldo, 1987). In turn, the decline in digestive cancer (chiefly stomach cancer) has a special significance, due to its extraordinarily high incidence in Costa Rica. The risk of dying from digestive cancer was 46 per cent lower in 1989–90 than in 1951–2 at young adult ages, and 18 per cent lower than in 1961–2 at older adult ages.

Table 9.4 shows the estimated contributions of each cause of death to the overall mortality decline. This 'attributable decline' depends on both the pace of change in a particular cause and its baseline level. About three-quarters of

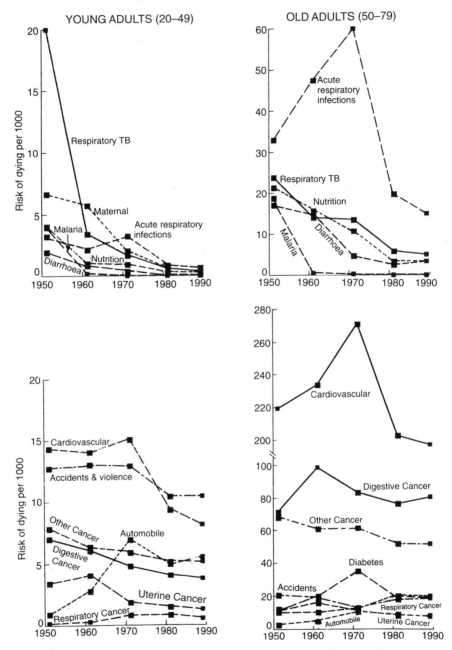

Fig. 9.4. Risk of dying by selected causes of death: Costa Rican adults, 1951–90
Source: Table 9.2 and 9.A1.

Table 9.4. Attributable decline in adults' risk of dying in 1951–71 and 1971–89

Cause of death	Percent attributable decline			
	Ages 20–49		Ages 50–79	
	1951–71	1971–89	1951–71	1971–89
Respiratory TB	37.0	4.4	16.5	4.1
Malaria	7.9	0.1	29.7	0.1
Diarrhoeal diseases	3.0	1.1	20.0	0.6
Acute respiratory infections	−0.1	8.7	−44.8	22.1
Other infections and parasitic	12.9	7.0	34.0	3.0
Malnutrition	6.3	2.3	17.2	3.4
Maternal	9.4	5.5	0.0	0.0
Subtotal: infection–nutrition	76.4	29.1	72.7	33.3
Digestive cancer	4.4	3.5	−19.4	1.2
Respiratory cancer	−1.2	0.7	−3.8	−3.5
Uterus cancer	3.1	1.9	2.3	1.7
Other cancers	3.9	2.7	11.5	4.6
Subtotal: cancer	10.2	8.8	−9.3	4.1
Cardiovascular	−1.5	23.4	−108.6	45.5
Diabetes	−1.7	0.7	−38.4	7.4
Subtotal: cardiovascular–diabetes	−3.2	24.1	−147.0	52.9
Automobile accidents	−12.1	4.7	−12.9	1.1
Accidents and violence	−0.5	8.4	12.3	−2.8
Subtotal: accidents–violence	−12.6	13.1	−0.6	−1.7
Cirrhosis	1.5	−2.4	−1.7	−2.4
Ill-defined, senility	15.0	11.0	92.1	19.7
Residual	12.7	16.4	93.8	−5.9
Total	100.0	100.0	100.0	100.0

Source: Table 9.A1.

the mortality reduction at both young and older ages from 1951–2 to 1971–2 can be attributed to the control of infectious diseases and malnutrition. This contribution declined to about 30 per cent in the 1970s and 1980s. In this later period, cardiovascular diseases accounted for approximately one-quarter of the decline at young adult ages and one-half at older adult ages. An increase in accidents and violence counteracted the adult mortality decline in the 1950s and 1960s by 13 per cent, whereas in the 1970s and 1980s external causes contributed 13 per cent to the decline. The contribution of tuberculosis and malaria to the early mortality transition is outstanding. The control of these two diseases alone explains about 45 per cent of the adult-mortality decline from 1951–2 to 1971–2 in the two age groups studied. A 9 per cent contribution of maternal deaths to the decline in young adult mortality in this early period is also noteworthy.

A large decline of ill-defined causes of death, which is almost as large as the decline in all other causes, confounds analysis of the components of the early mortality transition in the older age group (Table 9.4). Part of the negative contributions of cardiovascular diseases (–109 per cent), acute respiratory infections (–45 per cent), diabetes (–38 per cent), and digestive cancer (–19 per cent) is probably due to the reduction in ill-defined causes of death. However, this artifact could only explain a fraction of these negative contributions (44 per cent at the most). It seems that the increases in these causes of death and automobile accidents diminished by more than one-half the potential mortality decline brought about by other causes. This adverse effect may be ascribable to the negative influence of economic development and affluence: the increase in automobile accidents is a clear example of this. Part of the increase in diabetes, cardiovascular diseases, respiratory cancer and, perhaps, respiratory infections can be linked to modern lifestyles, including obesity, smoking, sedentary habits, and consumption of animal fats. It seems, however, that these deleterious consequences of progress were neutralized in the 1970s and 1980s.

Data by sex on the cause-specific mortality (Table 9.5), are only available for the period since 1971. They corroborate the aforementioned trends, such as the large contribution of cardiovascular disease to the mortality decline. At young adult ages, the most important factor in the mortality decline among men was the control of accidents and violence (23 per cent contribution). These causes of death made almost no contribution to the decline among women. Cardiovascular diseases played a more important role in women (29 per cent) than in men (18 per cent). Maternal mortality was the second most important component (12 per cent contribution) among women. At older adult ages, the contribution of digestive and respiratory cancer exhibits major sex-differences. Mortality from these tumours increased among men and made a negative contribution to the transition. Among women, there was almost no increase in respiratory cancer and digestive cancer decreased. Therefore, the widening of the sex differential in mortality at young ages was a result of the reduction in maternal mortality and a more rapid decline of cardiovascular mortality among women. At older adult ages, the increasing differential resulted largely from an increase in deaths from respiratory and digestive cancer among men.

How does the cause of death profile of Costa Rican adults compare with that of other populations? A comparison with Argentina and Chile has shown that infectious and parasitic diseases mortality (including pneumonia and bronchitis) is relatively low in Costa Rica, whereas men's mortality from accidents is higher (Arriaga, 1991; Table 9.4). Other international comparisons single out Costa Rica for its high mortality from stomach cancer and accidents and its relatively low mortality from lung cancer and cardiovascular diseases (Brouard and Lopez, 1985; Meslé, 1985).

Table 9.5. Risk of dying by sex for 17 groups of causes of death, young and older adults, Costa Rica, 1971–90

Cause of death	Male risk per 1000			Female risk per 1000			Attributable decline 1971–89 (%)	
	1971–2	1981–2	1989–90	1971–2	1981–2	1989–90	Males	Females
Young adults (20–49)								
Respiratory tuberculosis	1.7	1.1	0.5	1.7	0.6	0.2	3.6	5.3
Diarrhoeal diseases	0.5	0.1	0.1	0.3	0.1	0.1	1.5	0.6
Acute respiratory infections	3.6	1.0	0.7	2.8	0.7	0.5	8.9	8.6
Other infections and parasitic	2.8	1.1	1.0	3.1	0.8	0.7	5.4	8.8
Malnutrition	1.1	0.2	0.3	0.8	0.4	0.2	2.6	2.0
Maternal	0.0	0.0	0.0	4.0	1.2	0.7	0.0	11.9
Digestive cancer	6.2	4.3	4.5	3.4	3.8	3.0	5.3	1.4
Respiratory cancer	1.0	1.2	0.5	0.6	0.5	0.6	1.5	−0.2
Uterus cancer	0.0	0.0	0.0	3.7	3.0	2.6	0.0	3.9
Other cancer	4.8	4.5	4.4	7.2	5.9	5.9	1.3	4.5
Cardiovascular	15.8	10.8	9.8	14.3	7.9	6.3	18.5	29.0
Diabetes	0.9	0.9	1.0	1.8	1.1	1.3	−0.5	2.0
Cirrhosis	2.4	3.3	3.5	1.0	0.9	1.3	−3.4	−1.2
Automobile accidents	12.0	8.4	9.5	1.7	1.5	1.5	7.9	1.0
Other accidents, and violence	22.5	18.3	17.7	3.2	2.4	3.1	15.1	0.7
Ill-defined, senility	5.8	1.9	1.4	2.7	2.2	0.4	13.4	8.1
Residual	13.9	7.4	7.8	10.2	7.0	6.5	18.7	13.7
Total	91.4	62.7	61.2	60.8	39.3	34.3	100.0	100.0
Old adults (50–79)								
Respiratory tuberculosis	18.4	8.4	7.9	9.3	3.6	2.6	5.7	3.0
Diarrhoeal diseases	4.4	3.4	3.6	4.8	1.8	3.3	0.4	0.6
Acute respiratory infections	61.4	22.6	17.2	59.0	16.9	13.3	24.6	20.6
Other infections. and parasitic	15.9	8.4	9.0	9.9	7.1	4.2	3.8	2.5
Malnutrition	11.3	4.7	3.9	10.1	2.1	3.0	4.0	3.1
Digestive cancer	99.5	102.1	108.9	67.5	52.4	55.2	−5.6	5.7
Respiratory cancer	17.1	30.0	30.3	8.3	11.6	10.3	−7.2	−0.9
Uterus cancer	0.0	0.0	0.0	21.2	16.5	14.4	0.0	3.0
Other cancer	72.0	63.4	63.0	52.4	42.7	43.3	5.1	4.2
Cardiovascular	299.0	233.8	231.4	245.6	174.5	166.0	49.0	43.4
Diabetes	27.5	13.7	14.1	41.9	22.5	25.1	7.3	7.5
Cirrhosis	12.6	12.7	18.5	5.5	9.5	9.4	−3.2	−1.7
Automobile accidents	16.8	15.7	13.2	4.8	1.9	3.6	2.0	0.5
Other accidents, and violence	20.4	25.9	28.7	6.2	9.9	9.6	−4.6	−1.5
Ill-defined, senility	60.8	53.3	14.4	42.4	42.4	7.7	25.7	15.4
Residual	98.6	101.0	110.3	71.9	72.3	82.9	−7.0	−5.3
Total	597.6	526.5	514.6	507.3	400.5	378.9	100.0	100.0

Table 9.6 compares the risks of dying from selected causes in Costa Rica and the USA in the late 1980s. Heart disease and respiratory cancer are the key to the comparatively low mortality of Costa Rica (see risk-differences in Table 9.6). Consumption of cigarettes is substantially lower in Costa Rica than in the USA and is a likely explanation of some of this differential (Ravenholt, 1990). Other plausible explanations of lower heart disease mortality in Costa Rica are a less stressful lifestyle, less sedentary habits, particularly in rural areas, less fat and protein in the diet, and a lower prevalence of obesity among men. The sharp decline in cardiovascular mortality in both Costa Rica and the USA

Table 9.6. Risk of dying at ages 25–74 years for selected causes of death, comparison between Costa Rica, 1988 and the USA, 1987

Cause of death (ICD Codes[a])	Mortality per 1000			
	CR-1988	US-1987	Difference CR-US	Ratio CR/US
Males				
Heart disease (390–429)	117.8	204.5	−86.7	0.58
Respiratory cancer (162)	18.8	68.5	−49.7	0.27
Other cancer (140–208, exc. 151, 162)	72.9	101.1	−28.2	0.72
Diabetes (250)	11.3	10.7	0.6	1.05
Other accidents and violence (800–9, 820–999)	38.5	35.2	3.3	1.09
Cirrhosis (571)	17.7	14.1	3.6	1.25
Automobile accidents (810–819)	18.4	12.7	5.7	1.45
Stroke (430–438)	34.0	26.6	7.4	1.28
Stomach cancer (151)	47.8	5.8	42.0	8.30
Females				
Heart disease (390–429)	71.7	99.9	−28.2	0.72
Respiratory cancer (162)	5.7	28.5	−22.9	0.20
Other cancer (140–208, exc. 151, 162, 180)	67.6	86.5	−19.0	0.78
Other accidents and violence (800–9, 820–999)	9.2	10.9	−1.7	0.85
Automobile accidents (810–819)	3.9	5.3	−1.5	0.72
Cirrhosis (571)	6.8	6.2	0.6	1.09
Stroke (430–438)	27.0	21.1	5.9	1.28
Cervical cancer (180)	11.0	2.8	8.3	3.96
Diabetes (250)	20.0	9.7	10.3	2.06
Stomach cancer (151)	18.5	2.4	16.1	7.56

[a] International Classification of Diseases (ICD), 9th Revision.
Source: PAHO, 1990, Vol. I, Tables III-9.

in the 1970s and 1980s is an encouraging development, suggesting that progress need not necessarily result in an increase in such mortality. The future of mortality from respiratory cancer in Costa Rica is less appealing. An increase in smoking in young generations in the 1960s, which probably took place because of the boom in television and communications, will have an impact on mortality from respiratory cancer thirty to fifty years later, that is after 1990.

In the group 'other cancer' Costa Ricans are again fortunate (Table 9.6). The differences from the USA under this rubric come mostly from bladder and prostate cancer in men and breast cancer in women. The future evolution of bladder and prostate cancer in Costa Rica is uncertain, but breast cancer will probably increase substantially. A slight increase of breast cancer mortality has already been observed and a substantial increase (32 per cent in twenty years) in the incidence of this cancer has been projected just as a consequence of past fertility reductions (Rosero-Bixby *et al.*, 1987).

Mortality from stomach cancer is eight times higher in Costa Rica than in the USA. Nevertheless, an encouraging decline has already occurred in Costa Rica and will probably continue in the future. Stomach cancer mortality has been decreasing dramatically in the USA (more in women than in men) for several decades: in 1973–4, this rate was one-fifth its level in 1935 among white females (Devesa and Silverman, 1978; Table 9.4). Although the causes of this decline are still unknown, it seems reasonable to expect a similar trend in Costa Rica.

The comparison with the USA also suggests that Costa Rica could achieve important mortality reductions from the death rates due to stroke in both sexes, automobile accidents in men, and diabetes and cervical cancer in women. Several technologies are already available to intervene against these causes of death.

6. Areal Variation in Adult Mortality

The data examined so far have shown puzzling relationships between socio-economic development, expenditure on health services and adult-mortality transition in Costa Rica. National indicators of adult mortality, socio-economic progress, and health interventions follow disparate trends. Moreover, adults in Costa Rica face similar, or even lesser, mortality risks than their counterparts in the USA, despite the enormous differences between them in income, social organization, and availability of health facilities. The analysis of causes of death offers hints about the forces that reduced adult mortality in Costa Rica but also raises questions regarding the possible determinants of cardiovascular mortality trends. An examination of areal variation in adult mortality and its correlates might provide additional clues about the role that socio-economic development and health interventions play in determining adult mortality in Costa Rica.

The areal (or ecological) analysis uses a territorial division of Costa Rica into 100 'counties' defined for other purposes (Rosero-Bixby, 1991*b*). Four-fifths of the counties are in the range of 6000 to 60,000 population. The analysis covers two three-year periods centred on the census years 1973 and 1984. The adult mortality rates at young ages (20 to 49 years) and older ages (50 to 79 years) are analysed separately. Three mortality rates are studied in each age group: all causes of death; infectious diseases and malnutrition; and cardiovascular diseases and diabetes. It is important to keep in mind the considerable random variation existing in these county-level rates because of the small numbers involved, particularly in the young adult age group.

Are there geographical regularities in adult mortality in Costa Rica? The choropleth map of cardiovascular mortality at older ages in 1973 (Figure 9.5) suggests geographical clustering: counties with higher cardiovascular mortality tend to line up along an interoceanic axis between the ports of Puntarenas and Limón, including the Central Valley and the capital city, San José. It is precisely along this axis that Costa Rica traditionally concentrated its socio-economic and demographic development (Hall, 1985). The map therefore suggests a correspondence between cardiovascular mortality and development. Other choropleth maps (1984, all causes of death, young adult ages) present less clear geographical clustering. Maps (not shown) for the young adult ages and infection-malnutrition conditions, in particular, resemble a chess board, without spatial regularities.

Figure 9.5 also includes a map describing the pace of decline in cardiovascular mortality between 1973 and 1984. The geographical pattern is less clear in this than in the 1973 mortality level map. Nevertheless, a 'regression to the mean' phenomenon is clearly present: those counties with the lowest rates in 1973 tend to be the ones where the rate increases most in the following decade.

Pearson correlation coefficients (r) can be used to check the existence of ecological covariations between adult mortality in Costa Rican counties and their socio-economic and health status (Table 9.7). To illustrate, correlation coefficients smaller than 0.20 in absolute value indicate lack of, or non-significant, association; coefficients between 0.20 and 0.39 indicate a modest but significant association; and coefficients of 0.40 or larger indicate a close association. Mortality rates at young and older adult ages are weakly correlated (Table 9.7). The largest correlation coefficient between young and adult mortality is a modest 0.31 for infections and malnutrition in 1973. In addition, neither young nor older adult mortality rates are correlated meaningfully with infant mortality. The only two correlations with infant mortality of a significant magnitude are negative in sign. Mortality from cardiovascular disease tends to be high in counties with low infant mortality in 1973, a pattern consistent with that shown in Figure 9.5. The lack of a positive association

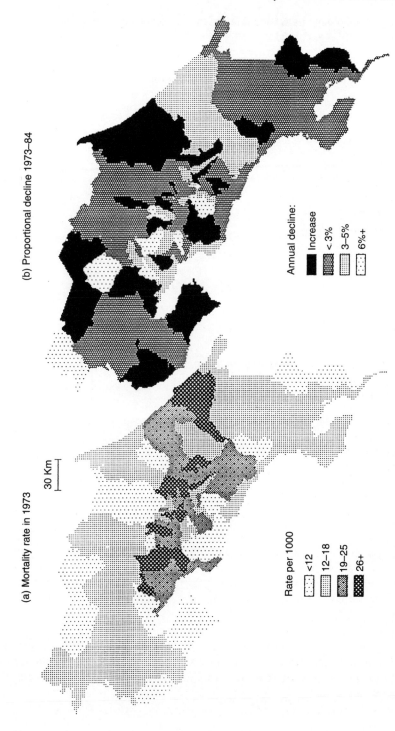

(a) Mortality rate in 1973

30 Km

Annual decline:

- Increase
- < 3%
- 3–5%
- 6%+

Rate per 1000

- <12
- 12–18
- 19–25
- 26+

Fig. 9.5.   Level and change in the mortality rate from cardiovascular diseases and diabetes at ages 50–79

Table 9.7. Relationship between adult mortality and selected variables, 100 Costa Rican counties, 1973 and 1984

Variable[a]	All causes		Infection–nutrition		Cardiovascular–diabetes	
	1973	1984	1973	1984	1973	1984
Correlations between young adult mortality and:						
Mortality among:						
Older adults (50–79 years)	0.18	−0.06	0.31	−0.08	0.21	0.22
Infants	0.06	0.04	0.14	0.08	−0.10	−0.02
Socioeconomic development:						
10 years earlier	0.12	0.02	0.16	0.04	0.29	0.22
contemporary	0.11	0.01	0.16	0.04	0.32	0.23
Social security	0.14	−0.06	0.10	0.03	0.33	0.06
Medically assisted deaths	0.08	−0.18	0.20	−0.08	0.38	−0.09
Primary care	—	−0.05	—	−0.03	—	−0.12
Travel time to San José	−0.3	0.08	−0.02	0.17	−0.27	−0.14
Correlations between older adult mortality and:						
Mortality among:						
Young adults (20–49 years)	0.18	−0.06	0.31	−0.08	0.21	0.22
Infants	−0.31	0.01	0.15	−0.01	−0.35	−0.06
Socioeconomic development:						
10 years earlier	0.52	0.48	0.19	0.28	0.60	0.59
contemporary	0.49	0.46	0.22	0.26	0.58	0.59
Social security	0.53	0.43	0.21	0.29	0.59	0.57
Medically assisted deaths	0.48	0.42	0.17	0.11	0.67	0.54
Primary care	—	−0.24	—	−0.17	—	−0.24
Travel time to San José	−0.48	−0.44	−0.17	−0.21	−0.51	−0.53

[a] For definitions see text.

between adult and infant mortality suggests that conclusions from previous studies about the determinants of the breakthrough in the Costa Rican infant mortality in the 1970s cannot be extrapolated to explain the adult mortality transition.

Young adult mortality shows almost no association with indicators of development and health services (Table 9.7). In contrast, older adult mortality, especially cardiovascular deaths, correlates closely with socio-economic and health indicators, with mortality tending to be lower in backward counties and areas farther away from San José. These inverted correlations are modest for death rates linked to infection and nutrition (about 0.20 to 0.30), whereas they are substantial (0.50 to 0.60 at older ages) for cardiovascular diseases and diabetes.

Data errors, such as differential integrity in the registry of deaths or biased reports of the place of residence of the dead, are unlikely explanations for the odd behaviour of adult mortality rates, since the problem is not present in infant mortality rates based on the same data source. For example, an earlier study shows that the infant mortality rate in 1972–5 and 1982–4 was negatively and significantly correlated with such characteristics as the proportion of deaths medically-certified, coverage of social security, and proportion of dwellings with plumbing (Cervantes and Raabe, 1991; Tables 9.1 and 9.2).

One plausible explanation of the inverse association is reverse causality between adult mortality and place of residence: sick adults may tend to migrate to places with better health facilities and higher levels of development, artificially increasing mortality rates in the better-off counties. The targeting of health interventions on backward areas could also generate reverse causality since high mortality counties would appear as being better-off in terms of health services. Another explanatory mechanism is the existence of 'frailty', or selection effects: backward counties may have low adult mortality rates because historically high child mortality eliminated the frail children in each cohort, leaving alive a select group of more resistant individuals (Vaupel *et al.*, 1979). A more straightforward explanation is that economic progress and modern lifestyles indeed raise adult mortality, particularly that of cardiovascular origin.

A further step in the analysis is modelling mortality decline, rather than its level, as a function of changes in the potential explanatory variables. An analysis based on changes rather than levels has advantages like controlling the effect of unmeasured variables (e.g. the 'targeting' problem); in addition, some data errors neutralize each other by the computation of changes (Liker *et al.*, 1985). Random and other errors, however, can be magnified by the computation of changes, and the 'regression to the mean' phenomenon can introduce considerable noise into the variance of changes (Bohrnstedt, 1969). Due to these problems, the magnitude of correlations for changes is usually lower than for levels (Freedman and Takeshita, 1969).

Table 9.8 shows the results of estimating, with generalized least squares, multiple regression models of the percentage decline in mortality during 1973–84 for: young adults, all causes of death; older adults, all causes; older adults, infection and malnutrition; and older adults, cardiovascular diseases and

Table 9.8.   Standardized regression coefficients (t-ratios) on the relative decline in adult mortality from 1972–4 to 1983–5, 100 Costa Rican counties

Explanatory variables	Young adults (20–49 years)	Older adults (50–79 years)		
		All causes	Infection-nutrition	Cardio-vascular
Initial mortality level (1972–74)	0.159 (1.45[a])	–0.059 (–0.55)	0.158 (1.54[a])	0.007 (0.07)
Pace of socioeconomic development				
A decade earlier (1963–73)	0.102 (0.81)	–0.040 (–0.32)	0.219 (1.80[b])	–0.028 (–0.23)
Contemporary (1973–84)	–0.002 (–0.02)	–0.014 (–0.11)	0.027 (0.22)	–0.163 (–1.32[a])
Relative decline in travel time to San José 1970–84	–0.107 (–0.86)	–0.091 (–0.74)	–0.146 (–1.24)	0.113 (0.93)
Increase in Social Security System coverage 1973–84	–0.099 (–0.73)	–0.233 (–1.78[b])	–0.158 (–1.25)	–0.047 (–0.36)
Increase in the proportion of MD assisted deaths	–0.144 (–0.96)	–0.086 (–0.74)	–0.106 (–0.94)	0.126 (–1.10)
Increase in primary health care services 1972–84	0.077 (0.51)	0.009 (0.06)	0.061 (0.42)	–0.153 (–1.04)
Improvement in access to secondary health care 1970–84	–0.055 (–0.41)	–0.022 (–0.17)	–0.055 (–0.43)	–0.030 (–0.23)
Adjusted R^2	0.033	0.006	0.059	0.014

[a] Significant at 0.90.
[b] Significant at 0.95.

diabetes. Cause-specific mortality decline at young adult ages cannot be analysed because the small number of deaths involved yields highly unreliable estimates.

In the four multiple regression models in Table 9.8 only a few regression coefficients appear statistically significant. Initial mortality levels exert a positive and significant influence on the declines in young adult and in older adult mortality from infections and malnutrition. These significant effects are manifestations of the regression to the mean trend: mortality is easier to lower where it is high initially. The speed of socio-economic progress ten years earlier appears to be a significant factor in the speed of decline in older age mortality from diseases of infectious and nutritional origin, whereas contemporary progress exerts a negative influence on the decline in mortality from cardiovascular disease. Social security coverage also has a significant negative effect on older age mortality from all causes.

A perturbing result in Table 9.8 is that the data fail to show any meaningful impact of interventions like the development of new clinics or the expansion of primary health coverage upon adult mortality. This is in sharp contrast with the findings of earlier studies that showed a clear linkage between these interventions and the infant mortality decline in the 1970s (Rosero-Bixby, 1986).

7. Conclusions

Mortality at young adult ages has declined during the present century to a similar degree to infant mortality (80 per cent from 1920 to 1990). The proportional decline at older adult ages was also substantial but represented only about one half of that at younger ages. Women's mortality decreased more than men's, giving rise to a widening sex differential. The most fruitful period in the control of young adult mortality was after the Second World War; at older adult ages it was the late 1980s. This exceptionally fast decline has allowed Costa Rica to close the gap with industrialized countries. At present, adult men in Costa Rica face lower risks of dying than men in countries such as the USA and France (women face similar or slightly higher risks than their counterparts of these nations).

It is hard to trace an association between the pace of adult mortality decline and trends in socio-economic development and in health interventions in Costa Rica. The decade of fastest economic growth and expansion of expenditure on health was the 1960s. Most of the Costa Rican fertility transition also occurred in these years. It was precisely in this decade, however, when the mortality transition presented signs of stagnation. Conversely, it was in the decade of stalling, or even deteriorating, socio-economic conditions and public health interventions—the 1980s—that the greatest reductions in older adult mortality occurred. On the other hand, the most fruitful period for young adult mortality—the 1950s—was the decade with the fastest progress in educational enrolment and sanitation, as well as in the expansion of basic hospital care like institutional childbirth. The existence of cohort effects, long latency periods, and complex lagged reactions might be the cause for these puzzling temporal relationships. It is also possible that some degree of independence actually exists between adult mortality and the socio-economic and programmatic environment. In this case, the key factors explaining adult mortality trends might be the diffusion of innovations among health professionals and of life styles (good and bad) and health practices among the general population.

Areal analyses of adult mortality suggests that cardiovascular and diabetes mortality is higher in more prosperous communities. Moreover, the decline in such mortality between 1973 and 1984 correlated negatively—and significantly—with socio-economic improvement. In contrast, the decline in mortality from infections and malnutrition was positively associated with ten-year lagged improvements in well-being. This, of course, is not a conclusive proof that development has a negative effect on adult mortality. Bad data, frailty, and the reversed causal linkages discussed already could explain all or part of this correlation. A longitudinal study in selected communities would give more conclusive answers about the impact of progress and health interventions upon the components of adult mortality and, in particular, cardiovascular deaths. Nevertheless, the results of this somewhat simplistic exercise match other pieces of evidence, such as the higher mortality rates in the USA and the adverse trends in some causes of death in the 1950s and 1960s. They suggest a picture in which socio-economic development does not necessarily enhance survival chances at adult ages.

The analysis of mortality trends by cause of death gives additional insights into the existence of a dark side to the development of the epidemiologic transition. The period from 1951–2 to 1971–2 saw substantial mortality increases from cardiovascular diseases, diabetes, automobile accidents, respiratory cancer, and respiratory infections. These probably offset more than one half the mortality decline generated by the control of other conditions. Improved diagnoses alone can hardly explain these mortality increases. Some increases were probably linked to affluence and features of modern lifestyles like smoking, sedentary habits, obesity, consumption of animal fats, and an increase in the use of motor-vehicles. It seems, however, that these deleterious consequences of progress were largely neutralized during the 1970s and 1980s.

A comparison with causes of death in the USA showed that Costa Rica's adult mortality is comparatively low because of substantially lower risks of dying from heart disease and respiratory cancer. Cigarette smoking, a habit associated with modernity, seems likely to play a central role in this difference.

The classic shift in the cause of death profile from infectious diseases and malnutrition to degenerative and man-made conditions is observed in the adult mortality transition in Costa Rica. At present, the leading causes of death are accidents and violence at young adult ages and cardiovascular diseases at older adult ages (each represents almost 40 per cent of deaths in the corresponding age group). In the early stages of Costa Rica's epidemiologic transition, the control of infections and malnutrition was the key factor of mortality decline. About three-quarters of the decline between 1951 and 1971 at both young and older adult ages can be ascribed to infectious and nutritional diseases. In particular, respiratory tuberculosis and malaria account for about 45 per cent of the decline in the two age groups, an outstanding contribution linked to the importation of cost-effective technological advances (chiefly streptomycin and DDT). The contribution of infections and malnutrition to the adult-mortality decline shrank to about 30 per cent during the period from 1971–2 to 1989–90. During this second stage, the control of cardiovascular diseases became the key factor in the decline at older ages, whereas both cardiovascular disease and accidents and violence fuelled the decline at young ages.

Trends under way and a comparison with the epidemiological profile of the USA suggest that substantial adult reductions in mortality might come in the future from control of stomach cancer, as well as from mortality from stroke, automobile accidents, diabetes (particularly in women), and cervical cancer. In addition, it is an important challenge for Costa Rica to keep its comparative advantage in heart disease mortality. Increases must be expected in lung and breast cancer mortality as consequence of past rises in smoking and reduced fertility respectively.

Shifting the focus from infant to adult mortality has exposed new facets of the epidemiologic transition in Costa Rica. Trends in the pace of adult mortality decline differ from those in infant mortality. Geographical patterns and ecological correlates are also different. The determinants of these disparate trends and geographical patterns are thus probably different as well. In particular, while the breakthrough in child survival in the 1970s can be ascribed largely to programmatic interventions, the explanation for the recent decline in adult mortality is more elusive.

Appendix 9.1

Table 9.A1. Risk of dying for 17 groups of causes of death, young and old adults, Costa Rica 1951–90

Causes of death	Risk of dying per 1000				
	1951–2	1961–2	1971–2	1981–2	1989–90
Young adults (20–49)					
Respiratory tuberculosis	19.94	3.37	1.70	0.86	0.38
Malaria	3.95	0.17	0.03	0.00	0.00
Diarrhoeal diseases	1.91	0.80	0.40	0.10	0.07
Acute respiratory infections	3.19	2.16	3.24	0.86	0.61
Other infections and parasitic	9.35	2.80	2.94	0.95	0.84
Malnutrition	4.06	1.01	0.95	0.28	0.26
Maternal	6.68	5.74	1.99	0.61	0.34
Digestive cancer	6.99	6.07	4.82	4.07	3.76
Respiratory cancer	0.20	0.29	0.79	0.85	0.58
Uterus cancer	3.42	4.06	1.88	1.49	1.31
Other cancer	7.87	6.37	5.94	5.20	5.14
Cardiovascular	14.31	14.08	15.06	9.37	8.09
Diabetes	0.51	0.67	1.36	0.97	1.15
Cirrhosis	2.43	1.02	1.69	2.10	2.41
Automobile accidents	0.92	2.79	6.94	4.97	5.52
Other accidents, and violence	12.74	12.99	12.98	10.44	10.47
Ill-defined, senility	11.67	4.92	4.23	2.03	0.92
Residual	18.29	12.92	12.05	7.20	7.14
Total	121.21	79.28	76.26	51.15	47.96
Old adults (50–79)					
Respiratory tuberculosis	23.9	14.0	13.6	5.8	5.0
Malaria	18.7	0.5	0.2	0.0	0.0
Diarrhoeal diseases	17.1	15.1	4.6	2.6	3.4
Acute respiratory infections	33.1	47.4	60.0	19.6	15.1
Other infections and parasitic	33.7	17.5	12.7	7.7	6.4
Malnutrition	21.4	16.1	10.7	3.3	3.4
Digestive cancer	71.6	98.6	82.9	76.1	80.5
Respiratory cancer	10.1	10.4	12.5	20.3	19.7
Uterus cancer	12.6	15.8	11.2	8.7	7.6

Table 9.A1. *Continued*

Causes of death	Risk of dying per 1000				
	1951–2	1961–2	1971–2	1981–2	1989–90
Other cancer	68.2	60.7	61.4	52.3	52.2
Cardiovascular	219.4	234.1	271.1	202.9	197.0
Diabetes	11.5	19.8	35.1	18.3	20.0
Cirrhosis	7.8	10.4	8.9	11.1	13.8
Automobile accidents	2.5	5.1	10.6	8.5	8.2
Other accidents, and violence	20.7	19.2	13.1	17.7	18.9
Ill-defined, senility	104.7	63.3	51.1	47.4	10.7
Residual	137.3	140.3	84.6	85.8	95.8
Total	579.6	569.7	552.2	463.3	446.3

References

Arriaga, E. E. (1991), 'Similarities and differences in the adult mortality transition in developing countries', IUSSP Seminar on Causes and Prevention of Adult Mortality in Developing Countries, Santiago, Chile, 7–11 October.

Behm, H. (1976), *La Mortalidad en los Primeros Años de Vida en Países de la América Latina. Costa Rica 1968–69*, CELADE, Series AN. 1024, San José, Costa Rica.

Bohrnstedt, G. W. (1969), 'Observations on the measurement of change', in: E. F. Borgatta (ed.) *Sociological Methodology*, Jossey-Bass, San Francisco.

Bourgeois-Pichat, J. (1985), 'Recent changes in mortality in industrialized countries', in: J. Vallin and A. Lopez (eds.) *Health Policy, Social Policy and Mortality Prospects*, Ordina Editions, Liège, Belgium.

Brouard, N., and A. Lopez (1985), 'Cause of death patterns in low mortality countries: a classification analysis', in: *International Population Conference, Florence, 1985*. Vol. 2, International Union for the Scientific Study of Population, Liège, Belgium.

Caldwell, J. C. (1986), 'Routes to low mortality in poor countries', *Population and Development Review*, 12: 171–220.

Centro Latinoamericano de Demografía (CELADE), Ministerio de Salud & Universidad de Costa Rica (1987), *Los Grupos Sociales de Riesgo para la Sobrevida Infantil 1960–1984*, Series A 1049, San José, Costa Rica.

Cervantes, S., and C. Raabe (1991), 'Determinants of the evolution of the health situation of the population', *Scandinavian Journal of Social Medicine*, Supplement 46: 43–52.

Devesa, S. S., and D. T. Silverman (1978), 'Cancer incidence and mortality trends in the United States: 1935–74', *Journal of the National Cancer Institute*, 60: 545–71.

Freedman, R., and J. Y. Takeshita (1969), *Family Planning in Taiwan: An Experiment in Social Change*, Princeton University Press, Princeton.

González-Vega, C. (1985), 'Health improvements in Costa Rica: the socio-economic background', in: S. Halstead, J. Walsh, and K. Warren (eds.) *Good Health at Low*

Cost: Proceedings of a Conference Held at the Bellagio Conference Center, The Rockefeller Foundation, New York.

Hall, C. (1985), *Costa Rica, a Geographic Interpretation in Historical Perspective*, Westview Press, Boulder, Colo.

Hanushek, E. A., and J. E. Jackson (1977), *Statistical Methods for Social Scientists*, Academic Press, Orlando, Fl.

Kleinbaum, D. G., D. G. Kupper, and H. Morgenstern (1982), *Epidemiologic Research*, Van Nostrand Reinhold, New York.

Liker, J. K., S. Augustyniak, and G. J. Duncan (1985), 'Panel data and models of change: a comparison of first difference and conventional two-wave models', *Social Science Research*, 14: 80–101.

Mata, L., and L. Rosero-Bixby (1988), *National Health and Social Development in Costa Rica: A Case Study of Intersectorial Action*, PAHO, Technical Paper No. 13, Washington, DC.

Meslé, F. (1985), 'Evolution des causes de décés dans quelques pays á faible mortalité', in: *International Population Conference, Florence, 1985*, Vol. 2, International Union for the Scientific Study of Population, Liège, Belgium.

Meza-Lago, C. (1985), 'Health care in Costa Rica: boom and crisis', *Social Science and Medicine*, 21: 13–21.

Mohs, E. (1991), 'General theory of paradigms in health', *Scandinavian Journal of Social Medicine*, Supplement 46: 14–24.

Omran, A. R. (1982), 'Epidemiological transition: theory', in: *International Encyclopedia of Population*, The Free Press, New York, 172–83.

Pan American Health Organization (PAHO) (1990), *Health Conditions in the Americas, 1990 Edition*, Vol. I, Scientific Publications 524, Washington, DC.

Preston, S., N. Keyfitz, and R. Schoen (1972), *Causes of Death: Life Tables for National Populations*, Seminar Press, New York.

Ravenholt, R. T. (1990), 'Tobacco's global death march', *Population and Development Review*, 16: 213–40.

Rosero-Bixby, L. (1985a), 'The case of Costa Rica', in: J. Vallin and A. Lopez (eds.) *Health Policy, Social Policy and Mortality Prospects*, Ordina Editions, Liège, Belgium.

——(1985b), 'Infant mortality decline in Costa Rica', in: S. Halstead, J. Walsh, and K. Warren (eds.) *Good Health at Low Cost: Proceedings of a Conference held at the Bellagio Conference Center*, The Rockefeller Foundation, New York.

——(1986), 'Infant mortality in Costa Rica: explaining the recent decline', *Studies in Family Planning*, 17: 57–65.

——(1991a), 'Socioeconomic development, health interventions, and mortality decline in Costa Rica', *Scandinavian Journal of Social Medicine*, Supplement No. 46: 33–42.

——(1991b), *Interaction Diffusion and Fertility Transition in Costa Rica*, Doctoral dissertation, University Microfilms International, University of Michigan, Ann Arbor.

——and H. Caamaño (1984), 'Tablas de vida de Costa Rica 1900–1980', in: *Mortalidad y Fecundidad en Costa Rica* (pp. 7–19), Asociación Demográfica Costarricense, San José, Costa Rica.

——and C. Grimaldo (1987), 'Descriptive epidemiology of cancer of the breast and uterine cervix in Costa Rica', *PAHO Bulletin*, 21: 250–60.

——M. W. Oberle, and N. C. Lee (1987), 'Reproductive history and breast cancer in a population of high fertility, Costa Rica, 1984–5', *International Journal of Cancer*, 40: 747–54.

Rytchtaríková, J., J. Vallin, and F. Meslé (1989), 'Comparative study of mortality trends in France and the Czech Republic since 1950', *Population (English Selection No. 1)*, 44: 291–321.

Saenz, L. (1985), 'Health changes during a decade: the Costa Rican case', in: S. Halstead, J. Walsh, and K. Warren (eds.) *Good Health at Low Cost: Proceedings of a Conference held at the Bellagio Conference Center*, The Rockefeller Foundation, New York.

Vaupel, J. W., K. G. Manton, and E. Stallard (1979), 'The impact of heterogeneity in individual frailty on the dynamics of mortality', *Demography*, 16: 439–54.

Part IV

Causes of Adult Death: Issues for Prevention

10 Epidemiology and Demography of Tuberculosis

CHRISTOPHER MURRAY

Harvard University, Cambridge, Mass. USA

The purpose of this chapter is to bring together the rather disparate lines of research into the demography and epidemiology of tuberculosis and to provide a general picture of the historical decline in tuberculosis and its current levels in developing countries. Tuberculosis is the largest single infectious cause of death in the world (Murray *et al.*, 1990). It has also been at the centre of debate on the historical decline of mortality in Europe and developing countries. Unfortunately, tuberculosis is not only an old disease, it is quite complex and difficult to understand. To work on tuberculosis, it is essential at least to understand the epidemiological approach. Developing an understanding of this approach to tuberculosis is complicated by the near total isolation of tuberculosis specialists even within the public health community. Their unique vocabulary and analytical methods have perpetuated this insular mentality.

This review is timely because there is a widespread resurgence of interest in tuberculosis. This resurgence can be traced to at least three factors: first, with the HIV epidemic tuberculosis has again become a clinical issue in industrialized countries and threatens to become much worse in some developing countries; second, the World Health Organization has taken a lead in tuberculosis control for the first time in nearly two decades; and finally, as part of the World Bank Health Sector Priorities Review, chemotherapy for tuberculosis has been identified as one of the three most cost-effective health sector interventions (Jamison and Mosley, 1991). As part of the new WHO programme on tuberculosis, there will be a substantial operational research effort to which demographers could make an important contribution.

1. Pathogenesis

Some knowledge of the natural history of tuberculosis is required to understand levels and trends in tuberculosis morbidity and mortality. Tuberculosis is caused by the bacillus *Mycobacterium tuberculosis,* which usually attacks the lungs. Infection is most commonly transmitted from cases of pulmonary tuberculosis to other persons, in particular when coughing or sneezing. The most important exception to the airborne route of infection is infection of the digestive tract through contaminated milk containing *Mycobacterium bovis* from cows suffering from tuberculosis, which causes a disease clinically similar to tuberculosis.

If one or more bacilli reach the lung tissue, they can cause a non-specific inflammatory response that may result in a primary complex. The primary complex has two components, one in the lung and the other in the corresponding lymph node(s). Usually, both the primary pulmonary lesions and lesions in lymph nodes heal spontaneously leaving behind a focus of a few 'dormant' bacilli that can be reactivated and cause clinical disease at any moment during an individual's lifetime.

Before the development of allergy and immunity, some bacilli may escape from the primary lesions into the blood stream and set up blood-borne foci in other parts of the body, for example in the kidneys, ends of long bones, spine or brain. In newborn babies and small children, the infection progresses either in the primary site or metastatic foci and serious forms of tuberculosis may develop, in particular miliary tuberculosis and/or tuberculous meningitis. These forms of tuberculosis also occur in adolescents and adults but much less frequently.

Two to six weeks after the primary infection, the body's immune system develops a certain level of cell-mediated immunity to *M. tuberculosis* antigens. This leads to the formation of granulomas around the focus of the bacilli. When these areas become calcified, they may be detected on a chest X-ray. Clinical disease, on the other hand, may occur weeks to years after the primary infection with the bacillus. The key aspect of the natural history of tuberculosis is that infection may lead to clinical disease later. Consequently, the process of elimination of tuberculosis in a community is very slow because the development of latent infections into active tuberculosis (endogenous exacerbation) cannot be prevented completely.

There are four major diagnostic strategies used to detect tuberculous infection and/or clinical disease:

(a) A recently or remotely infected person, whether or not (s)he has clinical disease, develops a certain degree of immune response to *M. tuberculosis* antigen. An injection of tuberculin under the skin will cause a hard lump in 48 to 72 hours. This skin test, the Mantoux test, enables relatively easy detection of the prevalence of tuberculous infection in any population. Studies by Canetti (1939, 1972) indicate that most patients who have been infected and have a positive skin test maintain viable bacilli within their bodies. However, the tuberculin test does not distinguish between recent and remote infections, nor whether the infection was caused by *M. tuberculosis* or *M. bovis* or by another mycobacterium. In spite of these limitations, tuberculin sensitivity surveys in a representative sample of a population are one of the mainstays of tuberculosis epidemiology.

(b) Detection by microscopy of acid-fast bacilli, which are nearly always identical with tubercle bacilli, in sputum and other specimens (e.g. gastric washings) is the most important tool to detect highly infectious cases of tuberculosis. There is strong evidence (Rouillon *et al.*, 1976; Styblo, 1984) that those patients whose sputa contain sufficient bacilli to be detected by microscopy are highly infectious. These cases are referred to as *smear-positive.*

(c) The culture of specimens for mycobacteria detects, in about four to six weeks, tubercle bacilli in sputum containing insufficient bacilli to be detected by microscopy. These cases are then classified as sputum smear-negative but *culture-positive* pulmonary tuberculosis. Patients whose sputum is smear-negative and culture-positive are several times less infectious than smear-positive cases.

(d) In smear- and *culture-negative* patients, particularly children and young adults, diagnosis of tuberculosis is made by clinical examination and interpretation of pathology on chest X-ray.

Extra-pulmonary tuberculosis is diagnosed in some cases by bacteriology (in patients with tuberculous meningitis, lymphadenitis, genito-urinary tuberculosis, etc.) or by histology of biopsy material. Depending on the site of infection, roentgenological and other special examinations are required to diagnose extra-pulmonary tuberculosis. It is important to stress that extra-pulmonary tuberculosis is either non-infectious or the degree of infectivity is very low.

2. Progress from Infection to Disease: 'Breakdown'

Breakdown from infection to disease can be classified into three types. Progressive primary infection is where breakdown occurs within five years of the initial infection. Breakdown after a person who was infected in the distant past is infected again, is called exogenous reinfection. Finally, endogenous reactivation is when a patient develops tuberculosis many years after infection. Prospective studies of breakdown to clinical disease after primary infection (Styblo, 1991; Sutherland, 1976) suggest that about 7 to 10 per cent develop clinical disease over the first seven years after infection. The risk of breakdown appears to be highest in the first year thereafter decreasing exponentially (Sutherland, 1968). Breakdown rates after exogenous reinfection appear to be about 75 per cent lower than after primary infection (Sutherland, 1976). Nevertheless, breakdown after reinfection is much higher than the long-term rate of endogenous reactivation; approximately 25–40 per 100,000 infected break down each year (Styblo, 1991; Sutherland, 1976).

Progression from infection to clinical disease or breakdown depends on the immunological status of the individual. There are at least three recognized risk factors for breakdown relevant to demographic analysis of tuberculosis. The strongest known factor is concurrent infection with HIV (Elliot *et al.*, 1990; Chaisson *et al.*, 1987; Colebunders *et al.*, 1989; Selwyn *et al.*, 1989). Individuals infected with both diseases appear to have an annual breakdown rate between 5 and 10 per cent per year.

The second risk factor for breakdown is related to pregnancy or, at least, the female reproductive period. While women have lower rates of infection in the young adult age groups in virtually every survey (e.g. Roelsgaard *et al.*, 1964; National Tuberculosis Institute, 1974; Narain *et al.*, 1966; Korea, 1985; People's Republic of China, n.d.), the incidence of tuberculosis in young women is equal to that of men or higher. Lower infection rates but higher incidence rates must mean that the breakdown rate for young women is higher than for men. This statistical conclusion is supported by the long-standing clinical observation that pregnancy and tuberculosis are related. Unfortunately, not much research has been undertaken on the patterns of tuberculosis in young women in developing countries.

The third factor that may contribute to an increased rate of breakdown from infection to disease is the individual's nutritional status. Severe malnutrition is known to affect immune function (Scrimshaw *et al.*, 1968; Tomkins and Watson, 1989). Evidence comes from World War II, where tuberculosis rates increased in European countries affected by the war particularly in some special groups, such as in camps (Cochrane, 1948) and in the Warsaw Ghetto (Schechter, 1953). However, a careful controlled demonstration is missing, since crowding, recirculating air and poor sanitation seem at least as important. It is also evident that the case fatality rate for tuberculosis remained unchanged in the USA, England, Denmark, and other developed countries from the turn of the century until the introduction of chemotherapy, despite improvements in nutritional intake—see below. Improvement in nutritional status may alter the probability of developing clinical tuberculosis in those who are infected.

Both the probability of becoming infected and the probability of breakdown after infection to disease are age dependent. The highest rates of infection and apparently of breakdown occur in the young adult age groups, that is 15 to 29 years (Sutherland, 1976). Combined with the typical developing country age structure, this incidence pattern concentrates most tuberculosis in the productive adult ages. Figure 10.1 provides the age distribution of detected smear-positive pulmonary cases in four developing country programmes: more than three-quarters of cases are in adults aged 15 to 59 years.

The clinical spectrum of tuberculosis is thought to be quite constant (Styblo, 1991; Murray *et al.*, 1990). The accepted rules of thumb are that 50 per cent of pulmonary tuberculosis is sputum smear-positive and 50 per cent is sputum smear-negative. Of 100 tuberculosis patients, 15 per cent usually have extra-pulmonary forms. With *M. bovis* infection the clinical spectrum may be shifted to extra-pulmonary forms. Except in rare circumstances, deviations from the expected clinical spectrum are due to poor diagnostic systems.

Without appropriate chemotherapy, tuberculosis is highly fatal. Two types of source provide information on the relationship between disease incidence

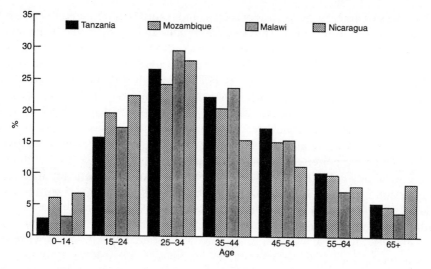

Fig. 10.1. Age-distribution of smear-positive tuberculosis in four developing country programmes

and tuberculosis mortality: data from before chemotherapy was available in developed countries and survey data from South India. First, Drolet (1938) investigated the relationship between the tuberculosis mortality rate and reported incidence in selected American cities from 1915 to 1935. He found that the case-fatality rate for all types of tuberculosis in Detroit and New Jersey was 58.8 per cent and 54.9 per cent respectively. The estimated case-fatality rate varied little during that twenty-year period. Similar case-fatality rates for all forms of tuberculosis were recorded in European countries—Denmark 1925–34: 51.2 per cent (Lindhart, 1939); Norway 1925–44: 50.6 per cent (Galtung Hansen, 1955); and England and Wales 1933–5: 49.1 per cent (Drolet, 1938). The most detailed study is from Berg (1939) who followed 6162 smear-positive cases over periods of up to twenty years. After two years, 40.1 per cent died, increasing to 60.7 per cent at five years and 73.3 per cent at ten years. Berg found that even fifteen to nineteen years after diagnosis, smear-positive patients had mortality rates five times higher than the general population of the same age. Secondly, a five-year study of the natural history of tuberculosis in Bangalore, India, found that 49 per cent of smear-positive and culture positive cases detected on the first round of the survey were dead after five years (National Tuberculosis Institute, 1974; Olakowski, 1973). Taken together, these data suggest that, without treatment, from 50 to 60 per cent of tuberculosis cases die of the disease.

The case-fatality rate for smear-positive cases is thought to be higher than for all forms of tuberculosis combined. Rutledge and Crouch (1919) followed

1229 cases of smear-positive tuberculosis and found that 66 per cent of them were dead after four years. Lindhart (1939) found in Denmark that 66 per cent of cases that were bacteriologically positive died. Berg's (1939) results for smear-positive patients provide the most direct evidence on the higher case-fatality of smear-positive tuberculosis. Higher mortality among smear-positive cases was also shown in the South Indian study (Olakowski, 1973). For the 126 bacillary cases detected in the first round, the death rate was 45.2 per cent at five years in the culture-positive and smear-negative group (62 cases) and 53.1 per cent in the smear-positive group (64 cases). Even X-ray suggestive, culture-negative pulmonary tuberculosis has a considerable mortality rate. In the Bangalore study, the mortality rate after five years for this group was over 30 per cent, more than twice the baseline mortality rate for the population. Case-fatality rates also must be expected to vary between communities due to other factors such as nutrition and concurrent infections.

Thus, the overall transmission dynamics of tuberculosis in the absence of chemotherapy seem extremely stable. Figure 10.2 provides a summary in schematic form. Each 100 smear-positive cases cause about 2000 to 2400 infections over a two-year period. Of these newly-infected people, about 100 will develop smear-positive tuberculosis and 120 will develop smear-negative or extra-pulmonary tuberculosis. Fifty of the 100 smear-positive cases will die and another 50 will die in the smear-negative and extra-pulmonary group. The transmission cycle will begin again as the 100 smear-positives infect another 2000 to 2400 people. To maintain such stable transmission dynamics, the absolute number of smear-positive cases or new infections would have to

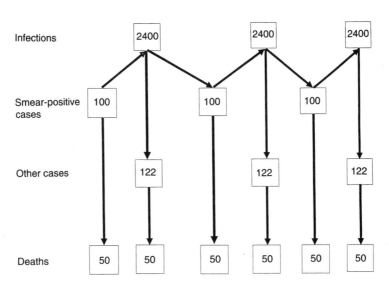

Fig. 10.2. Transmission schematic

remain constant over time. The validity of this assumption is discussed in more detail below.

3. Epidemiology

Since the pioneering work of Styblo and Sutherland (Styblo *et al.*, 1969; Sutherland *et al.*, 1971), the primary tool for monitoring the epidemiological situation of tuberculosis has been the annual risk of infection. The annual risk of infection is 'the proportion of the population that will be primarily infected, or reinfected (in those who have been previously infected) with tubercle bacilli in the course of one year' (Styblo, 1991: p.40). Population surveys with tuberculin skin tests provide data on the prevalence of infection in different age groups. The prevalence of infection at a given age is the cumulative effect of the annual risks of infection since birth. In a manner analogous to estimating child mortality from data on children ever born and children surviving, Styblo and Sutherland developed techniques for estimating the annual risk of infection and its trend from skin test prevalence data.

Analysing annual tuberculin skin test data for Dutch military recruits, they found that the decline in the risk of infection was well approximated by an exponential decay. Before 1940, the annual risk of infection was declining by 5.4 per cent annually; after 1940 the annual decline accelerated to 13 per cent each year (Figure 10.3). Although not shown, the annual risk of infection has continued to decline at a rate over 11 per cent since the 1960s (Sutherland, personal communication).

With a high annual risk of infection, many cases of primary and exogenous reinfection tuberculosis occur especially in young adults. As the annual risk of infection declines, there will be an equally rapid decline in primary and exogenous reinfection cases. Cases due to the endogenous reactivation, in other words cases caused by infections that occurred long ago, will not decline rapidly. As most infected individuals maintain viable bacilli for the rest of their life, cases due to endogenous reactivation decline only as the older cohorts with a higher cumulative infection rate die and are replaced with younger cohorts with lower prevalences of infection. Sutherland and Svandova (1972) used a regression analysis of the incidence in the Netherlands of pulmonary tuberculosis in specific age groups, the proportion newly infected, the proportion with reinfection, and the proportion with distant infection to estimate the proportion of tuberculosis due to progressive primary infection, exogenous reinfection, and endogenous reactivation over time. According to their regression model, the proportion of tuberculosis due to reactivation increases progressively as the risk of infection declines.

With a shift in the proportion of cases due to primary or exogenous reinfection, as opposed to endogenous reactivation, the age distribution of tuberculosis also will change. Primary and exogenous reinfection tuberculosis

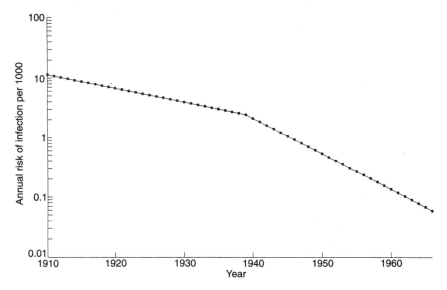

Fig. 10.3. The decline in the annual risk of infection in the Netherlands, 1910–66
Source: Styblo *et al.* 1969.

is characteristically a disease of younger people. In contrast, with an exponentially declining annual risk of infection, older cohorts have much higher rates of infection and thus higher incidence rates of reactivation tuberculosis. The classic shift in the age-pattern of tuberculosis deaths manifested in nearly all industrialized nations is easily understood in these terms. The changing distribution of ages of death with tuberculosis, after adjusting for changes in age-structure, in Chile, is shown in Figure 10.4.

Many demographers may be familiar with the work on the cohort effects in tuberculosis mortality (Collins, 1982; Frost, 1939; Spicer, 1954; Springett, 1950; Stevens and Lee, 1978). Tuberculosis mortality data show a clear cohort effect, where each subsequent birth cohort has lower tuberculosis mortality at each age. This has often been interpreted as the effect of some factor at young age such as nutritional status or accumulated insults due to other diseases. Such life-long effects are not necessary to explain the cohort effect. In Europe, such a cohort effect can be largely explained by an exponentially declining annual risk of infection. The lower mortality in each cohort is due, not only to a lower accumulated prevalence and thus a lower rate of endogenous reactivation, but also to a lower annual risk of infection for each cohort at each particular age and thus lower rates of primary and exogenous reinfection tuberculosis. Figure 10.5 illustrates the estimated prevalence of tuberculosis infection by age for a series of cohorts assuming a 5 per cent decline in the annual risk of infection each year. Most of the cohort effect before chemotherapy must be due to

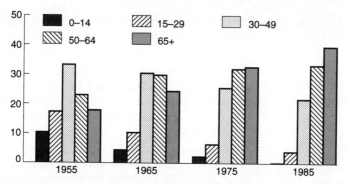

Fig. 10.4. The shifting age-structure of tuberculosis deaths in Chile from 1955–85
Note: Adjusted for age-structure changes.

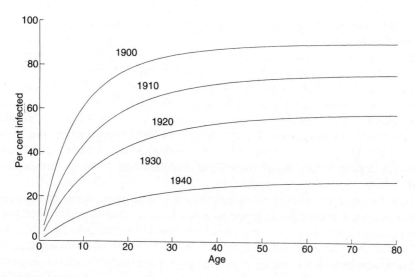

Fig. 10.5. Prevalence of infection by cohort and age with an annual risk of infection decreasing 5% per year

decreased transmission as the data reviewed earlier showed no significant change in case-fatality rates during the first part of this century.

4. Mortality Decline and Tuberculosis

Tuberculosis played a pivotal role in the European mortality decline. McKeown and colleagues (McKeown, 1976*a*, 1976*b*; McKeown and Brown,

1955; McKeown and Record, 1962; McKeown *et al.*, 1975) found that respiratory tuberculosis accounted for 17.5 per cent of mortality decline in England and Wales from 1848–54 to 1971. Preston (1976) analysed an extensive set of cause of death data for most industrialized countries and some developing countries. In the regressions of age-standardized mortality rates, tuberculosis accounted for 11 to 12 per cent of each unit decline in mortality for women and men respectively. Notably the correlation coefficients were 0.86 for women and 0.87 for men. A more recent analysis of cause of death data focused on adults aged 15 to 59 (Murray *et al.*, 1992) also found that tuberculosis mortality is highly correlated with the probability of dying between 15 and 60 years ($_{45}q_{15}$) in men and women. Linear regressions of each cause on total mortality showed that for each unit decline in $_{45}q_{15}$, 19 and 16 per cent were due to tuberculosis in men and women respectively. Only a few other diseases were highly correlated with overall adult mortality levels measured by $_{45}q_{15}$. In other words, there is substantial evidence that tuberculosis is a major contributor to mortality decline and tuberculosis mortality is highly correlated with overall mortality, especially in adults.

From the perspective of tuberculosis epidemiology, we can divide the decline in tuberculosis mortality into a possible direct decrease in the risk of infection and a decrease in the breakdown rate, leading to an indirect decrease in the risk of infection. Direct decreases in the risk of infection could have been due to a decrease in transmission from each smear-positive case, because of improved housing or work conditions with less overcrowding and better ventilation; isolation of the sick so that the number of contacts was substantially decreased; or decreased transmission of *M. bovis* through contaminated milk.

In a steady state, each case of tuberculosis must infect more than twenty other people. Improvements in the degree of overcrowding and ventilation in both the workplace and the home could have decreased the average number of infections per smear-positive case. McFarlane (1989) has argued that the decline of tuberculosis mortality in Glasgow was closely related to improvements in housing.

We know that, during the same period, the sanatorium movement meant that many infectious cases were isolated from the rest of the community. The impact of isolation either at home or in sanatoria depends on how soon after the onset of infectiousness the patient is isolated from the rest of the community and what percentage of the time (s)he is isolated. The public health impact of sanatoria has remained controversial (Smith, 1988; Bryder, 1988; McFarlane, 1989). Evidence that sanatoria were ineffective in decreasing transmission is often extremely weak. Data from one or two hospitals have been used to try to show that only advanced cases were admitted, or that many patients did not like the surroundings and left. The fact remains that a considerable share of smear-positive patients spent many years in sanatoria isolated from the community. Transmission would have been higher if they had not been isolated.

In some European countries, such as the Netherlands, *M. bovis* played a significant role in tuberculosis. For example, the frequency of mesenteric primary tuberculous foci decreased, indicating a substantial decline in enterogenic infections (Styblo, 1991). In fact, the number of cases of tuberculosis due to peritoneal tuberculosis was higher than pulmonary tuberculosis in England and Wales until around the turn of the century. Improvements in milk supply may have contributed to the decline in the risk of *M. bovis* infection. The impact of decreasing exposure to *M. bovis* on the trends in pulmonary tuberculosis remain unclear.

Alternatively, a decline in the annual risk of infection and thus tuberculosis mortality could have been due to a decrease in the breakdown rate. First, general resistance to disease could have improved because of the decline of other infectious diseases, especially those contracted in childhood. Such non-specific theories of general insult accumulation are not persuasive without identification of more specific biological pathways through which they may act. Mortality analysis by cohort, however, shows that such effects may well exist for overall mortality. As discussed in the previous section, cohort effects in tuberculosis mortality can be explained by declining annual risks of infection without invoking a change in the breakdown rate.

Second, rising food intake per head could have improved nutritional status and resistance to disease. The strongest advocate of the link between nutritional status and tuberculosis has been McKeown. The explanation of the decline in tuberculosis mortality in Europe is central to the McKeown thesis (1976a) that rising living standards, essentially improved per capita food intake, were largely responsible for mortality decline. McKeown argued that 38.5 per cent of the decline was due to airborne infections and could only have been brought about by improved resistance due to better nutritional status. Szreter (1988), in a powerful critique of McKeown's nutrition thesis, has reminded us that 7.5 percentage points of decline were attributable to scarlet fever and smallpox, both of which were probably unrelated to improving nutritional status. Of the remaining decline in airborne infectious diseases, 6.5 percentage points of decline were due to 'other' diseases, 17.5 due to respiratory tuberculosis and 7.0 to bronchitis, pneumonia and influenza. Most of the remaining decline in mortality was attributable to respiratory tuberculosis. If tuberculosis declined due to other factors, much of the support for the McKeown thesis is eroded.

There is insufficient evidence to accept or reject the McKeown thesis as applied to tuberculosis. Severe malnutrition is thought to contribute to increased breakdown but the importance of mild malnutrition and, by inference, rising food intake is unknown. One might expect that improving nutrition could contribute to a lower case-fatality rate as well as a lower breakdown rate depending on the mechanisms through which nutrition affects cellular immunity. However, no change in the case-fatality rate was observed before the introduction of chemotherapy. To explain the rather consistent decline in the risk of infection over time, food intake per head would have had to have increased at a steady rate throughout the period. Economic growth over this period, however, was far from constant.

Finally, tuberculosis may be like scarlet fever, an epidemic that is 'burning itself out' through natural selection of the host or the bacillus. Neither the natural selection nor the nutrition thesis are appealing hypotheses. Without further empirical data, one cannot refute a rational case for any of these possibilities. One cannot, however, argue that the *only* possibility is improving nutritional status.

What has been the contribution of BCG immunization to tuberculosis mortality decline? BCG only became commercially available after 1920. The effectiveness of BCG in preventing tuberculosis in prospective clinical trials and case-control studies has ranged from 0 per cent to 80 per cent (Aronson *et al.*, 1958; Great Britain, 1972; Smith, 1987; Clemens *et al.*, 1983). Styblo and Meijer (1976) illustrated that, even where BCG is effective, it will have little or no impact on the epidemiology of the disease. BCG is given at birth in most countries. While indiscriminate adult revaccination is performed in a few European countries, the British MRC trial (1972) showed that BCG has no protective effect beyond fifteen years. As children are rarely smear-positive and do not contribute substantially to transmission, BCG will have little or no effect on continued transmission in the community. In those communities where BCG is effective, it may contribute to the decline of tuberculosis mortality in the population aged under 15. The decline in the risk of infection after 1920, however, cannot be attributed to BCG immunization.

5. Tuberculosis in Developing Countries

Cauthen *et al.* (1988) reviewed all available risk of infection data for developing countries (Table 10.1). In South America, the risk of infection ranges from 0.5 per cent or less in countries such as Venezuela or Chile to 1.5 per cent or more in Bolivia and Peru. The annual risk of infection is declining at a rate of 2 to 5 per cent per year in South America but by less than 2 per cent in many developing countries of Africa and Asia. There were almost no examples of increasing risks of infection between two surveys. Allowing for population growth, the absolute number of smear-positive tuberculosis patients would be constant or slightly increasing. The assumptions in the transmission schematic (Figure 10.2) are thus a reasonably close approximation of the truth in most of the developing world.

Murray *et al.* (1990) use these figures by regions to estimate the morbidity and mortality from tuberculosis based on the known epidemiological pattern of the disease. Revised estimates of the burden of tuberculosis are presented

Table 10.1. Estimated risks of tuberculosis infection in developing countries, 1985–90

Area	Annual risk of infection (%)	Annual decrease in risk (%)
Sub-Saharan Africa	1.5–2.5	1–2
North Africa and Western Asia	0.5–1.5	4–5
Asia	1.0–2.0	1–3
South America	0.5–1.5	2–5
Central America and Caribbean	0.5–1.5	1–3

Source: Cauthen *et al.* (1988), Murray *et al.* (1990).

here based on the same methodology. In brief, there is a strong relationship between incidence of smear-positive tuberculosis and the annual risk of infection as long as the annual risk is greater than 0.5 per cent. At lower risks, endogenous reactivation begins to predominate, so that there is a weaker correspondence between the annual incidence and the risk of infection. Using this relationship, estimates of the incidence of smear-positive tuberculosis were generated; these were multiplied for specific age groups by the expected relationship between smear-positive tuberculosis and total tuberculosis.

The close relationship between HIV infection and clinical tuberculosis that has been observed widely will substantially affect the predicted incidence of clinical tuberculosis in regions with high levels of HIV sero-positivity. Using the most recent estimates of country specific sero-prevalence for sub-Saharan Africa provided by the World Health Organization, we estimate that there were approximately 4.9 million HIV sero-positive individuals in sub-Saharan Africa in 1985–90. Using estimates of the prevalence of tuberculosis infection in the region, there are approximately 2.1 million patients with dual HIV and tuberculosis infections. Individuals with dual infections have much higher rates of breakdown from infection to clinical disease (Selwyn *et al.*, 1989). A range for the annual breakdown rate in dually infected individuals of 5 to 10 per cent has been used to estimate that an additional 105,000–210,000 cases of tuberculosis occur each year in sub-Saharan Africa. If sero-prevalence continues to rise, the tuberculosis burden attributable to the HIV epidemic will also rise. For these estimates, we assume the same clinical spectrum between smear-positive and other tuberculosis for HIV positive patients (Chaisson and Slutkin, 1989).

The annual incidence of 7.3 million total cases and 3.3 million smear-positive cases leads to substantial mortality (Table 10.2). By estimating the percentage of patients receiving treatment and thus suffering lower mortality, mortality attributable to tuberculosis was estimated to be 2.7 million deaths per year. Based again on the age-distribution of cases, the known relationship between the case-fatality rate and age and an assumption that all ages are

Table 10.2. Estimated annual incidence of smear-positive tuberculosis, total tuberculosis, and deaths from tuberculosis in developing countries, 1985–90 (in thousands)

Area	New smear-positive cases	New cases (all forms)	Deaths
Sub-Saharan Africa	591	1313	586
North Africa and Western Asia	146	323	91
Asia	2298	5102	1825
South America	160	356	111
Central America and Caribbean	83	185	80
Total	3279	7280	2692

Source: Murray *et al.* (1990).

equally likely to be detected, more than three-quarters of these deaths are in adults aged 15 to 54 years. This is more than was estimated for adults in the World Bank adult health project (Murray *et al.*, 1992). The discrepancy could be due to four possibilities. First, routine cause of death data may underestimate mortality from tuberculosis. Second, the epidemiological model may overestimate total tuberculosis mortality. Third, the estimated age-distribution for tuberculosis deaths based on cases detected in African control programmes may overestimate the percentage of deaths in prime-aged adults. This is a likely possibility as younger patients may be more willing and perhaps more able to seek treatment than older patients. Finally, the relationship between tuberculosis $_{45}q_{15}$ and total $_{45}q_{15}$ is curvilinear. To estimate a consistent set of cause of death estimates for each level of mortality, linear equations had to be used. At higher levels of adult mortality, the linear regression equation underestimates tuberculosis and other infectious disease mortality.

While tuberculosis declined steadily by 5 to 6 per cent annually in Europe before chemotherapy was introduced, a similar rate of decline is not evident in most developing countries. Interventions are available that can accelerate the decline in the risk of infection. The limited role of BCG has been discussed, but chemotherapy of smear-positive patients can accelerate the decline in the risk of infection. A striking illustration of the effectiveness of case detection and treatment is provided by the Inuit (Gryzybowski *et al.*, 1976). The risk of infection was in excess of 25 per cent per year. With the introduction of an aggressive case detection and treatment programme, the annual incidence of smear-positive tuberculosis in Greenland declined from 208 per 100,000 in 1955–6 to 8.7 per 100,000 in 1972–4. This represents an annual decline in incidence of 17 per cent. This decrease in tuberculosis occurred in all age groups, not just at young ages. Thus tuberculosis control efforts can substantially accelerate the decline in tuberculosis.

Studies of the national tuberculosis programmes in Malawi, Mozambique, and Tanzania show that short-course chemotherapy for smear-positive tuberculosis is among the most cost-effective health interventions available (Murray *et al.*, 1990, 1992; Jamison and Mosley, 1991). In a low-income country, short-course chemotherapy costs between US $1 and $4 per discounted year of life saved. Tuberculosis continues to be a major cause of death in developing countries, but, fortunately, a cost-effective solution is available that can work in even the most difficult circumstances. We do not need to wait for socio-economic development to have a major impact on tuberculosis morbidity and mortality.

6. Conclusion

Tuberculosis remains an enormous problem in developing countries. It is unique among the world's great killer diseases, in that it is concentrated in adults. The impact of tuberculosis on the welfare of households is likely to be great because of this age-distribution but has been little studied so far. Because of the transmission dynamics of tuberculosis, prompt detection and appropriate treatment of smear-positive cases can accelerate the decline in the incidence of tuberculosis infection and disease. Studies have shown that short-course chemotherapy in well-managed programmes can be cost effective. Wider application of these proven methods of tuberculosis control would have significant benefits for the developing world.

References

Aronson, J., C. Aronson, and H. Taylor (1958), 'A 20-year appraisal of BCG vaccination in the control of tuberculosis', *Archives of Internal Medicine*, 101: 881–93.

Berg, G. (1939), 'The prognosis of open pulmonary tuberculosis. A clinical-statistical analysis', *Acta Tuberculosea Scandinavica* Supplement IV.

Bryder, L. (1988), *Below the Magic Mountain*, Clarendon Press, Oxford.

Canetti, G. (1939), *Les Réinfections tuberculeuses latentes du poumon*, Vigot Edit., Paris, France.

——(1972), 'Endogenous reactivation and exogenous reinfection. Their relative importance with regard to development of non-primary tuberculosis', *Bulletin of the International Union Against Tuberculosis*, 47: 116–22.

Cauthen, G. M., A. Pio, and H. G. ten Dam (1988), *Annual Risk of Tuberculous Infection*, WHO/TB/88.154, Geneva, Switzerland.

Chaisson, R. E., G. F. Schecter, C. P. Theuer, G. W. Rutherford, D. F. Echenberg, and P. C. Hopewell (1987), 'Tuberculosis in patients with the acquired immunodeficiency syndrome', *American Review of Respiratory Disease*, 136: 570–74.

——and G. Slutkin (1989), 'Tuberculosis and human immunodeficiency virus infection', *Journal of Infectious Diseases*, 159: 96–100.

Clemens, J. D., J. J. H. Chung, and A. R. Feinstein (1983), 'The BCG controversy. A methodological and statistical reappraisal', *Journal of the American Medical Association*, 249: 2362–9.

Cochrane, A. L. (1948), 'Tuberculosis among prisoners of war in Germany', *British Medical Journal*, 2: 656.

Colebunders, R., R. Ryder, N. Nzilambi *et al.* (1989), 'HIV infection in patients with tuberculosis in Kinshasa, Zaire', *American Review of Respiratory Disease*, 139: 1082–5.

Collins, J. J. (1982), 'The contribution of medical measures to the decline of mortality from respiratory tuberculosis: an age-period-cohort model', *Demography*, 19: 409–27.

Drolet, G. J. (1938), 'Present trend of case fatality rates in tuberculosis', *American Review of Tuberculosis*, 37: 125–51.

Elliott, A. M., N. Luo, G. Tembo, B. Halwiindi, G. Steenbergen, L. Machiels, J. Pobee, P. Nunn, R. J. Hayes, and K. P. W. J. McAdam (1990), 'Impact of HIV on tuberculosis in Zambia: a cross sectional study', *British Medical Journal*, 302: 412–15.

Frost, W. H. (1939), 'The age selection of mortality from tuberculosis in successive decades', *American Journal of Hygiene*, 30: 91–6.

Galtung Hansen, O. (1955), *Tuberculosis Mortality and Morbidity and Tuberculin Sensitivity in Norway*, World Health Organization, European Regional Office, Copenhagen, Denmark.

Great Britain Medical Research Council (1972), 'BCG and vole bacillus vaccines in the prevention of tuberculosis in adolescence and early life', *Bulletin of the World Health Organization*, 46: 371–85.

Grzybowski, S., K. Styblo, and E. Dorken (1976), 'Tuberculosis in Eskimos', *Tubercule*, 57 (supplement 4): 1–58.

Jamison, D. H., and W. H. Mosley (1991), 'Selecting disease control priorities in developing countries: health policy responses to epidemiological change', *American Journal of Public Health*, 81: 15–22.

Korea, Ministry of Health and Social Affairs and Korean National Tuberculosis Association (1985), *Report on the 5th Tuberculosis Prevalence Survey in Korea*, Ministry of Health and Social Affairs, Seoul, Korea.

Lindhart, M. (1939), *The Statistics of Pulmonary Tuberculosis in Denmark, 1925–1934. A Statistical Investigation on the Occurrence of Pulmonary Tuberculosis in the Period 1925–1934, Worked Out on the Basis of the Danish National Health Service File of Notified Cases and of Deaths*, Ejnar Munkshaard, Copenhagen, Denmark.

McFarlane, N. (1989), 'Hospitals, housing and tuberculosis in Glasgow, 1911–51', *Social History of Medicine*, 2: 59–85.

McKeown, T. (1976*a*), *The Modern Rise of Population*, Edward Arnold, London.

——(1976*b*), *The Role of Medicine: Dream, Mirage or Nemesis*, Nuffield Hospitals Trust, London.

——and R. G. Brown (1955), 'Medical evidence related to English population changes in the eighteenth century', *Population Studies*, 9: 119–41.

——and R. G. Record (1962), 'Reasons for the decline of mortality in England and Wales during the nineteenth century', *Population Studies*, 16: 94–122.

—— ——and R. D. Turner (1975), 'An interpretation of the decline of mortality in England and Wales during the twentieth century', *Population Studies*, 29: 391–422.

Murray, C. J. L., K. Styblo, and A. Rouillon (1990), 'Tuberculosis in developing countries: burden, cost and intervention', *Bulletin of the International Union Against Tuberculosis and Lung Disease*, 65: 6–26.

—— Ganghuan Yang and Xinjian Qiao (1992), 'Adult mortality: levels, patterns and causes', in: R. G. A. Feachem, T. Kjellstrom, C. J. L. Murray, M. Over, and M. A. Phillips (eds.) *The Health of Adults in the Developing World*, Oxford University Press, New York.

Narain, R., S. S. Nair, R. Rao, and P. Chandrasekhar (1966), 'Distribution of tuberculous infection and disease among households in a rural community', *Bulletin of the World Health Organization*, 34: 639–54.

National Tuberculosis Institute, Bangalore (1974), 'Tuberculosis in a rural population of India: a five-year epidemiological study', *Bulletin of the World Health Organization*, 51: 473–88.

Olakowski, T. (1973), *Assignment Report on a Tuberculosis Longitudinal Survey, National Tuberculosis Institute, Bangalore*, World Health Organization Project: India 0103, SEA/TB/129, Regional Office for South East Asia. Published in Geneva.

People's Republic of China, Ministry of Public Health (no date), *Nationwide Random Survey for the Epidemiology of Tuberculosis in 1984/85*, Ministry of Public Health, Beijing, China.

Preston, S. H. (1976), *Mortality Patterns in National Populations*, Academic Press, New York.

Roelsgaard, E., E. Iversen, and C. Blocher (1964), 'Tuberculosis in tropical Africa. An epidemiological study', *Bulletin of the World Health Organization*, 30: 459–518.

Rouillon, A., S. Perdrizet, and R. Parrot (1976), 'Transmission of tubercelle bacilli: the effects of chemotherapy', *Tubercule*, 57: 275–99.

Rutledge, C. J. A., and J. B. Crouch (1919), 'The ultimate results in 1,694 cases of tuberculosis treated at the Modern Woodmen of America Sanatorium', *American Review of Tuberculosis*, 2: 755–63.

Schechter, M. (1953), 'Health and sickness in times of starvation and food shortage', *Harofe Haivri*, 2: 191.

Scrimshaw, N. S., C. E. Taylor, and J. E. Gordon (1968), *Interactions of Nutrition and Infection*, World Health Organization, Geneva, Switzerland.

Selwyn, P. A., D. Harterl, V. A. Lewis, *et al.* (1989), 'A prospective study of the risk of tuberculosis among intravenous drug users with human immunodeficiency virus infection', *New England Journal of Medicine*, 320: 545–50.

Smith, F. B. (1988), *The Retreat of Tuberculosis: 1850–1950*, Croom Helm, London.

Smith, P. G. (1987), 'Case-control studies of the efficacy of BCG against tuberculosis', in: *XXVIth IUAT World Conference on Tuberculosis and Respiratory Diseases; Singapore, 4–7 November 1986*, Professional Postgraduate Services.

Spicer, C. C. (1954), 'The generation method of analysis applied to mortality from respiratory tuberculosis', *Journal of Hygiene*, 52: 361–8.

Springett, V. H. (1950), 'A comparative study of tuberculosis mortality rates', *Journal of Hygiene*, 48: 361–95.

Stevens, R. G., and J. A. H. Lee (1978), 'Tuberculosis: generation effects and chemotherapy', *American Journal of Epidemiology*, 107: 120–6.

Styblo, K. (1984), 'Epidemiology of Tuberculosis', in: G. Meissner *et al.* (eds.) *Infektionskrankheiten und ihre Erreger. Mykobakteria und mykobakteriellen Krankheiten*. Vol. 4 *Jena*, Gustav Fischer Verlag.

Styblo, K. (1991), *Epidemiology of Tuberculosis*, Royal Netherlands Tuberculosis Association Selected Papers, Vol. 24, The Hague, Netherlands.

——and J. Meijer (1976), 'Impact of BCG vaccination programmes in children and young adults on the tuberculosis problem', *Tubercule*, 57: 17–43.

—— ——and I. Sutherland (1969), 'The transmission of tubercle bacilli: its trend in a human population', *Bulletin of the International Union against Tuberculosis*, 42.

Sutherland, I. (1968), 'The ten year incidence of clinical tuberculosis following "conversion" in 2,550 individuals aged 14 to 19 years', TSRU Progress Report, KNCV, The Hague, Netherlands.

——(1976), 'Recent studies in the epidemiology of tuberculosis based on the risk of being infected with tubercle bacilli', *Advances in Tuberculosis Research*, 19: 1–63.

——K. Styblo, M. Sampalik, and M. A. Bleiker (1971), 'Risques annuels d'infection tuberculeuse dans 14 pays d'après les résultats d'enquêtes tuberculiniques effectivées de 1948 à 1952', *Bulletin of the International Union against Tuberculosis*, 45: 75–96.

——and E. Svandova (1972), 'Endogenous reactivation and exogenous reinfection: their relative importance with regard to the development of non-primary tuberculosis', *Bulletin of the International Union Against Tuberculosis*, 47: 123–4.

Szreter, S. (1988), 'The importance of social intervention in Britain's mortality decline, 1850–1914: a reinterpretation', *Social History of Medicine*, 1: 1–37.

Tomkins, A., and F. Watson (1989), *Malnutrition and Infection: A Review*, Administrative Committee on Coordination/Sub-Committee on Nutrition, Nutrition Policy Discussion Paper No. 5, United Nations, New York.

11 Malaria Mortality in Brazil

DIANA OYA SAWYER

Universidade Federal de Minas Gerais, Belo Horizonte, Brazil

1. An Overview of Malaria in the Americas

There are currently twenty-one countries in the Americas with active and continuous malaria control programmes. They will be referred to as malaria transmitting countries (MTC). The annual number of cases of the disease reported in 1990–1 in the MTC was 1,077,278, which represents an annual parasitological index (API) of 2.67 per 1000 inhabitants. That API, compared with an API of 1.32 in 1970, indicates the increasing seriousness of the situation regarding malaria transmission (PAHO/WHO, 1992). The pace of growth in malaria for the MTC overall is shown more clearly in Table 11.1. The number of cases notified annually increased from 332,600 around 1970 to 1,077,278 in 1990–1, which represents an annual growth rate of 5.9 per cent, whereas these countries' population increased at a rate of 2.4 per cent.

Breaking down the MTC into regions and countries, using the regional classification proposed by the Pan American Health Organization (PAHO), the diversity of the pattern of increase in malaria is clear. El Salvador and Costa Rica are two countries where the number of malaria cases has decreased in recent decades. The former had a rising tendency from the mid-1960s until 1980, when the opposite trend developed. In the 1980s there was a spectacular decrease in the number of cases. While the number of cases in 1970 represented 12 per cent of all cases in the MTC, in 1990–1 it represented only 0.9 per cent. According to PAHO this reflects a successful example of an integrated and diversified control programme (PAHO/WHO, 1992). In contrast, Belize in Middle America; Brazil, French Guyana, Guyana in the Amazon Region; and Peru in the Andean Region had a malaria case growth rate of above 10 per cent. It is worth noting that the population growth rates of these countries were all below 3 per cent. The regional distribution of cases has also changed. In 1970, 26.8 per cent of the MTC population was living in Middle America and this region generated 50.1 per cent of all cases. By 1990, cases had become concentrated in the Amazon Region, where 35.6 per cent of the MTC population experienced 55.6 per cent of the cases.

The diversity of the case distribution within countries is an important factor to take into account if one is to obtain an accurate picture of the malaria

Table 11.1.   Per cent distributions and growth rates of the population and of malaria cases in countries with malaria control programmes in the Americas

Region/ country	Population		Notified cases of malaria[a]		Annual growth rate	
	1970	1990	1970	1990	Population	Malaria
Middle America						
Belize	0.05	0.05	0.01	0.29	2.11	23.07
Costa Rica	0.69	0.75	0.13	0.09	2.79	3.81
El Salvador	1.41	1.30	11.99	0.88	1.98	−7.20
Guatemala	2.10	2.28	2.99	3.91	2.78	7.22
Honduras	1.05	1.27	11.30	4.60	3.33	1.38
Mexico	20.19	21.96	15.69	6.76	2.79	1.67
Nicaragua	0.73	0.96	6.88	3.80	3.74	2.90
Panama	0.60	0.60	1.16	0.04	2.37	−11.28
Total	26.81	29.17	50.13	20.35	2.79	1.37
Caribbean						
Dominican Republic	1.62	1.78	0.06	0.08	2.84	7.35
Haiti	1.69	1.61	2.71	1.30	2.15	2.21
Total	3.30	3.39	2.76	1.38	2.50	2.39
Amazon						
Brazil	37.10	35.20	19.23	52.81	2.11	10.93
French Guyana	0.02	0.02	0.03	0.57	2.95	20.81
Guyana	0.28	0.26	0.01	2.02	1.91	34.19
Suriname	0.15	0.10	0.33	0.15	0.41	2.03
Total	37.55	35.58	19.60	55.55	2.10	11.09
Andean						
Bolivia	1.96	1.81	1.94	2.09	1.97	6.25
Colombia	8.17	7.89	9.43	9.27	2.19	5.79
Ecuador	2.37	2.67	8.87	4.41	2.96	2.38
Peru	5.36	5.54	1.18	2.83	2.54	10.25
Venezuela	4.09	4.89	4.78	3.64	3.26	4.52
Total	21.96	22.80	26.20	22.24	2.56	5.06
Southern Cone						
Argentina	9.46	8.01	0.09	0.15	1.54	8.77
Paraguay	0.92	1.06	1.22	0.32	3.10	−0.80
Total	10.37	9.07	1.30	0.47	1.70	0.80
Total	251,111[b]	403,463[b]	332,600	1,077,278	2.37	5.88

[a] Notified cases of malaria were averaged for 1969–71 and 1990–1.
[b] In thousands.

Source: PAHO/WHO (1992). Population for Brazil is adjusted.

situation in the MTC. In some countries the whole population lives in malaria transmitting areas. On the other hand, elsewhere only a small portion of the population is at risk. In particular, in Brazil only 8.5 per cent of the population is at risk (Table 11.2). Considering only the population in malarious areas, the malaria incidence rate for 1990 can be as high as 6.6 per 1000 (French Guyana). Belize, Guatemala, Honduras, Nicaragua, Brazil, French Guyana, and Guyana have malaria incidence rates above 1 per 1000 (Table 11.2). Considering only malarious areas emphasizes the high concentration of cases in Amazonia. As only 9.2 per cent of the region's population is from malaria-transmitting areas, less than 10 per cent of the MTC population generated about 55 per cent of all cases of malaria. Special attention should be directed to Brazil within the Amazon Region, as it accounts for 52.8 per cent of all cases in the twenty-one countries.

Although notified numbers and statistics of malaria control programme inputs are relatively abundant, very little is known about case-fatality or malaria death rates in the region. An account of deaths is not part of routine malaria control programme activities and the vital statistics system is not very reliable in most of these countries. Brazil has the largest malarious area in the Amazon Region. To a large extent, what happens to malaria prevalence in the Brazilian Amazon determines this region's profile. To some extent it shapes the profile of the Americas. This chapter focuses on some aspects of high internal migration to the Brazilian Amazon which have led to an increase in the number of cases of the disease and on the estimation of the malaria mortality, which is believed to be low compared with the African and Asian situations.

2. The Case of Brazil

The number of malaria cases in Brazil has been increasing steadily since the early 1960s. The average number of cases annually in 1990–1 was 568,958. Compared with the 1970s, this represents an annual increase of 10.9 per cent and is five times the national population growth in the same period. The picture is more striking if we examine the regional distribution of those cases. Currently, 90 per cent of reported cases are concentrated in Amazonia, where the number of reported cases grew at an annual rate of 16 per cent but population increase was 4.9 per cent. Within the region, the API is highest in the settlement projects in Rondônia and the gold mining areas in the southern parts of the state of Pará (Marques, 1987).

The increase in the prevalence of malaria parallels the massive migration of population to the area. A vast network of roads has been constructed in recent decades connecting both areas within the region and the region to the highly urbanized and industrialized southern part of Brazil. During the late 1960s and 1970s, direct incentives were given by the state to attract agricultural capital

Table 11.2. Population of malarial areas; percentage of each country's population in malarial areas; per cent distribution by country of the population of malarial areas (%) and central notified malaria rate (per 100,000), countries with malaria control programmes, 1990

Region/ country	Population of malarial areas	Proportion of the country's population	Distribution of the population of malarial areas	Central malaria incidence rate
Middle America				
Belize	183	100.00	0.12	1726
Costa Rica	835	27.69	0.57	111
El Salvador	4,727	90.00	3.20	200
Guatemala	3,429	37.28	2.32	1227
Honduras	4,620	89.92	3.13	1072
Mexico	40,000	45.15	27.07	182
Nicaragua	3,871	100.00	2.62	1056
Panama	2,325	96.15	1.57	17
Total	59,990	50.98	40.60	366
Caribbean				
Dominican Republic	7,127	99.40	4.82	11
Haiti	5,360	82.41	3.63	262
Total	12,487	91.32	8.45	119
Amazon				
Brazil	12,000[a]	8.45	8.12	4741
French Guyana	92	100.00	0.06	6627
Guyana	768	73.85	0.52	2832
Suriname	302	74.94	0.20	548
Total	13,162	9.17	8.91	4547
Andean				
Bolivia	2,645	36.16	1.79	852
Colombia	22,555	70.89	15.27	443
Ecuador	6,250	57.97	4.23	760
Peru	7,199	32.24	4.87	424
Venezuela	15,519	78.63	10.50	253
Total	54,168	58.89	36.66	442
Southern Cone				
Argentina	4,241	13.12	2.87	39
Paraguay	3,706	86.65	2.51	93
Total	7,947	21.71	5.38	64
Total	147,754	36.62	100.00	729

[a] From Demographic Census.
Source: PAHO/WHO (1992).

and labour. Taxes and credit incentives, optimistic predictions for ranching, the low price of land (the land price differential between the region and the South was about 1:1000), and discovery of timber and mineral resources attracted many investors from the South.

Small-scale farmers were attracted either to the new open areas or to the state-sponsored colonization projects. These new migrants are part of a large population surplus that originated first in the very unequal land tenure system of Brazil and, second, in the recent shifting of crops from coffee and rice to soybean, that liberated many workers in the well-established agricultural areas. Because of lack of capital and credit, insecurity about land tenure, high transportation costs, and uncertainty about prices, among many other problems, these small-scale farmers settled on a temporary basis. Very few have permanent crops and they do not invest in land improvement. Instead, they adopt shifting agriculture, with constant encroachment on new forest areas (Sawyer, 1990). In addition, extraction of natural resources, mainly timber and minerals, received some incentives from the State, leading large corporations and small itinerant independent panners to penetrate into the forest for prospecting and extraction.

Thus, the last decades have been characterized by the arrival of a highly mobile, non-immune population engaged in activities which bring them into intense and quasi-permanent contact with the habitat of *A. darlingi*, the main species of the mosquito vector which breeds in fresh and undisturbed water with the forest as a natural shelter. Some common features of the malaria transmission conditions in this frontier area, termed by Sawyer (1988) 'frontier malaria', are:

(a) Vector contact features: high vector density, intense exposure to vectors, and outdoor transmission;

(b) Population features: low immunity, limited knowledge of the disease, high morbidity and low fatality, high proportion of falciparum malaria, high spatial mobility and political marginality;

(c) Institutional features: difficulty of conventional control measures and weak presence of other institutions (Sawyer, 1988).

The states of Rondônia, Acre, Amazonas, Amapá, Pará, and Roraima of the Northern Region are regrouped for this study into Rondônia, Pará, and other states. It is in Rondônia that many of the state-sponsored colonization projects were initiated and it has been one of the most malaria-prevalent states. In 1985, Rondônia was responsible for 42.1 per cent of the malaria in Brazil. In the state of Pará there is a high concentration of mining activities, especially panning for gold.

Results from surveys of the socio-economic and environmental conditions affecting malaria transmission and control, conducted in southern Pará and in a state-sponsored colonization project in Machadinho, have shown that in southern Pará, in 1984, gold miners had a malaria prevalence rate of 1265 malaria-months per 1000 population per year, compared with 722 for those with rural occupations, 248 for those with urban occupations and 158 for the inactive. Residents aged over 15 years had a prevalence rate six times higher than those aged under four years (Fernandez and Sawyer, 1988). After controlling for other socio-economic and environmental variables, those adult males engaged in gold mining had a prevalence rate twice as high as the average. Machadinho, with a more homogeneous population, exhibited less striking differentials, although the overall prevalence of malaria was much higher (Sawyer and Monte-Mor, 1992).

The conditions of malaria transmission in these non-immune populations living and working in extremely high risk areas would suggest a high mortality rate. However, one of the most commonly cited features of frontier malaria in Brazil is its low fatality, which implies low mortality rates. Studies have shown that the overall malaria mortality rate in Brazil did not increase between 1979 and 1982, but fluctuated around 5 to 6.5 per 100,000, and that lethality decreased in this period from 10 to 5 deaths per 1000 cases (Ministério da Saúde, 1985). These are very low figures but, as no other study has been published on this subject, very little more is known about the level and regional and age differentials in malaria mortality. The lack of reliable death statistics, especially in the Amazon Region, is one of the major constraints that has prevented researchers investigating this subject. This chapter represents an initial approach to a more systematic presentation of the data on deaths from malaria.

In areas of high immigration with an incoming population with low immunity, we would expect malaria mortality to follow the migrant's disease exposure pattern. In Pará, where a large number of male adult migrants engage in extractive activities, high male adult mortality rates should prevail compared with the overall, all-cause mortality pattern. In Rondônia, where the colonization projects attracted family migration, the malaria mortality pattern should be less concentrated by age and sex.

3. Data and Methods

Since 1977, the Ministry of Health has published mortality statistics for Brazil at the state and capital city levels. The publications provide data on number of deaths by age group, gender, and cause of death. The Ministry also publishes the number of municipalities and the estimated population covered by the vital statistics system in each state. Systematic malaria mortality statistics have been available since 1979 for the states of the Northern Region. The published data from 1979 to 1985 are used to estimate central death rates from malaria for the years of 1980, 1982, and 1984, according to gender in selected age groups, for Rondônia, Pará, and the other states of the Northern Region. These years correspond to a period when malaria cases were increasing rapidly. Unfortunately reliable data are not available for the 1970s, when malaria prevalence started to rise.

One of the major problems in using vital statistics data in Brazil, with a few exceptions, is that they are unreliable because of a considerable degree of under- and misreporting. For example, according to the official reports, only ninety-eight out of the 169 municipalities of the Northern Region were sending information to the vital statistics system in 1984. The estimated proportion of population covered was 79 per cent for the region: 77 per cent for Pará; 96 per cent for Rondônia and 76 per cent for the other states of the region.

The degree of under-reporting of deaths by gender for the region in 1980, according to the growth balance method of estimation, is 16 per cent for males and 20 per cent for females (Martin and Jardim, 1988). Misreporting of the underlying cause of death is also very frequent, either because of ignorance of the proper procedure for filling in death certificates or because the death was not preceded by adequate medical assistance. Lima and Silva (n.d.) carried out a study of malaria death reporting in hospitals and health units in Rondônia in 1985 and found 27.5 per cent under-reporting for the state, with variations by gender and age. Instead of malaria, coma, renal insufficiency, and 'ill-defined' were frequently indicated as the underlying cause of death.

Assuming that the degree of under-reporting by age and sex are independent, the correct number of malaria deaths has been estimated from the reported data as:

$$d_{x,g,i,y} = \frac{D_{x,g,i,y}}{c_{g,i,y}}\left[1 + m_g \cdot m_x\right]$$

where:

$$c_{g,i,y} = c_g \frac{pc_{i,y}}{pc_y}$$

and:

- x: age groups ($1 = 0\text{–}4$; $2 = 5\text{–}14$; $3 = 15\text{–}29$; $4 = 30\text{–}49$; $5 = 50$ and over);
- g: gender ($1 = $ male; $2 = $ female);
- i: states of Northern Region ($1 = $ Rondônia; $2 = $ Pará; $3 = $ other states);
- y: years ($1 = 1979$; $2 = 1980$; $3 = 1981$; $4 = 1982$; $5 = 1983$; $6 = 1984$; $7 = 1985$);
- d: correct number of deaths from malaria;
- D: published number of deaths from malaria;
- c: coverage of number of deaths;
- m: rate of misreporting;
- pc: proportion of population covered by the vital statistics system.

The values adopted for the c_g parameter were 84 per cent for males and 80 per cent for females (Martin and Jardim, 1988). Values of m_g ($1 = 0.4426$, $2 = 0.5574$,) and m_x ($1 = 0.2414$, $2 = 0.1528$, $3 = 0.1818$, $4 = 0.2931$, $5 = 0.1870$) are based on Lima and Silva (n.d.). Values of $D_{x,g,i,y}$ and of $pc_{i,y}$ were taken from data published by the Ministry of Health (Ministério da Saúde, 1982–90).

The population by age and sex for 1979 was estimated by interpolation between the 1970 and 1980 Censuses using the forward and reverse survival methods. For the 1980s, the total population of each state was estimated by interpolation between the 1980 and 1991 Censuses. The population by age and sex for the Northern Region was estimated by interpolation between the 1980 Census data and the projected population for 1990 (adjusted to take into account Census data on the total population). A 1990 projected age structure for the Northern Region was provided by Dr Kaizô Beltrão, who has projected the Brazilian population by region up to year 2010. These disaggregated data are not published. Finally, detailed population estimates for each state were obtained by an interactive procedure, taking into account the region's composition by state in 1980 and the interpolated regional estimates.

4. Recent Short Term Trend and Age Pattern

The malaria mortality rate for all ages in the state of Pará increased over the period from 20 to 27 per 100,000 for males and from 13 to 16 for females. There was no clear trend in Rondônia, where the respective rates for males and females were around 87 and 80 per 100,000. For other states of the region, there was an increasing trend; the rates rose from 9 to 17 for males and 9 to 11 for females. The age pattern of mortality in each of the areas considered varies substantially.

Table 11.3 shows gender and age-specific mortality rates from malaria and from all causes and the ratio of malarial to all-cause mortality. (The number of deaths from all causes was also corrected for under-reporting.) In the state of Pará, higher male malaria death rates were recorded for the adult population, aged 15 to 50 years, than for children. For the most recent period, these rates are around 34 to 50 per 100,000, which is considerably higher than in 1980. The age pattern of low child mortality and higher adult mortality differs from the pattern for all causes, which is J-shaped for the three years and shows no tendency to decline. For females, the malaria mortality pattern by age is the opposite of that for males. The rates are highest for those aged under 15 years, with rates around 20 to 25 per 100,000. These rates are higher than the rates for boys. The rates decline with age and are around 10 per 100,000 among women over 50 years. For males, the contribution of malaria to all-cause mortality is greatest in the ages of 5 to 50 years. At these ages, the ratio of malaria to all-cause mortality varies from 10 to 20 per cent. For females, the contribution of malaria deaths to total mortality is most striking in the low mortality ages of 5 to 14 years, ranging from 18 to 21 per cent.

In the high malaria prevalence state of Rondônia, the level and the age pattern of malaria death rates differ from those in the state of Pará. For both sexes, the age pattern conforms to the classical J-shape curve, exhibited by the

Table 11.3. Malaria death rates, overall death rates and malaria deaths as a percentage of overall deaths by region, year, sex, and age group

Region		Males					Females				
		0–4	5–14	15–29	30–49	≥50	0–4	5–14	15–29	30–49	≥50
Malaria death rates (per 100,000)											
Rondônia	1980	195	38	55	115	168	149	24	41	51	132
	1982	116	26	43	85	134	103	24	26	38	84
	1984	171	44	56	144	237	155	39	39	57	136
Pará	1980	20	8	26	38	8	19	22	3	4	4
	1982	22	9	25	50	12	22	26	3	10	6
	1984	17	9	34	53	11	22	21	3	10	4
Others	1980	15	5	8	12	8	14	6	3	4	13
	1982	24	7	13	10	16	24	5	5	7	5
	1984	29	6	14	20	20	21	6	8	8	5
Overall death rates (per 100,000)											
Rondônia	1980	4126	279	797	1676	5318	3713	292	382	814	4155
	1982	3267	226	623	1294	4914	2640	156	335	653	3525
	1984	3757	240	986	1543	5436	3022	193	336	588	4148
Pará	1980	2709	175	497	952	5205	2161	106	237	580	4011
	1982	2311	150	444	901	5316	1801	101	222	451	3954
	1984	2552	167	489	1050	5649	2025	119	225	442	4324
Others	1980	2598	165	245	947	4918	2052	84	237	561	3542
	1982	2795	169	478	1003	5064	1427	111	237	514	3575
	1984	3069	184	551	1002	3083	2279	130	262	543	3981
Malaria deaths as a percentage of total deaths											
Rondônia	1980	4.7	13.6	6.9	6.8	3.2	4.0	8.1	10.8	6.2	3.2
	1982	3.5	11.4	6.8	6.6	2.7	3.9	15.4	7.8	5.9	2.4
	1984	4.5	18.1	5.7	9.3	4.4	5.1	20.3	11.6	9.8	3.3
Pará	1980	0.7	4.5	5.1	4.0	0.2	0.9	21.1	1.1	0.6	0.1
	1982	0.9	6.3	5.7	5.5	0.2	1.2	25.4	1.2	2.2	0.2
	1984	0.7	5.4	6.9	5.1	0.2	1.1	17.7	1.5	2.3	0.1
Others	1980	0.6	3.0	3.2	1.3	0.2	0.7	7.7	1.3	0.8	0.4
	1982	0.9	4.2	2.6	1.0	0.3	1.7	4.1	2.0	1.4	0.1
	1984	0.9	3.2	2.6	2.0	0.7	0.9	4.8	3.0	1.5	0.1

Source: Data from 7 volumes published by the Ministry of Health (1982–90), corrected for under- and misreporting.

rates for all causes, but are relatively high in the intermediate age groups. For the most recent period, the rates for those aged 0–4 years were 171 and 155 per 100,000 for males and females respectively. They were 237 and 136 respectively in the oldest age group. The relative importance of malaria as a cause of death is highest in the age group 5 to 14 years; in this group about 20 per cent of all deaths were due to malaria. In the other age groups, this share was about 6 to 10 per cent for both sexes.

In the region's other states, there is a clear tendency for male malaria mortality to increase, especially for younger and older age groups. For 1984, the rate for those aged 0–4 years was 29 per 100,000 and that for the elderly 22 per 100,000. In the intermediate groups, the rates were around 6 to 14 per 100,000. The relatively high child mortality produces a U-shaped age pattern in male malaria mortality. Women suffer lower malaria mortality than males in all age groups and a transition occurs from a U-shape to an inverted J-shape due an increase in the level of child mortality and decrease in elderly mortality. For both sexes, the contribution of malaria to mortality is highest at intermediate ages, especially among adolescents. The proportion of deaths from malaria does not surpass 10 per cent.

The age and gender pattern across the region follows that expected. The mortality of economically active men is considerably higher in the state of Pará, reflecting the occupations of the in-migrants. The high proportion of the male population in activities like mining, timbering, and ranching renders this group most prone to the risk of malaria infection. In Rondônia, the population at highest risk are those involved in new colonization projects, which attract

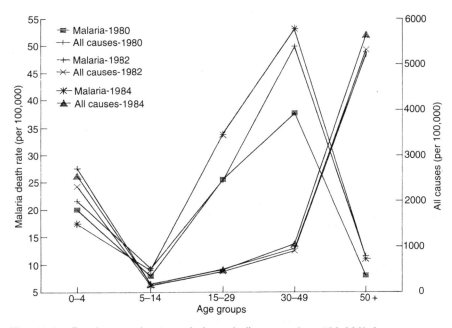

Fig. 11.1. Death rates due to malaria and all causes (per 100,000), by age group, state of Pará, males 1982–4

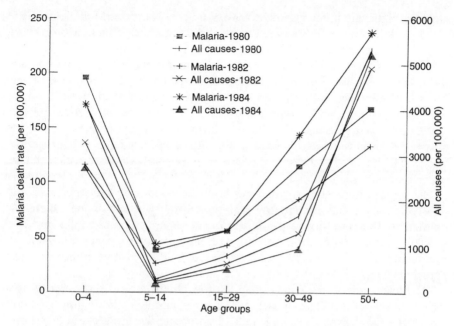

Fig. 11.2. Death rates due to malaria and all causes (per 100,000), by age group, state of Rondônia, males, 1982–4

migratory families rather than a male labour force, and mortality patterns very similar to the overall mortality pattern result, with some upward shift for adult males. In Rondônia, where there is some evidence that female mortality may be higher for children and young adults, mortality patterns conform to the overall pattern of gender-specific mortality. This is an issue for further investigation, focusing on the gender differential in health assistance and care at these ages. To illustrate more clearly the distinct patterns of male mortality in Rondônia and Pará, the results are presented in Figures 11.1 and 11.2.

Unfortunately the data needed to calculate case fatality by age and gender are not available. However, these results suggest that a considerable proportion of the rise in malaria cases may be reflected in an increase in the malaria mortality rates.

5. Discussion

Many difficulties arise in any attempt to study mortality from malaria and the literature approaches the subject in several ways. For the most part the reverse situation to that in Brazil is dealt with. It is sought to assess the effect of declining malaria on overall mortality by models comparing mortality before and after a decline in malaria (see, for example, Gray, 1974; Molineaux, 1985; Cohen, 1988). In this literature, the impact of malaria reduction on overall mortality, especially infant mortality, has been cited as considerable.

In Brazil's Northern Region, the level of malaria mortality, compared with the level of malaria prevalence, is low. The relatively low resistance of the parasite to the available drugs and the extensive action of the Brazilian malaria control programme are probably the main factors which account for the low fatality of the disease. A reduction in malaria mortality would not have much impact on the overall crude death rate or life expectancy, because the ages at which malaria mortality is relatively important are those ages with low overall mortality.

The large differential between mortality in Rondônia and other areas is, however, an indication that low malaria mortality is not to be taken for granted. If the conditions of Amazon development remain similar and the incidence of malaria continues to rise without delivery of proper treatment, it is possible that malaria will come to parallel other leading infectious and parasitic causes of death.

The burden posed to the new and old settlers in the area arises from the high incidence of malaria. The malaria action programme in the region has kept mortality at low levels, but it has failed as a preventive strategy. In fact, both the current and most of the alternative strategies are based on curative procedures and very few preventive measures have been proposed. The general framework for prevention is to cut the transmission chain by means of mosquito and parasite elimination. Such procedures face many difficulties inherent in the process of Amazon settlement. The dimensions of the forest, the vector's natural breeding and sheltering place; the influx of highly mobile non-immune populations in constant proximity with high risk areas; very poor housing and working conditions; lack of knowledge about the disease; and the lack of a vaccine with attested efficacy against infection combine to sustain transmission of malaria.

Ultimately, the increase in malaria in the Amazon Region is linked to those social and economic conditions outside the region which fuel migration to it and the unfavourable conditions in the region which lead the population to expand into new areas. The incorporation of efficient preventive measures in the control programme requires multisectoral action with other sectors besides health acting in a well-orchestrated programme. To consolidate human settlement in those areas that are already occupied and to improve economic conditions outside the Amazon Region might be the only effective measures to cut down migration to new areas and decrease the incidence of the disease.

References

Cohen, J. E. (1988), 'Estimating the effects of successful malaria control programmes on mortality', *Population Bulletin of the United Nations*, 26: 6–26.

Fernandez, R. E., and D. O. Sawyer (1988), 'Socio-economic and environmental factors affecting malaria in an Amazon frontier area', in: A. N. Herrin and P. L. Rosenfield (eds.) *Economics, Health and Tropical Diseases*, The University of the Philippines School of Economics, Manila, Philippines.

Gray, R. H. (1974), 'The decline of mortality in Ceylon and the demographic effects of malaria control', *Population Studies*, 28: 205–29.

Lima, J. T. F., and M. A. Silva (n.d.), 'Sub-registro de mortalidade por malaria em Rondonia, Brasil, 1985', unpublished manuscript.

Marques, A. (1987), 'Human migration and the spread of malaria in Brazil', *Parasitology Today*, 3: 166–70.

Martin, C. F., and M. L. T. Jardim (1988), 'Analisis de la información sobre muertes ocorridas en el ultimo año declaradas en el Censo Demográfico Brasileño de 1980', in: *Encontro Nacional de Estudos Populacionais, 6, 1988, Olinda*, vol. iv, Associação Brasileira de Estudos Populacionais, São Paulo, Brazil.

Ministério da Saúde, Fundação Serviços de Saúde Pública (1985), 'Mortalidade por malária, Brasil—1977/82', *Boletim Epidemiológico*, 12:19–20.

Ministério da Saúde (1982–90), *Estatísticas de mortalidade: Brasil—1979/87*, Ministério da Saúde, Secretaria Nacional de Ações Básicas de Saúde, Divisão Nacional de Epidemiologia, Centro de Documentação do Ministério da Saúde, Brasília, Brazil.

Molineaux, L. (1985), 'The impact of parasitic diseases and their control, with an emphasis on malaria and Africa', in: J. Vallin and A. D. Lopez (eds.) *Health Policy, Social Policy and Mortality Prospects*, Ordina, Liège, Belgium.

Pan American Health Organization (PAHO) and World Health Organization (WHO) (1992), *Situacion de los programas de malaria en las Americas*, XXXIX Informe, PAHO, Washington, DC.

Sawyer, D. R. (1988), 'Frontier malaria in the Amazon Region of Brazil, types of malaria situations and some implications for control', presented to the PAHO/WHO/TDR Technical Consultation on Research in Support of Malaria Control in the Amazon, Brasília, 28–30 April, Brazil.

——(1990), 'The future of deforestation in Amazonia: a socioeconomic and political analysis', in: A. B. Anderson (ed.) *Alternatives to Deforestation: Steps Toward Sustainable Use of the Amazon Rain Forest*, Columbia University Press, New York.

——and R. L. Monte-Mor (1992), 'Malaria risk factors in Brazil', background paper presented to the Inter-Regional Meeting on Malaria, Brasília, Brazil.

12 AIDS in Brazil

EUCLIDES A. CASTILHO, CÉLIA L. SZWARCWALD,
and CYNTHIA BOSCHI-PINTO
Fundaçao Oswaldo Cruz, Rio de Janeiro, Brazil

Brazil is the fifth largest country in the world (8.5 million km²) with a total population of 146 million inhabitants in 1991 (FIBGE, 1992). It has the eighth largest GNP in the world (Medici, 1988) but wide disparities in socio-economic conditions. The national morbidity and mortality data conceal considerable regional variation for many diseases, including infectious disease.

In 1990, the cumulative absolute number of AIDS patients in Brazil was the highest in Latin America and the third highest in the world. The overall cumulative incidence of AIDS was the sixth highest in Latin America and forty-ninth highest in the world (PAHO, 1990; WHO, 1991). This cumulative incidence rate rose from 0.05 per million in 1982, to 178 per million population in November, 1991. By this time, the cumulative absolute number of AIDS patients in Brazil was 23,660 (MS, 1992). Of those individuals with AIDS, 77 per cent were reported from the states of São Paulo and Rio de Janeiro, although the disease has spread throughout the whole country (MS, 1992). Among males, the modal age is 30 to 40 years, while for females it is 15 to 20 years (MS, 1992). The male to female ratio has decreased from 120:1 in 1984 to 6:1 in 1991 (MS, 1992). This decrease has been considered an indicator of heterosexual transmission to women, who are infected with HIV as a result of the high rates of HIV infection among bisexual men, and among male hetero-sexual intravenous drug users with female partners (Quinn *et al.*, 1989). This view should be regarded with caution however, since 328 out of 799 (41 per cent) AIDS cases among females diagnosed in 1988–90 were of women who were themselves intravenous users (MS, 1990) and less than 30 per cent of the women were sexual partners of bisexual men.

The distribution of cases by age and exposure category is shown in Table 12.1. Among adults and adolescents, the distribution is roughly the same as that found in Europe and in the United States. However, among children

The authors thank Dr Pedro Chequer for his permission to use his presentation at the VI International Conference on AIDS. Special thanks are given to Cassia M. Buchalla for her assistance in obtaining data on AIDS deaths in São Paulo City. In addition the authors thank Dr Roberto Becker for the mortality data (1986–7), and Rômulo Viel for his efficiency in typing the manuscript.

Table 12.1. Total AIDS cases by exposure category and age. Brazil, 1980–90

Exposure category[a]	Adults/ adolescents		Children under 15 years old		Total	
	N	%	N	%	N	%
Male homosexual/bisexual	6,749	56.5	1	0.2	6,750	54.5
Intravenous drug user	1,963	16.4	12	2.8	1,975	15.9
Haemophilia/coagulation disorder	219	1.8	94	21.6	313	2.5
Blood transfusion recipient	544	4.5	94	21.6	638	5.1
Heterosexual contact	1,354	11.3	1	0.2	1,355	10.9
Mother with/at risk of HIV	—	—	211	48.5	211	1.7
Other/undetermined	1,141	9.5	22	5.1	1,163	9.4
Total	11,970	100.0	435	100.0	12,405	100.0

[a] Hierarchical classification.

Source: Adapted from Ministério da Saúde (1990).

under 15 years of age the proportion (48.5 per cent) of cases attributed to mother-to-child transmission is lower than the 84 per cent observed in the United States. The proportion of children infected through blood transfusion/ blood components (43 per cent) is higher than in Europe (30 per cent) and in the United States (14 per cent) (ECEMA, 1990; CDC, 1991). In Brazil, 48 per cent of all AIDS cases are in homosexual or bisexual men who do not report intravenous drug use (MS, 1990). However, the proportion of cases in homosexual men has decreased from 64 per cent of the total cases of sexual transmission before 1986 to 54 per cent in 1988–9 (Table 12.2). Sixteen per cent of all AIDS cases are in intravenous drug users. The percentage of intravenous drug users among the cases in the parenteral transmission

Table 12.2. Per cent distribution of types within the sexual transmission category by year of diagnosis, Brazil, 1980–9

Type of sexual transmission	%		
	1980–5	1986–7	1988–9
Homosexual (male)	63.6	61.9	54.2
Bisexual (male)	31.4	29.2	25.9
Heterosexual (male and female)	5.0	8.9	19.9

Source: Rodrigues *et al.* (1990).

Table 12.3. Per cent distribution of types within the blood transmission category by year of diagnosis, Brazil, 1980–9

Type of blood transmission category	%		
	1980–5	1986–7	1988–9
Intravenous drug users	16.4	44.9	72.9
Haemophiliacs	62.7	16.7	8.7
Other blood transfusion recipients	20.9	38.4	18.4

Source: Rodrigues *et al.* (1990).

category has increased from 16 before 1986 to 73 per cent in 1988–9 (Table 12.3).

The spectrum of opportunistic infections and malignancies associated with AIDS is very wide in Brazil. Among Brazilian AIDS patients, candidiasis, *Pneumocystis carinii* pneumonia and tuberculosis are the most frequent infections, affecting 55.8, 31.3, and 14.7 per cent of patients respectively (MS, 1990). The high frequency of tuberculosis is one of the most striking characteristics of the epidemiological profile of the AIDS epidemic in Brazil.

It is well known that the number of AIDS cases grossly under-represents the magnitude of the problem since they do not account for the total number of HIV-infected individuals. In Brazil, estimates of the prevalence of HIV infection have been derived from serologic studies carried out among selected groups, such as homosexual or bisexual men, intravenous drug users, prostitutes, haemophiliacs, pregnant women, prisoners, street children, beggars, and blood donors. No population-based survey has been mounted so far. Inferences derived from these studies must be viewed with great care since selection biases and methodological problems are usually present. Most such studies remain unpublished but a few examples can be seen in Table 12.4.

A second method for generating HIV estimates involves the use of mathematical models. In this way, reported AIDS cases through December 1989 were used by one of the authors (Castilho) to estimate the number of HIV-infected people according to the approach adopted by the Centers of Disease Control (CDC, 1987). Data were adjusted for reporting delays. In the model, the number of AIDS cases diagnosed each year, t, was considered as being a convolution of the number of persons infected in each preceding year, and the number of those expected to be diagnosed with AIDS. The disease progression rates were assumed to be the same as those observed in the San Francisco cohort and the number of newly infected persons, $i(t)$, in a specific year, was assumed to be described by firstly an exponential and secondly a logistic function. The parameters of $i(t)$ were estimated using nonlinear least

Table 12.4. Sero-prevalence rates for HIV infection in selected groups in Brazil

Groups	Number studied	% infected	Reference
Homosexual/bisexual men	128	25.0	Cortes *et al.* (1989)
	197	32.5	Costa *et al.* (1990)
Beggars	100	5.0	Carvalho *et al.* (1987)
Street children	55	0	Ude *et al.* (1990)
Female prostitutes	290	1.7–6.2	Cortes *et al.* (1989)
			Castelo-Branco *et al.* (1988)
Heterosexual partners of at-risk individuals	13	38.5	Cortes *et al.* (1989)
Blood donors	11,807	0.09–7.0	Castro *et al.* (1987)

Source: Adapted from Quinn *et al.* (1989).

squares estimators based on the pseudo Gauss-Newton iteration. As of December 1989, the estimated number of HIV-infected persons was approximately 50,000 and 300,000 assuming logistic and exponential infection functions, respectively. The range of estimated values is large, reflecting both uncertainty about progression rates for AIDS and the shape of the underlying infectious curve (CDC, 1987). Thus, the projected estimates should be considered only as broad estimates of what may be occurring.

1. Survival Following Diagnosis of AIDS-Related Disease in Adult Cases in Brazil, 1980–89*

In 1989, the Brazilian National Division of STD/AIDS in the Ministry of Health carried out a special study to evaluate the length of survival for adult Brazilian AIDS cases and to assess the possible influence of sex, age, exposure category, year of diagnosis, and initial AIDS-related disease on survival.

A sample of 948 cases stratified by year of diagnosis and place of residence was selected from 7182 total cases reported to the National Surveillance System as of 30 June 1989. Cases were reviewed through a specific and detailed form designed to obtain both more accurate data and additional information not collected on the initial reporting form. This included survival status on 30 June or date of death. The median survival time was estimated by the Kaplan-

* This section summarizes a paper presented orally at the VI International Conference on AIDS, held in San Francisco in June, 1990 (Chequer *et al.*, 1990). The results and conclusions discussed here are those obtained from a sample of the total number of AIDS cases analysed in the above quoted abstract. Thus, some of the results may vary slightly.

Table 12.5. Survival by gender, age and year of diagnosis for a sample of adult Brazilian AIDS cases, Brazil, 1980–9

Variable	Number of cases	Median survival (months)	P-value (level of significance)
Gender			
Male	898	5.1	0.8595
Female	50	4.7	
Male—age group (years)			
15–24	120	8.2	
25–39	575	5.8	0.0026[a]
40–59	190	2.9	
Male—year of diagnosis			
<1987	149	5.0	0.9100
1987	749	5.1	
All cases	948	5.0	

[a] Statistically significant.

Meier product limit function (SAS, 1985). Multivariate analysis with Cox life-table regression was used to evaluate the relative importance of different conditions occurring simultaneously. The statistical significance of each variable was measured using the Wald-statistic (BMDP, 1982). The main results are shown in Tables 12.5, 12.6 and 12.7. Median survival did not differ by sex. Female cases were not included in further analyses due to their small number. Survival curves were found to be related to age at diagnosis. The higher the age at diagnosis, the shorter survival. No significant differences were found in survival among the exposure categories of adult male AIDS cases. However, it is worth noting that the large difference found between survival in transfusion recipients (1.9 months) and in homosexual or bisexual men (6.0 months). Median survival time varied significantly with initial diagnosis. The median survival for those with toxoplasmosis as an initial diagnosis (3.0 months) was significantly different from the value observed for those with Karposi's sarcoma (8.7 months). It has been found elsewhere that individuals first diagnosed with Karposi's sarcoma have longer survival than those first diagnosed with *Pneumocystis carinii* pneumonia or other AIDS diagnoses (Hessol *et al.*, 1990; Rothenberg *et al.*, 1987). The overall median survival time of 5.0 months in Brazilian AIDS cases is shorter than that observed in San Francisco in 1981–7 (12.2 months) and in New York City, in 1981–6 (11 months) (SFEB, 1988; Bacchetti *et al.*, 1988). When the survival curves were compared by period of diagnosis, a significant improvement in the survival was not found. Since survival is related to the first AIDS-related disease diagnosed, it must be taken into account, in the present analysis, that the possible effect of the period of diagnosis for each AIDS-related disease was not considered.

Table 12.6. Survival by exposure category and initial diagnosis for a sample of adult male AIDS cases, Brazil, 1980–9

Variable	Number of cases	Median survival (months)	P-value (level of significance)
Exposure category			
Homosexual	415	5.1	
Bisexual	249	7.5	
Heterosexual	55	2.8	0.1355
IV drug user	76	6.4	
Transfusion recipient	35	1.9	
Haemophiliac	28	4.7	
AIDS manifestations at diagnosis			
PCP	239	3.8	
Toxoplasmosis	80	3.0	
Candidiasis	311	5.0	0.0027[a]
Tuberculosis	71	5.9	
Kaposi's sarcoma	41	8.7	
Others	156	6.1	

[a] Statistically significant.

Table 12.7. Coefficients of the Cox regression model for survival for adult male PCP patients, controlling for selected variables, Brazil, 1980–9

Variable	Coefficient	P-value (level of significance)
Included in the model		
Age	0.0145	0.0015[a]
PCP	0.2331	0.0149[a]
Excluded from the model		
Year of diagnosis	−0.0315	0.4076
Exposure category	0.0142	0.5542

[a] Statistically significant.

Neither was the interaction between the year of diagnosis and the kind of AIDS-associated disease.

2. Differentials in Mortality Trends: An Impact of AIDS?

In Brazil, death certificates were standardized for the whole country in 1975. Since 1977, a computerized national mortality information system has been in operation, and annual tabulations of the number of deaths have been published by age, sex, and place for each of the major causes of death (Boschi-Pinto and Coleman, 1990). Despite high under-reporting, mainly in rural areas, the system has allowed studies of mortality trends in recent years, at least in metropolitan areas, where data are of good quality.

At the very beginning of the AIDS epidemic, changes in mortality patterns were hypothesized. Two questions should be addressed: first, what, if any, is the increase of death rates among young adult males; and second, to what extent are HIV-related deaths contributing to the change in mortality patterns. To evaluate such changes, mortality trends have been examined in three Brazilian metropolitan areas: Rio de Janeiro, São Paulo, and Curitiba. The two first areas were chosen due to their high AIDS incidence rates; Curitiba is used as a control, since it has low AIDS incidence rates. In all three cities vital statistics are of good quality, and socio-economic and demographic status is similar (Szwarcwald and Castilho, 1990).

Mortality trends were analysed first among men aged 30 to 39 years for two different periods of time, 1977–83 and 1984–7. The criterion used to split the time period is that a low number of AIDS cases were reported before 1984. In order to exclude the effect of accidents and violent deaths, which are increasing in Brazil among young adult males (Szwarcwald and Castilho, 1990), they were subtracted from the total number of deaths. The death rates thus obtained are presented in Table 12.8. From 1977 to 1983, mortality rates showed a significant decreasing linear trend in the three cities ($P < 1\%$). From 1984 to 1987, a significant increasing linear trend was observed. These results confirm that there were changes in the mortality patterns of the cities under study.

Cause-specific mortality trends for the endocrine, nutritional and metabolic diseases, and immunity disorders, respiratory diseases, and infectious diseases were also analysed. These broad groups of diseases include either AIDS itself, when specified (ICD 9th Revision, code 279.3), or AIDS-associated diseases which are often reported as the underlying cause of death. The first group is the one recommended for coding AIDS deaths. However, these deaths are commonly classified as *Pneumocystis carinii* pneumonia, which can be coded as 136.3 ('infectious diseases') or as 484.8 ('respiratory diseases') according to the 9th Revision, or even as tuberculosis, candidiasis, toxoplasmosis, herpes simplex and so on, or included in the broad 'infectious diseases' group.

In the areas under study, endocrine, nutritional and metabolic diseases, and immunity disorders showed no significant trend from 1977 to 1983. However, between 1984 and 1987, death rates from this group of diseases increased significantly from 8.4 to 34.3 per 100,000 in Rio de Janeiro, and from 6.2 to 18.8 in São Paulo. No significant increase was found in Curitiba. Deaths from respiratory diseases exhibited a decreasing linear trend in all the three metropolitan areas in the first period. From 1984 to 1987, mortality rates continued

Table 12.8. Crude mortality rates (per 100,000) for all natural causes (except accidents and violence) for men aged 30 to 39 years in selected Brazilian cities, 1977–87

Year	Rio de Janeiro	São Paulo	Curitiba
1977	248.7	271.1	280.3
1978	243.4	250.8	240.6
1979	235.2	256.6	259.0
1980	237.1	258.3	226.0
1981	215.9	231.2	236.2
1982	225.3	220.4	227.0
1983	216.1	225.2	219.4
$b_1{}^a$ (1977–83)	−5.48	−8.00	−8.31
1984	249.8	238.5	200.8
1985	234.4	233.0	203.6
1986	265.4	257.2	177.6
1987	279.3	263.8	199.3
$b_2{}^a$ (1984–7)	11.95	10.01	−3.05

[a] Slope of the regression line/growth rate of mortality by year, in the two time periods.

Source: MS (1977–87); FIBGE (1986).

to decrease in Curitiba but in both Rio de Janeiro and São Paulo an increase was observed. Similar results were observed for the infectious diseases. Although the death rate from infections rose in all three metropolitan areas after 1984, Curitiba experienced the slowest rise.

In order to reinforce these results, expected death rates based on trends in the first period were calculated for the second period for Rio de Janeiro and São Paulo (Table 12.9). In 1984 and 1985, the excess deaths were classified mainly as respiratory diseases. In the last two years, however, the excess of deaths was evenly distributed among respiratory diseases, infectious diseases, and endocrine, nutritional and metabolic diseases, and immunity disorders. Needless to say, this analysis is not exhaustive. However, the results are consistent with the hypothesis and the possibility cannot be excluded that the upturn in young adult male mortality rates is largely due to AIDS.

3. Impact of AIDS on Life Expectancy

As of 31 January 1990, more than 160,000 cases of AIDS and 100,813 AIDS-related deaths had been reported in the United States (CDC, 1991). AIDS was ranked fifteenth among causes of death in 1987 and was the seventh most important cause of premature mortality, as measured by years of potential life

Table 12.9.   Differences between observed and expected[a] mortality rates per 100,000 for selected causes for men aged 30 to 39 years, Rio de Janeiro and São Paulo, 1984–7

Cause	Rio de Janeiro				São Paulo			
	1984	1985	1986	1987	1984	1985	1986	1987
Infectious diseases	0.2	3.9	10.9	16.2	2.4	−0.2	10.9	16.2
Endocrine and metabolic diseases	−0.2	4.7	12.3	24.8	0.5	3.9	9.0	13.2
Respiratory diseases	4.8	5.7	10.6	15.1	9.3	9.1	16.3	18.1
All causes (not including accidents and violence)	40.0	30.1	66.6	86.0	25.7	28.2	60.4	75.0

[a] Based on the linear trend observed in 1977–83.
Source: MS (1984–7).

lost (YPLL) before age 65 (Berkelman and Curran, 1989; Curran *et al.*, 1985). The high case-fatality rate and the relative youth of those affected by AIDS produce a strong effect on the life expectancy of groups with a high incidence of the disease. In 1984, the YPLL due to AIDS among single men aged 25 to 44 years in the United States was only slightly less than YPLL attributable to cancers. In Manhattan, in 1984, AIDS increased YPLL due to all causes among single men aged 25 to 44 years by 43.5 per cent (Curran *et al.*, 1985).

In São Paulo City, Brazil in 1983–6, among single and married men aged 25 to 44 years, YPLL due to AIDS (12.7 per cent) was less than YPLL due to homicides and suicides (24.3 per cent) but ranked above YPLL due to accidents or cancers (Table 12.10). This city can be used for comparisons between

Table 12.10.   Years of potential life lost before age 65 by selected causes of death and geographic area for men aged 25 to 44 years

Region	Cause of death[a]				All causes
	Accidents	Homicide/ Suicide	Cancer	AIDS	
Manhattan	1,400	4,800	800	7,000	16,100
United States	188,000	174,600	39,500	32,300	642,400
São Paulo City	19,200	41,300	11,300	21,700	170,200

[a] Manhattan and US AIDS data are for 1984; all other causes are for 1980. São Paulo data are for the period 1983–6.
Source: Curran *et al.* (1985); Buchalla (1991).

the United States and Brazil because it has a good AIDS notification system, presenting low under-reporting. In addition, certifications of deaths in 1983–6 among men aged 25 to 44 years were linked to the local AIDS surveillance data and the underlying cause of death was reviewed applying the new criteria proposed in the forthcoming 10th Revision of the ICD (Buchalla, 1991).

References

Bacchetti, P., D. Osmond, R. E. Chaisson, *et al.* (1988), 'Survival patterns of the first 500 patients with AIDS in San Francisco', *Journal of Infectious Diseases*, 157: 1044–7.

Berkelman, R. L., and J. W. Curran (1989), 'Epidemiology of HIV infection and AIDS', *Epidemiologic Reviews*, 11: 222–8.

BMDP Statistical Software, Inc. (1982), *BMDP User's Digest: A Condensed Guide to the BMDP Computer Programs*, Los Angeles, Calif.

Boschi-Pinto, C., and M. P. Coleman (1990), 'Cancer mortality in Rio de Janeiro', *International Journal of Cancer*, 46: 173–7.

Buchalla, C. M. (1991), (personal communication).

Carvalho, M. I. L., L. R. Castelo-Branco, J. Z. A. Habib, B. Galvão-Castro, and M. S. Pereira (1987), 'HIV antibodies in blood donor beggars in Rio de Janeiro, Brazil', *Memórias do Instituto Oswaldo Cruz*, 82: 587–8.

Castelo-Branco, L., M. I. L. Carvalho, E. A. Castilho, H. E. Perieira, and B. Galvão-Castro (1988), 'Frequency of antibody to human immunodeficiency virus (HIV) in male and female prostitutes in Rio de Janeiro, Brazil', *Fourth International Conference on AIDS*, Montreal, Canada.

Castro, B. G., J. C. Fernadez, E. A. Castilho, H. G. Pereira, M. S. Pereira, and F. O. Cruz (1987), 'Human immunodeficiency virus infection in Brazil' (letter), *Journal of the American Medical Association*, 275: 2592–3.

Center for Disease Control (CDC) (1987), 'Human immunodeficiency virus infection in the United States: A review of current knowledge', *Morbidity and Mortality Weekly Report*, 36(S-6): 1–21.

—— (1991), 'HIV/AIDS Surveillance: US AIDS cases reported through January, 1991', Atlanta, US Department of Health and Human Services, Atlanta, Ga.

Chequer, P., N. Hearst, E. Castilho, L. A. Loures, L. Rodrigues, and G. Rutherford (1990), 'Survival in adult AIDS cases, Brazil, 1980–1989', *Sixth International Conference on AIDS*, San Francisco, Calif.

Cortes, E., R. Detels, Aboulafia, *et al.* (1989), 'HIV-1, HIV-2 and HTLV-1 infection in high-risk groups in Brazil', *New England Journal of Medicine*, 320: 953–8.

Costa, M. F. F. L., M. R. Oliverira, E. I. Oliveira, *et al.* (1990), 'Factors associated with AIDS and AIDS-like syndrome among homosexual and bisexual men in Minas Gerais, Brazil', *International Journal of Epidemiology*, 19: 429–34.

Curran, J. W., M. W. Morgan, A. M. Hardy, H. N. Jaffe, W. W. Darrow, and W. R. Dowdle (1985), 'The epidemiology of AIDS: current status and future prospects', *Science*, 229: 1352–7.

European Centre for the Epidemiological Monitoring AIDS (ECEMA) (1990), 'AIDS surveillance in Europe', *Quarterly Report*, 28: 1–33.

Fundação Instituto Brasileiro de Geografia e Estatística (FIBGE) (1986), *Anuário Estatístico do Brasil, 1985*, Rio de Janeiro, Brazil.
—— (1992), *Censo Demográfico 1991: Resultados Preliminares*, Rio de Janeiro, Brazil.
Hessol, N. A., R. H. Byes, A. R. Lifson, *et al.* (1990), 'Relationship between AIDS latency period and AIDS survival time in homosexual and bisexual men', *AIDS*, 3: 1078–85.
Medici, A. (1988), 'Crise econômica e políticas sociais: a questão da saúde no Brasil', (Masters dissertation), Universidade de Campinas, Campinas, São Paulo, Brazil.
Ministério da Saúde, Brazil (MS) (1977–87), *Estatísticas de Mortalidade: Brasil*, Brasília, Brazil.
—— (1986), 'Estatísticas de Mortalidade: Brasil', unpublished data.
—— (1987), 'Estatísticas de Mortalidade: Brasil', unpublished data.
—— (1990), *AIDS. Boletim Epidemiológico, Brasil*, 11, Divisão Nacional de Doenças Sexualmente Transmissíveis e AIDS, Brasília, Brazil.
—— (March, 1992), unpublished data, Brazil.
Pan American Health Organization (PAHO) (1990), *Vigilancia Epidemiologica del SIDA en las Americas*, Washington, DC.
Quinn, T. C., F. R. K. Zacarias, and R. K. St-John (1989), 'HIV and HTLV-1 infections in the Americas: a regional perspective', *AIDS*, 68: 189–209.
Rodrigues, L. G. M., P. Chequer, and E. A. Castilho (1990), 'A epidemia de AIDS no Brasil: 1980–1989', *Revista Brasileira de Alergia e Imunologia*, 13: 187–90.
Rothenberg, R., M. Woelfel, R. Stoneburner, J. Milberg, R. Parker, and B. Truman (1987), 'Survival with the acquired immunodeficiency syndrome', *New England Journal of Medicine*, 317: 1297–302.
San Francisco Epidemiologic Bulletin (SFEB) (1988), 'Survival following diagnosis of AIDS-related opportunistic infections in San Francisco, 1981–1987', Bureau of Communicable Disease Control, Department of Public Health, San Francisco, Calif.
SAS Institute Inc. (1985), *SAS User's Guide: Statistics, Version 5*, Cary, NC.
Szwarcwald, C. L., and E. A. Castilho (1990), 'Regiões metropolitanas: violência na vida e na morte', *RADIS/DADOS 14*, Fundação Oswaldo Cruz, Rio de Janeiro, Brazil.
Ude, W., R. Campos, M. Amado, *et al.* (1990), 'Risk behaviour for HIV infection among street youth in Brazil', *Sixth International Conference on AIDS*, San Francisco, Calif.
World Health Organization (WHO) (February 1991), 'Update: AIDS cases reported to surveillance, forecasting and impact assessment unit', Global Programme on AIDS, Geneva, Switzerland.

13 Cholera in the Americas in 1991

A. DAVID BRANDLING-BENNETT, MARLO LIBEL,
and AMÉRICO MIGLIÓNICO
Pan American Health Organization, Washington, DC, USA

1. Introduction

Cholera is an acute diarrhoeal illness caused by the bacterium *Vibrio cholerae*.
In its fullest manifestation, cholera presents as a profuse, watery diarrhoea
that leads to dehydration, shock, and even death. However, mild and
subclinical infections are common. Epidemic cholera is produced by the
serogroup *V. cholerae* O1, of which there are two biotypes, classical and El
Tor, the latter first identified in Egypt in 1905 (Greenough, 1990). There are
also two principal serotypes, Inaba and Ogawa. Other members of the genus
Vibrio cause disease in man, including non-agglutinating or non-O1 vibrios,
but it is the species *V. cholerae* O1 that has caused epidemics of disease and
death throughout history.

V. *cholerae* produces diarrhoea by elaborating an enterotoxin that affects
the small intestine, causing a profuse secretion of electrolytes and water.
Only toxigenic strains are associated with epidemic diarrhoea. Studies
have shown that glucose in the intestinal lumen can partially reverse the effect
of the toxin, lessening the loss of water and electrolytes. A highly effective
treatment of cholera and other diarrhoeal diseases has been developed
utilizing solutions of salts and glucose which are given orally (Nalin and Cash,
1970).

The incubation period for cholera, or the interval between infection and
onset of diarrhoea, is typically 1 to 2 days but can range from 12 hours to 6
days. The diarrhoea often begins abruptly and is most severe in the first 24 to
36 hours. Abdominal pain and vomiting are common, and painful muscle
cramps result from electrolyte imbalance that accompanies the diarrhoea.
Death may occur in 50 per cent of persons presenting with profuse diarrhoea
if they are not treated, but vigorous replacement of lost water and electrolytes,
either orally or intravenously, can prevent virtually all deaths. Treatment with
antibiotics to which the organism is sensitive will reduce the duration and
severity of diarrhoea, but such treatment is not essential and is secondary to
rehydration.

In areas that are endemic for cholera, adults maintain an acquired immunity from repeated exposure to infection, and illness and death are more likely to occur in children under 5 years of age, as is true for diarrhoeal diseases of other aetiology. Epidemics in previously uninfected areas will affect all age groups (Mosley, 1970). One would expect deaths to be more likely at the extremes of age in individuals less able to tolerate the physiological impact of dehydration, but little information is available about the characteristics of persons dying from cholera before treatment of dehydration became widely used.

Seven large pandemics of cholera have swept the world since the early nineteenth century. The high fatality rate in previous pandemics has caused the disease to be widely feared and underlies much of our public health response to epidemic disease. For example, the First International Sanitary Conference held in Paris in 1851 was stimulated largely by the second pandemic of cholera (Duffy, 1977), and international health regulations were formulated in an effort to control the spread of cholera, as well as other diseases.

It is almost certain that all countries of the Americas were infected at various times during the first five pandemics. With the construction of water and sanitation systems in the larger cities, cholera disappeared from the Americas at the turn of the century, and the hemisphere was spared the sixth pandemic that occurred early in the twentieth century and the first thirty years of the seventh pandemic, which began in Indonesia in 1961. After 1970, imported cases were reported in North America, and the United States identified a focus of persistent infection along the Gulf Coast which caused sporadic cases related to the consumption of inadequately cooked shellfish. The strain of *V. cholerae* causing the latter infections was of the El Tor biotype but was genetically distinct from the pandemic El Tor strain.

2. Mortality from Intestinal Infectious Diseases

Over the period from 1950–5 to 1985–90, life expectancy at birth increased from 51.8 to 66.6 years in Latin America and from 56.4 to 72.4 years in the non-Latin Caribbean. In general, the greatest contributor to these increases was reduced mortality from infectious and parasitic diseases, which resulted from direct influences (improved nutrition, immunization, availability of drinking water and waste disposal, and safer food handling) and indirect influences (lower birth rates, increased literacy rates among women, outreach of mass communications) (McKeown, 1988). While these improvements unquestionably had an impact, they were not distributed equitably throughout the population of the hemisphere, as is seen in the persistence of a problem which is one of the most preventable and yet one of the most common: the intestinal infectious diseases—basically, the diarrhoeal diseases (categories 001–009 in the International Classification of Diseases, 9th Revision). Diarrhoea continues to kill large numbers of children in their first years of life and, in some countries, diarrhoea remains an important cause of death in other age groups as well.

Analysing available mortality data by five-year periods since 1965, the Pan American Health Organization (PAHO, 1991*c*) found a decrease in the number of deaths from intestinal infectious diseases for all ages in almost all countries, ranging from only 10 per cent in Peru and Ecuador to 90 per cent in Costa Rica and Chile. The declining trend was also seen in proportional mortality, that is, the relative importance of deaths from intestinal infections as a percentage of total deaths from all causes. Since overall mortality from all causes declined, the downward trend in mortality from intestinal infections was much greater than that seen for all causes combined. Therefore, reduced mortality from intestinal infectious diseases, as a single cause, contributed substantially to the decline in mortality from all causes and to the increase in life expectancy at birth observed in the Americas.

While the relative weight of deaths due to intestinal infectious diseases is greatest in children under 5 years of age, the importance of this cause varies by age group according to its overall impact. When proportional mortality from diarrhoea is high for all ages, that is in excess of 20 per cent of all deaths, mortality is high not only in children under 5 but in other age groups as well. When the importance of diarrhoea relative to other causes begins to decrease, deaths tend to occur more in young children, suggesting that gains from reductions of deaths due to intestinal infections are greater in older age groups. Finally, when proportional mortality due to diarrhoea is low, mortality from this cause occurs mostly in older age groups, indicating that a decline in mortality from diarrhoea has occurred in young children.

Over 6 million deaths from intestinal infectious diseases were registered by twenty-three countries of Latin America and the Caribbean between 1965 and 1990, corresponding to nearly 1 out of every 11 deaths from all causes. Almost 5 million of these deaths occurred in children under 5 years of age, representing 7 per cent of deaths from all causes in all age groups and meaning that 1 out of every 14 deaths in the general population was from intestinal infection in a child aged under 5. In some countries the proportion is even greater. For example, 1 death from diarrhoea occurs in a child under age 5 years for every 6 deaths in Nicaragua.

Despite the progress that has been made in preventing deaths from diarrhoea during the last thirty years, figures for the period 1985–90 indicate that, at a minimum, 130,000 children under 5 years of age were dying from diarrhoea each year in Latin America and the Caribbean.

3. The Cholera Epidemic in 1991

Given this background, it was with considerable alarm that the Pan American Health Organization and the rest of the international community learned about the appearance of cholera in Peru in late January 1991 (PAHO, 1991*a*). *V. cholerae* O1 El Tor Inaba had been isolated from persons with diarrhoea in Chancay, on the coast. Within a week, infection was confirmed along a 1200 km stretch of the northern coast from Chancay to Piura and, within the next month, the disease spread to the interior of the country. At the peak of the epidemic in March, 20,000 cases were being reported each week (Figure 13.1). After that, the intensity of transmission decreased in the coastal departments but increased in the two departments east of the Andes that form part of the Amazon basin. The interior departments in the high plateau of the Andes were less affected. The epidemic in Peru was one of the largest ever reported, with a total of 322,562 cases and 2909 deaths by the end of the year (Table 13.1). Every department was involved, and it is estimated that at least 1.5 per cent of the Peruvian population was infected (PAHO, 1991*d*). At the end of the year, transmission remained intense in the two departments of the Amazon basin, where an estimated 4 per cent of the population had been infected (WHO, 1992). Moreover, new outbreaks were reported along the southern coast.

Ecuador was the second country to be infected, reporting its first case on 1 March in a community of shrimp fisherman who worked in Peruvian waters. As in Peru, the disease spread to all provinces and produced 46,320 reported cases and 697 deaths. The areas of highest incidence were those with the highest population density and greatest commerce with other provinces and countries. While cases declined after May, high transmission continued

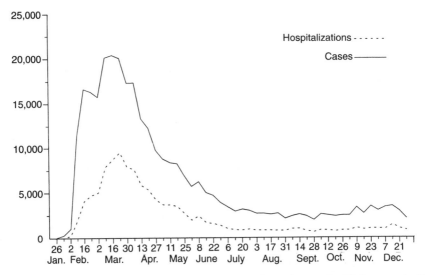

Fig. 13.1. Cholera cases and hospitalizations in Peru, by week, 26 January to 28 December 1991
Source: Ministry of Health.

Table 13.1. Cholera in the Americas, 1991

Country	First report	Total cases	Hospital cases	Deaths	Death-to-case ratio (%)
Peru	23 Jan.	322,562	119,523	2909	0.9
Ecuador	1 Mar.	46,320	37,342	697	1.5
Colombia	10 Mar.	11,979	5,166	207	1.7
USA	9 Apr.	26[a]	11	0	—
Brazil	10 Apr.	1,567	1,032	26	1.6
Chile	12 Apr.	41	38	2	4.8
Mexico	13 June	2,690	836	34	1.2
Guatemala	24 July	3,674	1,510	50	1.3
El Salvador	19 Aug.	947	481	34	3.6
Bolivia	26 Aug.	206	115	12	5.8
Panama	10 Sept.	1,177	276	29	2.5
Honduras	13 Oct.	11	9	0	—
Nicaragua	12 Nov.	1	1	0	—
Venezuela	29 Nov.	15[b]	9	2	13.0
French Guyana	14 Dec.	1[c]	—	0	—
Canada		2[d]	2	0	—
Total		391,219	166,349	4002	

[a] 18 cases related to travel in Latin America.
[b] 10 imported cases from Colombia.
[c] 1 imported case from Brazil.
[d] 2 imported cases from India.

through July and August and new outbreaks occurred in some coastal provinces and in Guayaquil, Ecuador's largest city. Disease incidence began to increase in December, exceeding 500 cases per week.

The third country to be infected, Colombia, reported its first case on 10 March near the southern Pacific coast but over 500km from the nearest epidemic focus in Ecuador. The disease spread more gradually and with a lower intensity than in Peru or Ecuador, though just as inexorably, and by the end of the year twenty-eight states and municipalities had been involved, including the entire Pacific and Caribbean coasts. A total of 11,979 cases and 207 deaths were reported. Disease incidence exceeded 500 cases for 3 of the last 4 weeks of the year.

The United States of America had its first imported case on 9 April and subsequently had eighteen cases related to the epidemic in Latin America. Twelve cases resulted from eating crab brought in non-commercially in the luggage of persons returning from Ecuador. The other six cases were imported by travellers from Peru and Ecuador. In addition, the Latin American strain of *V. cholerae* was isolated from oysters collected from the Gulf coast of Alabama, though the source of infection of these waters remains unknown.

Brazil reported its first case on 10 April in Amazonas State on the border between Peru and Colombia. Cholera initially appeared to remain localized in that area but an eight-fold increase in cases occurred in July and August as the disease began to spread eastward along the Amazon River. By November, cholera had passed Manaus, the capital of Amazonas State, and had reached at least three neighbouring states. By December, the disease was present in Belem, the capital of Pará State located on the Atlantic coast, so that in ten months the epidemic had crossed the 3500 km width of the South American continent.

Chile reported 41 cases between 12 April and 23 May, with 33 of these in the metropolitan area of Santiago and no cases occurring after May. Control of the outbreak appeared to have been achieved by limiting the distribution and consumption of raw fruit and vegetables. However, *V. cholerae* was isolated from waste waters at several locations in Chile later in the year, indicating the possibility that infection was persisting and could reappear as clinical disease.

As it was expecting the disease to continue its spread into contiguous geographic areas, PAHO was disturbed to receive on 13 June a report from Mexico about cholera in a small, isolated community in the State of Mexico. In spite of vigourous control measures, the disease could not be confined to that community and infection spread to the Federal District and sixteen states of Mexico, affecting primarily the southern areas of the country on the Gulf coast and the border with Guatemala.

Guatemala itself reported cases on 24 July, after which the disease spread to all departments, with the majority of cases occurring along the Pacific coast and in the Department of Guatemala. El Salvador became infected in mid-August, with cases initially in the metropolitan area of San Salvador but extending to all departments before the end of the year. In Panama, cholera was introduced in early September from Colombia to the Pacific coast of Darien Province and spread rapidly, infecting over 1 per cent of the population of that province. After mid-October, the disease also reached other provinces of Panama, including the Atlantic coast, producing 1177 cases or 47 cases per 100,000 population, the third highest case rate after Peru and Ecuador. Honduras and Nicaragua were infected in October and November, respectively, but it appears that only limited transmission occured in Honduras and no transmission in Nicaragua. By the end of 1991, intense transmission was still occurring in Guatemala, El Salvador and Panama. On 26 August, seven months after the epidemic began in its neighbour to the west, Bolivia reported its first cases, in the region around La Paz. The disease remained largely confined to that department during the year, with only two cases in Cochabamba, but the continued rise in cases during December was cause for concern.

Venezuela was the last country in the Latin America to become infected in 1991, initially having cases imported from Colombia into two western

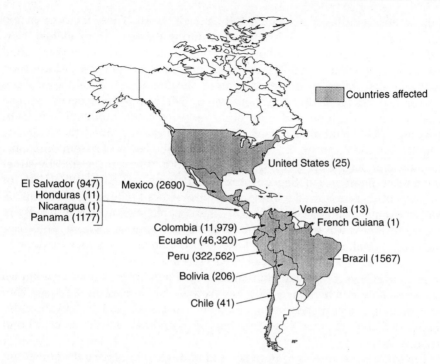

Countries affected

United States (25)

El Salvador (947)
Honduras (11)
Nicaragua (1)
Panama (1177)

Mexico (2690)

Venezuela (13)
French Guiana (1)

Colombia (11,979)
Ecuador (46,320)
Peru (322,562)
Bolivia (206)

Brazil (1567)

Chile (41)

Fig. 13.2. Cholera cases in the Americas, 1991

districts and then transmission locally. French Guyana had one case imported from Brazil in mid-December. The two cases in Canada were both imported from India.

The 391,219 cholera cases reported from fourteen countries in the Americas accounted for 70 per cent of cases worldwide in 1991, a year in which more cases were reported than in any other year of the seventh pandemic. The almost inexorable geographic spread had infected an average of one new country per month between January and December, reaching from Chile in the south to the United States in the north and across the entire width of South America (Figure 13.2). By the end of 1991, active transmission extended from southern Mexico to Peru and from the Atlantic to the Pacific, strongly suggesting that many, if not most, countries of Latin America and the Caribbean would be infected in the next one to two years.

4. Transmission of Cholera in the Americas

Cholera is almost always introduced into new areas by infected travellers. The El Tor biotype produces a higher proportion of mild or sub-clinical infections than the classical biotype and has a greater tendency to persist in the infected human host and the environment (Greenough, 1990). These factors may explain in part its extensive dissemination during the seventh pandemic. New infection is seldom introduced by commercial food products or contaminated river or coastal waters, though the latter may lead to infection of local food and water. However, within infected areas, the disease is transmitted between persons by contaminated food and water. Direct person-to-person spread is probably rare, though it may occur between close household contacts. Investigations in urban areas of the coast of Peru identified the following risk factors for acquiring infection: drinking unboiled water from municipal systems and superficial wells; consuming food and beverages sold by street vendors, especially drinking beverages containing ice; eating food left for more than three hours at room temperature without reheating; and drinking water from a container into which other people had put their hands. In Ecuador, illness was also shown to be associated with eating raw fish or raw shellfish, as well as with drinking beverages obtained from street vendors. In Chile, disease appeared to be associated with eating raw vegetables and salads, which are grown in irrigated fields around Santiago. Irrigation water is known to be heavily contaminated with raw sewage discharged by Santiago into surrounding rivers. Later investigations in Guatemala and El Salvador also implicated contaminated water and improperly prepared foods as vehicles of transmission.

Environmental studies in Peru showed that many municipal water systems had high counts of faecal coliform bacteria, indicating contamination of the water and inadequate chlorination. *V. cholerae* was isolated from at least three water systems and from rivers and coastal waters at several locations in Peru. Epidemic strains of *V. cholerae* were also isolated from rivers in Chile, Mexico, Guatemala, and El Salvador. The Latin American strain of *V. cholerae* was found in oysters harvested from the Gulf coast of the United States without known association with human disease.

In all the infected countries of the Americas, cholera was predominantly a disease of adults. In Peru, 80 per cent of cases occurred in persons 5 years of age and older, while 75 per cent of diarrhoea in that country normally occurs in children under 5 years of age. Basically the same pattern was seen in the other Latin American countries. In fact, fewer cases were reported in children under 10 years of age than would be expected, though this may be an artifact of surveillance. More cases were reported in men than women. However, detailed information characterizing infected persons is lacking from many countries and for most cases, because of the limitations of surveillance in the region.

5. Cholera Mortality

The overall death-to-case ratio from cholera in Latin America has been 1 per cent, shaped largely by the figures in Peru, which maintained a ratio below 1

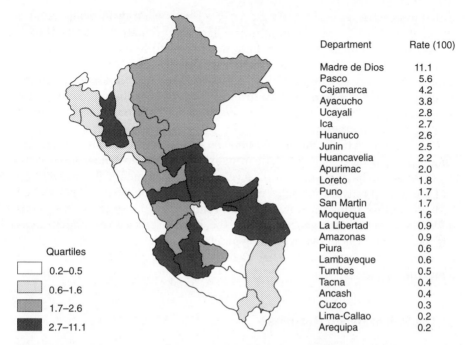

Department	Rate (100)
Madre de Dios	11.1
Pasco	5.6
Cajamarca	4.2
Ayacucho	3.8
Ucayali	2.8
Ica	2.7
Huanuco	2.6
Junin	2.5
Huancavelia	2.2
Apurimac	2.0
Loreto	1.8
Puno	1.7
San Martin	1.7
Moquequa	1.6
La Libertad	0.9
Amazonas	0.9
Piura	0.6
Lambayeque	0.6
Tumbes	0.5
Tacna	0.4
Ancash	0.4
Cuzco	0.3
Lima-Callao	0.2
Arequipa	0.2

Quartiles

0.2–0.5

0.6–1.6

1.7–2.6

2.7–11.1

Fig. 13.3. Cholera deaths per 100 cases in Peru by department, 26 January to 28 December 1991
Source: Ministry of Public Health, Department of Epidemiology.

per cent for much of the epidemic, but ranging as high as 13 per cent in Venezuela, which had two deaths during December (Table 13.1). Five countries had death-to-case ratios over 2 per cent. These figures are similar to the 1.1 per cent death-to-case ratio reported from Asia and are much better than the 10 per cent death-to-case ratio reported from Africa. Generally, death rates were higher at the beginning of epidemics in each country but declined as medical staff became more aware of the disease and its proper treatment. This was the case in Peru, at the beginning of the epidemic, and in Venezuela, which experienced its initial cases in December.

Too little detail regarding cholera deaths was provided by the countries to characterize them by age and sex. The impression is that cholera deaths followed basically the same pattern as the disease itself, indicating that susceptibility to the effects of diarrhoea or dehydration did not play a dominant role. Access to and use of health services were more important. In Peru, death-to-case ratios ranged from under 0.2 per cent in large municipalities to over 3 per cent in remote departments with predominantly indigenous populations (Figure 13.3). (Madre de Dios had only nine cases and one death.) Staff in several countries noted that deaths occurred in those who arrived late at health services or who never arrived at all.

These observations regarding cholera deaths in the Americas are consistent with those made elsewhere. Tauxe *et al.* (1988) working in Mali found a 29 per cent death-to-case ratio in four villages where patients received little or no care. In Bangladesh, Islam and Shahid (1986) found that *V. cholerae* was associated with unusually high case fatality that was unrelated to patient characteristics, and Glass *et al.* (1989) found no relation between the severity of cholera and undernutrition. The overwhelming determinant of the outcome of infection with *V. cholerae* O1 is prompt and adequate treatment of dehydration.

The greater than twenty-fold range in death-to-case ratios should not diminish the achievement of Peru in maintaining a ratio below 1 per cent. This was due in large part to a well-developed programme for the distribution and use of oral rehydration salts, which was rapidly mobilized and resupplied with donations from the international community. In spite of enormous difficulties, including a general strike, the health services responded courageously to care for an overwhelming number of patients. Peru set a standard for case management which other countries of the Americas must strive to maintain.

6. The Public Health Response

The cholera epidemic revealed serious weaknesses in surveillance systems and the ability to conduct field investigations in the Americas. Several countries were initially reluctant to report detected cases, fearing adverse effects on tourism and exports. Many countries attempted to limit reporting to laboratory-confirmed cases until they realized that isolation and identification of *V. cholerae* can be accomplished only for small numbers of patients at any one time. Even after that realization, the countries did not agree upon and apply a uniform, simple case definition designed to facilitate reporting. In most of the infected countries, fewer cases were probably reported than actually occurred because of these and other failures in their surveillance systems.

Field investigations of the epidemic were even weaker. Little information beyond case counts and little analysis beyond documentation of time and place appear to have been done or made available to PAHO. The few studies seeking risk factors for disease, which are essential for effective and targeted control, were conducted largely with assistance from international consultants. Previously, cholera has demanded and stimulated improvements in surveillance and field investigations. This should be one positive outcome of the cholera epidemic in this hemisphere.

By contrast, the health services did relatively well, as is clearly shown by the low death-to-case ratios. Even so, too great a reliance was placed on intravenous therapy, which is more expensive and potentially more risky than oral therapy. Antibiotics were overused, with instances of mass treatment and prophylaxis, contrary to World Health Organization guidelines. A possible result was the emergence of multiple antibiotic-resistant strains of *V. cholerae* in Guayaquil, Ecuador.

The 4002 deaths from cholera in 1991 represent a small contribution to mortality, even among adults. From available mortality data for 1965 and 1990, it has been estimated that 240,000 deaths occur each year in Latin America from intestinal infectious diseases; 20 per cent of these deaths are in adults (PAHO, 1991*c*).

It is not deaths *per se* that make cholera so important. Rather, it is the tremendous demand placed upon the health services to prevent deaths. Applying the death rate among untreated cases of approximately 30 per cent observed by Tauxe *et al.* (1988) in Mali to the Peruvian data, the health services succeeded in preventing over 35,000 deaths that would have occurred among hospitalized patients had adequate rehydration therapy not been available. A conservative estimate is that throughout the Americas at least 50,000 deaths were prevented. At the height of epidemics in some locations, hospitals and staff were taken over by the need to care for cholera cases. The cost of oral rehydration salts, intravenous fluids, antibiotics, hospital supplies, laboratory reagents, and measures to provide safe water and excreta disposal on an emergency basis were enormous, totalling hundreds of millions of dollars in the region (PAHO, 1992). The community and social disruption that accompany a cholera epidemic undoubtedly had even greater consequences.

Though tourists are usually at low risk of acquiring cholera and commercially exported foods are seldom responsible for transmitting disease, loss of revenues from tourism and embargoes on food products also imposed economic costs on infected countries. Instances of unjustified refusal to import products from infected countries did occur initially but decreased later in the epidemic. At the very least, commercial enterprises had to make significant investments to assure that their exports were free of *V. cholerae*.

7. The Future

Classically, cholera has been a disease of poverty, affecting those living under the poorest conditions, without safe water, adequate sanitation, the proper means to prepare and store food, and access to basic health care. Epidemic cholera in the Americas in 1991 was no different. Its presence provides clear evidence that water, sanitation, and health services remain inadequate. Major efforts and investments will be needed to control the spread of cholera and limit its effects during the 1990s. Even with these commitments, cholera can be expected to spread to much of Latin America and the Caribbean. The elimination of cholera from the region, which must be the ultimate goal, can be achieved only by major investments to improve water, sanitation, and health services and extend them to the significant proportion of the population that has not yet been reached (PAHO, 1991*b*). This must be regarded as one of the greatest public health challenges and opportunities of the last decade of the century.

References

Duffy, J. (ed.) (1977), *Ventures in World Health. The Memoirs of Fred Lowe Soper*, Pan American Health Organization, Scientific Publication No. 355, Washington, DC.

Glass, R. I., A. M. Svennerholm, B. J. Stoll, M. R. Khan, S. Huda, M. I. Huq, and J. Holmgren (1989), 'Effects of undernutrition on infection with *Vibrio cholerae* O1 and on response to oral cholera vaccine', *Paediatric Infectious Diseases Journal*, 8: 105–9.

Greenough, W. B. (1990), 'III. Vibrio cholerae', in: G. L. Mandell, R. G. Douglas Jr, and J. E. Bennett (eds.) *Principles and Practice of Infectious Diseases*, 3rd Edn., Churchill Livingston, New York.

Islam, S. S., and N. S. Shahid (1986), 'Morbidity and mortality in a diarrhoeal diseases hospital in Bangladesh', *Transactions of the Royal Society of Tropical Medicine and Hygiene*, 80: 748–52.

McKeown, T. (1988), *The Origins of Human Disease*, Basil Blackwell, Oxford.

Mosley, W. H. (1970), 'Epidemiology of Cholera', in: *Principles and Practice of Cholera Control*, Public Health Papers No. 40, World Health Organization, Geneva, Switzerland.

Nalin, D. R., and R. A. Cash (1970), 'Oral and nasogastric therapy for cholera', in: *Principles and Practice of Cholera Control*, Public Health Papers No. 40, World Health Organization, Geneva, Switzerland.

Pan American Health Organization (PAHO) (1991*a*), 'Cholera situation in the Americas', *Epidemiological Bulletin*, 12(1): 1–10, Washington, DC.

——(1991*b*), 'Environmental health conditions and cholera vulnerability in Latin America and the Caribbean', *Epidemiological Bulletin*, 12(2): 5–10, Washington, DC.

——(1991*c*), 'Mortality due to intestinal infectious diseases in Latin America and the Caribbean, 1965–1990', *Epidemiological Bulletin*, 12(3): 1–6, Washington, DC.

——(1991*d*), 'Update: the cholera situation in the Americas', *Epidemiological Bulletin*, 12(3): 11–12, Washington, DC.

——(1992), 'The economic impact of the cholera epidemic, Peru, 1991', *Epidemiological Bulletin*, 13(3): 9–11, Washington, DC.

Tauxe R. V., S. D. Holmberg, A. Dodin, J. V. Wells, and P. A. Blake (1988), 'Epidemic cholera in Mali: high mortality and multiple routes of transmission in a famine area', *Epidemiology and Infection*, 100: 279–89.

World Health Organization (WHO) (1992), 'Cholera in the Americas', *Weekly Epidemiological Record*, 67: 33–9.

14 Adult Mortality from Chronic Diseases in Chile, 1968-90

ERICA TAUCHER, CECILIA ALBALA, and GLORIA ICAZA
Universidad de Chile, Santiago, Chile

1. Introduction

Great demographic changes have taken place in Chile over the last four decades against a background of industrialization, urbanization, increasing levels of education, and extended access to health care and family planning services. Perhaps the most important demographic events have been the decrease in infant mortality and the simultaneous fertility decline. Between 1970 and 1990, infant mortality declined from 78.8 to 16.0 per 1000 and life expectancy at birth increased by about ten years, to reach 68.5 years for males and 75.6 years for females in 1990. Fertility declined from a total fertility rate of 4.5 in 1965, levelling off at around 2.5 from 1985 onwards. The proportion of population below the age of 15 fell from 39.1 in 1970 to 30.6 per cent in 1990, raising the proportion between 15 and 64 years of age from 55.8 to 63.4 per cent. The population of age 65 and over experienced only minor changes from 5.1 to 6.0 per cent.

All these developments had an important impact on the structure of mortality by age as well as by cause. In 1970, deaths below 1 year of age accounted for 25 per cent of all deaths. By 1990 this proportion had declined to 6 per cent. Conversely, the proportion of deaths at age 15 and over increased from 68 per cent in 1970 to 91 per cent in 1990. Changes in the structure of mortality by cause relate closely to the decline in infant mortality. Between 1970 and 1990 the proportion of infant deaths caused by diarrhoea declined from 16.5 per cent to 0.1 per cent and the proportion caused by pneumonia from 30.7 to 0.9 per cent, while deaths from congenital abnormalities in this age group increased from 3.9 to 22.9 per cent. As a consequence, the proportion of total deaths caused by infectious diseases declined from 10.9 in 1970 to 3.2 per cent in 1990.

The chronic diseases examined in the present analysis include malignant neoplasms of the stomach, gall bladder, respiratory organs, breast, cervix uteri, and prostate, diabetes mellitus, hypertensive diseases and stroke, ischaemic heart disease, chronic respiratory diseases, and liver cirrhosis. These diseases cause the majority of adult deaths in Chile, as in most developed countries. Between 1970 and 1990 their relative weight among total deaths increased from 27.9 to 38.9 per cent. In Canada, the lowest mortality country in the Americas, these causes were responsible for more than 42 per cent of all deaths in 1988, whereas the proportion of deaths from infectious diseases was only 0.6 per cent. Therefore, in Chile at present, the advantages and problems of developing and developed countries coexist.

There is epidemiological evidence that deaths from cardiovascular diseases, from diabetes, from some malignant neoplasms, from chronic respiratory diseases, and from cirrhosis can be delayed or reduced by adopting positive changes in lifestyle or by timely diagnosis and treatment (Belloc, 1982). Therefore it is an important challenge for the health sector to develop strategies that diminish, or prevent the increase of, mortality from such diseases.

Before any action can be implemented the first step is to gain an accurate picture of the situation. The present study updates the information on time-trends and regional differentials presented in earlier investigations of Chilean adult mortality (Taucher and Pérez, 1989). In addition, rural and urban differentials are analysed in an attempt to relate some causes to environmental and lifestyle determinants. The influence of individual socio-economic factors is sought by examining the structure of deaths by educational level. Finally, comparison with other countries of the Americas and some detailed comparison with USA mortality are used to evaluate the Chilean situation.

2. Sources and Quality of Data

Analyses in this study are based on vital statistics data published by the National Institute of Statistics (INE) in *Demografía*, the official yearbook of the country, and on some special tabulations prepared at the Institute of Nutrition of the University of Chile and at the Ministry of Health. The population data used to calculate mortality rates come from INE estimates and projections, which are the official figures for the country.

Until 1981, data on births and deaths were processed by both the Ministry of Health and the Institute of Statistics. The former published the list of 999 causes of deaths in the International Classification of Diseases (ICD) for deaths under 28 days of age, from 28 days to 11 months and for 1 year and over. On the other hand, *Demografía* presented the A-list of 150 causes for ages under 1 year, from 1 to 4 years and, from then on, for five-year age groups until age 85 and over. Since 1982, as a consequence of an agreement between INE, the Civil Registrar and the Ministry of Health, *Demografía* has published the 999 causes by five-year age groups. Since knowledge of the age structure of deaths is essential for any analysis of adult mortality by cause, the study of time trends for years prior to 1982 has to be adapted to the 150 categories of the A-list. This does not apply to deaths from cancer, which have been published in the mortality yearbook of the National Health Service, by single codes of the ICD and sex and age group since 1960.

During the period under study, cause of death was coded following the rules of the 8th Revision of the ICD from 1968 to 1978 and of the 9th Revision from 1979. Neither revision differed in codes or rules for the causes of deaths included in the present analysis. Mortality rates from breast cancer were calculated for women. Therefore, though code 174 for both sexes in the 8th Revision was separated into 174 and 175 in the 9th Revision for females and males respectively, this fact is of no importance. The codes for hypertensive diseases were expanded from 401–4 in the 8th Revision, to 401–5 in the 9th Revision. However these codes cover exactly the same causes of deaths. Thus ICD changes do not interfere with the trend analysis presented here.

Data for comparison with other countries of the Americas are available in PAHO (1990) and, for the more detailed comparison with USA mortality, in a publication of the National Center for Health Statistics (1988).

With respect to the quality of vital statistics data in Chile, under-registration is believed to be minimal for adult deaths, whereas doubts exist with respect to the completeness of registration of neonatal deaths, especially those of low birth weight. INE estimated 1.4 per cent under-registration of total deaths for 1980–5 (INE, 1987).

Between 1970 and 1990, the medical certification of deaths from all causes increased from 81 to 95 per cent. In 1990, except for ill-defined causes for which medical certification is 23 per cent, 99 per cent or more of all causes were certified by physicians. Obviously some proportion of the 6 per cent of deaths occurring from ill-defined causes may correspond to the causes under study. However, for at least some chronic diseases, especially malignant neoplasms, it seems likely that the length of the period of illness that precedes death would give time for medical consultation, correct diagnosis, and accurate medical certification.

Medical certification is more common in urban than rural areas: 98 per cent of deaths are medically certified as opposed to 80 per cent. The implication is that rural mortality rates from well-defined causes will be underestimates of real mortality if those deaths not certified by physicians have the same cause distribution as certified ones. Differential medical certification among the thirteen administrative regions into which the country is divided is related to the proportion of rural-urban residents in each region. In 1982 the lowest proportion of deaths medically certified was 97.3 per cent and in eleven regions it was over 98 per cent. In 1990, two regions had lower levels—81.1 and 86.3 per cent. In the other eleven regions over 90 per cent of deaths were medically certified.

In both 1970 and 1990 the proportion of deaths from ill-defined causes was 6 per cent. The apparent failure to improve the data is due to the shift in the age structure of deaths. In 1970, a high proportion of deaths occurred under 1 year of age and about 30 per cent of causes of infant death were ill-defined. On the other hand, except for sudden deaths, recording of ill-defined causes was unusual for an infant death in 1990. Nevertheless, the overall percentage remains constant due to the increase in the proportion of deaths occurring at older ages, where the proportion of ill-defined causes remains relatively high. For this reason most of the comparative analyses in the present study are restricted to adult deaths below the age of 75. Above this age, ill-defined causes surpass 8 per cent in both 1970 and 1990.

3. Methods of Analysis

Age-specific mortality rates are complemented by summary standardized rates for 15 years and over, 15 to 64 years and 15 to 74 years. These eliminate the effect of differences in age-composition over time, among regions and between countries. Age and sex-adjusted rates are calculated for comparison of rural and urban areas, since the sex ratio differs widely between them. Rates of malignant neoplasms of breast, uterus, and prostate are adjusted using the age distribution of the population of the sex concerned. The standard population used is the population at 30 June 1982, the census year in Chile.

Standardized rates are presented for several ranges of age because, although adults are defined as those between the ages of 15 and 64, mortality from most chronic diseases is very important after the age of 64. However, as already mentioned the proportion of ill-defined causes increases above 74 years of age, which makes cause-specific rates less reliable. In addition, after age 74 the size and age structure of the population greatly influences the level of mortality from cardiovascular diseases, cancer of the gallbladder, and other causes which are more common in one sex than the other. Therefore, the best cut-off point for rates seems to be at age 74, especially for comparisons.

Average rates for two or three years are calculated to compare regions and to measure changes over time in order to diminish the influence of annual variations. In an attempt to relate some causes to socio-economic status, comparison of the structure of deaths by educational level within causes is attempted as education-specific rates cannot be calculated because recent census information on the educational structure of the population is unavailable.

4. Characteristics of Chilean Mortality

4.1. Mortality by Sex and Age Group

During the last twenty years mortality has declined in all age groups from 15 years of age upwards and in both sexes. Average rates for three-year periods centred on 1969, 1979 and 1989 are shown in Table 14.1. The decline is summarized further by means of the overall mortality rate at 15 years and over and three age-standardized rates.

During the twenty-year period, the decline in mortality has been greater in younger groups, up to 44 years of age, where mortality from avoidable causes, like tuberculosis, pneumonia and others has diminished. It is worth emphasizing the much greater decline in female than male mortality after the age of 45. This may be due to the lower mortality of women from cardiovascular diseases, which are responsible for a substantial proportion of male deaths. As a consequence, the male to female ratio of mortality rates increased in the period under study.

Declines in the standardized mortality rates are smaller in the period 1979 to 1989 than in the previous decade. During the last twenty years the emphasis on mother and child health care programmes in Chile has been identified as an important determinant of infant mortality decline. In a previous investigation (Taucher and Pérez, 1989) an attempt was made to find out whether, as a consequence of the simultaneous deterioration of health care for adults, there was a stagnation or an increase in levels of adult mortality. The results did not support this conclusion. Perhaps the time-lag needed to show effects on adult mortality from chronic diseases, which by definition have a long evolution, is much longer.

Table 14.1. Mortality rates from all causes by sex and age group, Chile, 1969, 1979 and 1989[a] (per 1000)

Age	Both sexes			Male			Female		
	1969	1979	1989	1969	1979	1989	1969	1979	1989
15–24	1.61	1.14	0.86	1.92	1.53	1.26	1.28	0.73	0.44
25–34	2.83	1.77	1.34	3.52	2.42	1.96	2.14	1.16	0.71
35–44	5.40	3.63	2.43	6.88	4.84	3.34	4.00	2.46	1.54
45–54	9.71	7.96	5.69	12.65	10.55	7.55	7.02	5.60	3.96
55–64	19.38	16.01	13.40	24.41	21.10	18.08	14.79	11.69	9.41
65–74	40.26	36.44	31.12	49.30	46.81	41.30	33.36	28.44	23.22
⩾75	101.07	99.27	98.61	107.83	111.43	115.58	96.43	91.34	88.77
Total ⩾15	10.08	8.58	7.70	11.33	9.76	8.71	8.90	7.47	6.74
Age-adjusted rates									
⩾15	10.08	8.64	7.45	11.03	9.76	8.54	9.14	7.58	6.42
15–74	7.30	5.86	4.65	8.67	7.28	5.93	5.95	4.51	3.41
15–64	5.33	4.04	3.07	6.55	5.21	4.09	4.12	2.91	2.08

[a] Average rates for years 1968–70, 1978–80 and 1988–90.
Source: INE (1968–90).

4.2. Time Trends of Mortality from Selected Chronic Diseases

The rates in Table 14.2 show total mortality and cause-specific mortality by age in both the initial and final triennium of the period under study. The overall decline in mortality is related closely to the decline in two important causes—cardiovascular diseases and stomach cancer. Decreases are also observed in mortality from liver cirrhosis and, to a minor degree, in mortality from malignant neoplasms of the cervix. Conversely, the most important increases are those in mortality from malignant neoplasms of the gallbladder and breast cancer. Mortality from malignant neoplasms of respiratory organs has increased slightly, especially in the age group 15 years and over. All other causes show only minor changes.

It is very difficult to relate time trends in mortality to previous or simultaneous changes in variables believed to be risk factors, since time series data for the latter are not usually available or are only estimates. This is a problem, for instance, with data on dietary change. Each year the Food and Agricultural

Table 14.2. Age-standardized mortality rates at 15 years and over, 15 to 64 years and 15 to 74 years of age, Chile, 1969 and 1989. (Average rates per 100,000 for 3 years, centred on the year shown)

Causes	15 and over		15–74		15–64	
	1969	1989	1969	1989	1969	1989
Total	1008.34	744.50	729.70	465.32	533.15	307.49
Malignant neoplasms of						
Stomach (151)	54.74	27.48	39.31	18.95	22.64	10.64
Gall bladder (156)	6.55	14.09	5.19	10.51	3.27	6.43
Respiratory organs (161, 162)	13.37	15.99	11.13	12.64	7.30	7.61
Female breast[a] (174)	13.53	16.17	11.63	13.14	9.12	10.08
Cervix uteri[a] (180)	17.34	15.98	16.18	13.93	13.87	11.61
Prostate[a] (185)	9.54	10.78	5.03	6.74	1.84	1.70
Diabetes mellitus (250)	14.96	13.58	11.97	9.17	7.36	4.84
Cerebrovascular diseases (401–405, 430–438)	118.67	85.44	72.53	45.48	39.92	23.03
Ischaemic heart disease (410–414)	107.78	81.27	63.25	39.40	32.81	17.98
Chronic respiratory diseases (490–493)	16.81	16.83	10.33	8.14	5.16	3.58
Liver cirrhosis (571)	55.53	35.71	54.45	33.58	32.81	22.04

[a] With respect to the sex-specific population.

Source: INE (1968–90).

Organization (FAO) publishes food balance sheets for most countries of the world, based on statistics of national food production, exports, and imports. Food availability, which is not necessarily synonymous with food intake, can be calculated from these food balance data. The estimates for Chile from 1961 to 1988 show very little change in food availability from vegetable and animal sources with respect to calories, proteins, and fats (FAO, 1988 and 1991).

Sometimes, data on risk factors are available from isolated studies of special groups or sectors of the population which do not permit generalization or comparison. For instance, several surveys on cigarette smoking have been carried out in Chile in the last twenty years. Although methods and geographical coverage vary, the general trend seems to be towards an increase in smoking frequency in the population of age 15 years and over. This could explain much of the increase in cancer of the respiratory organs.

In CASEN, a survey on socio-economic characteristics of the population conducted by the Ministry of Planning (1990), questions on cigarette smoking in the two weeks before the survey were asked using a national sample that provides estimates for each of the thirteen regions of the country as well as for other sub-groups of the total population. No data exist that permit comparison with smoking habits at other points in time. However, if it can be assumed that the ratios of smoking behaviour between different regions have remained constant over time, the information is of interest in exploring relationships between mortality from certain causes and smoking behaviour by region. It is even more difficult to relate the evolution of other aspects of personal behaviour, like sedentarism, to mortality time trends. Therefore, at this stage, only some aspects of mortality trends will be analysed.

The great decline in mortality from malignant neoplasms of the stomach and the steep increase in cancer of the gall bladder are shown in Figure 14.1. The decrease in mortality from stomach cancer mortality seems to be a worldwide phenomenon. On the other hand, no evidence has been found of an increase in mortality from malignant tumours of the gall bladder in other countries like that in Chile. The lack of importance assigned to this disease internationally is shown by the fact that there is no separate category for this location of malignant neoplasms in the basic list recommended in the 9th Revision of the ICD. The association with gallstones, which are very frequent in the Chilean population, especially among women, and deterioration in the timely surgical elimination of the gall bladder in the last two decades, may explain the increase (Serra, 1988). The magnitude of this problem has led health authorities to support a programme of laparoscopic surgery around the country, to shorten the waiting list for cholecystectomy.

The fluctuating trend in mortality from liver cirrhosis, a disease associated with alcoholism, has been studied in relation to alcohol availability. This variable is assumed to be strongly related to consumption and shows similar oscillating patterns over time and a high positive correlation with cirrhosis mortality, as can be seen in Figure 14.2 (Medina, 1989). The association with

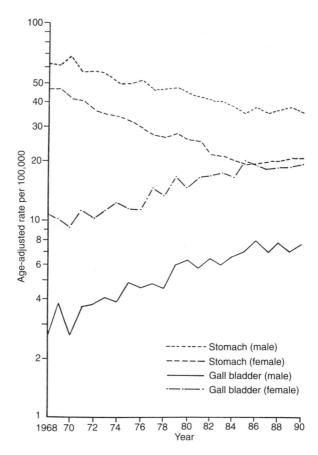

Fig. 14.1. Malignant neoplasm of stomach and gall bladder, by sex. Chile, 1968–90

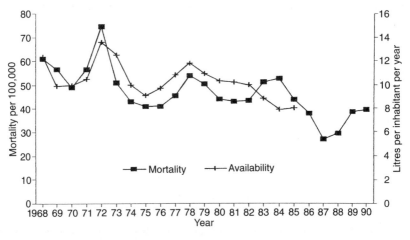

Fig. 14.2. Adult mortality from cirrhosis of the liver and availability of ethanol, Chile 1968–90, both sexes

Hepatitis B found in other places does not extend to Chile since the frequent epidemic outbreaks of hepatitis in this country are due to Hepatitis A. For instance, in 1990, of 456 total cases of hepatitis reported, 66 per cent were identified as Hepatitis A, 1 per cent as Hepatitis B and the rest had no specification, but were probably for the most part of type A (Ministerio de Salud, 1991). Consequently, the fluctuating time trend of hepatitis morbidity exhibits no relationship with the cycles in mortality from cirrhosis.

The increase in breast cancer follows the trend observed in developed countries. The disease has been associated with the use of contraceptive pills which, initially, contained large amounts of oestrogen. There also seems to have been an increase in oestrogen treatment of menopause, which could increase the risk of breast cancer in older women. However, other factors, such as fewer children, later first births, lack of breastfeeding, and obesity, increase with development and have been found to be associated with breast cancer (Ravera *et al.*, 1991).

The very small decline in mortality from cancer of cervix uteri is rather disappointing in light of the existence of an official programme of free Pap smears to prevent this type of cancer. One would also expect that the high prevalence of use of IUDs, which have to be inserted by a health professional who at the same time takes the Pap smear, should have lowered the risk of dying from this cancer. However, IUD users are women of reproductive age, who are at lower risk of cervical cancer than older women.

The most important contribution to the decline in total adult mortality has come from cardiovascular diseases. These account for about 18 per cent of all deaths between 15 and 74 years of age, and about 13 per cent of deaths between the ages of 15 and 64. Neither proportion has changed between the triennia at the ends of the period under study. Comparing age-adjusted rates in the open-ended group, 15 years and over, the relative weight of mortality from these diseases increased from 22.5 to 26.0 per cent during the period under study.

Comparisons of mortality from hypertension and stroke and ischaemic heart disease illustrate the influence of using open-ended or closed age-adjusted mortality rates for interpretation of the data. It is commonly believed that mortality from hypertension and cerebrovascular diseases is higher in women than in men, whereas ischaemic heart disease is a more frequent cause of death among men. In a previous paper (Taucher *et al.*, 1990), an analysis of age-specific mortality rates confirmed the excess in male mortality from ischaemic diseases. However, except for greater mortality in the 15 to 24 and 35 to 44 age groups, where the rates are negligible compared with older ages,* male mortality from hypertension and cerebrovascular diseases exceeds female mortality. The higher female mortality according to the age-adjusted rates for 15 years and over in Figure 14.3 reflects the much greater proportion of old women than old men in the population. Thus, by limiting the upper end of the rate to 74 years of age, one observes in Figure 14.3 that male mortality

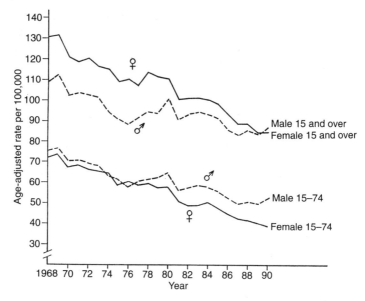

Fig. 14.3. Mortality from hypertensive diseases, by sex, Chile 1968–90

exceeds female mortality for this disease. Possible explanations for the decline of mortality from cardiovascular diseases are discussed in the last section.

4.3. Regional Differences

Chile, in its continental part, extends along the west coast of South America, from latitude 17°30′ in the north to latitude 56°30′ in the south. The country is about 4000 km long, with an average width of 200 km between the Andes Mountains and the Pacific Ocean. The climate is desertic in the north, mild in the central part and cold in the extreme south. The country is divided into thirteen regions. Regions I to XII are ordered from north to south. Region XIII, also called the Metropolitan Region, where the capital of the country lies, is in approximately the centre of the country.

As a consequence of the differences in climate and economic activity, regions vary significantly with respect to their predominant type of food intake, socio-economic levels, exposure to occupational and environmental risks, and access to health services, which is related to the proportion of population in urban and rural areas. Thus, the regions are characterized by a whole spectrum of conditions related to specific causes of death. Unfortunately, the study of mortality differentials by region is obstructed by the great disparity in their population sizes, which range from 81,000 inhabitants in Region XI to 5.3 million in the Metropolitan Region. The analysis of mortality by cause is hindered further by differences in the proportion of deaths medically certified, as discussed in the section on data quality. In spite of these problems, there is such great and consistent excess mortality from certain causes in some regions that areal analysis is worthwhile.

Special tabulations from the tapes for 1981 and 1982, provided by INE, were made for an earlier study (Taucher and Pérez, 1989) since deaths by causes and regions were not available at that time. For this study, six causes from which there are sufficient deaths to calculate stable rates and for which significant differences by region were found in the earlier study, were extracted from the tabulations for 1989 and 1990 available at the Ministry of Health.

The standardized average rates for 1981–2 and for 1989–90 for ages 15 and over are presented in Table 14.3. The patterns repeat themselves in both biennial periods. The mortality rate from stomach cancer declines during the period but is consistently highest in the VIIth Region, which has the most rural population of all regions of the country (40 per cent). The second highest rates for this cause are found in the VIIIth Region, which has a predominantly urban population. However, analysing deaths in the four health service areas of Region VIII, one observes that the high gastric cancer mortality comes from the two areas with more rural populations, which may be characterized by food consumption or other risk factors that are similar to the adjacent VIIth Region. Results of a case-control study, which explored principally the influence of nitrates in the diet, showed no association with this component nor with any other of the risk factors investigated (Armijo *et al.*, 1981).

Mortality from malignant tumours of respiratory organs is highest in the IInd Region, followed by the Ist Region. This has already been described by Haynes (1983) and others. The percentage of population age 15 and over, smoking ten or more cigarettes a day was investigated using the CASEN survey of 1990 and showed no relationship with respiratory cancer mortality rates among regions. It has to be remembered that to justify analysis of this association, one has to assume that the ratios of the percentages smoking among regions in 1990 reflect earlier ratios. Even though Regions II and I, with 5.3 and 4.5 per cent of heavy smokers, lag far behind Region XIII with 7.8 per cent, the three regions with lowest mortality rates from this disease also have the lowest percentage of heavy smokers. They are the regions with the most rural population and smoking is less frequent in rural areas.

The most likely explanation of the high mortality rate from respiratory cancers in the IInd Region is environmental contamination by arsenic, an element that has been identified as a risk to health (Tchernitchin and Tchernitchin, 1991), especially for producing lung and skin cancer (Maclure and Macmahon, 1980; Leefeldstein, 1989). Unacceptably high levels of arsenic used to be present in drinking water in Antofagasta, the largest city in the IInd Region (Borgoño and Greiber, 1971). Whereas the international norm permits maximum levels of 50 micrograms per litre, the arsenic content of water in Antofagasta fluctuated between 80 and 130 micrograms per litre in measure-

Table 14.3. Age-standardized mortality from malignant neoplasms of the stomach and respiratory organs, from bronchitis, emphysema and asthma, from cerebrovascular diseases, ischaemic heart diseases and from liver cirrhosis by region (per 100,000)

Regions	Malignant neoplasms				Bronchitis, emphysema and asthma (490–493)	
	Stomach (151)		Respiratory Organs			
	1981–2	1989–90	1981–2	1989–90	1981–2	1989–90
I	28.11	17.22	29.94	33.20	7.18	18.02
II	27.96	21.01	52.14	51.54	18.70	19.89
III	27.26	26.46	18.58	25.00	6.70	13.53
IV	28.09	28.01	15.33	13.77	7.56	13.48
V	35.58	23.24	17.22	16.78	12.01	14.74
VI	34.03	28.63	10.02	11.12	9.98	22.14
VII	53.18	39.26	9.18	9.75	12.96	17.98
VIII	43.12	37.58	7.94	7.53	9.86	13.72
IX	33.44	31.08	7.86	6.96	6.88	11.76
X	25.86	29.94	10.66	12.90	7.91	11.08
XI and XII	27.50	28.98	21.85	23.35	17.48	26.20
XIII	26.76	23.58	19.06	18.74	12.77	16.86

Regions	Ischaemic heart disease		Cerebrovascular diseases		Liver cirrhosis	
					1981–2	1989–90
	1981–2	1989–90	1981–2	1989–90		
I	105.38	83.84	71.34	73.65	42.79	36.27
II	136.18	118.36	86.47	85.07	44.12	36.19
III	67.91	57.75	85.49	80.68	20.12	21.05
IV	84.36	79.11	70.51	72.35	11.56	13.60
V	109.56	99.88	115.48	96.22	47.55	33.40
VI	76.64	76.14	95.82	76.84	42.36	41.96
VII	81.70	88.62	101.01	106.34	35.52	57.74
VIII	73.52	76.88	115.13	115.40	65.34	71.84
IX	51.42	54.94	86.08	90.42	23.44	26.71
X	68.91	74.24	71.40	74.03	25.10	27.62
XI and XII	145.96	100.42	82.78	74.76	30.60	23.78
XIII	87.53	80.88	96.20	73.18	47.48	37.28

Source: Ministry of Health, special tabulations.

ments made between 1957 and 1968. Borgoño also studied the effect of a water treatment plant that was installed in 1970 to prevent arsenic-related diseases (Borgoño *et al.*, 1977). The plant reduced the level to below 120 micrograms per litre. A new plant was installed in 1980 and finally stabilized the level of arsenic in water below 50 micrograms. However, arsenic-related diseases are still a problem at present. This may be because Chuquicamata, the largest open-cast copper mine in the world, is located in the IInd Region. The copper refinery pollutes the air with arsenic far beyond the international norm of 0.02 micrograms per cubic metre. The annual average in Chuquicamata in 1990 was 1.96 micrograms. The peak that year was 41.5 and the level surpassed 10.0 several times. Moreover, the winds blow this polluted air into the snow of the Andes which, on melting, contaminates the ground water and, as a consequence, vegetables and fish of the region. The problem is under study at this moment in order to develop further preventive programmes in addition to water treatment plants, especially related to reducing the air pollution from the copper refinery. In fact, a modern reverberator, replacing two older ones, has already reduced pollution by arsenic from 2.75 micrograms per cubic metre in the first half of 1991 to 1.06 in the second half of the same year. No equivalent explanations can be suggested for the high mortality from similar diseases in the Ist Region. Migration data from the 1982 census do not reveal a large population flow from the IInd to the Ist Region among adults.

Similar comments apply to deaths from chronic respiratory diseases. Again, in Region II, arsenic is a risk factor for bronchial diseases, specifically for bronchiectasis. The rise in the rate in the VIth Region, immediately south of Santiago, the capital of the country, is important. A big copper refinery has been expanded in that region producing significant air pollution. The consistently high mortality from chronic respiratory disease in Regions XI, XII and XIII could be related to the fact that they are regions with high percentages of heavy smokers. However, the high rates in Region VII, which is predominantly rural, are difficult to explain.

Mortality from hypertension and cerebrovascular diseases appears highest in three regions that have little in common. The VIIth and the VIIIth Regions have already been discussed with reference to the frequency of stomach cancer. They had the lowest percentage of cigarette smokers in the CASEN survey of 1990. The Vth Region is composed of a very heterogeneous population, with the majority living in or near the most important seaport of the country and the rest in agricultural areas. The region is in a mid-position with respect to cigarette smoking.

Ischaemic heart disease mortality is highest in Region II and in Regions XI and XII, which are grouped together because of the small size of their populations and because they have similar environmental and dietary characteristics. The explanation of the high mortality must differ between Regions II and XI and XII. Again, smoking is not significant in Region II according to the CASEN survey. However Regions XI and XII have the highest smoking levels in the country. The IInd Region may have a high rate because of arsenic contamination, which has already been commented on extensively and which has been shown to provoke heart infarcts due to arteritis. On the other hand, the southern regions, XI and XII, in contrast to the rest of the country, have both a high proportion of heavy smokers and above average consumption of beef and lamb, which have a high saturated fat content which is known to be a risk factor for high cholesterol and, in consequence, ischaemic heart disease.

Finally, liver cirrhosis, a disease related to alcoholism, is highest in the VIIIth Region in both periods. Comparing the situation in the four health services of that region again, this time the contribution of the urban areas is greater than that of the rural parts of the region. Alcoholism among coal miners and industrial workers has been recorded as a health problem in the region. However, remembering the fluctuating time trends in mortality from this cause, any discussion based on a two-year period should be interpreted with caution.

Surprisingly, the Metropolitan Region XIII, with the highest percentage of heavy smokers, with all the negative aspects of urban lifestyles, and with air pollution that reaches dangerous levels every winter, shows below average mortality rates from all the diseases analysed by region. In addition, all rates diminish between the two biennia, except for a slight increase in mortality from chronic obstructive respiratory diseases. It is possible that better access to medical care explains the lower mortality from chronic diseases in the Metropolitan Region.

It seems important to investigate some of the hypotheses that have been raised in the discussion of differences between regions in this section and to continue to pay attention to the evolution of the rates in future studies.

4.4. Urban–Rural Differentials

Comparison of urban and rural mortality is significant because the exposure to risk factors of the population differs by residence. The rural population is only 15 per cent of the whole population of Chile. However, this represents 2 million people, which is sufficient to obtain stable rates. Mortality for both sexes is higher in rural than in urban areas up to the age of 54. Thereafter urban mortality exceeds that of rural residents (Table 14.4). This crossover takes place earlier for males than for females, but occurs in both sexes before the age of 50.

The sex ratio of the urban population is always below unity and is very different from the rural population, where this ratio is considerably greater than one until age 75. Since mortality levels from some causes differ between the sexes, the rates shown in Table 14.5 have been adjusted both for the sex and age composition of the population. Analysis of urban–rural mortality differentials by cause is hampered by the difference in the frequency of non-medical certification of deaths, which is about 2 per cent in the urban population and approximately 20 per cent in the rural one. This may distort the cause-specific mortality rates: one would expect that mortality from most causes would be about 18 per cent lower in rural than in urban areas for this reason alone. On the other hand, if for some causes higher mortality is found in rural areas, this should be interpreted as a higher risk associated with rural

Table 14.4. Urban and rural mortality rates by sex and age group, 1990 (per 1000)

Age	Both sexes		Male		Female	
	Urban	Rural	Urban	Rural	Urban	Rural
15–19	0.60	1.10	0.84	1.41	0.37	0.72
20–24	0.92	1.53	1.42	2.22	0.42	0.65
25–29	1.15	1.66	1.76	2.38	0.57	0.69
30–34	1.38	2.13	2.04	2.76	0.76	1.30
35–39	1.79	2.62	2.57	3.44	1.04	1.57
40–44	2.99	3.77	4.19	4.82	1.89	2.43
45–49	4.70	4.78	6.61	5.79	2.99	3.49
50–54	7.23	7.38	9.87	9.50	4.93	4.73
55–59	10.88	9.79	14.89	11.83	7.58	7.33
60–64	17.50	16.22	24.33	19.42	12.21	12.41
65 and over	57.30	52.81	69.93	59.16	49.22	46.30

Source: Ministry of Health, special tabulation.

Table 14.5. Urban and rural adult mortality from chronic diseases, Chile 1990 (age and sex-adjusted rates per 100,000)[a]

Causes of death	15–74		15–74 (Corrected)[b]	
	Urban	Rural	Urban	Rural
Malignant neoplasms of				
Esophagus (150)	3.87	4.27	3.97	5.30
Stomach (151)	18.59	19.72	19.05	24.50
Colon (153)	3.47	1.75	3.56	2.17
Gall bladder (156)	10.90	10.53	11.17	13.08
Respiratory organs (161, 162)	14.71	4.90	15.07	6.09
Female breast (174)	14.52	6.79	14.88	8.43
Cervix uteri (180)	14.63	9.56	14.99	11.88
Prostate (185)	8.02	4.03	8.22	5.01
Diabetes mellitus (250)	10.57	6.44	10.83	8.00
Cerebrovascular diseases (401–405, 430–438)	46.84	40.14	47.99	49.86
Ischaemic heart disease (410–414)	41.94	29.28	42.97	36.37
Chronic respiratory disease (490–493)	8.11	5.02	8.31	6.24
Liver cirrhosis (571)	41.62	18.38	42.60	22.83

[a] Standard population: Chile 1982. Rates from cancer of breast, cervix uteri and prostate, age-adjusted by sex-specific population.
[b] For non-medical certification.

Source: Ministry of Health, special tabulation.

conditions. In Table 14.5, rates corrected for this difference by assuming that the deaths not certified by physicians have the same structure as the certified ones are added for comparative purposes.

The most outstanding differences in mortality by residence are found for malignant neoplasms of the respiratory organs and for liver cirrhosis. Mortality rates for the two diseases are definitely higher in the urban population. To a lesser degree, differences in the same direction are also found for all cancers of sexual organs, for cancer of colon and for diabetes, chronic respiratory and ischemic heart disease. It is known that most of these diseases are related to factors, such as smoking habits, alcoholism, obesity, stress, sedentary habits, and air pollution, that are typical of urban populations. According to the CASEN survey data, 6.2 per cent of the urban population smokes ten or more cigarettes a day but this proportion is only 3.6 per cent in rural areas. No information on other risk factors is available. On the other hand, mortality from cancer of oesophagus and stomach is higher in rural areas, perhaps because of dietary habits that have not been identified yet.

4.5. Mortality and Educational Level

As it is ten years since the last census, it is difficult to estimate the structure of the population by educational level. Therefore it is not possible to calculate education-specific mortality rates like those presented for the regions or the rural–urban population. However, since education is one of the few variables on the death certificate that is related to the individual's socio-economic level, we attempt to come to some conclusions by comparing, for every cause, the proportion of deaths by age occurring to those with a low level of education, defined as lacking formal education or only reaching or completing primary school. Only the age range of 25 to 64 years is considered because the proportion of the population with a low level of education is greater in older persons and, in addition, not all causes have the same age-distribution. Because of this last consideration, the simple average of the four age groups was chosen as a summary measure. One would expect that the proportion of deaths pertaining to lower levels of education in the age span under consideration should be somewhere between 60 and 75 per cent of all deaths. The constraints on interpretation resulting from differences between categories of educational level with respect to the proportion of deaths medically certified have to be overcome by assuming that deaths from all causes are affected in the same way and, therefore, that comparisons of the proportions among causes are valid.

The proportion of the deaths that are of people with low levels of education for selected causes and the above-mentioned average, arranged in ascending order of magnitude, are shown in Table 14.6 and in Figure 14.4. Liver cirrhosis and malignant neoplasms of the colon are at the two extremes of the ordered series. This is consistent with the discussion earlier. In Chile, one would expect alcoholism to be more frequent among the lower social strata. However, dietary factors like foods low in fibre content and high in saturated fats, which

Table 14.6. Percentage of adult deaths from each cause occurring to those with no education or primary schooling for selected chronic diseases, Chile, 1990

Causes of death	Age group				
	Average	25–34	35–44	45–54	55–64
Cancer of colon (153)	40.5	37.5	21.4	39.6	63.4
Respiratory cancer (161, 162)	45.3	23.1	41.2	52.9	64.2
Cancer of breast (174)	51.8	39.1	49.0	56.4	62.8
Cerebrovascular diseases (401–405, 430–438)	62.0	42.6	62.0	67.4	75.8
Ischaemic heart disease (410–414)	62.7	52.9	61.4	66.4	70.1
Cancer of stomach (151)	68.1	58.3	62.0	73.1	78.9
Diabetes mellitus (250)	68.3	66.7	66.7	65.9	74.1
Cancer of cervix uteri (180)	71.9	60.0	66.7	80.6	80.2
Chronic respiratory diseases (490–493)	72.0	62.5	72.2	76.7	76.5
Cancer of gall bladder (156)	72.5	70.6	77.3	67.1	74.9
Liver cirrhosis (571)	77.0	82.6	77.0	74.6	73.6

Source: Ministry of Health, special tabulation.

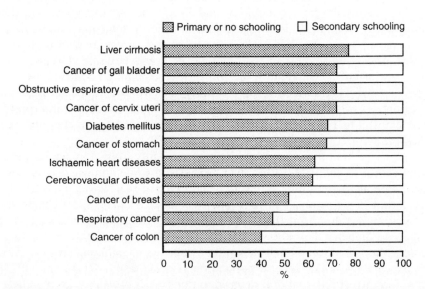

Fig. 14.4. Per cent distribution according to level of education of deaths at 25 to 64 years for selected causes, Chile, 1990

have been found to be associated with colon cancer (Bristol and Heaton, 1985), are probably more prevalent among the better educated and, therefore, well-off sectors of the population. The greater proportion of deaths to the educated within deaths from lung cancer and other respiratory neoplasms occurring to the educated also coincides with what is expected according to smoking habits. Breast cancer is related to high-fat food consumption, obesity, and other factors that have been discussed already in relation to breast cancer trends and may be more common in higher social strata.

The remaining causes appear more evenly distributed according to the general distribution by education of the population and to the distribution of deaths from all causes.

5. Chilean Mortality in the Context of Mortality in the Americas

The Pan American Health Organization publication (PAHO, 1990) on health conditions in the Americas contains valuable data for comparison of mortality among countries in this region. After examining the data, it was decided to use 1986 for comparison of different countries since this was the last year for which most countries provided information. Only countries with at least 20,000 deaths per year were considered in the analysis. Age-adjusted mortality rates from the most common chronic diseases for all the countries fulfilling both requirements are shown in Table 14.7.

With respect to overall mortality, Canada, the USA, Cuba, and Puerto Rico have the lowest levels and Ecuador and Brazil the highest, while all other countries are in an intermediate position. In order to interpret cause-specific mortality, it is important to look at the rates and percentages of ill-defined causes. These are highest in Brazil, Venezuela and Ecuador. Uruguay and Chile are at an intermediate level and in the remaining countries they are relatively low. This means that low mortality rates from some specific causes in the countries with large proportions of ill-defined causes cannot be interpreted as low mortality. However, higher rates would be an underestimate of the real situation.

With these limitations in mind, the high mortality from stomach cancer in Chile and in Ecuador and from liver cirrhosis in Chile and Mexico, as compared with all other countries, has to be accepted as real. The same is true for the extremely high mortality from diabetes in Mexico and for somewhat lower, but still high, rates from this disease in Puerto Rico and Venezuela. With respect to diabetes, it is known that mortality from this disease is due to its complications and it has been shown that well-treated patients have the same life expectancy as the general population (García de los Ríos *et al.*, 1972). Therefore, irrespective of other considerations, early mortality from diabetes may serve as an indicator of access to medical care.

With regard to rates that are higher in more developed countries with a lower proportion of ill-defined causes, the clearest example case is respiratory cancer. Even if the ill-defined deaths of the remaining countries are attributed proportionally to this cause, respiratory cancer mortality in the USA, Canada, Uruguay, Cuba, and Argentina greatly surpasses that in other countries. These

Table 14.7. Mortality from selected chronic diseases in countries of the Americas with at least 20,000 deaths per year, 1986 (Age-adjusted rates per 100,000)

	Argentina	Brazil	Canada	Chile	Cuba	Ecuador	Mexico	P. Rico	Uruguay	USA	Venezuela
Total mortality	465.3	516.1	315.5	444.4	385.7	579.6	496.9	392.4	462.3	364.9	461.7
Ill-defined causes (780–799)	12.1	104.4	7.0	33.6	0.9	82.7	21.2	3.1	36.4	9.9	79.5
Percent ill-defined	2.6	20.2	2.2	7.6	0.2	14.3	4.3	0.8	7.9	2.7	17.2
Malignant neoplasms											
Total	72.7	46.6	78.8	72.2	66.5	46.9	40.8	58.6	92.4	77.4	49.9
Stomach (151)	5.2	5.8	3.4	13.3	3.2	12.2	4.9	5.0	7.0	2.1	7.2
Colon (153)	4.9	1.6	6.4	2.5	4.4	1.2	1.4	4.1	7.1	7.0	1.9
Respiratory (162)	12.3	5.5	19.6	7.1	15.4	2.6	5.7	7.0	15.7	20.8	5.9
Breast (174)	6.6	3.1	7.8	4.0	4.5	1.8	2.4	4.1	8.7	7.4	2.9
Cervix uteri (180)	1.8	1.7	0.9	4.4	2.1	1.9	4.9	1.3	1.7	1.0	2.9
Diabetes (250)	7.3	9.2	5.2	7.0	8.8	7.0	29.9	16.1	7.8	5.7	13.8
Hypertension (401–405)	5.3	9.3	1.8	5.6	4.6	5.4	7.0	12.7	4.2	4.4	10.4
Ischemic heart disease (410–414)	36.6	39.4	66.9	38.0	73.9	16.9	24.7	48.7	44.4	69.9	41.5
Cerebrovascular (430–438)	38.2	46.5	18.5	35.7	32.7	25.0	21.9	17.5	43.7	19.1	28.0
Cirrhosis (571)	6.0	8.2	4.2	20.1	4.0	6.8	21.7	15.3	3.9	5.6	6.3

Source: PAHO/WHO (1990).

countries also have the highest mortality from breast cancer and from cancer of the colon. Except for Argentina and Uruguay, they also share high mortality from ischaemic heart disease. It is perhaps dangerous to infer common risk factors from these outcome data. However, the conjunction of smoking habits, diets rich in saturated fats and low in fibre, and obesity are partial explanations for excess mortality from these causes (Berríos *et al.*, 1990).

In an earlier study (Taucher and Pérez, 1990), a detailed comparison was made for 1986 between mortality from cardiovascular diseases in Chile and the USA. Having found that in Chile, compared with the USA, the proportion of ill-defined causes of death increased significantly with age, and that, in both countries, mortality before the age of 35 was rare, standardized rates were calculated for the age span 35 to 74 years. Mortality from ischaemic heart diseases was 187.2 in the USA and 89.3 in Chile, whereas cerebrovascular diseases showed the opposite trend with a rate of 91.9 in Chile and 39.9 in the USA. The ratios between the rates for Chile and the USA were lower than unity for ischemic heart disease and above one for cerebrovascular diseases in all age groups. The interpretation of these findings was that the USA diet, which is rich in saturated fats, leads to high cholesterol and ischaemic heart disease. The lower frequency of deaths from cerebrovascular diseases in the USA was attributed to better control of hypertension in that country.

6. Comments and Conclusions

Since most studies of cause-specific mortality studies are aimed at evaluating health situations either descriptively or comparatively in order to propose preventive measures, it is useful to remember that mortality is a partial indicator of the full health situation. Programmes based on this knowledge rely on the assumption that future generations can benefit from current action. The emphasis on mortality statistics reflects the fact that it is easier to obtain them than reliable and unbiased morbidity data, which is the information required ideally to develop programmes to prevent fatalities. Accepting the inherent limitations of information on mortality, a second issue is the quality of the data. Under-registration of deaths, non-medical certification, physicians with limited knowledge of how to complete death certificates or little motivation to provide the necessary information, and other factors may limit the quality of data.

Regarding the methodological aspects of comparative studies, the standard population used for calculating the age-adjusted rates by PAHO is a very young population: 74 per cent of it is below the age of 35, which is the age at which chronic diseases start to be a major problem. This means that differences in adult mortality and in mortality from chronic diseases have less opportunity to show their real dimensions and differences in rates adjusted with respect to the structure of this population than diseases or forms of injury that are common in younger age groups. The identification of risk factors for mortality from particular causes and the study of relationships between mortality and risk factors based on secondary data pose problems. For example, it is difficult to obtain reliable information on smoking, diet, and other components of lifestyles.

Sometimes the main difficulties lie in the interpretation of results. For instance, mortality from diseases which are believed to respond to the same risk factors sometimes exhibit opposite trends. This occurs in Chile with respect to the decrease in mortality from cardiovascular diseases and increase in mortality from cancer of respiratory organs, both of which have been related to smoking habits. It is also difficult to explain why, in Chile, mortality from cardiovascular diseases has decreased during a twenty-year period of modernization as such mortality is believed to be associated with negative changes in lifestyles like cigarette smoking, sedentarism, increases in the consumption of saturated fats and of refined sugars, and decreases in consumption of fibre-rich food. One possible explanation for this unexpected pattern could be that, in Chile, progress during the present century has been associated with a decline in infant and child mortality and of mortality from infectious diseases, which usually affect lower social strata. If development has failed to create social mobility, implying that the new survivors remained in the lower social strata, the proportion of people of low socio-economic status in the adult and elderly age groups will have increased over time. In Chile red meat and other foods linked to high blood cholesterol are expensive and inaccessible to the lower strata. People in the lower social strata get their calories mainly from bread, other carbohydrates, and vegetable proteins and fats which are healthy with respect to cardiovascular diseases (Albala *et al.*, 1989). Data on socio-economic mortality differentials by cause and information on changes in the population structure of older people, which will become available once the 1992 census is processed, would be of help in investigating this hypothesis.

In spite of all their limitations, studies of mortality by cause reveal important differences between countries and regions that coincide with what would be expected based on present knowledge of risk factors. They can therefore help both to identify the magnitude of problems and to set priorities for environmental interventions and for specific health and educational programmes addressing known determinants.

References

Albala, C., P. Villarroel, S. Olivares, I. Truffello, F. Vío, and M. Andrade (1989), 'Mujeres obesas de alto y bajo nivel socioeconómico; composición de la dieta y niveles séricos de lipoproteínas', *Revista Médica de Chile*, 117: 3–9.

Armijo, R., R. Detels, A. Coulson, E. Medina, M. Orellana, and A. Gonzalez (1981), 'Epidemiología del cáncer gástrico en Chile', *Revista Médica de Chile*, 109: 551–6.

Belloc, N. B. (1982), 'Personal behaviour affecting mortality', in: S. Preston (ed.) *Biological and Social Aspects of Mortality and the Length of Life*, Ordina Editions, Liège, Belgium.

Berríos, X., L. Jadue, J. Zenteno, M. I. Ross, and H. Rodríguez (1990), 'Prevalencia de factores de riesgo en enfermedades crónicas. Estudio en la población general de la Región Metropolitana 1986–1987', *Revista Médica de Chile*, 118: 597–604.

Borgoño, J. M., and R. Greiber (1971), 'Estudio epidemiológico del arsenicismo en la ciudad de Antofagasta', *Revista Médica de Chile*, 99: 702–7.

——P. Vicent, H. Venturino, and A. Infante (1977), 'Arsenic in the drinking water of the city of Antofagasta: epidemiological and clinical study before and after the installation of a treatment plant', *Environmental Health Perspectives*, 19: 103–5.

Bristol, J., and K. W. Heaton (1985), 'Sugar, fat and the risk of colorectal cancer', *British Medical Journal*, 26: 757–68.

Food and Agricultural Organization (FAO) (1988), *Food Balance Sheets (1975–77 Average) and per Caput Food Supplies (1961–65 Average, 1967 to 1977)*, Rome, Italy.

——(1991), *Food Balance Sheets, 1984–86 Average*, Rome, Italy.

García de los Ríos, M., S. Valiente, I. Canessa, I. Mella, and E. Taucher (1972), 'Complicaciones degenerativas y sobrevida de los diabéticos', *Revista Médica de Chile*, 100: 733–40.

Haynes, R. (1983), 'The geographical distribution of mortality by cause in Chile', *Social Science and Medicine*, 17: 355–64.

Instituto Nacional de Estadísticas (INE) (1968–90), *Demografía*, Santiago, Chile.

——and Centro Latinoamericano de Demografía (CELADE) (1987), *Chile: Proyecciones de Población por Sexo y Edad, Total del País 1950–2025*, Fascículo F/CHI.1, CELADE, Santiago, Chile.

Leefeldstein, A. (1989), 'A comparison of several measures of exposure to arsenic— Matched case-control study of copper smelter employees', *American Journal of Epidemiology*, 129: 112–24.

Maclure, M. R., and B. Macmahon (1980), 'An epidemiologic perspective of environmental carcinogenesis', *Epidemiologic Reviews*, 2: 19–48.

Medina, E. C. (1989), 'Consumo de sustancias psicoactivas en Chile', *Boletín Epidemiológico de Chile*, 16(4,5,6): 53–74.

Ministerio de Planificación (1990), 'Encuesta de Características Sociales y Económicas Nacionales (CASEN)', Santiago, Chile.

Ministerio de Salud (1991), 'Anuario de Enfermedades de Notificación obligatoria', Santiago, Chile.

National Center for Health Statistics (1988), Advance Report of Final Mortality Statistics, 1986, *Monthly Vital Statistics Report* (Supplement), 37: 6.

Pan American Health Organization (PAHO) and World Health Organization (WHO) (1990), *Health Conditions in the Americas*, Scientific Publication No. 524, Washington, DC.

Ravera, R., E. Medina, and I. López (1991), 'Epidemiología del cáncer de mama', *Revista Médica de Chile*, 119: 1059–65.

Serra, I. (1988), 'Perspectiva del cáncer biliar y otros cánceres importantes en Chile', *Cuadernos Médico Sociales*, 29(4): 126–33.

Taucher, E., C. Albala, and P. Pérez (1990), '¿Ha aumentado la mortalidad cardiovascular en Chile?', *Revista Médica de Chile*, 118: 225–34.

——and P. Pérez (1989), 'Mortalidad del adulto en Chile: 1975 a 1987', *Cuadernos Médico Sociales*, 30(2).

Tchernitchin, A., and N. Tchernitchin (1991), 'Posibles efectos en la salud de la contaminación de aire, aguas y alimento con arsénico en Chile', *Revista Chilena de Nutrición*, 19: 149–63.

15 Maternal Mortality

DANUTA RAJS

Instituto Médico Legal, Santiago, Chile

1. The Magnitude of Maternal Mortality

Although the risk that any of the 115 million women of childbearing age currently living in the Latin American and Caribbean countries will die from pregnancy, delivery or puerperal complications decreased by 54 per cent between 1970 and 1989, this is still a far cry from the levels that have been achieved by the industrialized countries. Maternal death is still one of the main causes of death of women aged 15 to 49 in a number of countries of the region (PAHO, 1987). Moreover, an even more worrying picture of the situation would emerge if the unreported maternal deaths that occur in almost all the Latin American and Caribbean countries could be identified (see Chapter 4).

Considering only maternal deaths registered and published by various national and international agencies, the probability of dying from maternal causes declined from 13 per 10,000 estimated births in 1970–4 to six per 10,000 estimated births in 1985–9. During this period, the region's infant mortality is estimated to have declined by 33 per cent while fertility dropped by 29 per cent. Compared with the industrialized countries of North America, where the probability of dying from maternal causes fell by 63 per cent between 1970 and 1989, the relative risk of death of Latin American and Caribbean women aged 15 to 49 has increased from 7.1 in 1970–4 to 8.8 during the last quinquennium of the period.

This chapter analyses data compiled for the Technical Information System of the Pan American Health Organization (PAHO) together with population estimates compiled by the Latin American Demographic Centre (CELADE). These data have been supplemented with information on vital statistics published by various countries.

2. Maternal Mortality and Fertility

The direct relationship between maternal mortality and fertility has been demonstrated and analysed in several publications (CELADE, 1990; US

National Research Council, 1989). The effect of parity and of intervals between pregnancies on the risk of complications in all the stages of pregnancy
and of the puerperium is well known (PAHO, 1987). Hence, the countries
covered by this study have been classified into three groups according to the
total fertility rate estimated for them in 1985–9, namely:

(a) The low-fertility countries (Argentina, Cuba, Chile, Puerto Rico, and
Uruguay) where, in 1985–9, the estimated total fertility rate was below 3.0
children per woman and fertility declined by a little over 20 per cent between
1970 and 1989;

(b) The medium-fertility countries (Brazil, Colombia, Costa Rica, Ecuador,
Mexico, Panama, the Dominican Republic, and Venezuela), where women
had estimated total fertility rates of 3.1 to 4.4 children in 1985–9 and fertility
declined by a little over 32 per cent in the 1970–89 period; and,

(c) The high-fertility countries (Guatemala, Honduras, Peru, and
Paraguay) where the estimated total fertility rate was 4.5 or more children per
woman in 1985–9 and fertility fell by nearly 26 per cent between 1970 and
1989.

In global terms, the information presented concerns a population of some 418
million people in 1990 who inhabit seventeen of the twenty-one countries of
the region. Of these people, 106 million are women of childbearing age. They
represent 95 per cent of the fertile female population of the region. Four
countries are omitted (Bolivia, El Salvador, Haiti, and Nicaragua) because it is
not possible to obtain sufficient information on maternal deaths from the
sources consulted.

Tables 15.1, 15.2 and 15.3 and the corresponding figures show the evolution
of maternal mortality in the three groups of countries by quinquennium and
the evolution of the risk of maternal death in relation to the ratio observed in
Canada, which is the American country with the lowest maternal mortality
rate. Each curve is accompanied by a fitted regression line that indicates the
underlying time trend in the indicator. In addition, each figure shows
the evolution of the overall total fertility rate for the group of countries. The
validity of comparing the maternal mortality ratio in each group of countries
with the Canadian ratio was established by regressing the maternal mortality
ratios on total fertility for each group of nations and for Canada, and assessing
whether the slopes of the fitted lines differ by means of a t-test. In all the cases
the differences were insignificant (P = 95%). Although maternal mortality
declined in all three groups of countries during the period, the relative risk in
comparison to Canada has increased.

There was a decline of about 57 per cent in the maternal mortality ratio in
the low fertility countries between 1970 and 1989. Nevertheless, their relative
risk of maternal death in comparison with Canada increased by some 61 per
cent during the period. The downward slope of the estimated trend in maternal mortality is 4 deaths a year per 100,000 births but the relative risk of dying

Table 15.1. Low fertility countries: quinquennial maternal mortality and relative risk in relation to the Canadian ratio, 1970–89

Country	Quinquennia							
	1970–4		1975–9		1980–4		1985–9	
	MMR	RR	MMR	RR	MMR	RR	MMR	RR
Argentina	11.41	7.71	8.74	12.75	6.55	13.58	5.64	14.28
Chile	14.80	10.00	9.50	13.86	3.94	8.17	4.23	10.71
Cuba	6.92	4.67	5.68	8.29	4.70	9.74	4.53	11.47
Puerto Rico	2.73	1.85	1.28	1.87	1.05	2.18	1.51	3.83
Uruguay	7.03	4.75	6.22	9.08	4.48	9.29	3.21	8.13
Total	10.70	7.23	8.03	11.72	5.31	11.01	4.59	11.62
Canada	1.48	1.00	0.69	1.00	0.48	1.00	0.40	1.00

Note: MMR: Maternal mortality ratio (per 10,000 births). RR: Relative risk in relation to the Canadian ratio.

Table 15.2. Medium fertility countries: quinquennial maternal mortality and relative risk in relation to the Candian ratio, 1970–89

Country	Quinquennia							
	1970–4		1975–9		1980–4		1985–9	
	MMR	RR	MMR	RR	MMR	RR	MMR	RR
Brazil	—	—	6.38	9.30	5.74	11.91	4.53	11.47
Colombia	14.90	10.07	12.69	18.52	9.71	20.12	7.78	19.70
Costa Rica	7.47	5.04	4.73	6.90	2.62	5.43	2.79	7.07
Dominican Republic	8.89	6.00	6.83	9.96	6.03	12.50	4.98	12.60
Ecuador	17.83	12.05	15.84	23.11	13.04	27.03	10.56	26.74
Mexico	12.87	8.70	10.56	15.41	8.93	18.52	6.92	17.53
Panama	10.39	7.02	7.82	11.41	6.11	12.68	4.94	12.51
Venezuela	8.18	5.53	6.35	9.27	5.30	10.99	5.06	12.81
Total	12.81	8.65	9.09	13.26	7.27	15.08	5.93	15.00
Canada	1.48	1.00	0.69	1.00	0.48	1.00	0.40	1.00

Note: MMR: Maternal mortality ratio (per 10,000 births). RR: Relative risk in relation to the Canadian ratio.

from maternal causes, in relation to the Canadian maternal mortality ratio, has increased by 1.5 each decade.

The medium fertility countries recorded the biggest decline in fertility and experienced a decline in the maternal mortality ratio of some 54 per cent,

Table 15.3. High fertility countries: quinquennial maternal mortality and relative risk in relation to the Canadian ratio, 1970–89

Country	Quinquennia							
	1970–4		1975–9		1980–4		1985–9	
	MMR	RR	MMR	RR	MMR	RR	MMR	RR
Guatemala	14.66	9.90	12.48	18.22	9.55	19.80	9.67	24.48
Honduras	13.53	9.14	9.77	14.26	5.48	11.36		
Paraguay	15.15	10.23	14.32	20.90	11.89	24.66	10.20	25.82
Peru	16.36	11.05	11.20	16.34	10.26	21.27		
Total	15.47	10.45	11.63	16.96	9.63	19.96	9.76	24.70
Canada	1.48	1.00	0.69	1.00	0.48	1.00	0.40	1.00

Note: MMR: Maternal mortality ratio (per 10,000 births). RR: Relative risk in relation to the Canadian ratio.

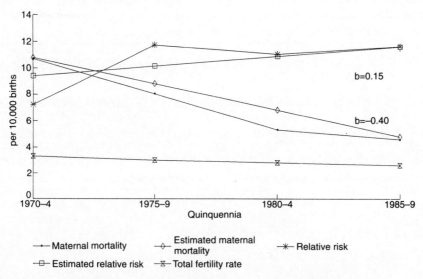

Fig. 15.1. Low fertility countries: quinquennial maternal mortality, relative risk in relation to Canadian maternal mortality ratio and quinquennial fertility, 1970–89

accompanied by an increase in the relative risk of dying from maternal causes in relation to Canada of about 73 per cent, between 1970 and 1989. The projected trend has a descending slope of 5 maternal deaths a year per 100,000 births. The relative risk of dying from maternal causes, compared with Canada, is increasing by 6.7 each decade.

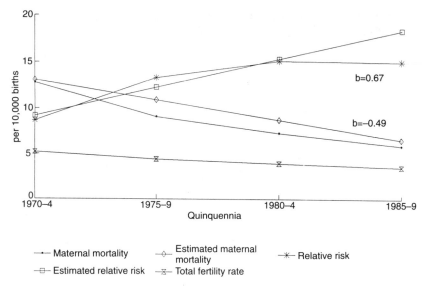

Fig. 15.2. Medium fertility countries: quinquennial maternal mortality, relative risk in relation to Canadian maternal mortality ratio and quinquennial fertility, 1970–89

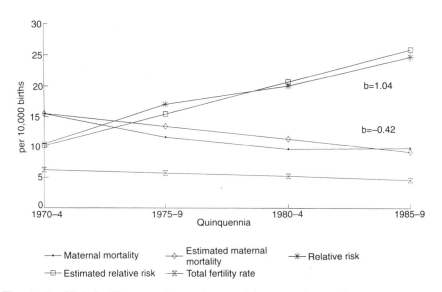

Fig. 15.3. High fertility countries: quinquennial maternal mortality, relative risk in relation to Canadian maternal mortality ratio and quinquennial fertility, 1970–89

For two of the four countries in the high fertility group, information on maternal deaths is available only for the period 1970–83. The decline in the maternal death ratio was in the order of 37 per cent, which is less than in the other groups of countries, although the adjusted downward slope is 4 deaths per 100,000 estimated births, which is similar to the ratio obtained for the low fertility countries. The slow decline could be due partly to the limited decline in the total fertility rate in these countries, which was about 26 per cent. However, although the decline in the total fertility rate of the low fertility countries was even smaller, they were able to reduce maternal mortality more rapidly. As a result of this slow decline, the relative risk of maternal death, compared with Canada, has risen by ten each decade.

2.1. Estimates of Excess Maternal Deaths

In order to illustrate the magnitude of differences in maternal mortality between the countries of the region, excess maternal deaths have been estimated controlling for the level of fertility in each country. Comparisons were made with countries with low maternal mortality ratios and fairly reliable death registers but similar fertility (Chackiel, 1986). Each comparison has been validated statistically and the differences between the slopes of the regressions predicting maternal mortality from fertility in each pair of countries are insignificant. The results of this exercise appear in Table 15.4, where a footnote indicates the origin of the maternal mortality ratios applied.

Estimated excess deaths vary between 2 per cent and 800 per cent of expected deaths. The most striking difference is observed in Cuba, where total fertility is estimated at 1.85 and 1.83 children per woman for the last two quinquennia of the period but the quinquennial maternal mortality ratios fluctuated between 4.7 and 4.5 deaths per 10,000 births. During the same period, Canada, with total fertility rates that were slightly lower than Cuba's, had a maternal mortality ratio of only 0.5 deaths per 10,000 births. Uruguay and Puerto Rico, whose total fertility rates were equal in the 1980–9 decade (PAHO, 1990), had different maternal mortality ratios; the excess in maternal deaths in Uruguay is approximately two to four times the excess in Puerto Rico. Argentina and Chile, with total fertility rates of over 2.7 children per woman in the last quinquennium of the series, have maternal mortality ratios which are about three times and four times higher respectively than in Puerto Rico, whose fertility rate is only 12 per cent lower.

These differences can be explained in various ways, one of the most important factors being the quality of maternal death records, which is discussed later in this chapter. Other factors that affect maternal mortality include the standard of living of the fertile female population of the various countries and differences in the coverage and quality of the maternal health services and fertility control services. These variables influence, in turn, the structure of causes of maternal death in each country.

Table 15.4. Excess maternal deaths estimated in relation to maternal mortality in countries with similar fertility rates, different periods between 1970 and 1989

Country and estimation period	Estimated births	MMR[a] applied	Maternal deaths			
			Expected	Observed	Absolute difference	Relative difference
Low fertility countries 1985–9	3,947,372	1.48[b]	584	1,811	1227	209.99
Argentina 1985–6	1,339,200	1.51[c]	202	755	553	273.36
Chile 1985–9	1,521,000	1.51[c]	230	643	413	179.97
Cuba 1985–8	733,600	0.50[d]	37	332	295	805.13
Puerto Rico 1985–7	191,572	1.48[b]	28	29	1	2.28
Uruguay 1985–7	162,000	1.51[c]	24	52	28	112.57
Medium fertility countries 1985–8	18,569,800	2.62[e]	4865	11,003	6138	126.15
Brazil 1985–6	8,179,400	2.62[e]	2143	3,706	1563	72.93
Colombia 1985–6	1,728,400	1.28[f]	221	1,345	1124	507.95
Costa Rica 1985–8	322,400	1.28[f]	41	90	49	118.09
Dominican Republic 1985	213,000	2.62[e]	56	106	50	89.94
Ecuador 1985–8	1,336,000	7.47[g]	998	1,411	413	41.38
Mexico 1985–6	4,885,600	2.62[e]	1280	3,383	2103	164.29
Panama 1985–7	184,200	1.28[f]	24	91	67	285.96
Venezuela 1985–7	1,720,800	4.73[h]	814	871	57	7.01
High fertility countries 1980–8	7,529,600	7.70[i]	5798	6,993	1195	20.61
Guatemala 1980–8	3,093,600	7.70[i]	2382	2,972	590	24.77
Honduras 1980–3	702,800	5.00[j]	351	385	34	9.56
Paraguay 1980–8	1,214,400	7.60[k]	923	1,052	129	13.98
Peru 1980–3	2,518,800	7.47[g]	1882	2,584	702	37.33

[a] MMR Applied: the country's expected maternal mortality ratio, given its total fertility rate. [b] Canada, 1970–4. [c] Puerto Rico, 1985–8. [d] Canada, 1980–8. [e] Costa Rica, 1980–4. [f] Puerto Rico, 1975–9. [g] Costa Rica, 1970–4. [h] Costa Rica, 1975–9. [i,j,k] Ratios estimated from the relationship between maternal mortality and fertility in Costa Rica.

In the medium fertility countries, the maternal mortality ratio usually applied, after ensuring that there were no significant differences between the respective slopes of the curves associating maternal mortality and fertility, was that of Costa Rica in the period when it had a total fertility rate similar to that of each of the medium fertility countries. The exceptions were Colombia, Costa Rica itself, and Panama, whose total fertility rates for the last quinquennium of the series are closer to the figures registered by Puerto Rico in 1975–9. There are some unusual figures among the results. These probably result from defects in the maternal death records of some countries. The calculated excess of maternal deaths varies between 7 per cent and 500 per cent.

Colombia, Costa Rica and Panama, with total fertility rates of around 3.2 children per woman in 1985–9, had maternal mortality ratios of between 3 and

8 deaths per 10,000 births, representing an excess of maternal deaths of between 120 per cent and 500 per cent in relation to those in Puerto Rico. Brazil and Mexico, whose total fertility rates for the last quinquennium of the series were both close to 3.5 children per woman, maintained maternal mortality ratios of between 4.5 and 7 deaths per 10,000 births. Excess maternal deaths in these countries exceed those predicted in Costa Rica by 73 per cent and 164 per cent. It should be noted, at least for Brazil, that the coverage of the register of deaths is not complete. Studies of the recording of maternal deaths in some areas of Brazil put such under-reporting at over 50 per cent (Laurenti, 1988).

Ecuador, with a higher total fertility rate of 4.3 children per woman in 1985–9 had a maternal mortality ratio of nearly 11 deaths per 10,000 births. It has been compared with the maternal mortality ratio of Costa Rica in 1970–4 which had a similar total fertility rate. This comparison yields an excess of maternal deaths of 41 per cent for the four-year period.

The maternal mortality ratio of Venezuela, which had a total fertility rate of 3.0 children per woman for 1985–9, is compared with that of Costa Rica during the period when the latter had a similar total fertility rate (1975–9) and shows a slight excess of 7 per cent over expected maternal deaths. Although death records in Venezuela seem to be more complete than those of other countries in the group, maternal deaths will be under-reported if they are classified as caused by other conditions.

The most striking results for this group are for Costa Rica. Although this country's total fertility rate fell by 25 per cent between 1970 and 1989, it is still high. Nevertheless quinquennial maternal mortality ratios declined by 63 per cent during the same period due to changes in other factors that affect the health of women going through the pregnancy–puerperal cycle. As studies performed in Costa Rica have pointed out (Jiménez, 1989), the fastest decline of maternal mortality occurred during the period when high levels of coverage of health and social security services were reached.

The estimates of excess maternal deaths in the high fertility group of countries are obtained from the regression predicting maternal mortality from fertility in Costa Rica. In Guatemala and Paraguay information is available on maternal deaths for the period 1980–8 and reported maternal deaths are 14 per cent and 25 per cent higher respectively than expected. In Honduras and Peru, reported maternal deaths are available only for the period 1980–3 and are 10 and 37 per cent respectively above expected maternal deaths. It should be noted that, given the poor quality of death registers in these countries, the validity of these comparisons is questionable.

2.2. Summary

The information presented in this section shows that, as documented by earlier studies (PAHO, 1985), differences in the levels of maternal mortality in this region have continued to be striking in recent years, even allowing for differences in fertility and in the completeness of recording of maternal deaths. On the other hand, there is no doubt that the most significant difference is in comparison with an industrialized North American country, Canada. This comparison indicates a widening gap between the developing and the industrialized countries. It should also be stressed that, although the association between maternal mortality and fertility has evolved along similar lines in all the countries mentioned, including Canada, disparities exist with respect to their achievements in reducing maternal mortality. This could be attributable in part to the impact on the main causes of maternal death of health care for women of childbearing ages.

Finally, judging from the similarity in the evolution of patterns of maternal mortality for at least the first two groups of countries in the four quinquennia studied, maternal mortality is declining in the region. This downward trend, however, differs from that observed in the industrialized countries. This probably reflects the influence of factors that are not related directly to fertility, such as differences in standards of living between the industrialized countries and the Latin American and Caribbean countries.

3. Data Quality

Studies of the completeness of maternal death records have demonstrated consistently and frequently that maternal deaths are under-reported even in the industrialized countries of North America (MMWR, 1985). Apart from the omission of cases that occur more than forty-two days after the termination of pregnancy, reflecting the current definition of maternal death, several factors lead to under-reporting of the actual number of deaths that result from complications of pregnancy, childbirth, and the puerperium in the countries of the region.

Some deaths are still not registered in a number of countries of Latin America and the Caribbean. However, in most cases, under-reporting of maternal deaths is due to misclassification of cause of death on the death certificate. The resulting differentials in the completeness of reporting of maternal deaths reduce the comparability of data from different countries. This factor probably explains the vast differences in the estimated excess of maternal deaths between Cuba and Honduras observed in Table 15.4. The completeness and accuracy of death and cause of death records in Cuba and the dubious quality of such registers in Brazil, Honduras, Peru, and the Dominican Republic, cast doubts on the validity of the comparison. Under-reporting of maternal deaths detected in various cities of Latin America at the end of the 1960s fluctuated between 6 and 50 per cent (Puffer and Griffith, 1968). More recent studies have confirmed that this situation persists, at least in countries where such studies have been carried out (Chapter 4; Cervantes and Watanabe, 1985; Laurenti, 1986 and 1988; Castellanos, 1991; Kestler, 1991).

The retrospective estimates of maternal mortality obtained from the application of indirect methods such as the sisterhood method (Graham and Brass, 1988) have also demonstrated the magnitude of under-reporting of maternal deaths in some countries of this region. Studies carried out in limited areas of three Latin American countries—Bolivia, Chile and Peru—showed that the maternal mortality ratio obtained by the sisterhood method for different periods between 1970 and 1989 exceeded the figure recorded by the vital statistics system of these countries by between 300 and 460 per cent (see Chapter 6). These facts demonstrate that, in Latin America and the Caribbean, indirect methods should be applied in order to obtain better estimates of maternal mortality and all deaths of women of childbearing age need to be verified before the cause of death recorded on the death certificate can be accepted.

4. Causes of Maternal Death and Health Care

More accurate explanations of the magnitude of mortality and its differentials (Vallin, 1988) can be obtained by analysing the causes of death. Before identifying a chronological series of groups of causes of death, factors that affect the comparability of the data available that stem not only from the quality of registration of such data but also from revision of the International Classification of Diseases (ICD) should be considered and, if possible, eliminated. Data on causes of maternal death analysed in this report have been classified according to the grouped lists in the 8th and 9th Revisions of the ICD. The grouped categories do not match completely and this limits the internal consistency of the series and makes it difficult to compare different periods.

Table 15.5 considers the correspondence between the grouped categories referred to and shows that:

(a) The category 'Toxaemia of Pregnancy' in the 9th Revision of the ICD (642.4–642.9, 643) cannot be obtained from List A of the 8th Revision, where code A112, 'Toxaemia of Pregnancy and of the Puerperium' covers more items from the Detailed List than in the 9th Revision; thus, the difference between the two is included in the residual group of the aggregate list in the 9th Revision.

(b) The category 'Puerperal Complications' in the 9th Revision cannot be isolated from List A in the 8th Revision, since item A116 corresponds only to 'Sepsis of Delivery and Puerperium'; the differences fall in the residual group of the grouped list of the 8th Revision.

(c) The category 'Indirect Obstetric Causes' in the 9th ICD Revision is not a separate item in List A of the 8th Revision; the equivalent codes were merged with the residual group in the earlier list.

Table 15.5. Correspondence of grouped causes of maternal death in the 8th and 9th Revisions of the International Classification of Diseases, Injuries and Causes of Death

Concept	Groups of causes			
	ICD 8th Revision		ICD 9th Revision	
	Codes: Detailed List	Codes: Tabulated List	Codes: Detailed List	Codes: Tabulated List
Total	(630–678)		(630–676)	
Indirect obstetric causes	Not applicable		(647, 648)	42.0
Abortion	(640–645)	A114 + A115	(630–639)	38.X
Haemorrhage	(632, 651–653)	A113	(640, 641, 666)	39.1
Toxaemia	(636–639)	A112	(642.4–642.9, 643)	39.2
Puerperal complications	(670, 671, 673)	A116	(670–676)	39.3
Others	(630, 631, 633–635, 650–654, 662, 672, 674–678)	A117 + A118	(642.0–642.3, 644–646, 651–665, 667–669)	39.9 + 41

(d) The grouped categories 'Abortion' and 'Haemorrhages' are equivalent in both revisions of the ICD.

The differences noted do not affect the overall group. This covers similar sets of causes in both revisions and does not contain categories from other chapters of the ICD. This was verified in the current study through the assessment of the magnitude of yearly variations in maternal deaths in each country in absolute terms. The same was done with groups of causes by comparing the periods 1970–8 and 1979–89, which correspond to the use of the two revisions of the ICD, to determine the variations attributable to changes in the standards of codification and tabulation of causes of death (Villalón and Orellana, 1990) and estimate what proportion of the residual group could be reclassified. The fact that this procedure produced appreciable results only in one country could be due in part to the small total number of maternal deaths registered each year in most of the countries. Therefore, it was decided to limit the study of the structure of causes of maternal death to the 1980s, which are covered by the 9th Revision, for all causes except abortion-related deaths, for which trends can be examined. Only countries with information for a sufficient number of years were selected.

Table 15.6 shows the percent distribution of maternal deaths according to three groups of causes in thirteen of the seventeen countries for different periods in the 1980–9 decade. Abortions (630–639) are relatively important in Argentina, Chile, Uruguay and Venezuela, where they account for over 20 per cent of maternal deaths. Indirect obstetric deaths predominate in Cuba, suggesting a future shift in the structure of causes of maternal death as the incidence of direct obstetric complications is reduced. In the other countries, this group accounts for less than 8 per cent of maternal deaths.

4.1. Maternal Mortality due to Abortion

Figures on maternal mortality due to abortion should be interpreted cautiously, as the completeness of the records is affected by legal considerations in most countries of the region except Cuba, where maternal deaths are also verified systematically (Farnot, 1985; Cabezas, 1988). Deaths caused by abortion can be avoided by preventing unwanted pregnancies and by providing

Table 15.6. Maternal deaths by cause grouping, varying periods between 1980 and 1989

Country	Deaths by cause grouping[a]							
	Total[b]	Abortion		Other direct obstetric causes		Indirect obstetric causes		
		Number	%	Number	%	Number	%	
Argentina 1980–6	2,957	1087	36.76	1,791	60.57	79	2.67	
Brazil 1980–6	15,170	2005	13.22	12,639	83.32	526	3.47	
Chile 1980–9	1,352	482	35.65	767	56.73	103	7.62	
Colombia 1980–6	5,430	1063	19.58	4,285	78.91	82	1.51	
Costa Rica 1980–8	190	31	16.32	158	83.16	1	0.53	
Cuba 1980–8	725	141	19.45	395	54.48	189	26.07	
Dominican Republic 1980–5	724	135	18.65	543	75.00	46	6.35	
Ecuador 1980–6	2,615	221	8.45	2,356	90.10	38	1.45	
Mexico 1980–6	9,881	843	8.53	8,801	89.07	237	2.40	
Panama 1980–7	272	46	16.91	220	80.88	6	2.21	
Paraguay 1980–6	1,052	150	14.26	859	81.65	43	4.09	
Uruguay 1980–7	183	43	23.50	138	75.41	2	1.09	
Venezuela 1980–6	2,015	469	23.28	1,409	69.93	137	6.80	
Total	42,566	6716	15.78	34,361	80.72	1489	3.50	

[a] Groups of causes, codes as in tabulated list, ICD 9th Revision: Abortion (630–639), other direct obstetric causes (640–646; 651–676), indirect obstetric causes (647 and 648).
[b] Total maternal deaths with known causes.

hospital services with the minimum facilities required for timely intervention in cases of complications resulting from abortion. Table 15.7 summarizes the evolution of quinquennial maternal mortality due to abortion in the region and contrasts it with the use of contraceptives as determined through various surveys (PAHO, 1989). The percentages presented for contraceptive use include all methods of birth control, including sterilization, local, barrier, and rhythm methods except in the case of the Dominican Republic. Most of the surveys refer to married women or women in conjugal unions.

The table emphasizes that maternal mortality due to abortion in Argentina, Chile, Colombia, Paraguay, Uruguay, and Venezuela is higher, even double, that in the other nations in the four quinquennia considered. The cases of the two Southern Cone countries are particularly striking. Abortion accounts for 36 per cent of maternal deaths and is the leading cause of death within the group of pregnancy, delivery, and puerperal complications. Although no data are available on the use of contraceptives in any of the low fertility countries, the high level of maternal mortality from abortion suggest that the incidence

Table 15.7. Quinquennial materal mortality from abortion and use of contraceptives, 1970–89

Country	Quinquennial ratios per 10,000 estimated births				Percentage use of contraceptives[a]		
	1970–4	1975–9	1980–4	1985–9	1970–9	1980–9	% difference
Argentina	3.64	2.51	2.45	1.98			
Brazil		0.84	0.76	0.59		65	
Chile	5.15	3.63	1.82	1.44			
Colombia	1.91	2.33	1.83	1.68	43	65	51.2
Costa Rica	0.94	0.89	0.37	0.53	70	71	1.4
Cuba	1.61	1.05	0.93	0.86			
Dominican Republic	0.48	0.52	1.13	0.85	32	50	56.3
Ecuador	0.96	1.27	0.83	0.87	34	44	29.4
Guatemala	1.22	1.20	0.95		19	23	21.1
Honduras	0.43	0.40	0.33			35	
Mexico	0.74	0.68	0.76	0.61	30	53	76.7
Panama	0.81	0.92	1.27	0.87	49	54	10.2
Paraguay	2.76	2.35	1.60	1.68	29	38	31.0
Peru	1.07	0.81	1.05		31	46	48.4
Uruguay	1.55	0.92	1.04	0.93			
Venezuela	1.62	1.23	1.30	1.09	49		
Total	1.36	1.19	1.07	0.90	35	58	66.6

[a] Percentage of women aged 15–49 currently using any contraceptive method from surveys performed in varying years of each decade.

of induced abortion is high in some of them. This has been borne out by other sources (Requena, 1990). Hence it can be assumed that induced abortion is partly responsible for the decline of fertility in a number of low-fertility countries.

Costa Rica and Venezuela experienced declines in maternal mortality from abortions of roughly 33 and 43 per cent. There is little variation in most of the other countries. The two striking exceptions are Panama and the Dominican Republic, where the maternal mortality ratio due to abortion increased in the second ten-year period by over 50 per cent and 100 per cent respectively.

These findings conflict with those of the fertility surveys, which show an increase in the use of contraceptives in every country for which data are available except Costa Rica. It seems likely that the considerable decline in maternal mortality due to abortion in Costa Rica has as much to do with the improved coverage of health services as with the high, but constant, level of use of contraceptives. Making due allowance for the shortcomings of maternal death records, the increased use of contraceptives does not seem to have reduced maternal mortality caused by abortion in this region, except in countries where this increase has gone hand in hand with improvements in other factors.

4.2. Maternal Mortality from Direct Obstetric Causes

The bulk of maternal deaths in the region stem from direct obstetric causes. Most of them could be prevented through the application of simple, low-cost technology, although some less-common complications can require more sophisticated therapeutic equipment. Generally speaking, maternal deaths due to haemorrhage can be prevented by making an early diagnosis, during pre-natal care, of those women who are prone to haemorrhage. The most important preventive measures, however, are hospital delivery and monitoring of the puerperium by professional staff equipped with essential facilities, especially adequate blood banks (WHO, 1986). Apart from exceptional acute cases, maternal deaths from toxaemia should be much less frequent. Although toxaemia is associated with poverty and malnutrition, preventive and therapeutic technology is now available that permits the early diagnosis and monitoring of hypertension in pregnant women. Deaths from puerperal complications can be prevented by carefully monitoring this stage of the pregnancy-puerperal cycle to stave off complications and by dealing in a timely and appropriate manner with any complications that do occur. In this connection, it has been known for some time now that there is a link between total maternal mortality and maternal mortality from puerperal complications and the incidence of caesarean sections (Cabezas, 1988; PAHO, 1990).

Table 15.8 shows proportional mortality from these three causes in those countries for the region for which sufficient data are available. Data has been

Table 15.8. Maternal deaths by group of direct obstetric causes and professional birth attendance, different periods, 1980–9

Country	Groups of causes[a]								
	Haemorrhage		Toxaemia		Puerperium complications		All causes	Coverage of professional birth attendance[b]
	Number	%	Number	%	Number	%	Number	
Argentina 1980–6	437	14.78	453	15.32	389	13.16	2,957	91.0
Brazil 1980–6	2809	18.52	4,633	30.54	2431	16.03	15,170	79.0
Chile 1980–9	97	7.20	194	14.39	254	18.89	1,346	98.0
Colombia 1980–6	933	17.18	1,230	22.65	474	8.73	5,430	70.0
Costa Rica 1980–8	32	16.84	34	17.89	44	23.16	190	94.0
Cuba 1980–8	32	4.41	52	7.17	107	14.76	725	99.0
Dominican Republic 1980–5	147	20.14	187	25.62	24	3.29	730	90.0
Ecuador 1980–6	575	16.57	665	19.16	252	7.26	3,471	61.0
Mexico 1980–6	2089	17.16	1,890	15.52	882	7.24	12,177	48.0
Panama 1980–8	42	15.44	44	16.18	15	5.51	272	84.0
Paraguay 1980–6	276	26.24	174	16.54	182	17.30	1,052	22.0
Uruguay 1980–7	7	4.05	40	23.12	16	9.25	173	97.0
Venezuela 1980–6	317	13.65	418	18.00	326	14.04	2,322	98.0
Total	7793	16.94	10,014	21.76	5396	11.73	46,015	72.5

[a] Groups of causes, as in tabulated list, ICD 9th Revision: Haemorrhage (640, 641, 666), Toxaemia (642.4–642.9, 643), Puerperium complications (670–676).
[b] Percentage deliveries with professional attendance. Estimated totals for the decade.

added on the proportions of births occurring in institutions or attended professionally during the 1980–9 decade. Figure 15.4 compares the structure of the three groups of direct obstetric causes for two groups of countries, classified according to whether coverage of professional delivery care is above or below the median level (90 per cent). The incidence of toxaemia and haemorrhage is, in relative terms, clearly higher in countries where coverage by

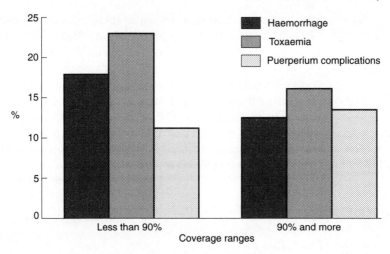

Fig. 15.4. Groups of countries with high and low coverage of professional birth attendance: percentage of maternal deaths caused by haemorrhage, toxaemia and puerperium complications, 1980–9

professional care at delivery is poorer. On the other hand, the group of countries with higher professional birth attendance have a higher incidence of deaths from puerperal complications. This may be linked to the incidence of caesarian sections. These findings indicates the need for investigation of the quality of care at delivery and evaluation of the resources available to maternity hospitals and centres. The high incidence of toxaemias calls for an analysis of prenatal care, on which little information is available.

Some of the fertility surveys conducted in recent years in the region established the coverage of prenatal care by asking women about pregnancies and deliveries in the five years prior to the interview. The data obtained from certain surveys contrast with the figures on institutional care at delivery from other sources. Thus, for example, while the coverage of institutional delivery care reported officially by Colombia, Ecuador, Guatemala, Honduras, Mexico, and Paraguay for the years prior to 1980 varies between 22 per cent and 70 per cent (PAHO, 1989), the coverage of prenatal checkups in the same countries, according to the surveys, was between 46 and 84 per cent. This conflicts sharply with official reports that in most of the countries the coverage of institutional care at delivery is much higher than that of prenatal care.

In any case, the relationship between maternal mortality due to toxaemia and the coverage of prenatal care is not consistent. In the last decade of the period under consideration, maternal deaths due to toxaemia ranged between 0.53 and 3.19 per 10,000 live births in countries like Brazil, Colombia, Costa Rica, Ecuador, Mexico, Panama, Paraguay, and the Dominican Republic, where coverage by prenatal care ranges between 73 and 95 per cent according to survey data. Only a few countries (Argentina, Costa Rica, Cuba, Chile, Mexico, and Panama), report the number of consultations and the majority of them report between two to six prenatal consultations per pregnant woman. Elsewhere, no information is available on the total number of prenatal consultations, although this is significant for the control of maternal morbidity. For example, Cuba differs from the rest of the region in that every pregnant woman receives over fourteen prenatal check-ups. This seems to have had an impact, given the impressive decline of about 90 per cent in maternal mortality from toxaemia during the period covered by the study.

5. Conclusions

The reduction of maternal mortality in Latin America and the Caribbean to the lowest level possible in line with the region's current fertility could be achieved even in the least developed countries through the implementation of integrated maternal health programmes. Although the neglect of women's health care is due to a host of factors, ranging from the living and working conditions of the population and its views on health care to the availability of resources and the organization of health services, the information that has been presented suggests that the coverage and quality of care for pregnant and puerperal women is insufficient. This was also demonstrated by a PAHO/HPM study carried out in 1987 in a number of countries of the region. It found that less than 15 per cent of outpatient obstetric services and less than 8 per cent of obstetric hospital services were satisfactorily effective.

The different structures of causes of maternal death documented in this chapter demonstrate that the reduction of maternal mortality should be based on different strategies and activities in each country. Nevertheless, efforts should focus mainly on controlling direct obstetric causes in all countries, in view of the ground that still remains to be covered in this regard. Argentina, Chile, and Uruguay need to focus their attention on the problem of maternal mortality due to abortion by reviewing contraceptive use in different segments of the population in order to make it easier to prevent unwanted pregnancies and by providing access to proper hospital care for complicated abortions. On the other hand, the challenge that Costa Rica and Cuba seem to be facing is to tackle those direct obstetric causes that require the establishment of specialized obstetric care in hospitals, since both countries have health services with widespread coverage. Current experience suggests that an uphill yet simpler task remains ahead for the rest of the countries. They need to establish primary maternal health care systems and make them accessible to the majority of the population.

At the end of the twentieth century, maternal mortality is an anachronism that society must do away with. Latin American and Caribbean countries must make the elimination of maternal mortality a priority goal in order to promote the right of the women of the region to safe and healthy motherhood.

References

Cabezas, E. (1988), 'Mortalidad materna en Cuba', paper presented at the Regional Meeting on Prevention of Maternal Mortality, PAHO-Ministry of Health of Brazil, Campinhas, São Paulo, Brazil.

Castellanos, M. (1991), 'Mortalidad de mujeres en edad reproductiva y mortalidad materna, Honduras 1990', paper presented at the first Latin American Workshop on Maternal and Child Health: Operational Strategies, 27 May–1 June. PAHO-IMSS, Metepec, Puebla, Mexico.

Latin American Demographic Centre (CELADE) (1990), 'La fecundidad: niveles, tendencias y determinantes próximos', Santiago, Chile.

Cervantes, R. , and T. Watanabe (1985), 'Muerte materna intrahospitalaria en el Perú', paper presented at the Interregional Meeting on Prevention of Maternal Mortality, World Health Organization, Geneva, Switzerland.

Chackiel, J. (1986), 'Studies of causes of death in Latin America. Current situation and future perspectives', paper presented at the Seminar on Comparative Studies of Mortality and Morbidity, 7–12 July. International Union for the Scientific Study of Population and the University of Siena, Soignee, Italy.

Farnot, U. (1985), 'Mortalidad materna en Cuba', paper presented at the Interregional Meeting on Prevention of Maternal Mortality, World Health Organization, Geneva, Switzerland.

Graham, W., and W. Brass (1988), 'Field performance of the sisterhood method for measuring maternal mortality', paper presented at the Seminar on Collection and Processing of Demographic Data in Latin America, 23–27 May. International Union for the Scientific Study of Population, Santiago, Chile.

Jiménez, Mora G. (1989), 'Mortalidad materna en Costa Rica', paper presented at the Sub-regional Meeting on Maternal Mortality in Central America and Panamá, September. PAHO-Ministry of Health of Nicaragua.

Kestler, L. E. (1991), 'Maternal mortality in Guatemala, a big gap but just start', paper presented at the first Latin American Workshop on Maternal and Child Health: Operational Strategies, 27 May–1 June. PAHO-IMSS, Metepec, Puebla, Mexico.

Laurenti, R. (1986), *Mortalidade materna em Quatro Municípios do Estado de São Paulo. Relatório final*, Centro da OMS para a Classificação de Doenças, São Paulo, Brazil.

—— (1988), 'Alguns marcos referenciais para estudos e investigações em mortalidade materna', paper presented at the Regional Meeting on Prevention of Maternal Mortality, April. PAHO-Ministry of Health of Brazil, Campinhas, São Paulo, Brazil.

Morbidity and Mortality Weekly Report (MMWR) (1985), *Maternal Mortality Pilot Surveillance in Seven States*, No. 34, Centers for Disease Control, Atlanta Ga.

Pan American Health Organization (PAHO) (1985), *La Salud de la Mujer en las Américas*, Scientific Publication No. 488, Washington, DC.

Pan American Health Organization (PAHO) (1987), *Elementos Básicos para el Estudio y para la Prevención de la Mortalidad Materna*, Programa de Salud Materno-Infantil, fascicle II, Washington, DC.

—— (1989), *Estrategias para la Prevención de la Mortalidad Materna en las Américas*, Programa de Salud Materno-Infantil, fascicle IV, Washington, DC.

—— (1990), *Health Conditions in the Americas: 1990 Edition*, 2 vols., Scientific Publication No. 524, Washington, DC.

Puffer, R., and G. Griffith (1968), *Características de la Mortalidad Urbana*, PAHO Scientific Publication No. 151, Washington, DC.

Requena, M. (ed.) (1990), *El Aborto Inducido en Chile*, Sociedad Chilena de Salud Pública, Santiago, Chile.

United States, National Research Council (1989), 'Reproductive patterns and women's health', *Contraception and Reproduction: Health Consequences for Women and Children in the Developing World*, National Academy Press, Washington, DC.

Vallin, J. (1988), *Seminario sobre Causas de Muerte. Aplicación al Caso de Francia* (LC/DEM/G.55), Latin American Demographic Centre (CELADE) and National Institute of Demographic Studies (INED), Santiago, Chile.

Villalón, G., and H. Orellana (1990), *Compatibilización de las Revisiones Séptima, Octava y Novena de la Clasificación Internacional de Enfermedades. Aplicación a Chile, 1960–1985*, National Statistics Institute of Chile (INE), Latin American Demographic Centre (CELADE) and Canadian International Development Agency (CIDA), Santiago, Chile.

World Health Organization (WHO) (1986), *Essential Obstetric Functions at the First Referral Level: Report of a Technical Working Group*, Geneva, Switzerland.

16 Induced Abortion as a Cause of Maternal Mortality

TOMAS FREJKA

United Nations Economic Commission for Europe, Geneva, Switzerland

LUCILLE C. ATKIN

The Ford Foundation, Mexico City, Mexico

1. Introduction

Among the principal causes of maternal mortality in Latin America today, induced abortion is probably the easiest to prevent from a technical viewpoint, but the most difficult to address socially and politically. It is an issue that touches at the heart of women's roles and status and thus causes heated debate between those who support and those who oppose women's rights to choose when and if to become mothers. It is an issue that is often ignored or minimized and one for which reliable and accurate information is often absent but sorely needed in order to inform public debate. Even without accurate statistics, however, it is clear that induced abortions occur frequently despite restrictive legislation and, if practised in unsafe conditions, provoke widespread hardship at the individual, family and society levels (Frejka *et al.*, 1989).

Knowledge about the incidence of induced abortions, as well as about the magnitude of maternal mortality due to such abortions, in Latin America is unreliable and approximate. The main reason for this is that, for the most part, induced abortion legislation in Latin American countries is restrictive (Henshaw, 1990) and therefore no official statistics exist. Nevertheless, it is important to try to calculate reasonable estimates of the frequency of induced abortion and its contribution to maternal mortality in order to provide stronger arguments for its prevention. This chapter generates an estimate of the actual number of abortion-related deaths in Latin America, and discusses the contribution of induced abortion to maternal morbidity.

As discussed in an earlier paper (Frejka and Atkin, 1990), there is little doubt that the incidence of induced abortion in Latin America is elevated and is probably among the highest in the world, comparable with several East Asian and East European countries. In individual countries the total abortion rate (i.e. lifetime induced abortions), seems to be between 1 and 2 per woman of fertile age, if not higher. Therefore, between 4 and 6 million induced abortions per year seems a reasonable estimate for Latin America.

Data and estimates regarding maternal mortality, especially maternal mortality due to spontaneous and induced abortions, are probably even less reliable than those about the incidence of induced abortion. Nevertheless, available data and estimates, though imprecise, provide sufficient information to gain a comparative perspective. Around 1990, the level of mortality attributable to abortions (estimated as case-fatality rates) was possibly 100 to 200 times higher in Latin America than in Europe and other developed countries. In all likelihood this was significantly lower than in several other developing regions, particularly Africa.

2. Maternal Mortality

In order to estimate the contribution of induced abortion to maternal mortality and morbidity, one should consider the factors related to under-registration of both maternal mortality or morbidity and induced abortion. To begin with, it is well established that there is considerable under-registration of maternal deaths even in the developed countries. For instance, a thorough investigation in the United States found a 39 per cent shortfall in registered maternal deaths (Koonin, 1988). A number of evaluations in the developing countries indicate that the under-reporting of maternal deaths can be as high as 70 per cent (PAHO, 1990). A recent study in Mexico City found that approximately 50 per cent of maternal deaths were not registered (Reyes and Bobadilla, 1990).

A variety of factors contribute to this under-reporting. In many places women do not go to hospitals to give birth. They may not do so even if they are dying. Women who die quickly or who live far away from a hospital will be under-represented. Other biases exist that are of particular importance in relation to induced abortion. Poor women who cannot afford to pay hospital fees and women who might be ashamed of being pregnant, for example single and/or very young women, may be less likely to go to a hospital even if they are seriously ill.

Furthermore, women who die more than forty-two days after the end of pregnancy are not at present included in the statistics on maternal mortality. WHO defines a maternal death as occurring 'while pregnant or within 42 days of termination of pregnancy'. Complications sometimes occur beyond this time period. New treatments used to avoid the woman's death may delay the death beyond forty-two days. A study in the United States found that 11 per cent of maternal deaths occurred between forty-two days and one year after pregnancy termination (Koonin, 1988). In Colombia, a study at the Maternal–Infant Institute (Muñoz et al., 1985) found that 8 per cent of the maternal deaths occurred more than forty-two days after pregnancy termination.

Table 16.1   Estimated number of maternal deaths as of 1990 in selected countries and territories in the Americas, based on adjusted rates obtained from five different sources[a]

County	Adjusted maternal mortality rate (per 100,000 live births)	Births (in thousands)	Maternal deaths
Argentina (1986)	140	669	936
Bolivia	600	293	1,758
Brazil (1986)	200	4086	8,172
Chile (1987)	67	301	202
Colombia (1984)	200	861	1,722
Costa Rica (1988)	36	80	29
Cuba (1988)	36	181	65
Dominican Republic (1985)	300	213	639
Ecuador (1987)	300	328	984
El Salvador (1984)	300	182	546
Guatemala (1984)	300	350	1,050
Guyana (1984)	200	26	52
Haiti	600	213	1,278
Honduras (1983)	300	189	567
Jamaica (1984)	115	65	75
Mexico (1986)	200	2569	5,138
Nicaragua	300	149	447
Panama (1987)	60	68	40
Paraguay (1986)	300	150	450
Peru (1983)	300	759	2,277
Puerto Rico	20	78	16
Trinidad and Tobago (1986)	111	31	34
Uruguay	36	54	19
Venezuela	200	569	1,138
Total			27,634

[a] For Argentina the adjustment was based on the under-registration observed in the Córdoba study (Illia, 1987). For Brazil, Colombia, Guyana, Mexico, and Venezuela the estimated rate for Brazil was used (Laurenti, 1988). For Ecuador, El Salvador, Guatemala, Honduras, Nicaragua, Paraguay, and Peru the estimated rate for Peru was used. For Canada, Chile, Costa Rica, Cuba, Panama, Puerto Rico, Trinidad and Tobago, United States, and Uruguay the correction was based on the 39% under-registration observed in a study in the United States (Koonin, 1988). For Jamaica the figure from a recent study (University of West Indies, 1989) was used. For Bolivia and Haiti the rate was estimated on the basis of data from the Bolivian Ministry of Social Welfare and Public Health (1989).

Source: PAHO (1990).

Table 16.2. Latin American and Caribbean countries by level of maternal mortality (maternal deaths per 100,000 live births)

Maternal mortality	Country
Less than 99	Puerto Rico
	Costa Rica
	Cuba
	Uruguay
	Panama
	Chile
100–199	Trinidad and Tobago
	Jamaica
	Argentina
Around 200	Brazil
	Colombia
	Guyana
	Mexico
	Venezuela
Around 300	Dominican Republic
	Ecuador
	El Salvador
	Guatemala
	Honduras
	Nicaragua
	Paraguay
	Peru
Around 600	Bolivia
	Haiti

Source: PAHO (1990).

Taking into account the problem of under-reporting, the Pan American Health Organization (PAHO) has generated country estimates of maternal mortality ratios (calculated per 100,000 live births) and of the corresponding numbers of maternal deaths (see Table 16.1). These add up to almost 28,000 maternal deaths occurring annually in Latin America and the Caribbean. The average maternal mortality ratio for the Latin America region is approximately 220 maternal deaths per 100,000 live births. Maternal mortality is about twice that level in Asia and three times higher in Africa (Royston and Armstrong, 1989).

Although the estimates in Table 16.1 are rather crude, they point to large differences between countries. A grouping of countries by the level of maternal mortality (see Table 16.2) indicates that those with the highest levels are Bolivia and Haiti, followed by a number of Central American countries together with the Dominican Republic, Ecuador, Paraguay, and Peru. Five countries, including the two largest ones (Mexico and Brazil), are estimated to have maternal mortality ratios around 200 maternal deaths per 100,000 live births. The countries with the lowest maternal mortality ratios are predictably those that have relatively advanced systems of health care or relatively high standards of living.

3. Maternal Mortality due to Induced Abortion

Compared with the United States, which had an estimated 13 maternal deaths per 100,000 live births, maternal mortality is from 3 to 45 times higher in the various countries of Latin America and the Caribbean. Compared with Canada, with an adjusted maternal mortality rate of only six, maternal mortality is from 6 to 100 times higher, with the latter figure relating to Bolivia and Haiti (see Table 16.1).

Assuming that an estimate of 28,000 maternal deaths for Latin America is reasonable, we need to assess what proportion of these deaths are attributable to abortions in order to estimate the number of abortion-related deaths. Basically, we apply a method outlined by Royston (1991), which she termed the 'maternal mortality route' of estimating the total number of deaths due to abortion.

In the twenty-one Latin America and the Caribbean countries that recorded direct obstetric causes of maternal deaths in the mid-1980s, the median percentage of deaths due to abortion was 17 (see Table 16.3). Note that the numbers of deaths in this table are considerably smaller than those in Table 16.1, because they are limited to those that appear in the official civil registration files rather than estimates which compensate for under-reporting. If one applies this percentage to the 28,000 estimated maternal deaths, the annual number of abortion-related deaths in the region is close to 5000.

This estimate has to be considered an absolute minimum. Many abortion-related deaths are reported in other categories of maternal causes of death, particularly infection and perhaps haemorrhage. If these were included in the estimates, the number of deaths due to abortion would increase considerably. Puffer and Griffith (1967), when evaluating abortion registration data in a number of Latin American cities, detected undercounts of deaths due to abortion ranging from 10 per cent in Santiago, Chile to 65 per cent in Bogota, Colombia. Although this investigation took place in the 1960s, in all likelihood considerable under-reporting of abortion as a cause of maternal death continues to be a reality.

Considering the legal and social stigma attached to induced abortion, it is not hard to understand that many people will not admit to induced abortion as the cause of death. Medical personnel also often fail to mention abortion in their diagnosis in order to protect themselves and the patient from legal involvement. In some cases it is not apparent that the woman was, or had been,

Table 16.3. Distribution of causes of maternal mortality in selected countries and territories of Latin America, c. 1986

Country	Percentage of maternal deaths by direct obstetric causes						Indirect
	Total maternal deaths	Abortion	Toxaemia of pregnancy	Haemorrhage of pregnancy and deliery	Puerperal complications	Other direct obstetric causes	
Argentina (1986)	369	35	—	14	14	35	2
Brazil (1986)	1814	13	29	16	16	19	7
Chile (1987)	135	35	12	8	24	16	5
Colombia (1984)	642	23	20	17	9	30	1
Costa Rica (1988)	15	7	27	27	13	26	—
Cuba (1988)	73	22	8	3	16	18	33
Dominican Republic (1985)	106	17	25	16	—	34	8
Ecuador (1987)	355	8	26	23	11	30	2
El Salvador (1984)	99	7	5	7	8	72	1
Guatemala (1984)	236	17	10	2	15	56	—
Guyana (1984)	17	29	18	41	6	6	—
Honduras (1983)	79	9	—	—	—	88	3
Jamaica (1984)	14	64	21	7	—	8	—
Mexico (1986)	1681	9	20	25	9	35	2
Panama (1987)	22	23	18	5	—	49	5
Paraguay (1986)	140	14	18	31	17	16	4
Peru (1983)	538	11	8	33	14	33	1
Puerto Rico (1987)	11	—	22	9	45	24	—
Surinam (1985)	7	14	14	71	—	1	—
Trinidad and Tobago (1986)	18	50	28	6	6	4	6
Uruguay (1986)	14	36	7	7	14	36	—
Venezuela (1980–1983)	291	23	23	15	15	18	6

Source: PAHO (1990).

pregnant. In such cases it is much easier to register the cause of death as a medical condition, such as infection, haemorrhage, sepsis, or even renal failure (which does not even appear as a maternal death). It is clear that a considerable percentage of deaths due to these causes are provoked by unsafe induced abortions. The fact that physicians, in general, tend to register the most immediate causes of death, rather than the antecedent or provoking condition, only exacerbates the under-reporting of induced abortion as a cause of maternal mortality. A study in Brazil found that 60 per cent of the deaths reported as being due to infection were abortion-related (La Guardia *et al.*, 1990). A study in Colombia (Muñoz *et al.*, 1985) found that 66 per cent of maternal deaths attributed to infection were actually due to induced abortion. In estimating abortion-related deaths it is therefore necessary to include a proportion of those deaths due to infection.

It is extremely difficult to quantify this form of under-reporting, but the number of abortion-related deaths in Latin America could be as large as double the minimum estimate specified above. In order to calculate measures that enable comparisons, we assume that the actual annual number of abortion-related deaths in Latin America is between 5000 and 10,000 per year. The latter figure represents over one third of all maternal deaths.

By comparing the 5000 to 10,000 estimated abortion-related deaths with the 4 to 6 million induced abortions estimated to occur annually in Latin America (Frejka and Atkin, 1990), the estimated abortion-related mortality rate ranges from 83 to 250 deaths per 100,000 abortions. The abortion-related death rate per 100,000 abortions in developed countries is far lower: ranging from 0 in New Zealand (1976–87) and Norway (1978–82) to 2 in Scotland (1976–87) according to Henshaw's (1990) calculations. The aggregate abortion-related mortality rate for countries where abortion is legal is 0.6 per 100,000 abortions.

4. Abortion-Related Morbidity (Complications)

While these estimates suggest that induced abortion makes a considerable contribution to maternal mortality in Latin America, it is important to remember that, when performed in unsafe conditions, induced abortion may also lead to a variety of medical and psycho-social complications. In contrast, wherever and whenever induced abortions are performed by qualified personnel under adequate conditions, complications are rare. This is the typical state of affairs in countries where induced abortion legislation is liberal and in specialized institutions elsewhere. Under safe circumstances, the percentage of induced abortions with subsequent complications requiring hospitalization rarely exceeds 5 per cent; usually it is much less.

In Brazil, a country with restrictive legislation, a community-based study conducted in 1990 among female employees of a university (Hardy and Costa, personal communication) found a complication rate of almost 20 per cent. The majority of the abortions were conducted by physicians in a clinic or a hospital, but even these resulted in complications in 10 per cent of the cases. Abortions that were performed at home by unqualified individuals resulted in complications in approximately 50 per cent of cases. Even though poorer women, who are more likely to be subject to unsafe abortions, may be under-represented in this study, the complication rates found indicate that a large proportion of women suffer health complications following induced abortions when they are conducted in an environment of restrictive legislation. Even when performed by physicians, the complication rates are higher than in the studies from countries with liberal abortion legislation. This may be because many of the physicians performing the induced abortions have not been trained adequately in this procedure and/or because they were using obsolete methods under less than optimal conditions.

Another study examining a large data set also implies high complication rates (morbidity) due to induced abortions. A thorough analysis of data for the 1980s from the Mexican Social Security Institute (Hernandez *et al.*, 1991) revealed that case-fatality rates differed significantly for distinct causes of maternal mortality (Table 16.4). Taken at face value, the data indicate that case-fatality rates for abortions are by far the lowest. (Although all deaths were evaluated by Maternal Mortality Committees which independently evaluated cause of death, it is difficult to assess whether any abortion-related deaths were registered as haemorrhage or sepsis.) The case-fatality rates for haemorrhage, toxaemia, and sepsis are ten, twenty-four, and twenty-seven times higher than those for abortions. Furthermore, according to the data in Table 16.4, 63 per cent of the patients treated for pregnancy-related problems were abortion patients, yet only 9 per cent of the deaths were caused by abortions.

Various interpretations of these findings are possible. First, induced abortions frequently result in complications requiring hospitalization, but these are rarely fatal. Second, a large number of induced abortions are initiated 'at home' and when bleeding (or any other symptom) starts the women can be admitted to a hospital with the understanding that these are spontaneous abortions in progress. Third, despite the evaluations of the Maternal Mortality

Table 16.4. Hospital discharges, selected causes, maternal deaths and case-fatality rates 1987–9 Mexico Social Security Institute

Cause	Hospital discharges[a]		Deaths[b]		Case fatality rate (per 1000)
	Number	%	Number	%	
Toxaemia	46,618	15	314	53	6.74
Haemorrhage	57,483	19	156	26	2.71
Sepsis	9,410	3	71	12	7.55
Abortions	189,911	63	54	9	0.28
Total	303,422	100	595	100	1.96

[a] Based on registration system of hospital discharges (Sistema Unico de Informacion—Subsistema 13).
[b] Based on confidential reports of National Mortality Committee.
Source: Hernandez *et al.* (1991).

Committees, many of the deaths recorded as caused by haemorrhage or sepsis may have been caused initially by unprofessionally performed induced abortions. Most probably the low case-fatality rate of the abortions is the result of a combination of these factors. If, however, the first and the third factors are the more important, it would indicate that relatively large numbers of women in Mexico suffer health complications as a consequence of having had an induced abortion.

Recent estimates relevant to this issue are also available for Chile. In 1987, 31,966 women were hospitalized due to complications of spontaneous and induced abortions. Requena (1990) estimated the total number of abortions as being approximately 195,000, of which 176,000 were induced. There was a total of forty-nine maternal deaths in 1988 and it is known that the abortion-related proportion tends to be between 33 and 42 per cent (Gayán, 1990); thus one can estimate that about nineteen abortion-related deaths occurred in 1988. Even though the data are from different years (i.e. 1987 and 1988), they are adequate for estimation of the order of magnitude of the problem. The resulting calculations indicate similar relationships to those found in the Mexican study. The abortion-related case-fatality rate is low, namely about 0.6 per 1000 hospitalized abortions. At the same time, the complication rate of all abortions is about 16 per cent. The complication rate for induced abortions is certainly higher since one can assume that, in Chile as elsewhere, induced abortions have a higher complication rate than spontaneous ones.

These data suggest that, at least in Mexico and Chile, incomplete and complicated abortions are the cause of a large proportion of pregnancy-related hospitalizations but that in most cases the women are treated successfully and do not die. It is important to note, however, that in other countries the situation may be far worse. The proportion of women who die from induced abortions in a given setting depends on many factors such as the quality of abortion services available, women's knowledge and beliefs about post-abortion symptoms of complications, their willingness to seek help in a hospital, and the quality of care available in the hospitals once they arrive. As pointed out by Singh and Wulf (1991), the proportion of women who obtain abortions who later need hospitalization is probably quite different in Brazil, Colombia, and Peru, the three countries in which they developed estimates of abortion levels based on hospital admissions. Since little is known about the conditions under which clandestine abortions are performed in other Latin American countries, it is not yet possible to conclude that case-fatality rates are as low in all countries as those reported for Mexico and Chile.

5. Discussion and Conclusions

It is clear that induced abortion is a serious public health problem in Latin America. Compared with the developed countries, induced abortions in Latin America are accompanied by relatively high abortion-related mortality. Furthermore, large numbers of women suffer serious health complications as a result of induced abortions. As has been pointed out by numerous authors, almost all these deaths and health complications are avoidable through the combination of accessible and appropriate family planning services combined with the provision of high quality abortion services.

To the extent that women's organizations have been effective in improving the informal networks that support women in need of abortions, women are probably seeking abortions sooner and choosing safer practitioners among those available. Once complications ensue, these same networks may have improved the women's chances of identifying the symptoms and seeking medical care more quickly and appropriately. In some places, health care personnel have received training in the identification and referral of patients with post-abortion complications. This should decrease the risk of severe morbidity and mortality. To the extent that women's overall living conditions have improved in some countries and sectors of the population, some women will be less vulnerable and more resilient in the face of abortion complications.

It is also possible that improvements in services, even without liberalization of abortion legislation, may be decreasing the degree of danger to physical health due to induced abortions in many countries of the region and many strata of the population. Even though legal statutes have undergone few modifications, a number of other circumstances have changed. As a result, a larger proportion of women may be able to obtain safe, induced abortions and abortion complications may be easier to remedy. The suction method, which is far safer and cheaper than dilation and curettage, is now being used more frequently than it was two or three decades ago. It is likely that a larger proportion of induced abortions is conducted by more qualified personnel. Decades of folk experience with induced abortions have been gained. Some drugs used for other purposes can also be employed quite safely to induce abortions.

Despite these trends, the deplorable circumstances of many women make them highly vulnerable to the complications which result from unsafe, induced abortions. Large numbers of induced abortions continue to be performed by unqualified individuals, often the women themselves, with inappropriate and dangerous methods and in hazardous conditions.

A great deal remains to be done to improve the quality of services available and to insure that women with abortion complications receive prompt and appropriate care. Liberalization of abortion legislation combined with provision of appropriate and accessible services is clearly the most effective solution. But, even within the context of restrictive legislation, efforts should continue to improve the quality of services and referral systems.

References

Frejka, T., and L. C. Atkin (1990), 'El papel del aborto inducido en la transición de la fecundidad de América Latina (The role of induced abortion in the Latin American fertility transition)', *Salud Pública de México*, 32(3): 276–86, Instituto Nacional de Salud Pública, Mexico.

——L. C. Atkin, and O. L. Toro (1989), 'Research program for the prevention of unsafe induced abortion and its adverse consequences in Latin America and the Caribbean', Working Paper No. 23, The Population Council, Mexico City, Mexico.

Gayán, P. (1990), 'Consecuencias medicas del aborto inducido en Chile', in: M. Requena (ed.) *Aborto Inducido en Chile*, Sociedad Chilena de Salud Publica, Santiago, Chile.

Hardy, E., and G. R. Costa, 'Abortion experience among female employees of a Brazilian University', unpublished report to The Population Council, Mexico City in fulfilment of grant 191.54E-1, CECICAMP, Campinas, Brazil.

Henshaw, S. K. (1990), 'Induced abortion: a world review, 1990', *Family Planning Perspectives*, 22(2): 76–89.

Hernandez, D., O. Mojarro, J. Fuentes, and J. Martíntez-Manautou (1991), 'Consideraciones sobre la muerte materna en el IMSS y sus causas', Instituto Mexicano de Seguro Social (IMSS), Mexico City, Mexico.

Koonin, L. (1988), 'Maternal mortality surveillance, United States', *Morbidity and Mortality Weekly Report*, CDC 37: SS-5, 19–29.

La Guardia, K. D., M. V. Rothoz, and P. Belfort (1990), 'A 10-year review of maternal mortality in a municipal hospital in Rio de Janeiro: A cause for concern', *Obstetrics and Gynecology*, 75: 27–32.

Muñoz, L. A., H. Ñañez, E. Becerra, and J. Klevens (1985), 'Mortalidad materna en el instituto materno infantil de Bogota (1976–80)', *Revista de la Facultad de Medicina*, 39(4): 331–51.

Pan American Health Organization (PAHO) and World Health Organization (WHO) (1990), 'Regional plan of action for the reduction of maternal mortality in the Americas', XXIII Pan American Sanitary Conference: XLII Regional Committee Meeting, CSP23/10, September, Washington, DC.

Puffer, R. R., and G. W. Griffith (1967), *Patterns of Urban Mortality*, Scientific Publication No. 151, PAHO, Washington, DC.

Requena, M. (1990), 'El aborto inducido en Chile', in: M. Requena (ed.) *El Aborto Inducido en Chile*, Sociedad Chilena de Salud Publica, Santiago, Chile.

Reyes, S., and J. L. Bobadilla (1990), 'Muertes maternas prevenibles en el Distrito Federal: resultados preliminares', *Gaceta Médica de México*.

Royston, E. (1991), 'Estimating the number of abortion deaths', *Methodological Issues in Abortion Research*, Population Council, IPAS, WHO, New York.

——and S. Armstrong (1989), *Preventing Maternal Deaths*, World Health Organization, Geneva, Switzerland.

Singh, S., and D. Wulf (1991), 'Estimating abortion levels in Brazil, Colombia and Peru, using hospital admissions and fertility data survey', *International Family Planning Perspectives*, 17(1): 8–24.

17 The Changing Structure of Deaths from Injuries and Violence

ELÍAS ANZOLA-PÉREZ
Pan American Health Organization, Washington, DC, USA

SHRIKANT I. BANGDIWALA
University of North Carolina, Chapel Hill, NC, USA

1. Introduction

In Latin America and the Caribbean the epidemiological profile indicates both that communicable diseases still persist and that injuries are a serious problem (PAHO, 1986). Despite large differences between the different countries and subregions, it can be said that, for the most part, activities in injury prevention and control are in the early phases of development.

In the last twenty years, the Latin American and Caribbean region has been characterized by rapid urbanization and population growth. To these trends can be added the scenario of economic crisis, especially notable in the region during the 1980s. Together, these circumstances have brought about the deterioration of living conditions and increased poverty. Despite the fact that death rates for most of the countries in the region have declined during this period and life expectancy has increased, injuries have risen as a cause of mortality, morbidity, and disability. Injuries disproportionately affect certain groups of the population such as young people (Suárez-Ojeda and Cusminsky, 1979; Cusminsky and Suárez-Ojeda, 1979), males, and the poor. With improved control of infectious and parasitic diseases, it is not surprising that injuries are taking on increasing importance. Because of the early age at which injuries occur, the years of potential life lost from them represent a serious loss for countries of the region. In about 1986, the proportion of the total years lost from injuries in most of the countries of the region represented one third of total loss from all causes of death in the population 1 to 24 years of age (Figure 17.1). In only one country, namely Peru, was the potential life lost due to influenza and pneumonia greater than that due to injuries.

Among the external causes of death, certain causes are of particular importance in this region. Traffic accidents are taking on epidemic proportions as a

The authors wish to thank Dr Armando Peruga and the Pan American Health Organization, Washington, DC, for processing the data that made it possible to carry out the study; Mr Sergio Muñoz, Universidad de la Frontera, Temuco, Chile, for performing the statistical computations and preparing the figures; and Ms Matilde Kelly, for arranging the final version.

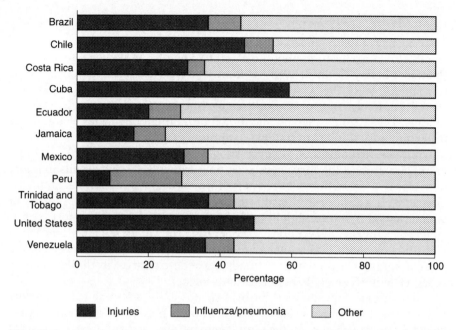

Fig. 17.1.   Sources of years of potential life lost by the population aged 1–24 years

result of a marked increase in registered motor vehicles (Bangdiwala and Anzola-Pérez, 1987). Violent acts—intentional traumatic events caused by individuals, groups, or governments—are another important aspect of the injury problem. Several health indicators for Latin America point to a troubling increase in violent acts (PAHO, 1990).

This chapter focuses on trends in mortality due to traffic accidents and acts of violence in the twenty-year period from 1968 to 1987 in selected countries of Latin America and the Caribbean.

2. Definitions

The International Classification of Diseases, 9th Revision (ICD-9) of the World Health Organization groups external causes of death into the following categories:

- E800–E949 Unintentional accidents
- E950–E959 Suicide
- E960–E969 Homicide
- E970–E979 Injury resulting from legal intervention
- E980–E989 Injury undetermined whether accidentally or purposely inflicted

- E990–E999 Injury resulting from operations of war

Accident is usually understood to refer to an occurrence, in a sequence of events, that produces unintentional injury, death, or damage to property (National Safety Council, 1984). Recently, preference has been given to the term injury, since the word accident erroneously implies that the event occurred randomly and, as a result, cannot be predicted or avoided (Hijar-Medina, 1991). Injury may be intentional or unintentional. This chapter uses the term injury to refer to traumatic injuries.

While any definition of violence should encompass its pyschological and moral dimensions, the focus here is on physical violence that results in injury to persons. A distinction between acts of violence and unintentional injuries is difficult to draw, since it is legal rather than conceptual in nature. Injuries of undetermined intention should probably be considered for the most part as violent acts. Legal interventions and operations of war do not lend themselves to a study of trends because they are by nature sporadic. For purposes of the present study, which compares trends between countries in the last twenty years, violent acts include homicide and suicide.

Unintentional injuries may be broken down by different causal factors involved, such as motor vehicles, fire, drowning, poisoning, etc. Injuries produced by motor vehicles are the most common cause and are the main focus of this study. Nomenclature for referring to injury victims suffers from lack of uniformity, which makes it difficult to draw comparisons between countries. For example, the World Health Organization defines as a death from a traffic accident one that occurs within thirty days from the occurrence of the event, whereas the European Union extends this period up to 1 year. However, especially in the developing countries, difficulties in follow-up make it unlikely that these conventions are applied. In several countries the period is shortened to the first twenty-four hours after the occurrence of the event and, in Mexico, only deaths that occur at the site of the crash are considered. This study uses information provided by the countries based on the definition of a traffic accident as contained in ICD-9 under categories E810–E829.

3. Studies in Latin America

Few studies have been conducted on the occurrence of injuries and violent acts in Latin America and the Caribbean. Alfaro-Alvarez and Díaz-Coller (1977) examined the growing public health problem represented by traffic accidents. The Pan American Health Organization (PAHO, 1984) and Bangdiwala and Anzola-Pérez (1987) have continued the study. Sharp increases in the number of registered vehicles in developing countries of the region, combined with the fact that traffic legislation, driver education, and highway and vehicle safety have not progressed at the same rate as the factors that created the problem, make it reasonable to expect an increasing rise in the risk of traffic accidents in these countries (Bangdiwala and Anzola-Pérez, 1987).

Apart from studies carried out by PAHO at the international level, few countries in the region have studied the problem of traffic accidents within their territory. Recently, Vilchis-Licón and Iturrioz-Rosell (1986) examined economic indicators and public health trends associated with traffic accidents in Mexico. A 1985–6 study of causes of emergencies in four general hospitals under Mexico's General Medical Services Directorate of the Federal District emphasized the pattern in Mexico City (Hijar-Medina *et al.*, 1989). In that study, the groups most affected were those aged 15 to 19 and 20 to 24, with males requiring attention in more than 70 per cent of cases.

PAHO sponsored a study of the incidence of injury in children and adolescents in selected communities and hospitals in Brazil, Chile, Cuba, and Venezuela (Bangdiwala and Anzola-Perez, 1990). Traffic accidents are a major cause of morbidity in these countries, and a positive association was found between the educational level of the head of household and probability of being a victim of a traffic accident (Bangdiwala and Anzola-Pérez, 1990).

PAHO (1990) has undertaken a descriptive study of violent acts in the Americas. Violent acts include the abuse of children and the elderly, sexual abuse and rape, torture, war injuries, suicide, and homicide. Despite the fact that only some of the aspects of violent acts are quantifiable and that indicators and available information are limited, it is possible to gain a rough idea of the magnitude and complexity of the problem from a review of information compiled and submitted by health services.

Recent studies of violent acts in Latin America include those in Brazil (Mello-Jorge and Bernardes-Marques, 1985), Mexico (Hijar-Medina *et al.*, 1986), Argentina (Danielsen *et al.*, 1989), and Chile (Aalund *et al.*, 1990). The study of violent deaths in Brazil concentrated on children and adolescents. The Mexican study focused on mortality due to accidents, violent acts, and poisoning in all age groups in the Federal District from 1970 to 1982. In Argentina, as part of a transcultural comparison between the Danes and the Argentinians of violent behaviour, investigators studied those injuries treated in the emergency department at two Buenos Aires hospitals which had resulted from deliberate acts of violence. Use of firearms and blunt instruments was considerably more frequent in Argentina than in Denmark. The same group of Danish investigators also studied violent acts registered at a hospital in Santiago. The most frequent act of violence was a blow with a blunt instrument. The incidents usually occurred on the street and, in most cases, the aggressors were members of the police force.

Most studies in Latin America have been cross-sectional and have not examined trends over time. The present study undertakes a preliminary review of trends in mortality from traffic accidents and violent acts in the region. It relies on the reports provided each year by member countries to PAHO through their Ministries of Health. The reports have been processed systematically with a view to making this presentation consistent across countries.

4. Analysis of Information from PAHO

For this analysis, twenty-three of the thirty-eight member countries of PAHO were considered initially since they had relatively complete information for the period of the study—namely from 1968 to 1987. For presentational purposes, detailed attention is given to the following nine countries: Chile, Colombia, Cuba, Ecuador, El Salvador, Mexico, Panama, the United States of America, and Venezuela. These countries cover both continents of the region and the Caribbean, as well as a variety of conditions that reflect the status of traffic accidents and violence. The other countries examined were: Argentina, Barbados, Canada, Costa Rica, The Dominican Republic, Guatemala, Martinique, Paraguay, Peru, Puerto Rico, Saint Lucia, Suriname, Trinidad and Tobago, and Uruguay.

The following age groups are considered: under 1 year, 1–4 years, 5–14, 15–24, 25–44, 45–64, and 65 years and over. In addition to mortality in general, the following specific causes of death are examined:

- Malignant neoplasms (140–209)
- Diseases of the circulatory system (401–459)
- Injury due to any external cause (E800–E999)
- Injury due to traffic accidents (E810–E829)
- Suicides (E950–E959)
- Homicides (E960–E969)
- Unintentional poisonings (E850–E869)
- Falls (E880–E888)
- Fire (E890–E899)
- Drownings (E910)
- Remaining injuries

The last eight causes sum to all injuries produced by external causes. Homicide and suicide are considered violent acts for purposes of this study.

The statistical analysis is essentially descriptive. Yearly age-adjusted (to the 1960 population distribution for the region) mortality rates per 100,000 for each sex and for each of the twenty-three countries mentioned above were computed for specific causes: malignant neoplasms, cardiovascular diseases, and external causes. Graphs are presented for the nine countries selected (Figures 17.A1–17.A9). The graphs are repeated for the three external causes of particular interest: traffic accidents, suicides, and homicides (Figures 17.A10–17.A18). Graphs of rates for traffic accident deaths are also presented for specific ages 0–14, 15–24, 25–44, 45–64, and 65 years and over (Figures 17.A19–17.A27).

In order to determine whether mortality from external causes and, specifically, mortality from traffic accidents are a growing problem in the region, the global age-adjusted rates by sex for the first three causes for the twenty-three countries for the period covered by the study were examined. (Note that graphs are presented for only the nine countries mentioned above, Figures 17.A1–17.A9). During this period, the major causes of death in most countries were cardiovascular diseases and malignant neoplasms. Generally speaking, death rates were higher for men and trends differed for the two sexes within a given country.

The data on Canada and the United States of America clearly reveal the well-known decline in mortality due to cardiovascular diseases for both sexes, but other, less-developed countries of the region had this trend as well: Argentina, Chile, Costa Rica (women only), Mexico (women only), Panama, Trinidad and Tobago, Uruguay, and Venezuela. The difference is that, while in Canada and the United States death rates from external causes have also been falling gradually in the last ten years, in the less-developed countries of the region the trend has been for them to rise or, at best, level off. In Argentina, there has been a small decline. In Chile, mortality from external causes is falling but still surpasses that from malignant neoplasms in men.

It is very important to note that in some Latin American countries overall mortality from external causes surpasses mortality from any other causes including chronic diseases. This is true for males in Ecuador, El Salvador, Guatemala, and Mexico. In Chile, Colombia, the Dominican Republic, Panama, Paraguay, Peru, Puerto Rico, Suriname, Trinidad and Tobago, and Venezuela, the death rate from external causes for males exceeds the death rate from malignant neoplasms. In Venezuela, the death rate from traffic accidents among males is so high that it alone almost equals the death rate from malignant neoplasms.

Overall mortality from external causes has tended to remain relatively stable or fluctuate very little in most countries; however, the level is already high compared with other diseases. In some countries an increase can be seen, especially among males. This is true for males in Colombia and for both sexes in El Salvador, Guatemala, Mexico, and Suriname. In Cuba, the death rate for men has risen to the level of malignant neoplasms. In contrast, in the United States, the death rate for men decreased during the study period.

The distribution of external causes of mortality from traffic accidents and violent acts across the period covered by the study by sex is shown in Figures 17.A10–17.A18. The distribution of external causes of mortality varies considerably between the sexes in almost all countries. In general, women who die from external causes tend to die from homicide less often than men in the same countries. Also, except in Cuba, suicide rates of women tend to be lower than the equivalent rates for men.

In the majority of the countries studied, traffic accidents are the main external cause of death. The pattern in the distribution of external causes of mortality is determined primarily by the percentage attributed to violent acts, in particular homicide. In Colombia, there has been a dramatic increase in deaths from homicide in men, whereas women die from other external causes (see Chapter 18). In El Salvador, the other country with high homicide rates in men, women tend to die more often from traffic accidents. The pattern in Mexico resembles that of Colombia, with men having high rates of homicide and women dying from other external causes.

Among external causes, mortality from suicide was relatively low in most countries studied and the pattern is similar in both sexes. Cuba is an exception: mortality from suicide is high relative to other external causes and suicide represented the most frequent cause of external mortality among women during the first ten-year period studied. Unfortunately, there is no information on death rates from specific external causes in this country for the last ten years. The United States and El Salvador are the only other countries where suicide was a frequent cause of external mortality. In Cuba, the already high proportion of suicides relative to other external causes of mortality increased during the ten years for which data are available. The proportion of external mortality from traffic accidents remained relatively stable.

In Colombia, although there was a sharp increase in the proportion of deaths from homicide among men (and also an increase in women), the increase in the proportion of deaths from traffic accidents has been relatively gradual. Chile, according to information from PAHO, experienced a steady decline in death rates from traffic accidents, homicide, and suicide during the study period. Ecuador and Panama had similar trends to each other, with a gradual increase in the proportion of mortality from traffic accidents.

In contrast to countries in Latin America, the United States had a rather static distribution of external causes of mortality over the study period. With the exceptions already noted, death rates from traffic accidents and violent acts are relatively high in comparison with most of the countries studied.

Trends in El Salvador, where homicide in men was the most common external cause of death, include a decline in rates of suicide in the late 1970s and a slight increase in the early 1980s. Homicides and suicides increased as causes of death in Salvadorian women in the course of the period. Mexico, on the other hand, stands out as having a low incidence of suicide relative to other external causes of mortality. Mortality from traffic accidents is low compared with other countries studied, but this proportion increases gradually in both men and women during the period. Although Mexico has high proportional mortality from homicide in men, rates are not as high as those in Colombia or El Salvador. Venezuela has the highest death rates from traffic accidents among countries studied, representing around 40 per cent of all external causes of mortality for both sexes and for the entire period of the study.

Mortality due to injuries caused by traffic accidents can also be studied within age groups (Figures 17.A19–17.A27). In general, males have higher rates across all age groups when compared with females. The rates follow a regular pattern in most countries of the region. Specifically, traffic accidents are not an important cause of mortality in children aged 0–14 years. The age group that has the highest death rates from traffic accidents is those aged 65 and over. This holds in eight of the nine countries studied. The exception is the United States, which exhibits a completely different pattern from that of the less-developed countries of the region. In the USA, young people aged 15 to 24, which is the age group that is just beginning to drive, have the highest death rates during the period of study, while rates for persons 65 years and over decline during the period.

In terms of young people (15–24 years) and adults (25–44 and 45–64 years), the trend in most of the Latin American countries studied is for older persons to have higher death rates. This pattern can be observed in Chile, Colombia, Ecuador, El Salvador, and Mexico. In Cuba, rates for the age groups 15–24, 25–44, and 45–64 years tend to be similar, although there is no information available for years after 1977. Chile had an appreciable reduction in mortality from traffic accidents among young people, adults, and the elderly during the twenty years of the study. In Colombia and El Salvador, there was an increase in the rates for adults and a sharp increase among the elderly. Ecuador, Mexico, and Venezuela follow a distinct pattern with a small increase at the end of the 1970s and a decline in the mid-1980s. In Panama, adult age groups (25–44 and 45–64) kept their rates steady during the period. Venezuela had the highest death rates from traffic accidents in the hemisphere. Rates increased for all groups over the age of 15 at the end of the 1970s, and, although they declined at the beginning of the 1980s, they increased once again during the last three years of the study period.

Violent acts in men were studied on the basis of suicide and homicide in the nine countries selected. In several countries, mortality from suicide is relatively low. This is true for Colombia, Ecuador, Mexico, and Panama. In most of the five remaining countries, suicide mortality tends to increase with age of the victim. This is seen in Chile, Cuba, the United States, and Venezuela. Cuba has the highest death rates from suicide of all the countries studied. In particular, the rate for persons over 64 is almost double that of any other age group in the country and of any age group in any of the other nine countries. Chile experienced a slight decline of suicide rates during the twenty years of the study period. In the United States, trends are very clear: rates for the 15–24, 25–44, and 45–64 age groups remained about the same during the 1980s while, among the elderly men, the rate rose rapidly during the decade. Venezuela, on the other hand, has experienced a dramatic reduction in its death rate from suicide among the elderly, which began to approach the rate for adults. Suicide rates in El Salvador increased during the period, with no clear differences between age groups, but there is no information available for 1975–80 or 1985–7. Age-adjusted suicide mortality rates are presented for five countries in Figure 17.2. Canada and Cuba have very high rates for men and Cuban women have rates close to seven times higher than women in the other selected countries.

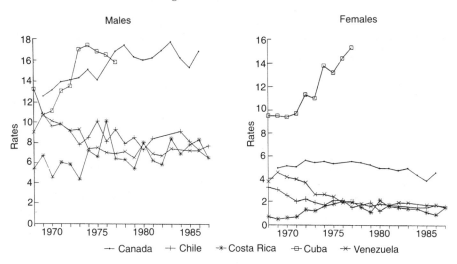

Fig. 17.2. Age-adjusted mortality rates for suicides in selected countries of the Americas (per 100,000)

Death rates from homicide in males are a good indicator of violent acts in the countries of Latin America (PAHO, 1990). Homicide is not a significant cause of mortality in 1–4 and 5–14 year old age groups. In Cuba, Chile, and Panama, death rates from homicide for all age groups are low compared with those in the other countries studied. In Cuba, the most consistently affected age group is young people aged 15 to 24 years. In other countries, the age group that tends to be most affected by homicide is those aged 25 to 44 years. This is seen in Colombia, Ecuador, El Salvador, Mexico, the United States, and Venezuela, with Colombia and El Salvador having the highest homicide rates of all. Colombian rates, which were already high, show an upswing during the period, with an approximate increase of 50 per cent in the homicide rate in the 25–44 age group between 1972 and 1982 and a less dramatic increase in other adult age groups (see Chapter 18). Death rates from homicide in El Salvador are double the already high rates in Colombia. Consistently, the 25–44, 45–64, and 15–24 age groups, in decreasing order, are the most affected in that country. Although already high at the beginning of the study period, the rates nearly doubled in fifteen years, not just among 25 to 44 year-olds, as in Colombia, but in all three adult age groups.

In Ecuador, death rates from homicide are relatively low in comparison with other countries studied. However, in all groups from age 15 onward, the rates increase gradually during the course of the period. The trend in Mexico is different from that in other countries studied. Death rates from homicide for groups over age 15 tended to remain stable during the period but their level is quite high. On the other hand, in the United States and Venezuela, which also had relatively stable rates during the period, rates were relatively low in adult

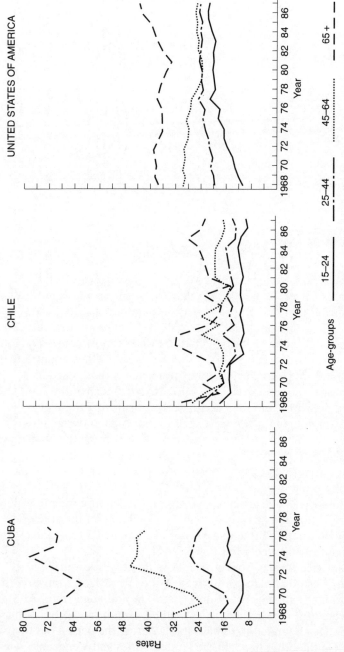

Fig. 17.3. Male age-specific mortality rates for suicides in Cuba, Chile and the USA, 1968–87 (per 100,000). *Source:* PAHO (1990).

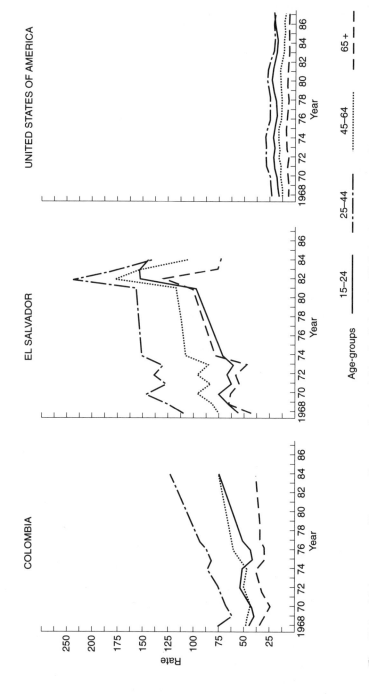

Fig. 17.4. Male age-specific mortality rates for homicides in Colombia, El Salvador, and the USA, 1968–87 (per 100,000).
Source: PAHO (1990).

age groups. Rates in Venezuela went up at the end of the 1970s and the beginning of the 1980s, but have been declining recently.

In order to contrast the striking differences in trends for suicides and homicides, mortality rates for men from selected countries are presented in Figures 17.3 and 17.4. Cuban men over 45 years of age have higher suicide rates than their counterparts in Chile and the United States. Suicide rates in Chile seem to be decreasing, while an upswing is noticeable in the United States. Homicide rates in Colombia and El Salvador are quite high and appear to be increasing when compared with rates in the United States.

5. Discussion

Mortality statistics are only the tip of the iceberg—or, in terms of the injury pyramid, the apex (Figure 17.5). It is estimated that for every fatal injury of a child or adolescent, forty-five traumatic injuries require hospitalization and nearly 1300 require medical care in emergency rooms or outpatient physician consultations (Gallagher *et al.*, 1984). Also, a great number of injuries are not treated medically and are therefore difficult to quantify, as are the numbers of victims who suffer for the rest of their lives from a disability resulting from a traumatic event. It is therefore safe to say that the damage to health from external causes can only be much worse than is suggested by the present study of trends in mortality.

The results of this descriptive review of information available from PAHO on external causes of mortality reflect not only the particular circumstances of the countries studied but also certain characteristics that they share in common. As in most of the world, death rates from external causes in countries studied here were greater for men than for women. In most of them, overall mortality from external causes has remained relatively stable or fluctuated very little, but it must be kept in mind that the level of such mortality is already quite high. In several countries the trend is rising, especially among males.

Differences between the circumstances of the countries are reflected in trends in mortality from selected causes and age groups. Thus, in developing countries, older age groups tend to have higher death rates from traffic accidents than young people, whereas in the United States it is the 15–24 year age group who have the highest rates. Among the countries studied, Venezuela has the highest rates of mortality from traffic accidents; Cuba, the highest rates from suicide; and El Salvador, followed by Colombia, the highest rates from homicide.

Traffic accidents and violent acts are not significant causes of death among children and adolescents in the countries studied, compared with older persons. However, injury and poisoning are affecting increasingly infant and adolescent populations for a number of reasons. In the first place, episodes of

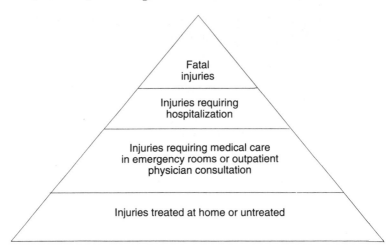

Fig. 17.5. The injury pyramid

infectious diseases are becoming less frequent (Figure 17.6). As infectious disease mortality declines, there is necessarily an increased probability that loss of life will result from other mechanisms—conspicuous among these being injury and poisoning (Gallagher *et al.*, 1984). In general, death rates from traffic accidents have tended to increase in adults but the pattern is not uniform among countries. Suicide rates are low throughout the region except in Cuba. Homicide occurs most frequently in the 25–44 age group, and more commonly among men than women.

In contrast to the United States, Latin American countries experienced relatively more variation over time in the distribution of external causes of mortality during the period. This may reflect the economic and political instability prevailing in most of the countries.

Consideration of the factors that account for the incidence of external causes of mortality suggests that the current situation will worsen. Bangdiwala and Anzola-Pérez (1987) note the significance of population growth and the increasing number of registered vehicles, as well as increases in the index of motorization (the number of motorized vehicles per inhabitant), in almost all countries of the region between 1969 and 1980. Bangdiwala *et al.* (1985) observed a positive correlation between death rates in the population and the index of motorization. These trends are compounded by the fact that, in most of the region, progress in traffic legislation, driver education, the use of protective devices for passengers, and highway and vehicle safety has not kept pace with factors that contribute to the problem. Thus, it can be expected that the risk of traffic accidents in these countries will increase.

Mortality may also be due to an inadequate system of medical or hospital care once a traumatic event has occurred. Emergency transfer systems, hospi-

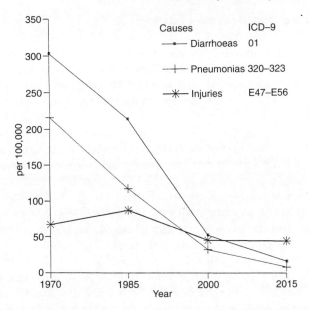

Fig. 17.6. Projection of mortality rates by cause in preschool[a] males, Latin America and the Caribbean, 1970–2015

[a] 1–4 years old.
Source: Bulatao and Stephens (1991).

tal installations, and other factors need to be considered and studied in order to identify preventive measures that could contribute to reducing mortality. Unless changes take place in the factors mentioned, increases can be expected in death rates from traffic accidents in the region.

In several Latin American countries the situation with respect to homicide is alarming. Factors recognized as relating to occurrence of homicide include: use of firearms, consumption of alcohol and/or drugs, involvement in drug trafficking or other illegal activities, socio-cultural aspects, socio-economic level, and poverty (NCIPC 1989). In Latin America, what also must be acknowledged is the reality of internal aggression in several countries, be it associated with civil wars (for example, El Salvador), drug trafficking (for example, Colombia), or government repression (for example, Argentina, Chile). With all these factors bearing on the problem, it is easy to understand why high rates of violence may get progressively worse.

Increasing death rates from traffic accidents and violent acts not only reflect a loss of lives but also have social and economic costs in terms of the negative impact on quality of life and living conditions for several sectors of the population, the concentration of the problem within productive age groups, and the burden on health services that are already stretched thin because of scarce resources (PAHO, 1990).

6. Conclusions and Recommendations

Like any statistical analysis, this study is limited by quality of information provided. The information available from PAHO is obtained from the countries and is based on national systems for registration of deaths. Death registration varies in terms of the percentage of deaths that cannot be classified according to ICD-9 (see Chapter 3). In addition, there are particular problems regarding the definition of different external causes of mortality, as already mentioned in relation to traffic accidents. It is unlikely that the relevant parts of ICD-9 are applied uniformly by countries of the region. One aspect of the definitions that it is difficult to measure is intentionality of the injury. This problem is aggravated by the fact that the proportion of notifications, which is low in any case, will vary between different population groups and according to type of violence. For example, certain types of injuries in children and adolescents, whether intentional or caused by negligence or abuse on the part of an adult, may go unreported due to legal problems that they entail. Differences between population groups, in turn, lead to biases in estimates of incidence rates. Suicide has such a negative stigma that agencies can expect appreciable under-reporting. It is also unlikely that homicides associated with assault by institutions of the State will always be reported to the governmental agencies that produce the information compiled by international agencies such as PAHO.

Despite these limitations of the information analysed, it is possible to make the following assessment of trends in mortality from external causes in the Americas:

- external causes of mortality are increasing in importance throughout the region;
- external causes of mortality affect males to a disproportionate extent;
- death rates from traffic accidents and violent acts increased during the twenty years of the study (1968–87);
- trends in factors affecting occurrence of traffic accidents and violent acts indicate they will continue to increase;
- direct and indirect damage/cost of external causes of mortality are appreciable; and
- mortality constitutes only the tip of the iceberg represented by the problem of injuries.

These conclusions bear out the view that violent acts and traffic accidents are among the most serious public health problems of the region. To these conclusions, the following observations may be added:

- injury is among the leading causes of years of potential life lost;
- policies relating to injuries on the part of the health and other sectors are inadequate in most Latin American countries;
- injuries are preventable in almost all cases;

- only limited information is available on the causes, circumstances and risk factors for injuries and violent acts in Latin America and on the morbidity and sequelae that result; and
- information available is not treated uniformly from the statistical point of view, which makes it difficult to compare situations among countries.

In order to plan intervention policies and prevention programs it is necessary to have relevant, up-to-date, and valid information. This information, at the very least, should permit identification of groups at greatest risk, most frequent types of traumatic injuries, and their distribution in time and space. In addition, knowledge of the environmental and individual circumstances that surround the occurrence of a traumatic event is indispensable for development of preventive measures in the future. A cost-benefit analysis of possible preventive measures requires information on the final outcome for persons involved, the care they received and the direct and indirect costs of the event.

For prevention of traffic accidents, it is recommended that the advances made in some countries in highway safety be reinforced and that other countries be encouraged to make similar progress. The experience of the industrialized nations should be enlisted creatively in this area and studies of the situation should be carried out in every country in order to develop adequate programmes (Bangdiwala *et al.*, 1991). Such objectives require multisectoral support based on highly centralized efforts, up-to-date information that is complete and valid and studies of the complex problem of providing adequate and timely care for the injured.

Although the study of violent acts is complex, this should not be an excuse for inaction. Violent acts are a social reality and their trend over time can be changed and controlled. Efforts should be multisectoral and interdisciplinary, involving rigorous and specific research, changes in individual and institutional attitudes from the local level up to national and international levels, redefinition of policies, allocation of resources, reorganization of services and assignment of priority to the subject (PAHO, 1990).

The growing problem represented by external causes of mortality in the Americas is of enormous social and economic importance and is largely preventable. Measures exist to control the trends that have been observed during the last twenty years, and these need to be implemented if the goal of *Health for All by the Year 2000* is to be reached.

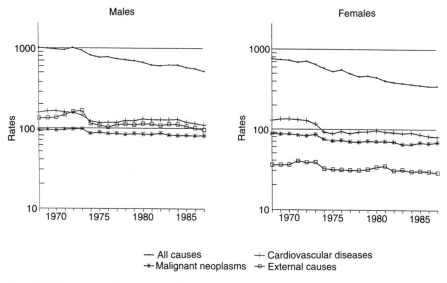

Fig. 17.A1. Age-adjusted mortality rates for all causes, cardiovascular disease, malignant neoplasms and external causes, Chile, 1968–87 (per 100,000) *Source*: PAHO (1990).

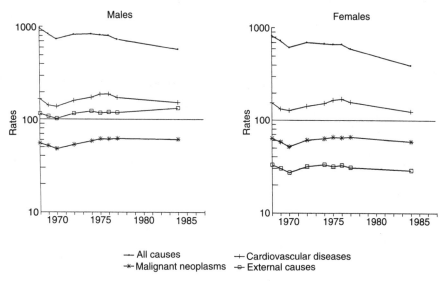

Fig. 17.A2. Age-adjusted mortality rates for all causes, cardiovascular disease, malignant neoplasms and external causes, Colombia, 1968–87 (per 100,000) *Source*: PAHO (1990).

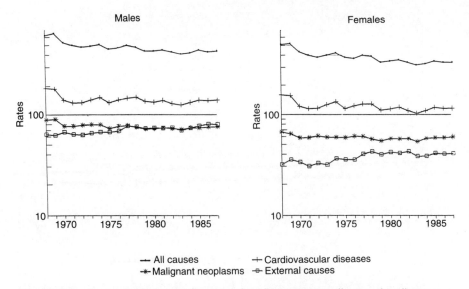

Fig. 17.A3. Age-adjusted mortality rates for all causes, cardiovascular disease, malignant neoplasms and external causes, Cuba, 1968–87 (per 100,000)
Source: PAHO (1990).

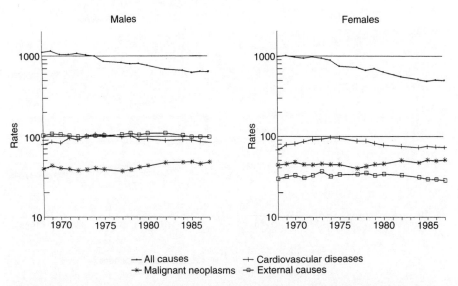

Fig. 17.A4. Age-adjusted mortality rates for all causes, cardiovascular disease, malignant neoplasms and external causes, Ecuador, 1968–87 (per 100,000)
Source: PAHO (1990).

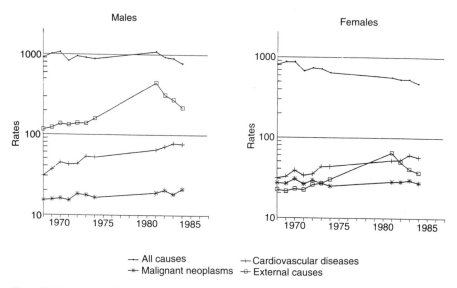

Fig. 17.A5. Age-adjusted mortality rates for all causes, cardiovascular disease, malignant neoplasms and external causes, El Salvador, 1968–87 (per 100,000)
Source: PAHO (1990).

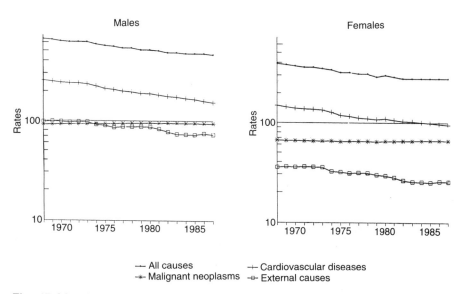

Fig. 17.A6. Age-adjusted mortality rates for all causes, cardiovascular disease, malignant neoplasms and external causes, USA, 1968–87 (per 100,000)
Source: PAHO (1990).

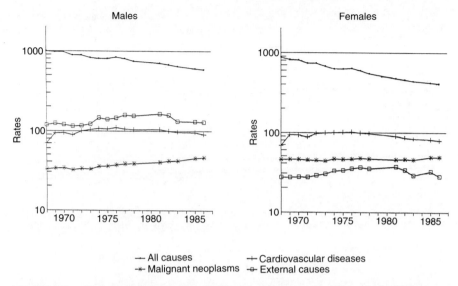

Fig. 17.A7. Age-adjusted mortality rates for all causes, cardiovascular disease, malignant neoplasms and external causes, Mexico, 1968–87 (per 100,000)
Source: PAHO (1990).

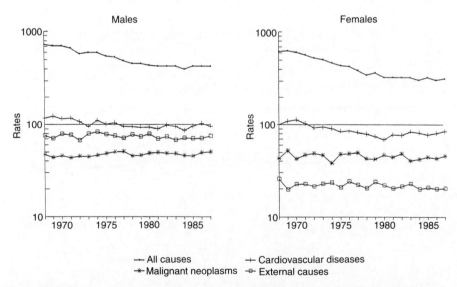

Fig. 17.A8. Age-adjusted mortality rates for all causes, cardiovascular disease, malignant neoplasms and external causes, Panama, 1968–87 (per 100,000)
Source: PAHO (1990).

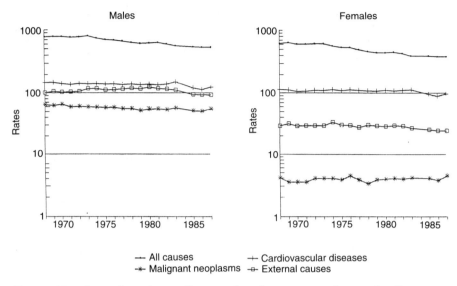

Fig. 17.A9. Age-adjusted mortality rates for all causes, cardiovascular disease, malignant neoplasms and external causes, Venezuela, 1968–87 (per 100,000)
Source: PAHO (1990).

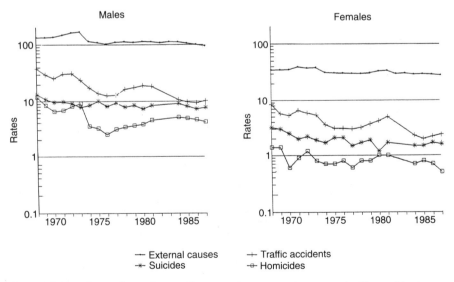

Fig. 17.A10. Age-adjusted mortality rates for external causes, traffic accidents, suicides and homicides, Chile, 1968–87 (per 100,000)
Source: PAHO (1990).

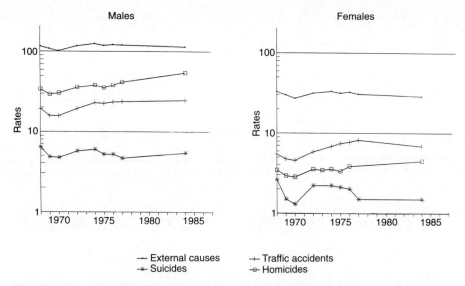

Fig. 17.A11. Age-adjusted mortality rates for external causes, traffic accidents, suicides and homicides, Colombia, 1968–87 (per 100,000)
Source: PAHO (1990).

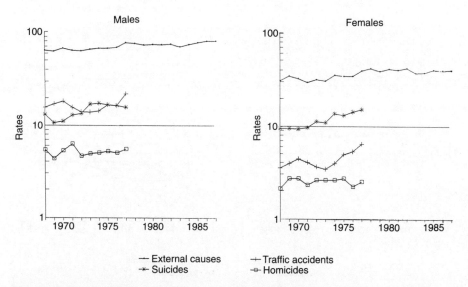

Fig. 17.A12. Age-adjusted mortality rates for external causes, traffic accidents, suicides and homicides, Cuba, 1968–87 (per 100,000)
Source: PAHO (1990).

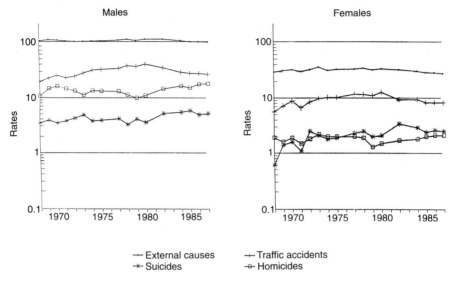

Fig. 17.A13. Age-adjusted mortality rates for external causes, traffic accidents, suicides and homicides, Ecuador, 1968–87 (per 100,000)
Source: PAHO (1990).

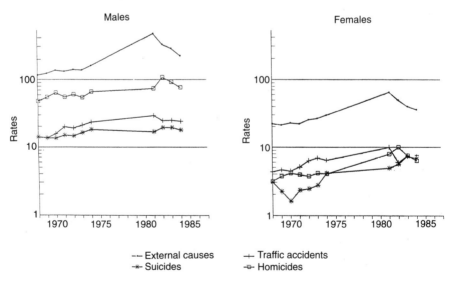

Fig. 17.A14. Age-adjusted mortality rates for external causes, traffic accidents, suicides and homicides, El Salvador, 1968–87 (per 100,000)
Source: PAHO (1990).

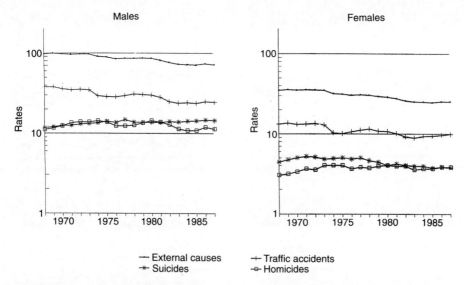

Fig. 17.A15. Age-adjusted mortality rates for external causes, traffic accidents, suicides and homicides, USA, 1968–87 (per 100,000)
Source: PAHO (1990).

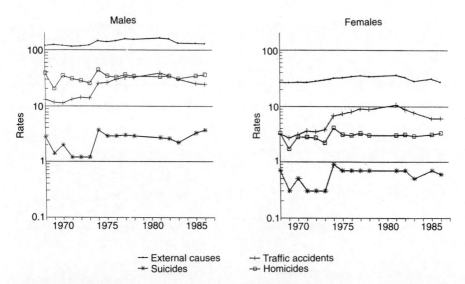

Fig. 17.A16. Age-adjusted mortality rates for external causes, traffic accidents, suicides and homicides, Mexico, 1968–87 (per 100,000)
Source: PAHO (1990).

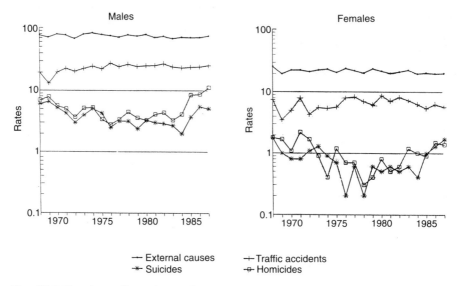

Fig. 17.A17. Age-adjusted mortality rates for external causes, traffic accidents, suicides and homicides, Panama, 1968–87 (per 100,000)
Source: PAHO (1990).

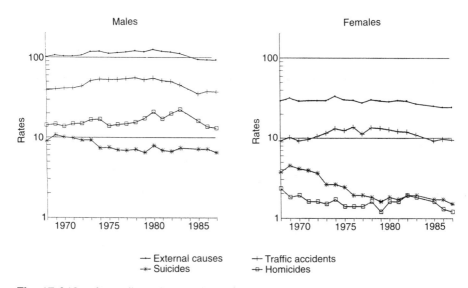

Fig. 17.A18. Age-adjusted mortality rates for external causes, traffic accidents, suicides and homicides, Venezuela, 1968–87 (per 100,000)
Source: PAHO (1990).

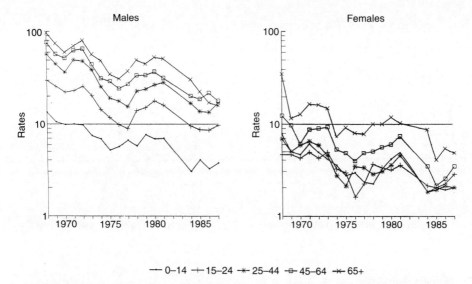

Fig. 17.A19. Age-specific mortality rates for traffic accidents, Chile, 1968–87 (per 100,000)
Source: PAHO (1990).

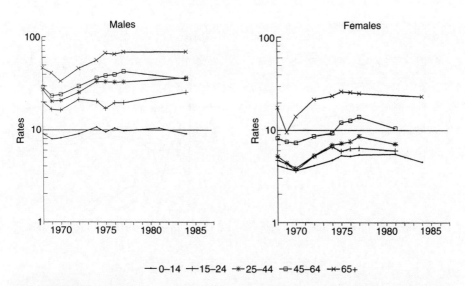

Fig. 17.A20. Age-specific mortality rates for traffic accidents, Colombia, 1968–87 (per 100,000)
Source: PAHO (1990).

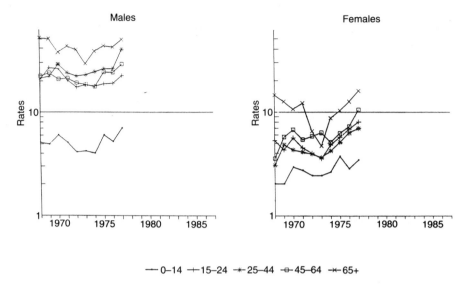

Fig. 17.A21.   Age-specific mortality rates for traffic accidents, Cuba, 1968–87 (per 100,000)
Source: PAHO (1990).

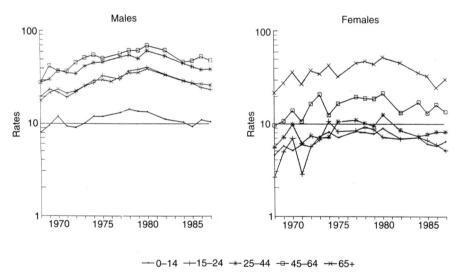

Fig. 17.A22.   Age-specific mortality rates for traffic accidents, Ecuador, 1968–87 (per 100,000)
Source: PAHO (1990).

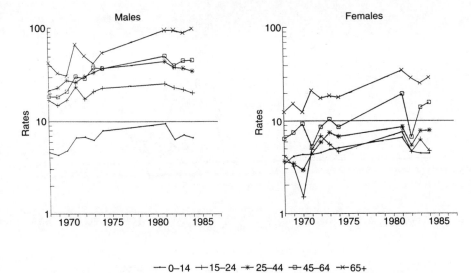

Fig. 17.A23.   Age-specific mortality rates for traffic accidents, El Salvador, 1968–87 (per 100,000)
Source: PAHO (1990).

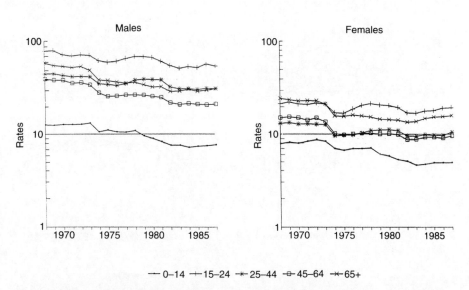

Fig. 17.A24.   Age-specific mortality rates for traffic accidents, USA, 1968–87 (per 100,000)
Source: PAHO (1990).

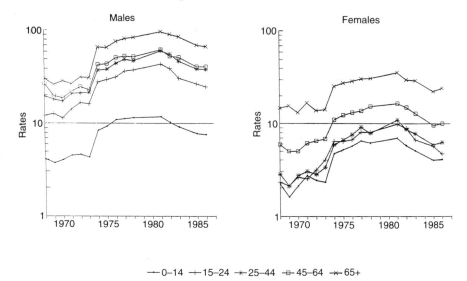

—— 0–14 —+— 15–24 —*— 25–44 —□— 45–64 —×— 65+

Fig. 17.A25. Age-specific mortality rates for traffic accidents, Mexico, 1968–87 (per 100,000)
Source: PAHO (1990).

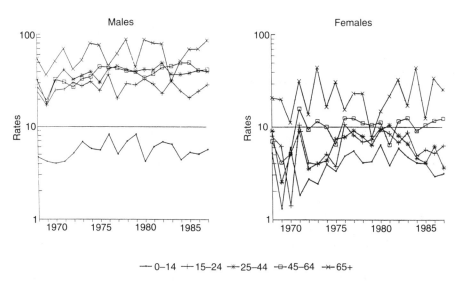

—— 0–14 —+— 15–24 —*— 25–44 —□— 45–64 —×— 65+

Fig. 17.A26. Age-specific mortality rates for traffic accidents, Panama, 1968–87 (per 100,000)
Source: PAHO (1990).

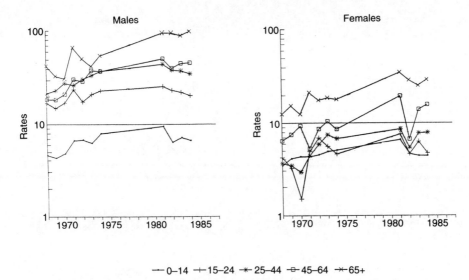

Fig. 17.A23. Age-specific mortality rates for traffic accidents, El Salvador, 1968–87 (per 100,000)
Source: PAHO (1990).

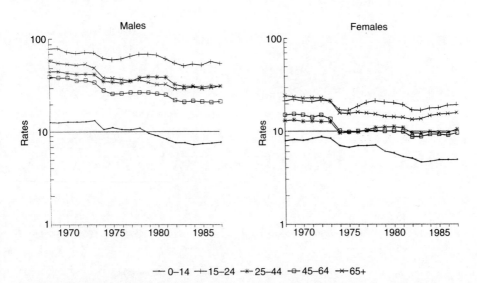

Fig. 17.A24. Age-specific mortality rates for traffic accidents, USA, 1968–87 (per 100,000)
Source: PAHO (1990).

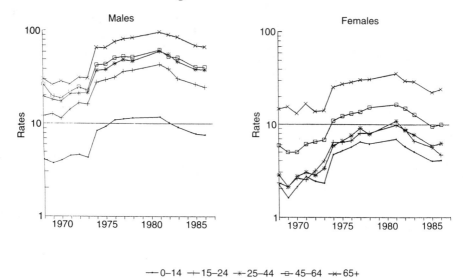

Fig. 17.A25. Age-specific mortality rates for traffic accidents, Mexico, 1968–87 (per 100,000)
Source: PAHO (1990).

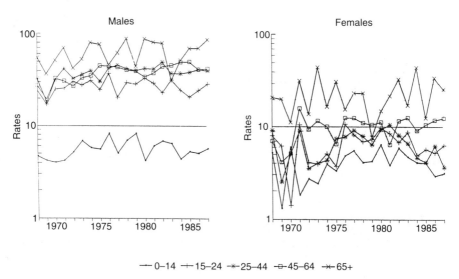

Fig. 17.A26. Age-specific mortality rates for traffic accidents, Panama, 1968–87 (per 100,000)
Source: PAHO (1990).

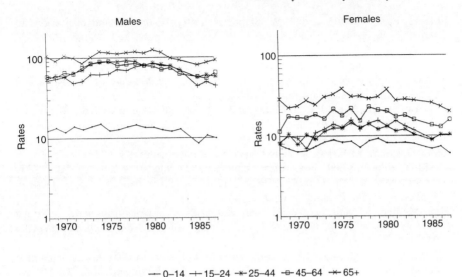

— 0–14 —+— 15–24 —*— 25–44 —□— 45–64 —✕— 65+

Fig. 17.A27.   Age-specific mortality rates for traffic accidents, Venezuela, 1968–87 (per 100,000)
Source: PAHO (1990).

References

Aalund, O., L. Danielsen, and R. O. Sanhueza (1990), 'Injuries due to deliberate violence in Chile', *Forensic Science International*, 46: 189–202.

Alfaro-Alvarez, C. and C. Díaz-Coller (1977), 'Los accidentes de tráfico: creciente problema para la salud pública', *Boletín de la Oficina Sanitaria Panamericana*, 83: 310–17.

Bangdiwala, S. I., and E. Anzola-Pérez (1987), 'Accidentes de tráfico: problema de salud en países en desarrollo de las Américas', *Boletín de la Oficina Sanitaria Panamericana*, 103: 130–9.

——(1990), 'The incidence of injuries in young people: II. Log-linear multivariable models for risk factors in a collaborative study in Brazil, Chile, Cuba and Venezuela', *International Journal of Epidemiology*, 19: 125–32.

——and I. M. Glizer (1985), 'Statistical considerations for the interpretation of commonly utilized road traffic indicators: implications for developing countries', *Accident Analysis & Prevention*, 17: 419–27.

——I. M. Glizer, C. J. Romer, and Y. Holder (1991), 'Método epidemiológico estructurado para planear la prevención de los accidentes de tránsito', *Boletín de la Oficina Sanitaria Panamericana*, 111: 186–9.

——C. J. Romer, B. Schmidt, F. Valdez-Lazo, J. Toro, and C. D'Suze (1990), 'The incidence of injuries in young people: I. Methodology and results of a collaborative study in Brazil, Chile, Cuba and Venezuela', *International Journal of Epidemiology*, 19: 115–24.

Bulatao, R., A. López, and P. W. Stephens (1991), 'Estimates and projections of mortality by cause: a global overview, 1970–2015', unpublished, The World Bank, Washington, DC.

Cusminsky, M., and E. N. Suárez-Ojeda (1979), 'Características de la mortalidad en el adolescente y el joven', in: *Condiciones de Salud del Niño en las Américas*, Pan American Health Organization, Washington, DC.

Danielsen, L., O. Aalund, P. H. Mazza, and E. Katz (1989), 'Injuries due to deliberate violence in areas of Argentina: II. Lesions', Copenhagen Study Group, *Forensic Science International*, 42: 165–75.

Gallagher, S. S., K. Finison, B. Guyer, and S. Goodenough (1984), 'The incidence of injuries among 87,000 Massachusetts children and adolescents: Results of the 1980–81 Statewide Childhood Injury Prevention Program Surveillance System', *American Journal of Public Health*, 74: 1340–7.

Hijar-Medina, M. (1991), 'Accidentes, violencias y lesiones traumáticas. Nuevo enfoque para el uso y análisis conceptual de los términos', *Salud Pública México*, 33: 278–82.

——L. Ortega-Mejía, and M. Dimas-García (1989), 'Traumatismos y envenenamientos como causa de demanda de servicios de urgencia', *Salud Pública México*, 31: 447–68.

——R. Rea-Castañeda, and C. Muggenburg-Rodríguez-Vigil (1986), 'Mortalidad por accidentes, violencias y envenenamientos en el Distrito Federal de 1970 a 1982', *Salud Pública México*, 28: 413–37.

Mello-Jorge, M. H., and M. Bernardes-Márques (1985), 'Violent childhood deaths in Brazil', *Bulletin of the Pan American Health Organization*, 19: 288–99.

National Committee for Injury Prevention and Control (NCIPC) (1989), 'Injury prevention: meeting the challenge', *American Journal of Preventive Medicine*, 5: 192–203.

National Safety Council (1984), *Accident Facts*, 1984 Edn., Chicago.

Pan American Health Organization (PAHO), Programa de Salud del Adulto (1984), 'Los accidentes de tránsito en las Américas', *Epidemiological Bulletin*, 5: 1–4.

Pan American Health Organization (PAHO) (1986), *Health Conditions in the Americas 1981–1984*, Vol. 1, Scientific Publication No. 500, Washington, DC.

——(1990), 'Violence: A growing public health problem in the Region', *Epidemiological Bulletin*, 11: 1–7.

Suárez-Ojeda, E. N., and M. Cusminsky (1979), 'Características de la mortalidad y morbilidad en menores de 10 años', in: *Condiciones de Salud del Niño en las Américas*, Pan American Health Organization, Washington, DC.

Vilchis-Licon, H., and P. M Iturrioz-Rosell (1986), 'Los accidentes de tránsito: una problemática actual', *Salud Pública México*, 28: 537–42.

18 Mortality from Accidents and Violence in Colombia

MAGDA RUIZ
Instituto Nacional de Salud, Bogotá, Colombia

MANUEL RINCÓN
Centro Latinoamericano de Demografía, San José, Costa Rica

1. Introduction

Continual study of the evolution of mortality is important for the understanding of a population's state of health and the development of appropriate policies and programmes. When, as with accidents and violence, disease and death affect large groups of the population at early ages, identifying their causes and methods for control becomes a priority. Violence refers to any act that impedes human rights, beginning with the fundamental right to life; an accident is any traumatic or morbid unforeseen act leaving temporary or permanent injuries or leading to death. Death occasioned by these causes must be interpreted as the tip of an iceberg; it represents an underlying social problem that has physical, psychological, moral, and economic consequences for its victims and society in general.

Mortality due to violence can and has been studied from various perspectives: as an epidemiological issue, as a socio-political problem, from the perspective of the criminality of the actors or agents provoking the violent acts, and from the point of view of the individuals that suffer their consequences. Analysis can also focus on the evaluation of the consequences that such acts have on such factors as a society's structures, conditions, and demographic dynamics. Analyses of accidents have been less frequent and require a different focus. The majority of such studies concentrate on accidents at work that result in decreases in the productivity of businesses. Motor vehicle accidents have also been the object of many investigations. Other accidents generally occur in homes and, despite their frequency, have not been given the same attention.

By considering death as the central focus, we propose to study the impact that various forms of violence and accidents have had on some demographic indicators and on the dynamics of populations. Measurement of the effect is considered, separating causes into accidents of all kinds, homicide, injuries inflicted intentionally by another person, and suicide. Those injuries for which it is not reported whether they were accidentally or intentionally inflicted, legal interventions, and war operations are included in some measures of homicide. The evolution of the problem over time, gender, and the age of the affected groups are considered. Other effects, such as the psycho-social consequences that can affect the survivors of violence, their relatives, and friends have been studied less and are not addressed in this chapter.

2. Background on Violence in Colombia

Colombia has had a particularly violent history marked by both internal wars between traditional political parties pursuing power and non-declared wars known simply as 'violence'. The war that took place in the 1950s and 1960s was one of the longest in Colombia's history. It resulted in 200,000 deaths (Sánchez *et al.*, 1989) and had innumerable social consequences felt even today. It was a political struggle and was resolved by negotiations and agreements between parties that were traditionally at odds. Another period of violence is taking place today. It is more complex and difficult to control than the previous one because other reasons and motives for violence have been added to its political aspects.

As a result of the National Front (an agreement between the Liberal and Conservative party by which they alternated in power during four consecutive presidential periods, between 1958 and 1974), traditionally irreconcilable parties identified other political forces as their principal enemies, ignoring the growth of common delinquency and drug trafficking. Combined with social and economic problems, this has led the country to the state of social, moral, and political disintegration it faces today. When the government of Betancur (1982–6) began its struggle against drug trafficking, prompt retaliations took place in the form of murders of ministers, attorneys, judges, journalists, and any other person or representative of the law that opposed drug trafficking interests. These retaliations have become increasingly bloody and indiscriminate, leading to the prevalence of drug-related terrorism as a measure for exerting pressure to obtain protection against extradition. Certain independent movements that entered the nation's democratic process, such as the Patriotic Union, have been eliminated.

The weakness of the State and its political class has been evident throughout this period. Political commitment is lacking and drug-trafficking and delinquency have contaminated various levels of government, the political class, the armed forces, and the judiciary. Petty thefts, muggings, and homicides go unpunished, resulting in increased violence due to the absence of exemplary punishment.

There have been many studies of violence in Colombia. Losada (1990) cites 112 studies from the 1980s and 24 from the previous decade. During the last twenty-five years, except for very short periods of stability, deaths attributable to various forms of violence have increased steadily and now constitute one of the principal causes of mortality. Thus 124,440 homicides of men and women were registered for the 1980–9 period along with 9230 suicides and 14,382 deaths where it was not specified whether they were accidental or intentional. These groups represent 10 per cent of all deaths. Once accidents are added to these homicides and violent deaths, deaths due to external causes represent 19 per cent of the total number of deaths during the period, that is a total of 272,768 deaths.

Violence continues to be a grave problem for Colombian society as indicated by the data collected by Castellanos (1991), a journalist with the daily newspaper *El Espectador*:

Violence is increasing. In 1990, there were 23,000 homicides, 65 per day, six per hour. According to known data, an average of four kidnappings took place per day. Attempts to mine pipelines, pylons and bridges take place continually as do ambushes of army vehicles and personnel. The murders of judges, Indians, and children fill television news and newspapers. The bloodbath continues; unsafety prevails.

Persistent social problems and guerrilla warfare as a response to those problems are identified as one of the principal causes of violence (Martínez, 1990). In addition, Colombian society has been assaulted during the last few years by violence involving hired assassins. According to research by the Ministry of Justice, the delinquents are usually men between 21 and 40 years of age who live in medium and large cities and have had little formal education. The victims of violence are frequently members of the civilian population with some kind of role as political, union or community leaders, teachers, priests, doctors or judges that come into contact with criminal activity, represent an unacceptable sector of society, or simply attempt to protect themselves against a mugging. The gamut of reasons for the homicides is so great that it is impossible to mention them all. However, the data, although fragmentary, indicates that it is not the confrontation between the army and the guerrillas that produces the greatest number of victims.

Apart from the impact that death by violence has on society, the problem of accidents is also important. As urbanization and society's level of development grow, so does the use of motor vehicles and other manifestations of technology that increase the risk of accidents. The absence of a clear and permanent policy for the prevention of accidents, of education for the community, and of sanctions against those who are irresponsible or negligent allows accidents to increase, resulting not only in deaths but also in temporary or permanent disabilities and related costs of care and rehabilitation.

The country has reduced mortality due to infectious and parasitic diseases, respiratory diseases, and many other pathological diseases. An epidemiological transition appears to be taking place that includes increases in cancer, cerebrovascular diseases, and other degenerative diseases related to ageing.

However, as was noted by Betancur (1987), by 1986 the magnitude of and growing tendency toward violence had become a new problem for public health that cannot be considered the exclusive responsibility of the medical community. Equally, the function of the medical community should include prevention and the control of the roots of the problem in collaboration with all sectors of society.

3. Sources, Materials and Methods

The basic information used for this study comes from vital statistics records compiled by DANE for 1973–84 that were published in 1987 as a result of the DANE-UNICEF agreement (DANE/UNICEF, 1987a, 1987b). Tables from this data base were consulted, together with published summaries from *Statistics Bulletins* (DANE, 1988, 1990) for the years 1985–90. The information for 1965 is taken from the general yearbook of statistics for 1965 (DANE, undated). The population estimates used for the tables on mortality were derived from the last official projection prepared jointly by DANE-DNP, with technical assistance from CELADE (Martínez and Escobar, 1989).

The deaths due to accidents and violence, that are the objects of this study, correspond to the chapter on external causes of death in the International Classification of Diseases and Causes of Death (PAHO, 1978). For the classification of causes of death, DANE used the 8th Revision of the ICD for the 1968–78 period, the 9th Revision for the period following 1979 and the 7th Revision for the years prior to 1968. The present study considers the groups described in Table 18.1.

In Colombia, as in most developing countries, the vital statistics system has serious deficiencies in terms of its coverage and the quality of the information. Recent studies demonstrate the existence of regional differences in the quality and coverage of registers. The mean coverage of the country is 85 per cent. It has been discovered that some regions lack registers for rural areas. Coverage of the one- to four-year age group is most deficient, followed by the age group less than one year. Deaths of those aged five or more years are reported more fully, although there has been no detailed evaluation within this age group and some differences by age may exist (Pabón and Ruiz, 1986, ch. 3).

It is very difficult to evaluate coverage by cause of death except indirectly by association with age. Some causes may be more unaccounted for than others, such as intestinal infections or acute respiratory diseases which are most frequent in young children. It might be thought that deaths due to accidents and violence would be more thoroughly registered than deaths by natural causes because of their greater effect on the adult population, their social impact and the need for procedures such as the removal of the corpse ('levantamiento del cadáver') and autopsy by a coroner. This may be true in populations that have a 'normal' number of deaths due to external causes. In

Table 18.1. Classification of the external causes of death into five groups of causes for the periods 1968–78 and 1979 to the present

Category used	9th Revision: 1979 on		8th Revision: 1968–78	
	Basic list (Vol. 1 p. 806)	List to three digits	Basic list (150 causes)	List to three digits
1. Suicide and self-inflicted injuries	E540	E950–E959	147	E950–E959
2. Intentional homicide and injuries inflicted by another person	E550	E960–E969	148	E960–E978
3. Injury, not specified whether accidentally or intentionally inflicted	E560	E980–E989	149	E980–E989
4. – Legal intervention and military operations	E562	E970–E978		
– War	E561	E990–E999	150	E990–E999
5. – All accidents	E470–E530	E800–E949	138–146	E810–E949
– All accidents and violence	E470–E562	E800–E999	138–150	E810–E999

Colombia, however, where violence occurs for so many reasons, the volume of deaths due to this cause throughout the national territory prevents registers from capturing all of the facts. Mass graves have been found containing numerous cadavers that obviously have not been accounted for in statistics. Even when relevant procedures are followed fully at the Institute of Legal Medicine, if a cadaver is not claimed by relatives and the victim cannot be identified, it is buried in a common grave after taking fingerprints for later identification. None of the information on the characteristics of the deceased that are usually compiled on the death certificate are available for such deaths.

During 1991 it was claimed that approximately three unclaimed cadavers were arriving daily at the Institute of Legal Medicine of Bogotá that had to be buried in a mass grave without prior identification (Moreno and Gómez, 1991). This number may be exaggerated, as it surpasses any estimate of deaths due to external causes, but it reflects an important fact that should be taken into consideration. If this issue arises in Bogotá, the city that houses all institutions responsible for these procedures, it can be assumed that the problem is even greater in more isolated regions.

According to data presented by the SER Institute that compare the statistics for homicide compiled by DANE (E960-E969) with those of the National Police (common homicide and aggravated homicide) for the 1976–86 period (Losada and Vélez, 1988), the police reported a greater number of homicides than DANE in every year. If the police data are accurate, the register of deaths due to homicide has a coverage of 86 per cent, which is a little higher than the coverage estimated for all causes among people over five years of age during the 1979–81 period of 82 per cent (Pabón and Ruiz, 1986). If we add to the homicide category deaths registered by DANE where it is not specified whether the injuries were accidental or intentional, the numbers approach those reported by the police. In conclusion, the number of deaths due to homicide is greater than the number registered and omission of homicide deaths is similar to omission of deaths from other causes.

When analysing data in the groupings shown in Table 18.1, it can be observed that the categories for 'injuries where it is not specified whether they were accidentally or intentionally inflicted', 'war operations', and 'legal intervention' show irregular behaviour. As Colombia is not under a declared state of war, deaths do not appear under this category but, as indicated by Losada and Vélez (1988), there is no good reason for the low number of deaths under 'legal interventions'. Deaths within the armed forces resulting from their struggle with the guerrillas, dead guerrillas and criminals killed by the police, who are not deemed to have been murdered, should fall under this category. The limited number of such reports reflects lack of familiarity with the death certificate on the part of the person issuing it; without noting the circumstances that surround the death, it is impossible for classifiers to select the appropriate category. Unless otherwise specified, deaths from injuries resulting from legal intervention are included under 'homicides' for the analyses contained in this chapter.

4. Demographic Aspects of Mortality

In the study of human mortality, various aspects can be considered individually. We can distinguish those that refer to the physical or biological characteristics of the individuals, those that are derived from the physical and ecological environment surrounding man, and those related to his economic and social surroundings. While this chapter focuses on mortality due to violence and accidents, mortality due to natural causes is considered briefly for purposes of comparison. This group includes deaths that result from a natural process associated with either exogenous or endogenous factors.

Like most developing countries, Colombia has experienced a decline in general mortality during the second half of this century. The crude mortality rate fell from 17 per 1000 deaths in 1950–5 to 6 per 1000 in 1985–90. During this period, life expectancy increased from 50.6 to 68 years, an average gain of half a year *per annum* (Martínez and Escobar, 1989). For those less than one year old, the gain was even more significant. The infant mortality rate fell from 123 to 40 per 1000 live births, a reduction of 67 per cent. Although these trends are encouraging, the decline in mortality would have been greater if not for the counterbalancing trend in deaths from accidents and violence. Given the differences according to sex in patterns of mortality, all indicators are analysed separately according to gender. Table 18.2 contains a summary of indicators according to sex.

The composition of mortality according to cause has varied. While homicide represented 2.5 per cent of all deaths in 1964, by 1990 it rose to 16 per cent. Meanwhile, accidents of all kinds rose from 4.3 to 7.8 per cent of deaths. These two causes plus suicide (the other category considered an external cause) grew from 7.1 to 23 per cent of deaths during this period. The risk of death by these causes varies significantly according to sex. In the decade 1980–9, 85 per cent of these deaths were of men. In the mid-1960s, it is estimated that the group of external causes constituted 11 per cent of male deaths and 3.9 per cent of female deaths. The increase is observed for both sexes and toward the end of the 1980s such deaths rose to 34 per cent in men and 7.4 per cent in women.

The number of deaths attributable to a specific cause gains special importance because awareness of such statistics permits the health sector to estimate the human, technical and economic resources required for opportune and efficient care of the affected population. It is striking to observe that the number of deaths among men due to external causes, which was 10,000 in 1965, had slightly more than tripled by 1990, while in women it had increased by 50 per cent, reaching 5000 in 1990. The change is even more spectacular in the case of homicide. Among men it increased by five times and among women by four times during the same period. This is in contrast to mortality by natural causes, which has declined in both sexes.

Figure 18.1 presents male mortality rates from broad groups of causes. In the 1970s, the average mortality rate from homicide among men was 37 deaths per 100,000 inhabitants. It grew to 56 between 1980 and 1985, and to 99 per 100,000 between 1985 and 1989, reaching a record level of 136 per 100,000 in 1990. For women, the rate remained between 3 and 5 per 100,000 until 1986 but reached a record level in 1990 of 11 per 100,000. As for mortality due to accidents, it remained at around 67 and 19 deaths per 100,000 inhabitants for men and women respectively until 1988. Then, in 1989 and 1990, a slight decrease occurred.

As is the case with crude mortality, mortality due to external causes varies according to age. Considering the motives that usually lie behind a death caused by aggression of others, it is clear that age is an important factor and key to the analysis of violence. Generally, the relative frequency of deaths due to external causes increases rapidly after five years of age, reaching a peak in the population between 15 and 30 years old, and falls gradually as age advances (Figure 18.2). There has been a notable increase in the proportion of

Table 18.2. Mortality according to cause by gender, Colombia, 1965–90

Years	Men							Women						
	Total	External causes					Natural causes	Total	External causes					Natural causes
		Suicide	Homicide	Other violence	Accidents	Subtotal			Suicide	Homicide	Other violence	Accidents	Subtotal	
Deaths by cause														
1965	94,001	698	4,140	(a)	5,701	10,539	83,462	84,371	410	449	(a)	2406	3265	81,106
1975	82,783	581	3,922	1259	6,747	12,509	70,274	70,455	261	405	300	2340	3306	67,149
1980	70,060	528	6,261	886	7,712	15,387	54,673	55,513	237	536	208	2529	3510	52,003
1985	88,443	792	11,266	560	10,449	23,067	65,376	65,504	226	675	154	3064	4119	61,385
1988	90,816	752	17,542	1663	10,532	30,489	60,327	62,253	174	1310	171	2966	4621	57,632
1990	92,982	680	22,237	672	9,237	32,826	60,156	61,703	200	1817	88	2799	4904	56,799
Death rates (per 1000 inhabitants)														
1965	10.22	0.08	0.45	(a)	0.62	1.15	9.07	9.07	0.04	0.05	(a)	0.26	0.35	8.71
1975	6.94	0.05	0.33	0.11	0.57	1.05	5.89	5.84	0.02	0.03	0.02	0.19	0.27	5.57
1980	5.24	0.04	0.47	0.07	0.58	1.15	4.09	4.10	0.02	0.04	0.02	0.19	0.26	3.84
1985	5.96	0.05	0.76	0.04	0.70	1.55	4.40	4.36	0.02	0.04	0.01	0.20	0.27	4.08
1988	5.76	0.05	1.11	0.11	0.67	1.94	3.83	3.90	0.01	0.08	0.01	0.19	0.29	3.61
1990	5.68	0.04	1.36	0.04	0.56	2.00	3.68	3.72	0.01	0.11	0.01	0.17	0.30	3.42

Structure of mortality according to cause

Year														
1965	100	0.7	4.4	(a)	6.1	11.2	88.8	100	0.5	0.5	(a)	2.9	3.9	96.1
1975	100	0.7	6.3	(a)	8.2	15.1	84.9	100	0.4	1.0	(a)	3.3	4.7	95.3
1980	100	0.8	10.2	(a)	11.0	22.0	78.0	100	0.4	1.3	(a)	4.6	6.3	93.7
1985	100	0.9	13.4	(a)	11.8	26.1	73.9	100	0.3	1.3	(a)	4.7	6.3	93.7
1988	100	0.8	21.1	(a)	11.6	33.6	66.4	100	0.3	2.4	(a)	4.8	7.4	92.6
1990	100	0.7	24.6	(a)	9.9	35.3	64.7	100	0.3	3.1	(a)	4.5	7.9	92.1

Average age at death

Year														
1965	26.6	34.6	33.8	(a)	29.2	31.4	26.0	28.9	26.8	32.1	(a)	28.0	28.4	28.9
1975	36.6	34.9	33.7	(a)	31.9	33.1	37.2	38.8	25.7	30.6	(a)	29.8	29.9	39.3
1980	41.0	34.8	32.8	(a)	31.5	32.4	43.4	45.3	26.5	30.4	(a)	31.0	30.7	46.2
1985	45.4	35.7	31.8	(a)	32.7	32.3	51.1	51.4	27.8	30.8	(a)	32.5	31.9	53.6
1988	46.1	34.6	31.1	(a)	34.2	32.2	53.8	53.8	27.9	30.4	(a)	34.8	33.1	56.2
1990	47.2	35.4	31.3	(a)	35.8	32.6	55.0	55.6	30.0	31.0	(a)	35.5	33.5	57.5

Changes in mortality rates by cause (Base year 1964 = 100)

Year														
1965	102.0	133.2	103.1	(a)	102.5	104.4	101.7	101.4	123.7	101.1	(a)	118.5	147.3	100.8
1975	89.9	110.9	97.7	(a)	121.3	123.9	85.7	84.7	84.5	91.2	(a)	115.3	118.8	83.5
1980	76.0	100.8	155.9	(a)	138.7	152.4	66.7	66.7	76.7	120.7	(a)	124.6	126.1	64.6
1985	96.0	151.1	280.6	(a)	187.9	228.4	79.7	78.7	73.1	152.0	(a)	150.9	148.0	76.3
1988	98.6	143.5	436.9	(a)	189.4	301.9	73.5	74.8	56.3	295.0	(a)	146.1	166.0	71.6
1990	100.9	129.8	553.4	(a)	166.1	324.9	73.4	74.1	64.7	409.2	(a)	137.9	176.2	70.6

Note: Injuries where it is not specified whether they were accidental or intentional, and injuries resulting from legal intervention and military operations are included with homicides

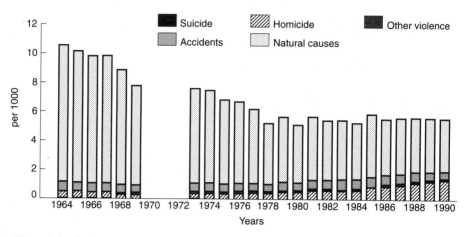

Fig. 18.1.   Male mortality rates by cause, Colombia, 1964–90 (per 1000)

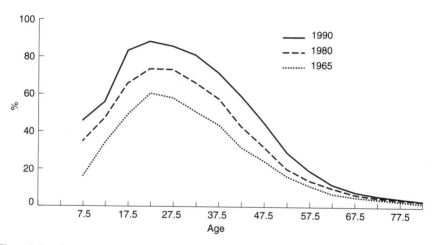

Fig. 18.2.   Proportion of male deaths from external causes, according to age, Colombia, 1965, 1980, and 1990

deaths attributable to external causes at all ages. While in 1965 this proportion reached a peak of 55 per cent in the male population between 20 and 24 years, the peak in this age group rose to 88 per cent in 1990. The pattern among women is similar, but at lower levels.

The average age at death due to suicide among women is almost eight years younger than in men. There has been a slow tendency for this age to increase with time in both sexes. In 1990, it was around 35 years for men and 30 years for women. In the case of homicide, there is not a great difference in the average ages of the sexes at death and a gradual decline is observed during the period studied. No important differences are found in the accidents category with the average age at death of both sexes falling around 34 years. In contrast to deaths from homicide, there is a tendency for this age to increase during the period.

The differential pattern of mortality by external causes in the two sexes is also reflected in the sex ratio of such deaths. In 1965, 323 men died from external causes for every 100 women but, by 1990, there were 670 male deaths for every 100 among women. The pattern of homicides allows us to see more clearly the selective nature of the risk of death from this cause. During the mid-1970s, nine men were murdered for every woman. In 1990 this ratio exceeded 12 (see Table 18.3).

The incidence of mortality due to external causes has been observed and the trend in the period under analysis has been described. Now the external causes are compared with natural causes. The discussion emphasizes male mortality given the greater relative importance of external causes for male mortality. Table 18.4 shows the primary causes of death in men, listed in order of importance in 1990, rates per 100,000 inhabitants and the proportion of deaths each cause represents for the period 1975–90. Homicide has become the leading cause of death and is considerably more common than malignant tumors, which occupy second place. The third most important cause is ischaemic heart disease. Motor vehicle and other accidents occupy the eighth and sixth place but would rise to fourth place if these two categories were combined.

It is useful to compare the situation in Colombia with the situation observed in other countries of the region (see Chapter 17). Some of these countries have a situation as serious as that of Colombia. In El Salvador in 1984 the death rate due to homicide was 41.6 per 100,000 inhabitants; the rate of deaths due to injuries for which it is not specified whether they were accidentally or intentionally inflicted was 26.2 per 100,000, and the death rate due to suicide was

Table 18.3. Sex ratio of deaths according to cause, Colombia, 1965–90

Years	Total deaths	Suicide	Homicide	Other violence	Accident	Total accidents and violence	Natural causes
1965	1.11	1.70	9.22	3.30	2.37	3.23	1.03
1975	1.17	2.23	9.68	4.20	2.88	3.78	1.05
1980	1.26	2.23	11.68	4.26	3.05	4.38	1.05
1985	1.35	3.50	16.69	3.64	3.41	5.60	1.07
1986	1.41	3.46	15.99	5.58	3.10	5.62	1.06
1987	1.41	3.91	14.01	7.07	3.42	6.08	1.04
1988	1.46	4.32	13.39	9.73	3.55	6.60	1.05
1989	1.48	3.68	13.47	8.67	3.27	6.74	1.06
1990	1.51	3.40	12.23	7.64	3.30	6.69	1.06

Table 18.4. Primary causes of male mortality, Colombia, 1975–90 (percentages and rates per 100,000 inhabitants)

Causes	1975			1980			1985			1990		
	Rank	Rate	%	Rank	Rate	%	Rank	Rate	%	Rank	Rate	%
Homicide	8	32.9	4.7	1	46.8	8.9	1	75.9	12.7	1	136.1	24.0
Malignant tumours	4	47.4	6.8	3	45.2	8.6	2	59.6	10.0	2	57.9	10.2
Ischaemic heart disease	3	49.6	7.1	5	37.9	7.2	3	58.8	9.9	3	57.4	10.1
Respiratory disease	1	85.8	12.4	2	45.9	8.8	4	47.6	8.0	4	41.1	7.2
Other heart disease	5	43.1	5.2	4	38.1	6.2	6	38.7	7.5	5	35.4	6.2
Other accidents	7	36.1	6.2	6	32.3	7.3	5	44.9	6.5	6	34.5	6.1
Cerebrovascular disease	9	32.2	4.6	9	26.5	5.1	7	35.2	5.9	7	27.4	4.8
Motor vehicle accidents	12	20.4	2.9	10	25.4	4.8	9	25.5	4.3	8	21.7	3.8
Perinatal causes	6	38.5	5.6	7	30.0	5.7	8	26.6	4.5	9	20.0	3.5
Other digestive disease	11	21.5	3.1	11	18.5	3.5	10	21.8	3.7	10	18.8	3.3
Hypertensive disease	14	12.2	1.8	12	14.5	2.8	13	12.3	2.1	11	13.8	2.4
Endocrine gland disease	—	0.7	0.1	14	10.1	1.9	14	10.7	1.8	12	10.6	1.9
Intestinal infections	2	55.4	7.9	8	28.7	5.5	11	16.8	2.8	13	8.8	1.5
Other circulatory diseases	—	9.7	1.4	15	8.5	1.6	—	9.4	1.6	14	8.1	1.4
Urinary disease	15	11.6	1.7	—	6.8	1.3	—	8.6	1.4	15	8.0	1.4
Ill-defined			8.9			6.3			4.7			3.4
Other causes			19.5			14.4			12.7			8.7

12.2 per 100,000 inhabitants (PAHO, 1990). According to the same source, in 1986 Colombia's death rates from these causes were 44.9, 6.8 and 4.5 per 100,000 respectively.

Guatemala (1984) and Chile (1987) have substantially lower mortality rates by homicide (3.6 and 2.3 per 100,000 respectively), but higher mortality rates due to injuries where it is not specified whether they were accidental or intentional (31 per 100,000 in both countries). In Chile, whose vital statistics system is trustworthy, the magnitude of this last category stands out. It could be explained by the application of criteria for classification that differ from those of other countries. If these deaths should be included with the homicides, Chile has a very high index of mortality due to violence compared with most other Latin American countries.

Regarding all deaths due to accidents, suicide, homicide and those injuries where it is not specified whether they were accidentally or intentionally inflicted, El Salvador also has the highest overall mortality due to external causes, followed by Colombia (the number of 41.4 deaths due to external causes per 100,000 inhabitants that appears in the PAHO *Bulletin* is incorrect). These countries are followed in importance by Mexico with 77.4, and Brazil, Cuba, Chile, Ecuador and Venezuela, where mortality from these causes nears 60 per 100,000. In most countries in the region, these causes of mortality principally affect the population between 15 and 44 years of age. Suicide, homicide and accidents rank among the first five causes of death, varying in importance according to country.

The comparison of Columbia with Costa Rica is instructive.* The latter country is characterized by more advantageous health conditions and, consequently, lower mortality rates. Both countries have experienced accelerated decreases in births since the beginning of the 1970s. As a consequence the age structures of their populations are similar. The crude mortality rate in Colombia was approximately 6 per 1000 during the entire 1978–88 period. In Costa Rica, it was less than 4 per 1000 and tended to decline. Mortality due to natural causes remained relatively constant in Costa Rica (with rates near 3.4 per 1000 inhabitants), while in Colombia a more accelerated decline occurred (from 5.1 to 4.5 per 1000). Thus mortality due to natural causes in Colombia would have to be reduced by at least 25 per cent from its 1988 level to reach the level that Costa Rica had achieved already at that time. The difference in mortality between the two countries is explained, however, not only by natural causes but by the contribution of external causes. In Colombia, the rate of mortality due to external causes, in addition to being higher, increased during the period from 79 per 100,000 in 1978 to 134 in 1988. The level for Costa Rica was 53 and 44 in these years. The principal differences in the composition of deaths due to external causes are found in suicides and homicides. The suicide rates of Costa Rica are generally greater. During the 1978–88 period the rates averaged 3.8

* Mortality tables for Costa Rica were provided by the General Statistics and Census Bureau, San José, Costa Rica.

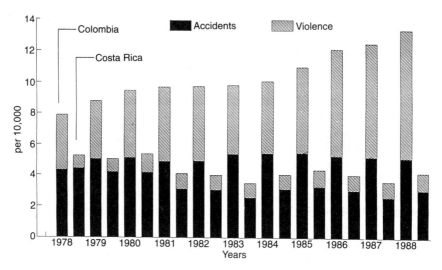

Fig. 18.3. Trends in mortality from external causes, Colombia and Costa Rica, 1978–88 (per 10,000)

in Colombia and 4.5 in Costa Rica per 100,000 inhabitants. In both countries, homicide and other forms of violence tend to increase. However, the situation is clearly much more unfavourable for Colombia. At the beginning of the period, the rate (32.1 per 100,000 in 1978) was seven times higher than that of Costa Rica. In 1988 it was 16 times greater (78.8 per 100,000). Finally, although mortality from accidents in Colombia is higher than in Costa Rica, accidents have a relatively similar impact on the general level of mortality in the two countries. Figure 18.3 compares the trend in mortality due to external causes in both countries, distinguishing two significant groups (accidents and violence).

5. Demographic Consequences

The changes observed over time in the structure of mortality according to cause are evident in the demographic indicators commonly used to analyse the characteristics and tendencies of a population's health conditions. This section considers the effects of changes in mortality due to external causes on life expectancy at birth and excess male mortality.

The pattern of mortality varies between the sexes according to age. Although male mortality is higher during childhood, the causes of death of boys do not differ much in order of importance from those in girls. In older age groups differences begin to emerge. During adolescence, complications of pregnancy, birth and the puerperium begin to appear as causes of female death while, in men, accidents of all kinds, homicides, and suicides prevail. In adult women, maternal mortality and female cancers rise in importance while, in men, mortality due to external causes increases. Further divergences take place in old age.

One of the priority groups for health care has been mothers and young children. Policies created for this group have resulted in the reduction of maternal mortality and technology for the early diagnosis and efficient treatment of malignant tumors has favoured women. The decrease of female mortality is accompanied by a growing excess in greater male mortality. If we add to this, as in Colombia, an increase in male mortality due to violence and accidents, then the excess mortality of men becomes extreme.

Figure 18.4 shows indices of excess male mortality according to age in Colombia for the years 1965 and 1988, in Costa Rica for 1988 and, as a reference, those of Level 21 of the Princeton West model life tables (Coale and Demeny, 1983). In all the populations, male mortality is higher at all ages. In the case of Colombia, the excess in male mortality increases between 1965 and 1988, particularly among men between 5 to 45 years of age. Cases of death due to external causes are concentrated in this age group. Costa Rica represents an intermediary pattern between Colombia and the model.

If the excess in male mortality can be interpreted as a measure of a relative risk of dying from external causes, it can be observed that the male population in Colombia has a greater excess risk over the female population of dying from external causes than its counterpart in Costa Rica. In both countries, the most extreme risk belongs to the population between 20 and 24 years of age. In Colombia a man of this age faces a risk of dying that is 4.5 times that of a woman while, in Costa Rica, this risk is a little more than 2.5 times higher. In Colombia, all men up to 50 years of age face higher relative risks than in Costa Rica. Given that the two countries have similar rates of mortality due to

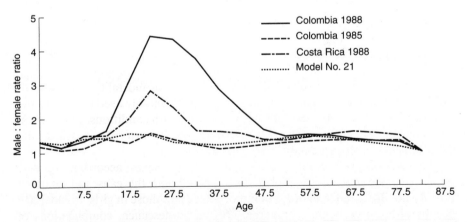

Fig. 18.4. Excess male mortality by age group

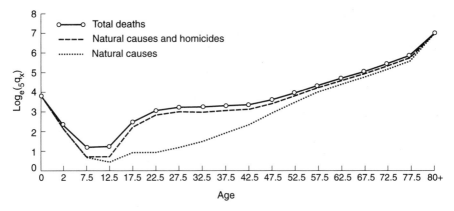

Fig. 18.5. Probabilities of dying by five-year age group ($_5q_x$) according to cause, males, Colombia, 1988

accidents, it can be deduced that the difference in excess male mortality is basically due to homicide.

Figure 18.5 shows the probabilities of death among the male population in 1988, differentiating the effects of homicide and accidents. The impact of homicides on the probabilities of death, particularly for members of the population between 15 and 44 years of age, is great. Accidents contribute to a significant but lesser degree. The excess in male mortality in 1988 is such that the probabilities of dying between 25 and 30 years for men surpass those for 1965 (Figure 18.6).

Throughout the world today, the life expectancy of women is greater than that of men. These differences tend to increase as mortality declines. Table 18.5 and Figure 18.7 present life expectancy at birth for Colombia during

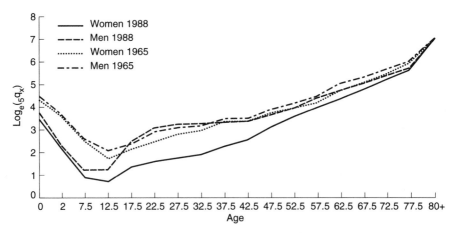

Fig. 18.6. Probabilities of dying by five-year age group ($_5q_x$) according to sex and age, Colombia, 1965 and 1988

Table 18.5. Life expectancy at birth, observed and with causes eliminated, Colombia, 1965–88

Life expectancy at birth	Years					Gain 1965–85
	1965	1975	1980	1985	1988	
Men						
1. Life expectancy at birth (without correcting data)	58.64	65.52	66.50	65.56	65.92	7.28
2. Life expectancy at birth (corrected deaths)	56.45	60.41	62.99	63.31	63.61	7.16
3. All external causes eliminated	59.76	63.67	67.18	68.47	69.64	9.88
4. Eliminating suicide (E 540)	56.73	60.62	63.18	63.52	63.80	7.07
5. Eliminating homicide (E 550)	57.87	61.82	64.96	66.06	67.28	9.41
6. Eliminating accidents (E 470–530)	58.08	62.10	65.01	65.44	65.66	7.58
(1)–(2) Effect of omitted deaths in registers	2.19	2.11	3.51	2.25	2.31	
(2)–(3) Effect of all external causes	−3.31	−3.26	−4.19	−5.16	−6.03	
(2)–(4) Effect of suicide	−0.28	−0.21	−0.19	−0.21	−0.19	
(2)–(5) Effect of homicide	−1.42	−1.41	−1.97	−2.75	−3.67	
(2)–(6) Effect of accidents	−1.63	−1.69	−2.02	−2.13	−2.05	
Women						
1. Life expectancy at birth (without correcting data)	62.91	67.47	71.83	71.90	73.09	10.18
2. Life expectancy at birth (corrected deaths)	60.81	65.53	68.85	70.07	71.35	10.54
3. All external causes eliminated	61.76	66.39	69.86	71.14	72.39	10.63
4. Eliminating suicide (E 540)	60.98	65.64	68.96	70.16	71.42	10.44
5. Eliminating homicide (E 550)	60.99	65.75	69.11	70.37	71.70	10.71
6. Eliminating accidents (E 470–530)	61.47	66.14	69.59	70.82	72.03	10.56
(1)–(2) Effect of omitted deaths in registers	2.10	1.94	2.98	1.83	1.74	
(2)–(3) Effect of all external cuses	−0.95	−0.86	−1.01	−1.07	−1.04	
(2)–(4) Effect of suicide	−0.17	−0.11	−0.11	−0.09	−0.07	
(2)–(5) Effect of homicide	−0.18	−0.22	−0.26	−0.30	−0.35	
(2)–(6) Effect of accidents	−0.66	−0.61	−0.74	−0.75	−0.68	
Differences between the sexes						
1. Life expectancy at birth (without correcting data)	4.27	4.95	5.33	6.34	7.17	
2. Life expectancy at birth (corrected deaths)	4.36	5.12	5.86	6.76	7.74	
3. All external causes eliminated	2.00	2.72	2.68	2.67	2.75	
4. Eliminating suicide (E 540)	4.25	5.02	5.78	6.64	7.62	
5. Eliminating homicide (E 550)	3.12	3.93	4.15	4.31	4.42	
6. Eliminating accidents (E 470–530)	3.39	4.04	4.58	5.38	6.37	

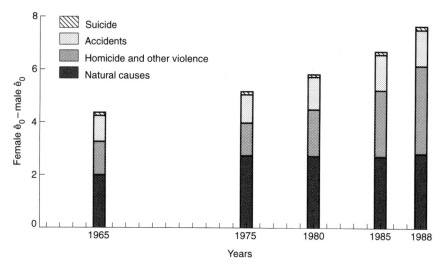

Fig. 18.7. Contribution of selected causes of death to the differential between the life expectancy at birth (e_0) of the two sexes, Colombia, 1965–88

the 1965–88 period. Life tables have been calculated both from the total number of deaths and eliminating external causes (see the Appendix for methodological details). During the twenty-three-year period, the male population increased its life expectancy by seven years and the female population by over ten years. Thus the differential between the sexes increased from four to over seven years. If deaths due to external causes had not been present, men would have gained nearly ten years and consequently the difference in life expectancy between the two sexes by 1988 would have been only 2.75 years.

If homicides alone had not been present, the gain in life expectancy at birth during the period would have been 9.4 years for men and 10.7 for women, 2.25 and 0.17 years respectively more than was observed. Excluding all external causes, these gains would have been 2.72 and 0.09 years for the two sexes. This means that the failure of life expectancy to increase as rapidly in the male population as the female population is explained largely by homicides. Equally, homicide accounts for almost 43 per cent of the differential in life expectancy by sex in the year 1988, while accidents account for 18 per cent of this differential.

6. Conclusions

During the last decades, Colombia has sustained health programmes that have assisted in the achievement of important goals in the struggle against disease and death. These programmes have succeeded in reducing the adverse effects of the environment and in significantly modifying the conditions of mortality that prevailed during the first half of the present century. However, conditions have coexisted in the social order that have resulted in a significant increase of mortality due to accidents and, in the last few years, of deaths due to various forms of violence. While, in 1964, external causes represented 7.1 per cent of deaths, by 1988 they rose to 23 per cent of all deaths. Homicide among men rose from a rate of 45 to 136 per 100,000. For women, the rate rose from 5 to 11 per 100,000 in the same period. This makes Colombia one of the most violent countries in the Americas. Thus, the incidence of homicides in Colombia was seven times higher than in Costa Rica in 1965. By 1988 it was sixteen times higher.

The group most affected has been young adult men. In Colombia, a young man of 20 to 24 years has a 4.5 times greater risk of dying than a woman of the same age in 1988. In contrast, in Costa Rica the same risk ratio was 2.5 in 1988 and only 1.5 in 1965. Changes in health conditions and the increase of mortality due to external causes have resulted in an abnormal increase in the differential in life expectancy at birth according to gender. By the end of the 1980s, it was almost eight years instead of the four years that would be expected given Colombia's present health conditions and progress towards development.

Appendix 18.1. Methodological Aspects

1. The Life Tables

The life table is a theoretical model used to analyse mortality according to age. It also constitutes an important tool for the study of mortality according to cause.

Mortality statistics according to causes of death permit the analysis of the importance that one cause or group of causes has on mortality in general. In more precise terms, they allow the study of how the level of mortality would vary as the effect of a cause of death is eliminated.

The gains that would be achieved in life expectancy at different ages are the differences between the observed and estimated life expectancy, assuming that a determined cause is eliminated. The gains from eliminating several causes are not additive: as one cause is reduced or eliminated, people who are no longer affected by it are still at risk of dying from other causes.

Abridged life tables are constructed, assuming the independent elimination of suicides, homicides (including other forms of violence) and accidents. The exclusion of all external causes results in the rate of mortality due to natural causes. The methodology used is explained in Preston *et al.* (1972).

2. Factors Related to the Adjustment of Deaths

For the life tables and the comparison with Costa Rica, deaths were adjusted according to the estimated average coverage (80 per cent coverage, 1.2 adjustment factor) except for 1980, which had greater coverage problems (74 per cent, 1.34 adjustment factor, Pabón and Ruiz, 1986).

3. Distribution of Deaths where Age is Ignored

Deaths for which an age at death is not reported represent nearly 1 per cent of the total number of registered deaths. For the construction of life tables, these deaths were distributed proportionally by age.

4. Definition of Indicators Used

Index of the increase in mortality: number of deaths in each year per 100 deaths during 1964.

Excess male mortality: the probability of death among men divided by the probability of death of women. It is also known as a relative risk.

5. Presentation of Results

Given limitations to the length of this chapter and the large quantity of information that had to be processed, the data bases used are not presented and the tables are summaries of more complete analyses on which the study is based.

References

Betancur, L. (1987), 'La violencia en Colombia', study presented at the Medical Association of Antioch in November 1986, *Journal of the Facultad Nacional de Salud Pública*, 10(2).

Castellanos, R. (1991), 'Misarabilismo', *El Espectador*, 19 January, Bogotá, Colombia.

Coale, A., and P. Demeny (1983), *Regional Model Life Tables and Stable Populations*, 2nd edn., with Barbara Vaughan, Academic Press, London.

DANE (undated), *Anuario Demográfico 1965*, Bogotá, Colombia.

——(1987a), *Registro de Defunciones en Colombia, 1970–1978*, DANE-UNICEF, Bogotá, Colombia.

——(1987b), *Registro de Defunciones en Colombia, 1979–1984*, DANE-UNICEF, Bogotá, Colombia.

——(1988), *Registro de Defunciones en Colombia, 1985–1986*, Statistics Bulletin No. 426, September, Bogotá, Colombia.

——(1990), *Registro de Defunciones en Colombia, 1985–1986*, Statistics Bulletin No. 447, June, Bogotá, Colombia.

Losada, R. (1990), *Los Estudios Sobre la Violencia Colectiva en Colombia*, SER Research Institute, Bogotá, Colombia.

——and E. Vélez (1988), *Muertes Violentas en Colombia*, Research Report IFT-138 SER Research Institute, Bogotá, Colombia.

Martínez, T. (1990), 'El "cañazo" de la paz en Córdoba', *El Espectador*, 9 September, Bogotá, Colombia.

Martínez, C., and G. Escobar (1989), *Colombia. Proyección de población 1950–2025*, DANE-CELADE-DNP, Bogotá, Colombia.

Moreno, C., and I. Gómez (1991), 'El drama de los N.N. Tumbas sin nombre', *El Espectador*, 3 February, Bogotá, Colombia.

Pabón, A., and M. Ruiz (1986), *La Mortalidad en Colombia*, Vol. v. *Niveles Ajustados 1979–1982, Análisis por Causa, Edad y Sexo 1979–1981*, Estudio Nacional de Salud INS ASCOFAME, Bogotá, Colombia.

Pan American Health Organization (PAHO) (1978), *International Statistical Classification of Diseases, Injuries and Causes of Death*, Scientific Publication No. 353, Washington, DC.

——(1990), *Epidemiological Bulletin*, 11(2).

Preston, S., N. Keyfitz, and R. Schoen (1972), *Causes of Death: Life Tables for National Populations*, Seminar Press, New York and London.

Sánchez, G., *et al.* (1989), 'Colombia: Violencia y Democracia', report presented to the Minister of Government, Universidad Nacional, Colciencias, Bogotá, Colombia.

Index

Note: A page number appearing in *italics* indicates that the reference on that page is to a table only and not to text.